Introducing Syntax

Syntax is the system of rules that we subconsciously follow when we build sentences. Whereas the grammar of English (or other languages) might look like a rather chaotic set of arbitrary patterns, linguistic science has revealed that these patterns can actually be understood as the result of a small number of grammatical principles. This lively introductory textbook is designed for undergraduate students in linguistics, English and modern languages with relatively little background in the subject, offering the necessary tools for the analysis of phrases and sentences while at the same time introducing state-of-the-art syntactic theory in an accessible and engaging way. Guiding students through a variety of intriguing puzzles, striking facts and novel ideas, *Introducing Syntax* presents contemporary insights into syntactic theory in one clear and coherent narrative, avoiding unnecessary detail and enabling readers to understand the rationale behind technicalities. Aids to learning include highlighted key terms, suggestions for further reading and numerous exercises, placing syntax in a broader grammatical perspective.

OLAF KOENEMAN is Assistant Professor of English Linguistics at Radboud Universiteit Nijmegen.

HEDDE ZEIJLSTRA is Professor of English Syntax at Georg-August-Universität Göttingen.

Cambridge Introductions to Language and Linguistics

This new textbook series provides students and their teachers with accessible introductions to the major subjects encountered within the study of language and linguistics. Assuming no prior knowledge of the subject, each book is written and designed for ease of use in the classroom or seminar, and is ideal for adoption on a modular course as the core recommended textbook. Each book offers the ideal introductory material for each subject, presenting students with an overview of the main topics encountered in their course, and features a glossary of useful terms, chapter previews and summaries, suggestions for further reading, and helpful exercises. Each book is accompanied by a supporting website.

Books Published in the Series
Introducing Phonology David Odden
Introducing Speech and Language Processing John Coleman
Introducing Phonetic Science Michael Ashby and John Maidment
Introducing Second Language Acquisition, Second Edition Muriel Saville Troike
Introducing English Linguistics Charles F. Meyer
Introducing Semantics Nick Riemer
Introducing Language Typology Edith A. Moravcsik
Introducing Psycholinguistics Paul Warren
Introducing Phonology, Second Edition David Odden
Introducing Morphology, Second Edition Rochelle Lieber

Introducing Syntax

OLAF KOENEMAN
*Radboud Universiteit
Nijmegen*

HEDDE ZEIJLSTRA
*Georg-August-Universität
Göttingen*

CAMBRIDGE
UNIVERSITY PRESS

CAMBRIDGE
UNIVERSITY PRESS

University Printing House, Cambridge CB2 8BS, United Kingdom

One Liberty Plaza, 20th Floor, New York, NY 10006, USA

477 Williamstown Road, Port Melbourne, VIC 3207, Australia

4843/24, 2nd Floor, Ansari Road, Daryaganj, Delhi – 110002, India

79 Anson Road, #06–04/06, Singapore 079906

Cambridge University Press is part of the University of Cambridge.

It furthers the University's mission by disseminating knowledge in the pursuit of education, learning, and research at the highest international levels of excellence.

www.cambridge.org
Information on this title: www.cambridge.org/9781107096745
10.1017/9781316156391

First published 2017

Printed in the United Kingdom by Clays, St Ives plc in 2017

A catalogue record for this publication is available from the British Library.

Library of Congress Cataloging in Publication Data
Names: Koeneman, Olaf, 1970– author. | Zeijlstra, Hedzer Hugo, 1975– author.
Title: Introducing syntax / Olaf Koeneman, Hedde Zeijlstra.
Description: New York, NY : Cambridge University Press, 2017. | Series: Cambridge introductions to language and linguistics
Identifiers: LCCN 2016041196 | ISBN 9781107096745 (hardback)
Subjects: LCSH: Grammar, Comparative and general – Syntax.
Classification: LCC P291 .K556 2017 | DDC 415–dc23
LC record available at https://lccn.loc.gov/2016041196

ISBN 978-1-107-09674-5 Hardback
ISBN 978-1-107-48064-3 Paperback

Contents

About this Book

Introducing Syntax

Whereas the grammar of English (or other languages) might look like a rather chaotic set of different patterns, syntactic theory has revealed that these patterns can actually be understood as the result of a small number of grammatical operations. Unravelling these is the science of syntax. This textbook describes state-of-the-art syntactic theory by addressing how and why certain combinations of words are 'proper' English sentences whereas other combinations are not. What is the mechanism behind that? What grammatical rules does English have and why? How is grammar related to meaning and to how sentences are expressed?

In this book we guide students through a variety of intriguing puzzles, striking facts and novel ideas, and let them discover the beauty of syntactic theory in both a bottom-up (data-driven) and a top-down (theory-driven) fashion. This book is primarily intended for students for whom this is a first (and hopefully not last) encounter with syntax and/or linguistic theory. We will primarily focus on the important insights that have been achieved in contemporary syntax. *Introducing Syntax* will offer students all the necessary tools to do this, without going into unnecessary technical detail.

Introducing Syntax is not the only available textbook on this topic. Why, then, the need for a new one? Introductory courses to (English) syntactic theory generally face three key challenges:

- First, syntax (and especially its level of formalisation and abstraction) can quite often be a surprise for students, especially those enrolled in an (English) language and literature/culture programme. The challenge is to make this formal theory accessible and interesting *without* oversimplifying.
- Second, since syntactic theory is formal, students have to learn a number of technical notions. A potential danger is that they learn the technicalities without understanding the insights behind them.
- Third, (English) syntactic theory deals with a number of phenomena that have shaped it. Many of these phenomena are part of the canon, and students have to know about them. However, they could be perceived as an arbitrary set of topics. It is a challenge to introduce all of these topics without losing the overall narrative that connects them in a coherent way.

On the basis of our teaching experience, we have felt a strong demand for an introductory textbook in syntactic theory that aims at addressing these three challenges. Such a textbook should be fully accessible, understandable and enjoyable for every student of English while reaching the same theoretical level as can be expected of textbooks in general linguistics programmes. We feel that our approach differs from existing ones in at least the following three respects:

- It offers insight beyond technical implementation. Textbooks often feel the need to be technically accurate and up-to-date, which can be detrimental to the clarity of the insights that syntax has to offer. In the worst case, they read like instruction manuals, and the explanations look as complicated as what they are trying to explain. In this book, particular subjects and phenomena are discussed not just because they are part of the syntactic canon but because (i) we can explicitly show how they have contributed to a crucial aspect of syntactic theory, and (ii) they clearly have the potential to intrigue students of modern languages, who as a result more readily acquire the relevant knowledge and skills.
- It begins with the state of the art. Although a historical perspective can be insightful, this book shows syntax as the present-day science that it is from the start, and overcomes the difficulties for student beginners by letting current insights prevail over technicalities.
- Most textbooks cover a range of syntactic topics treated in distinct thematic chapters. Although *Introducing Syntax* does not deviate from such a topical approach, it pays significantly more attention to an overall narrative that explains how these separate topics are related to one another and what exactly their role is in the general theory of syntax. This means that some of the topics and notions are introduced in different places from usual simply because we feel this better serves the development of the narrative. The desire to let the narrative prevail at all times has also forced us to make particular theoretical choices. Sometimes we have made fairly standard choices, sometimes more controversial ones. Whenever we had to make such choices, the narrative has been our guide, and less so our own theoretical preferences; and in all such cases we address these choices in the 'further reading' section at the end of every chapter.

Introducing Syntax, then, combines a *top-down* narrative, which connects the chapters and book parts, with a *bottom-up* data-driven discovery of intriguing syntactic regularities that feed syntactic theorising. It makes little sense to present an insight in the absence of data. Therefore, the insight is often very naturally introduced in a bottom-up fashion in which empirical – that is, data-driven – considerations pave the way to a particular insight. Ultimately, we don't want to just teach syntax, we want to teach how a syntactic theory is built up. Given these considerations, each chapter has the following tripartite structure:

(i) *Insight*

In this part we will present the major linguistic insight that forms the core of the chapter, the idea that aims to explain some key property of language. Insights are always justified: we show the central data that have led to them.

(ii) *Implementation*

Here the focus will be on the (technical) implementation of the insight, where students will learn to apply basic analytical skills.

(iii) *Consequences*

Here it is shown what predictions the insight and/or its implementation make(s) beyond the original data which gave rise to it/them and how these predictions can be confirmed.

We feel it is important that the insight is clearly distinguished from the implementation. First of all, this immediately reduces the risk of the insight getting buried under technicalities and details, because it clearly sets apart the idea which we want to turn into a fully-fledged theory. The implementation serves the purpose of developing the insight, and of making it more precise, but it is not the insight itself. After all, a particular insight may be correct but the implementation wrong. It is often the case that the insight is there, generally accepted, whereas the implementation is work in progress. By distinguishing the insight from the implementation we aim to make clear what their relation is. The consequences section is there to show what the benefits are of a particular implementation: 'If we do it this way, then we expect the following.' By distinguishing the implementation from the consequences, we aim to show that a particular implementation is never arbitrary. The way in which one shapes an insight into a fully-fledged theory has certain consequences, and leads to certain predictions rather than others. These consequences and predictions can be explored.

Every chapter also contains a number of exercises. These exercises will help students to recapitulate some of the main points raised in the chapter, and can also lead them to the conclusion that the theory leaves some data unexplained. Exercises are divided into categories A, B and C. 'A' questions typically involve tasks that can be carried out and questions that can be answered with the help of the main text. They help students train their basic syntactic understanding and skills, and apply the technique to concrete language data. 'B' questions are slightly harder, as they may involve additional examples or phenomena, but are still doable if one reads the text carefully. Students who do well on the 'A' questions and most of the 'B' questions can expect to pass an exam based on the book. 'C' questions, finally, are harder, and invite students to apply their knowledge and skills to novel phenomena or to point out potential counter-examples to the theory presented (and to hint at a solution to the theoretical problem). They generally require a more profound understanding of the theory. 'C' exercises are intended for more advanced or motivated students who seek an extra challenge or want to learn more about syntactic theory.

As a final note, what we derive in this book is a simple theory of something as complex as human language. Naturally, some of this simplicity follows from the fact that we have not discussed every phenomenon in its full complexity, and dismissed apparent counter-examples to the theory that are more likely to arise in a linguist's, than in a student's, head. After all, this is an introduction. Although additional data and studies might necessitate future revisions of this simple theory (as we explicitly illustrate in the afterword), it is nevertheless a striking fact about the organisation of the human mind that most of the complexity of human grammatical knowledge follows from a small number of simple operations. Reducing complex patterns to simple structures is the essence of beauty in science. It is this beauty that we hope to show in this book.

Foreword

This book is based on the syntactic approach known as minimalism and follows the generative paradigm as devised by Noam Chomsky. The literature on minimalist syntax is enormous and it is impossible to present a complete overview of all the relevant literature. In the main text we have spelled out what the major sources are for each chapter, as well as options for further reading. Please realise, though, that often we have simplified particular analyses for didactic or presentational purposes or represented them from another angle. Also realise that many of the references may not be easy to read (Chomsky's writings in particular can sometimes be very hard). For more accessible texts, we refer you to certain syntactic handbooks (e.g. Den Dikken 2013, Everaert et al. 2013 and Alexiadou & Kiss 2015) or the introductory works of our fellow syntax textbook writers, most notably Adger (2003), Haegeman (2006), Radford (2009), Tallerman (2011) and Carnie (2013).

Acknowledgements

The preparation of this book has benefited tremendously from people who have interacted with us at various stages of the project. We would like to take this opportunity to thank them here.

Ans van Kemenade advised us to contact Cambridge University Press about our idea for a new introduction to syntax at a time when our ambitions were rather more modest. We are glad that she did. We wish to thank her and Marion Elenbaas, Kees Hengeveld, Marjo van Koppen and the five anonymous reviewers invited by CUP for providing valuable comments on our book proposal.

Marc Richards commented on our manuscript, going far beyond the call of duty, and we are grateful for his very helpful suggestions. Stefanie Bode, Eva Csipak, Regine Eckardt, Hildegard Farke, Jovana Gajić, Beste Kamali and several others who were brave enough to use (parts of) the manuscript in their teaching generously sent us questions and lists of remarks, typos, infelicities and mistakes, the rectification of which has significantly improved the text.

We wish to thank Andrew Winnard and Maree Williams-Smith for their professional guidance of the reviewing, editing and production process at CUP. Virginia Catmur deserves our praise for her tremendously thorough editing work, and for pointing out so many aspects and textual details that have benefited from improvement. We feel humbled by her dedication and patience and have learned quite a bit from her during our collaboration.

This book is in large part a synthesis of lecture notes, assignments and ideas about how to teach syntax developed and used in our teaching over the years. This means that our own students, more than anybody else, have helped us shape this introduction into the form it now has, and we thank them for that. They have been, and will always be, a great source of inspiration and the main reason we like teaching syntax so much. We hope that we have succeeded in writing an introduction that reflects our enthusiasm for the classroom and that it will inspire students, including our own, for years to come.

Finally, we would like to thank Petra, Hedde's beloved partner, for having shared her home on Fridays for more than two years with two syntacticians dedicated to finishing the book that is now in your hands.

December 2016
Olaf Koeneman and Hedde Zeijlstra

Introduction: The Language Machine

We humans are surrounded by technology. We have machines for almost everything and computers allow us to achieve things that were long deemed impossible. We live in a day and age where dreams can become reality overnight due to technical innovation, and the amount of information that we have access to via a tiny machine in our pockets is simply astounding. There is talk right now about flying people to Mars and growing tomatoes there. Yes, we humans are a smart bunch.

Despite all this, there are some things we are still unable to do, and some machines we simply cannot build. And some of these failures have to do with language. A machine that can translate one language into another language perfectly? No, we don't have it (and please don't insult us by referring to Google Translate). Okay, how about something more modest, like a machine that can for any combinations of words in a single language (say, English) say whether it is a good sentence or not? It is perhaps hard to believe but even that is still out of our reach. Language, as it turns out, is an evasive and slippery creature.

At the same time, it is clear that such a machine, capable of stating for every English sentence whether it is grammatical or not, *does* exist. In fact, we have about 360 million of those machines on our planet. They are called *native speakers of English*. These speakers have at their disposal the knowledge of their mother tongue, English, and this knowledge can generate zillions of distinct combinations of English words and evaluate each of them, whether old or new, as being either a good sentence or not. Probably you have never heard someone say *Syntax is one of the most fascinating topics in linguistic theory*, but if you are a native speaker of English you know immediately that the sentence is grammatically correct (and hopefully after reading this book you will also find it to be correct content-wise). So these native speaker brains can do something that we cannot imitate with any man-made machine. The fact that we cannot mimic such everyday human language behaviour shows us that there is something worthwhile studying. There is something we apparently don't understand yet, namely the structure of English grammar. After all, if we already understood it, we would have no problem building some machine that imitates this behaviour. But, as said, we can't do that. This means we have to study the English language a bit harder. There is no other way.

But why would we want to know what makes some combination of English words a good English sentence? What is so interesting about knowing that *Maria drank some coffee* is good English, but *Maria some coffee drank* or *Maria drank some car* is not? They may just be facts of life. If so, asking these questions about English may sound like a good pastime for someone obsessed by the English language. Or an obsession for building the machine that we mentioned above. However, most theoretical linguists we know are not obsessed by a particular language. In fact, people obsessed by a particular language generally spend their time doing other things than comparing good and bad sentences. And most linguists we know don't really care that much about this language machine either.

They would be very happy doing their work realising that they will never come across such a machine.

So why are we doing this, if it is not some obsessive pastime over a language or a machine? Linguists are in this business for a different reason, namely the desire to understand the human brain itself. By studying human languages, linguists try to figure out not only the rule system – or the grammar – of the languages they study but also to understand the *nature* of these rules. Why are the rules the way they are? Why aren't they another way? If we know the answers to these questions, we think we will get closer to understanding how the human mind is used for thinking, talking, planning, fantasising, etc. and, therefore, ultimately how the human brain works. Linguistics, and therefore syntax, is a cognitive science, the science of the human mind. It is ultimately as much about the brain and the way the human brain works as it is about language. But why do we think that the study of a grammar is going to give us clues about the human brain? And even if that is true, how are we going to do it? Let us answer these questions in turn.

In this book, we are going to show you what the study of the English language can contribute to this bigger enterprise, understanding the human brain. But wait a minute. English is just English, right? And it differs from Japanese, or Swahili, or Russian. So to conclude after decades of research that English is the way it is because of properties of the human brain would be silly. Such a theory would predict that all humans speak English. And this is obviously not the case. Well, not so sure, actually. As stated above, we look at the rule system of English to discover what underlies these rules. To put it differently, what are the *principles* that underlie the rules of English? Other linguists at the same time look at the rule systems of Japanese, Swahili and Russian with the same goal in mind. What we discover is something quite extraordinary: *although the rules for English, Japanese, Swahili and Russian are quite distinct, the principles underlying these rules are the same for all these languages.* English, Japanese, Swahili and Russian look fundamentally different on the surface but when we look underneath that surface we discover that languages are much more alike than we would think by just looking at the surface.

The linguist Vivian Cook compared this kind of language variation with traffic rules. In the US, cars drive on the right-hand side of the road, whereas in Great Britain they drive on the left-hand side. On the surface, therefore, these traffic rules are completely different. However, they have one crucial principle in common: cars drive on one side of the road only, and drivers can't just pick their favourite side. All drivers, irrespective of where they are driving, therefore follow the same principle. Languages work the same: different on the surface but based on the same principles. So yes, in a deep sense all humans speak English, and all humans speak Japanese, Swahili and Russian, as well. Now, here is the point: these principles that languages have in common reveal properties of the human brain. Language is the way it is, and uses the principles that it does, because that is the way our human brain has evolved. The brain wouldn't allow other ways of doing language. And since English is obviously one of the languages that the human brain can do, studying it will contribute to the discovery of those principles that tell us something about the human brain.

This brings us to the next question: How do we study it? The grammar of English is present somewhere in brain tissue of a native speaker of English. However, just cutting away will not provide you with crucial information about what this grammar looks like. That would at best be a bloody affair. We could alternatively decide to do brain scans. Certainly less bloody, but this procedure has one serious thing in common with just cutting away: you first have to know what to look for. Without some prior understanding of the principles behind human grammars, it is like looking for the proverbial needle in the haystack. The best way to advance our knowledge about our linguistic capacities is to look very closely at the output of the grammar. What linguists do is just that. They 'reverse engineer' the grammar of English: if you can't look inside the machine, then make intelligent guesses about what it should look like inside based on what it can do. If you put coffee beans into a machine and press a button, hot coffee comes out. This means that there must be something in the machine that grinds the beans, heats the water and makes the coffee by combining the water and the ground coffee. You don't have to look inside the machine to know all this.

Doing linguistics works the same way. What is the output of the language machine? Well, it creates both correct and incorrect sentences, for instance, *Maria drank some coffee*, and *Maria some coffee drank*. *Maria drank some coffee* is a correct English sentence. We call that a grammatical sentence. And the sentence *Maria some coffee drank* is incorrect, or ungrammatical. Every native speaker of English can immediately tell you that. What we should do, therefore, is look carefully at grammatical and ungrammatical sentences of English and make educated guesses about how grammar in the brain of a native speaker makes the distinction. What components should grammar contain so that we get exactly the output that we see? Figuring this out is the job of a linguist. You formulate ideas that seem relevant to you, and test these against more (im-) possible sentences. And that is actually rather easy to do, since every native speaker of English knows whether a particular sentence is grammatical or not. Quite often, though, such first guesses about the internal workings of our language machine are not immediately correct, and more often than not you will have to go back to the drawing board. At some point, though, you will have an idea that works, and you will embark on the next problem. In this way, you try to slowly build a theory of English grammar. If all goes well, and we are pretty far ahead already, you end up with a plausible grammar for English. Not just a grammar of the surface rules, mind you, but a grammar that makes explicit which principles underlie these rules.

If you wished, you could then even build a machine that can generate only proper English sentences and never any bad ones. That is not where we will be at the end of this book (and no syntactician has actually ever got there), but we will take you on the road towards that point. It won't be a highway on which we speed past syntactic discoveries. It will be more like a crooked path that we have to cut for ourselves, and we will occasionally walk into dead ends. The reason for going the scenic route is to show you not just *what* we discovered but also *how* we discovered it. In this way, you will get a feel for syntax as a science and develop a better understanding of why the theory we end up with looks the way it does, and of how one builds theories in general.

Unfortunately, what we cannot do is look at every aspect of English grammar. As the title of this book reveals, we are going to look at syntax. So what is syntax anyway? Basically what we described above: that part of grammar that distinguishes between grammatical and ungrammatical sentences. Sentences are, simply put, combinations of words, and words can be thought of as simple units that mean something and sound a particular way. We know that a sentence can be ungrammatical even if it is put together with English words that are all perfect. If the words are perfect but the combination is not, it shows us that something must have gone wrong in the building process. Syntax is about the rules that guide that building process. If you obey the syntactic rules, you end up with a grammatical sentence, and if you violate a particular rule, the result will be ungrammatical. Now, what is true for words is also true for these multi-word utterances: they sound a particular way and they mean something specific. *Maria underestimates Harold* sounds different from *Adrian loves yellow chairs*, and it means something different from *Harold underestimates Maria*. What a sentence sounds like and means, then, depends on what you combine and how you combine. And this is determined by syntax. This gives us the following picture of the language machine (1), which you can call a *model of grammar*:

(1)

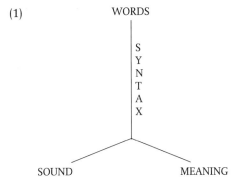

Syntax combines words into bigger units, and these units are uttered (by producing sound) and interpreted (by assigning meaning to them), and the focus of this book is on this combinatorial process. However, in the final chapters of this book we will also look at the sound and meaning systems of the grammar: how are sentences expressed and what exactly do they mean? In this way, we can show what syntax does in the overall grammar, and how we can tell syntax apart from sound and meaning.

This syntactic study has two significant outcomes, which we will highlight from the start. First of all, many factors can contribute to the ungrammaticality of a sentence. *Mary have loved Ahmed* is ungrammatical because there is something wrong with *have* (it should be *has*). *Why you have seen her?* is ungrammatical because there is something wrong with *you have* (it should be *have you*). *We love myself* is ungrammatical because there is something wrong with *myself* (it should be *ourselves*). *I want he to leave* is ungrammatical because there is something wrong with *he* (it should be *him*). And we could go on and on. However, what we will discover in this book is something profound. Although these sentences seem to violate different, unrelated rules, they in fact turn out to violate one and the same principle. English syntax can therefore be thought of as a lot of rules but also as the output of a severely restricted number of principles. And it is these principles we care about, remember?

The second outcome has to do with the model of grammar presented above. Note that this model has different components, apart from the words. There is a syntactic component, a sound component and a meaning component. This has an important consequence. If a sentence is ungrammatical, there can in principle be three reasons for it. It can be syntactically ungrammatical ('syntax error', so to speak), it can be uttered in the wrong way ('sound error'), or it could mean something weird or not mean anything ('meaning error'). You cannot know beforehand (that is, before you do some proper studying) what the cause is of ungrammaticality. And once you have done some research, your conclusions may be different from your initial expectations. Now, recall the sentences that we presented at the beginning of this introduction: *Mary drank some car* and *Mary some coffee drank*. Both are bad English sentences. At the end of this book, however, you will understand that the first sentence is not syntactically ungrammatical at all. It has a weird meaning but structurally the sentence is fine. And what about the second sentence, *Mary some coffee drank*? Well, it will turn out to be syntactically correct, too. It is just expressed in the wrong way. If you find this surprising, please realise that we've barely begun.

1 Categories and Features

CHAPTER OUTLINE

KEY TERMS
grammaticality
categories
features
subfeatures
substitution
nouns
verbs
open/closed classes

So, let's start. In the introduction we stated, very ambitiously, that by studying the rules underlying proper English sentences we may ultimately be able to better understand what is going on in the human mind or brain. So how do we study those rules? We will begin by looking at simple sentences and reveal an important insight: syntactic rules do not apply to particular words, but rather to particular categories that words belong to, e.g. nouns and verbs. That simple but fundamental insight already reduces the number of potential syntactic rules in a drastic way, and therefore saves us a lot of work. Moreover, we will see that words belong to a particular category because they carry features that are purely syntactic, and that must be distinguished from features that tell you how to pronounce those words or that tell you what they mean. These features will play a very important role throughout the book, and, for starters, they will help us make a first syntactic discovery: there are words that are never uttered.

1.1 Insight: Words and Categories

Syntax tries to understand why certain sentences (like *Mary loves Suzanne*) are good English sentences, whereas other ones (such as *loves Mary Suzanne* or *Mary snores Suzanne*) are bad English sentences. What causes them to be either good or bad?

Language consists of words. Words are elements that can be combined into sentences. In a way, you can think of words as the building blocks (like Lego blocks) with which sentences can be built. A simple sentence like *Mary loves Suzanne* consists of three words. The first idea therefore might be to say that there are certain rules in language (in this case, the English language) that allow the words *loves, Suzanne* and *Mary* to be combined in a particular order.

In essence, then, you need rules. If there weren't any rules, nobody could explain the correctness, often called the **grammaticality**, of some sentences and the ungrammaticality of others. There would be no way of stating the distinction if there were no rules. But how specific must these rules be? Arguably, there is no specific rule saying that the word *Mary* can be combined with the words *loves* and *Suzanne*, but not with the words *snores* and *Suzanne*. The reason is simple. If you replace the names of *Suzanne* and *Mary* by other names the same facts hold; *Bill loves Mary, Peter loves Helen* and *John loves Henry* are all equally good sentences of English. At the same time, *Bill snores Mary, Peter snores Helen* and *John snores Henry* are just as bad as *Mary snores Suzanne*. So it is not so much a property of *Mary* and *Suzanne* that allows them to be combined with *loves*, but rather a property of everything that has a name.

But even having a name is too restrictive: *Cats love fish* is as grammatical as *Mary loves Peter*. Saying that *love(s)* must be combined with things carrying a name is therefore missing a generalisation, an overall statement that correctly captures some property or behaviour of several individual cases. There is something fundamental that *Mary, Peter, cats* and *fish* share that makes it possible to combine these words with *love(s)* in a particular order.

We can take this one step further. That *Mary loves Suzanne* or *Peter loves Helen* is grammatical does not depend on the word *loves* either. If you replace *loves* by another word, such as *kills* or *kisses*, the sentences are equally fine. So just as much as *Mary, Peter, cats* and *fish* have something in common, so do *loves, kills* and *kisses*.

To conclude, a sentence consisting of three words like *Mary loves Suzanne* is not grammatical because these three words can be combined, but rather because these kinds of words can be combined. So here is the central insight of this chapter: syntax cares not about individual words but rather about kinds of words. The linguistic term for 'kind of word' is **category**.

The first task for a syntactician is now to identify all categories that exist in syntax. Once we know what categories play a role in a language, we can start to identify and explain the syntactic rules that apply to them. We have already identified two distinguishable categories, one that contains (proper) names and words like *cats* and *fish*, and one that contains words like *kisses, loves* and *kills*. These examples are all types of the two major categories in language: **nouns and verbs.** *Peter, Mary, cats* and *fish* belong to the first, and *loves, kisses* and *kills* belong to the second category. Other examples of nouns are **plural nouns** like *things*, **count(able) nouns** like *chair* and *table*, **mass nouns** like *butter* and *wine*, **abstract nouns**, such as *peace* and *democracy*; and there are many more. Examples of other verbs than *love* and *kiss*, which express a relation between two individuals and therefore require two nouns (*Mary loves Bill*), are verbs like *to snore* that require one element from the noun class (*Mary snores*) and *to give*, which require three other elements (*Mary gives John a book*), or other forms of the verbs we have already seen (*to love, loved*, etc.). But there are more categories than just nouns and verbs. For instance, there are **articles** (like *the* and *a(n)*), **complementisers** (like *that, if* and *whether*), **adjectives** (like *cold, blue* and *open*), **prepositions** (*in, on, after*, …) and, as we will see later on, a few more.

What is most interesting and striking here is not so much how many categories there are and how these categories are related to each other, but rather that every word belongs to some category. There is no word in any known human language that does not belong to a category. The fact that every word belongs to a category is a cornerstone of the way syntax works. Although nobody really knows how many words human beings know exactly (the estimates go from 50,000 to 90,000), the number of categories is much smaller. Compared to the number of words in a language, it's really just a handful. Now, suppose that syntactic rules were specific for every word in English. Then you would need thousands and thousands of syntactic rules, presumably several rules for every individual word. But if syntactic rules only apply to categories, the number of rules can be significantly reduced. To give an example, every noun can be combined with a definite article like *the*: *the chair, the table, the butter, the wine, the love, the democracy* and even **proper names**, as *the Mary* in *the Mary I used to love*. If you say that it is a property of the category noun that it can be combined with a definite article, you capture all these facts in one rule. On the other hand, if you have a rule that says that *chair* can be combined with *the*, and another rule that says that *table* can be combined with *the*, your set of syntactic rules would simply explode.

What we see is that words in the end are not the building blocks of syntax, but categories are. Syntactic rules dictate which categories can be combined, and which ones cannot. And if two categories can be combined, this holds for all elements that belong to that category. This is the first and one of the most important insights into syntax that we will discuss.

Exercises

A1 Say for the underlined words whether they are nouns. Try to justify your answer.
   a. We <u>booked</u> a <u>hotel</u> for three <u>days</u>.
   b. There is nothing better than <u>unprocessed</u> <u>food</u>.
   c. My <u>friend</u> from <u>Spain</u> speaks <u>Japanese</u>.
   d. I <u>finally</u> saw <u>Paul</u>'s <u>hamster</u>.
   e. Tina Turner is <u>singing</u> a <u>song</u> <u>about</u> <u>steamy</u> <u>windows</u>.
   f. Mary <u>sleeps</u> a <u>revolution</u> in three <u>sour</u> <u>ways</u>.

A2 Say for each underlined word whether it is a noun or a verb. Try to justify your answer.
   a. I <u>talk</u> way too much.
   b. An interesting <u>talk</u> on climate change was broadcast.
   c. There were <u>talks</u> that lasted for over an hour.
   d. No idea what he <u>talks</u> about!
   e. I want to <u>dream</u> that <u>dream</u> again.
   f. John started <u>singing</u> a song but his <u>singing</u> was not appreciated.

1.2 Implementation: Categories and Features

In this section, we will show how the major insight of this chapter (syntax deals with categories, not words) is implemented. An implementation is basically a way of turning your insight into a very precise and concrete proposal. This means, among other things, trying to understand how many categories can be distinguished, and figuring out how they can be distinguished. Once you have done this, you have a better understanding of what your insight amounts to. And then you have put yourself into a position in which you can determine what predictions the proposal makes. That will be the topic of section 1.3.

1.2.1 Distinguishing Categories

So far we have argued that every word belongs to a syntactic category. But how can we establish which word belongs to which category? To make this more concrete, let's focus on nouns and verbs. How do we know that one word (say, *car*) is a noun and that another word (e.g. *sing*) is a verb? Several possibilities arise. Perhaps it depends on the pronunciation of the word. Or on the meaning. Or maybe it is something else.

As for the first possibility, we can be brief. There is nothing in the pronunciation of the word *car* that makes it a noun. Other nouns have completely different pronunciations. Certain nouns can have one syllable (e.g. *cat*), others many more (the official name of the protein *titin*, for instance, has 189,819 letters). In addition, every possible vowel or consonant that can be part of a noun can be part of a verb, too. So the pronunciation of a word hardly ever reveals whether it is a noun, a verb or something else. In fact, some words can even be both nouns and verbs, for instance, *bike*, as in *the bike* and *to bike*. Both 'bikes' are pronounced the same way, showing that pronunciation is not telling.

Another guess: the meaning of a word reveals its category. This might be a much better hunch. It is a well-known fact that most nouns denote individual persons (*butcher*), animals (*cat*) or things (*table*), whereas most verbs denote actions (*to love, to kiss, to kill*). So, we could hypothesise (a hypothesis is a scientific assumption that you intend to test) that words denoting actions are verbs and words denoting individuals or things are nouns. Unfortunately, this guess cannot be correct either. There are nouns that actually denote actions (*war, dance*) and nouns that do not refer to persons or things (*eternity, mankind, love*), and there are verbs that do not denote actions (*to be, to seem, to own, to know*) and may even refer to individuals (*to pair up*). Even though nouns and verbs quite often show semantic (i.e. meaningful) differences, there is no clear-cut semantic difference between the two. This may perhaps be best seen in the following example:

(1)   Everybody was *dancing* well; John's *dancing* was the best.

In (1), the first *dancing* is a verb, but the second *dancing* is a noun. Still, what these words refer to is hardly different. So, even though the meaning hypothesis comes closer than the form hypothesis, it is simply not good enough. You cannot predict on the basis of the meaning of a word whether it is a noun or a verb, and a hypothesis that makes incorrect predictions is basically an incorrect hypothesis. We conclude, therefore, that something else must distinguish verbs from nouns.

Now, what is left? If the distinction between nouns and verbs does not ultimately lie in the form of the word nor in its meaning, it must have something to do with the combinatorial possibilities of words. And this turns out to be right, and there are two good diagnostics we can use.

The first diagnostic has to do with syntax. Nouns and verbs behave differently when it comes to the syntactic surroundings they can occur in. Nouns can be preceded by an article, for instance, but verbs cannot. We indicate that a combination is ungrammatical by putting an asterisk in front of it, as in the examples in (2b) and (3b). Also, nouns but not verbs can be modified by adjectives to create grammatical expressions, as (3) shows:

(2)   a.   the door/the wine/the democracy
       b.   *the was/*the seems/*the owns

(3)   a.   large doors/delicious wines/free democracy
       b.   *large was/*delicious seems/*red owns

Verbs, on the other hand, can appear after the infinitive marker *to*, which nouns cannot do:

(4)   a.   John wants to seem stupid.
       b.   John wants to own the original copy.
       c.   *John wants to door.
       d.   *John wants to democracy.

The second diagnostic has to do with word building, or morphology. We know that morphologically nouns and verbs behave differently. A verb, for instance, can be put in the past tense, but a noun cannot.

(5)   a.   The girl is/was ill.
      b.   The teacher seems/seemed ill.
      c.   Peter owns/owned the original copy.

On the other hand, nouns can be combined with the so-called plural morpheme -s (*door* – *doors*/wine – *wines*/democracy – *democracies*), unless these nouns have a so-called irregular plural (for instance, *mouse* – *mice*). You can of course also attach an -s to a verb but that would not be the plural -s but the -s indicating that the **subject** (*the girl, the teacher, Peter*) is 3rd person singular (distinguishing it from other persons of the verb, such as *I* and *they*).

So in short, a verb is a verb because it behaves grammatically like a verb, and a noun behaves grammatically in a different way. These grammatical differences are as robust as they can be. There is no single exception to the rule that nouns can be preceded by a definite article. Neither is there a single verb that lacks a past tense form (at best the past tense form is irregular, as is the case with *run* – *ran*, but nobody disputes that *ran* is the past tense of *run*). Now, why not take these exceptionless rules as a starting point and say that such grammatical properties (or syntactic properties) of a word determine its category? So we say that words that can be combined with an article are nouns, and words that have a past–present tense distinction are verbs – *by definition*.

This new way of defining categories already takes us quite far. To see this, have a look at the following sentence that contains some nonsense words, words that do not exist in English:

(6)   The glump flottered.

Clearly, you cannot say what this sentence means. We have no clue what *glump* or *flottered* mean, but on the basis of this example you can already tell that *glump* is a noun and *to flotter* is a verb (with *flottered* being its past tense). How do we know this? Well, we know that syntactically everything that can be combined with an article is a noun and that sentences must contain verbs. Since *glump* and *the* are not verbs, *flottered* must be. And since it ends in -ed and not in -s, it must be the past tense of the verb.

In conclusion, then, we can distinguish verbs from nouns because they have different combinatorial possibilities, both morphologically and syntactically. In the next section, we will extend these insights to figure out what other categories there are, and what underlies them.

1.2.2 Categories and Features

What distinguishes different grammatical categories has nothing to do with the form of words and very little to do with meaning: even though meaning can give you some pointers as to whether a word is a noun or a verb, it can't take you the whole way. Being a noun or a verb means that you behave in a certain way, irrespective of the way you are pronounced (a.k.a. your phonological properties) and of what you mean (a.k.a. your semantic properties). The consequence of this is that every word has three types of properties: phonological, semantic and syntactic. Let's illustrate this for *door* and *kill*.

(7) a. *door*: Phonological properties   /dɔː/
                  Semantic properties   PART OF A HOUSE

                                             HAS A HANDLE

                                             MADE OF A CERTAIN MATERIAL
                  Syntactic properties   being a noun (= [N])

     b. *kill*: Phonological properties   /kil/
                  Semantic properties   CAUSE TO DIE

                                             REQUIRES TWO PARTIES (THE

                                             KILLER AND THE KILLED)
                  Syntactic properties   being a verb (= [V])

Phonological properties are expressed by symbols in between slashes. These symbols are part of the so-called International Phonetic Alphabet (IPA) and simply describe how a word is pronounced; /dɔː/ reflects (Southern British English) pronunciation of the word *door*. The semantic properties are written in CAPS and taken together convey the meaning of a particular word. The exact way in which both phonological and semantic properties are represented is not really of any concern here, and shouldn't worry you at all. It's the syntactic properties that we're interested in. Syntactic properties are always displayed as a **feature**. To every noun is attributed the feature indicating that it is a noun, abbreviated as [N]; to every verb the feature indicating that it is a verb, ([V]). These features are sometimes related to, but are always independent of, the meaning, as we saw before.

A major advantage of distinguishing syntactic features from semantic and phonological properties is that we can distinguish ungrammatical sentences from grammatical sentences regardless of their meaning. Suppose we say: *I drank some coffee*. This sentence is grammatical, showing that any element with feature [N] is acceptable in the construction 'I drank some ... ' Is this correct? Suppose you say the following:

(8) I drank some furniture.

The sentence in (8) is crazy, because furniture is not something that you drink. But nothing is wrong *syntactically*. Speakers of English still feel that the sentence is proper English. The only reason why it is deviant is its meaning. On the other hand, if you say: *I some coffee drank*, you immediately feel that the sentence is bad English, even though it is not too hard to figure out what it could mean. This sentence is bad because English does not allow a word order in which the object (*some coffee*) precedes rather than follows the verb it belongs to (in this case: *drank*).

Maybe you find it hard to distinguish the two kinds of odd sentences (ungrammatical vs. grammatical but semantically weird). There is a simple test to tease these two apart, though, the so-called *cartoon test*. We cannot imagine a human being drinking some furniture, but we can very well imagine a cartoon in which some character first drinks a table, then a chair and finally a couch. It may take some wizard who can magically make furniture fluid, but in that context the wizard can say 'I drank some furniture' and there is nothing wrong with that English sentence any more. However, we cannot imagine any cartoon in which the wizard can make 'I some coffee drank' a sentence with which nothing is wrong. Whatever magical tricks (s)he performs, it will always be a bad sentence. So that is the test: if you can imagine a cartoon in which some weird sentence becomes normal, this sentence is grammatical. If you cannot imagine such a cartoon, the sentence is ungrammatical.

The cartoon test now gives us a great tool: in a sentence like (8), any word that can be inserted to replace the dots in *I drank some …* must be a noun and therefore have a feature [N]. The reason is that from (8) we can tell that syntax allows us to combine an element like *some* with an element carrying [N]. If you put in *coffee* you get a normal (sometimes called salient) meaning, if you add in *furniture*, the sentence has a weird meaning, but it is nevertheless grammatical, as is shown by the cartoon test. We can now, actually, turn this into a generalisation. Let's make a (first) attempt:

(9)   If two elements X and Y share the same syntactic features, then in every grammatical sentence that contains X you can replace X by Y (and vice versa) and the sentence remains grammatical.

To see what this means, let's assume X stands for *coffee* and Y for *furniture*. If *coffee* and *furniture* share the same features, every grammatical sentence with the word *coffee* will remain grammatical if you replace *coffee* by *furniture*, and vice versa. Since (9) is about substituting elements, it is often called the **substitution test**.

Equipped with this generalisation, we are now not only able to establish which elements are nouns, we can use it to see what other categories we can distinguish in syntax. Take the expressions *the wine* and *expensive wine*, both proper English expressions. Given (9), we must say that *expensive* is not a noun. After all, *the expensive* is bad, just as *I drank some expensive* is. This shows, then, that *expensive* and *wine* are not of the same category. *Expensive* is also not a verb, since *John wants to expensive the wine* is also bad. *Expensive* must then be of a different category, a category we know as adjectives.

Now let us look at articles, like *the*. Both *the wine* and *red wine* are fine. This may at first give the impression that *the* and *red* are of the same type: they can both be combined with the noun *wine*. But it is easy to see that not every article can be replaced by an adjective and vice versa: *expensive red wine* is fine, but if you replace *red* by an article the result is ungrammatical: **expensive the wine*.

So simple observations that use the diagnostic in (9) have led us to conclude that there are minimally four categories in English: nouns, adjectives, articles and verbs. But the search continues. We can identify words like *in* and *under*. Since *in* in *in the red car* cannot be replaced by an article, noun, adjective or verb, *in* must belong to a different category. We call words of this type **prepositions**. Now, you might say that you can replace *in* in the string *in the red car* with a verb, like *buy*, so you get the grammatical string *buy the red car*. Doesn't this show that *in* is actually a verb? No, because you cannot randomly replace a verb with a preposition. Verbs are always fine after *to* (*to buy*), but a preposition such as *in* is not (**to in*). Or take the sentence *We buy the red car*, and replace *buy* by a preposition: **We in the red car*. The result is again pretty bad. The conclusion is that we are forced to adopt a separate category for words like *in* and *under*, so that a distinct category for preposition is justified.

What other categories are there? Here we will not go through the evidence for each and every one of them, but just list the most important ones. (Proving that these elements are indeed categories is a fun exercise you can do yourself.) Apart from verbs, nouns, adjectives, articles and prepositions, we can also distinguish **complementisers**, such as *that, if, whether, because*, etc. All these complementisers can introduce a new clause in the sentence. Finally, there is also a category named **adverbs**, which in English fairly often (but not always) end in *-ly*: *quickly, rarely, possibly, immediately*, but also *soon* and *seldom*. Adverbs can all modify the meaning of the verb, even though the manner of modification might be quite different: *John walked quickly* means that the walking took place in a quick manner, whereas *John possibly walked* indicates that the speaker isn't sure whether the walking took place at all.

The categories described above are the most important ones in English, but the list is not complete. There are other words that in some sense look like nouns, but aren't in every respect. **Pronouns**, like *I, him* or *us*, and proper names, like *John* and *Mary*, can sometimes replace nouns (e.g. *Wine is red; It is red; John is red*), but sometimes the combination of a noun plus an article (*The wine is red → It is red; John is ill → He is ill*). To properly understand what is behind these categories, we will have to go further (and we will do so in the next section). First, let us take a closer look at the categories identified so far. We can observe that these categories differ in quite substantial ways. Suppose we asked you what articles there are in English. Probably you would say: *the* and *a(n)*. To come up with a list of all English complementisers is a harder job but not one that is impossible (try it yourself). But if we were to ask you to make a list of all nouns or verbs, then you would immediately realise that taking the rest of the day off would not suffice. The number of nouns and verbs easily exceeds tens of thousands, and we create new nouns and verbs every day. Think, for instance, of new nouns such as *selfie*, or verbs like *to whatsapp*. And furthermore, we can create new nouns on the spot: take a *dog trainer* (which, even though you write it separately, is really one word). A dog trainer trains dogs. But how about somebody who trains dog trainers? That would be a *dog trainer trainer*, and these people have been trained again by a *dog trainer trainer trainer*, etc. The fact that you can repeat this process endlessly shows that the number of nouns in a language is actually infinite.

So we can distinguish **closed classes**, categories like articles and complementisers, that have only a handful of members, and **open classes**, like nouns, verbs and also adjectives and adverbs. The latter have an unlimited number of elements. The reason why we introduce open- and closed-class categories is that there is another important difference between the two. It is generally harder to provide a meaning for an item from a closed class. You probably need to be a linguist to do this. Take for instance *that* in *I know that is true* and try to define what its meaning is. Or *that* in *I know that Harry is a fool*. Or try to say what the meaning difference is between the English articles *the* and *a*. A linguist can tell you that you are looking at a difference in definiteness. *The car* refers to one specific car, whereas *a car* has a much vaguer meaning. Saying *The car is mine* is much better than saying *A car is mine*. Definiteness is a linguistic property and a linguist can explain what is meant by it. This advantage that linguists have over non-linguists disappears, however, when we turn to items from open classes like nouns or verbs. If you want to know the difference between *to kill* and *to murder* you may have more luck asking a policeman or a lawyer than a linguist. And doctors can tell you the difference between a kidney and a liver. Closed-class categories like articles and complementisers, you might say, have a more grammatical function, and they are usually referred to as **functional categories**. Open-class categories like verbs and nouns, on the other hand, tell us much more about the world and are known as **lexical categories**.

In sum, we can say that the generalisation in (9) does an excellent job in distinguishing those categories that need to be distinguished in syntax, simply because they can be syntactically distinguished: different categories appear in different syntactic contexts. The noteworthy property of (9) is that it only cares about the feature of an element (for instance, whether it carries [N] or [V]), and is not concerned with the meaning of elements. From this it follows that the distinction between nouns and verbs cannot be derived from their meaning.

In the next section, we will see that (9) makes an important prediction. We will therefore explore the consequences of this prediction and show that this endeavour leads us to other features that, like categorial features, play a distinguishing role in syntax.

Exercises

A3   To what category do the underlined words belong?
a.   <u>I</u> <u>love</u> to read <u>a</u> book.
b.   Nobody <u>has</u> ever <u>helped</u> me.
c.   <u>The</u> red <u>car</u> is <u>parked in</u> the street.
d.   Did I <u>ever</u> say <u>that</u> you were crazy <u>about</u> <u>linguistics</u>?

A4 Take the following sentences, which are all odd. Are these ungrammatical (i.e. bad for syntactic reasons), or are they just bad for semantic reasons but still grammatical?
  a. I didn't say nothing to nobody about none of the students I never knew.
  b. The Queen of the USA is in love with the mayor of Vatican City.
  c. John and Mary is in the garden.
  d. Some of the students but David passed the test.
  e. The car is in garage the.
  f. Colourless green ideas sleep furiously.

B5 Does the cartoon test work for all cases in A4?

B6 The words *happy* and *happily* are visibly distinct. The second carries the affix *-ly* signalling that it is an adverb and not an adjective. Show that we can also distinguish adverbs from adjectives because of the different environments in which these two categories can (not) appear.

B7 If you want to establish whether a word is an adjective or adverb, the 'affix *-ly* test' turns out to be very unreliable. Show that this is true by discussing the behaviour of the words *jolly, silly, often* and *always*.

B8 The word *that* can be used both to introduce clauses (*I know that he cheated on his wife*) and to precede nouns (*I just love that book about syntax*). Use the substitution test to show that the two *that*'s are different words pronounced in the same way. Do the same for *to* (*I want to leave – I drove to Amsterdam*).

C9 We can distinguish open-class categories from closed-class categories using the criteria mentioned in the text. Discuss the status of prepositions with respect to this distinction. Do they belong to an open or closed class? Hint: arguments can go both ways.

C10 We observed that neither the way a word is pronounced nor what a word means is a reliable indicator of the category to which that word belongs. There is a third option that we have glanced at, however. Some words are morphologically complex; they consist of several morphemes put together. Take words like *thicken, deepen* and *strengthen* that are created by adding the morpheme *-en* to a stem morpheme. Since all these words end up being verbs, you may wonder whether the *-en* morpheme is a reliable clue for 'verbhood'. Discuss this, and do the same for *-er* in words like *killer, dancer* and *believer*.

1.3 Consequences: Features and Subfeatures

Now, where do we stand? We have figured out that every word belongs to a syntactic category, and we have established a way of determining which elements belong to the same category, and which elements belong to different categories. This was simply the result of implementing the insight that syntax does not care about particular words, but only about what categories these words belong to. On the basis of this, we have already concluded that English has verbs, nouns, adjectives, adverbs, prepositions, complementisers and articles. English syntax, therefore, has rules that are sensitive to the features [V], [N], [A] (for adjectives), [Adv] (for adverbs), [P] (for prepositions), [C] (for complementisers) and [D] (for articles). The reason that we say that articles have a feature [D], and not for instance [Art], is that articles are often referred to as **determiners** (the exact difference between articles and determiners will be explained in chapter 4). It is these features that the rules of syntax refer to. For instance, *the red car* is a proper English expression, since the rules of English allow elements carrying the features [D], [A] and [N] to be combined in this particular way. In our implementation, we define belonging to some syntactic category as carrying some syntactic feature. That seems like a small, technical step, but it has some important consequences that increase our understanding of syntax. After all, even though it is hard to think of certain words as belonging to more than one category, it is not so hard to think of words carrying more than one feature. And it turns out that words can indeed do that.

1.3.1 Subfeatures of Nouns

Let's start by observing that reality looks a little more complicated than what (9) may have suggested so far. To see this, take the following minimal pair. A minimal pair is a set of two examples that differ in only one way.

(10) a. John saw the red car.
     b. John saw the red cars.

Both sentences are grammatical, suggesting that *car* and *cars* belong to the same category. Both *car* and *cars* are nouns (after all, you can say *the car* and *the cars*), so that one can occur where the other can occur. But if two elements carry the same feature, it is predicted by (9) that the two can always be interchanged. This, however, is not correct, as we can see in the following pair:

(11) a. *John saw red car.
     b. John saw red cars.

The example in (11a) is bad, the one in (11b) is not. Does this mean that *car* and *cars* do not belong to the same category? If that were the case, we would have to conclude that the substitution test (that follows from the generalisation in (9)) is useless as a way of finding out the category of a particular word. This would mean that we could not even conclude for (10) that both *car* and *cars* are nouns, because one cannot always substitute *car* for *cars*, or vice versa. And the question would immediately arise what kind of category *car* or *cars* belong to, if not that of noun. We would essentially be back to square 1.

Luckily, this is only apparently the case. It turns out that the substitution test in (9) works even better than we thought. Let us explain. So far, we have restricted our attention to so-called categorial features, features that determine to what category some word belongs. We basically wanted to know how we can establish that a particular element is a verb or a noun, and the substitution test proved very helpful. But it is not the case that every verb is just a verb. Take, for instance, *repeats* in *He repeats himself. Repeats* has more properties than being a verb. For example, *repeats* can only be used with 3rd-person singular subjects. Saying it only carries [V] is not enough.

What this must mean is that elements can carry multiple features, not just one. Now, take a look again at what the substitution test says. It says that you can only replace element X by element Y if they share the same syntactic features (with 'features' in the plural). This now makes a very strong prediction: whenever we cannot substitute element X for Y, there must be *some* feature that distinguishes them. This can be a categorial feature but it does not have to be. Since elements carry multiple features, any feature can cause substitution to fail. The fact that we can replace *car* by *cars* in (10) shows us that both *car* and *cars* are nouns. We cannot replace *car* by *memorise*, showing that *memorise* is not a noun (**John saw the red memorise*). Since we cannot replace *cars* by *car* in (11), there must be a feature that *car* carries but *cars* does not, or vice versa.

Now, if we want to keep the substitution test as a useful tool, it is important that we can indeed identify a feature that distinguishes *car* from *cars*. If we cannot find reasons for such a distinguishing feature, this means that we have run into a mystery and must conclude that we do not understand our own generalisation in (9) any more. Now, luckily it is quite easy to see what distinguishes *car* from *cars*. We know that *car* and *cars* differ in meaning: *car* is **singular** and *cars* is **plural**. The singular–plural distinction, at least in English (and, as it turns out, in most languages of the world), is not just a semantic distinction but also plays a role in syntax. It must, therefore, also be a syntactic feature. This comes as no surprise when you think of it, because English grammar shows that the singular–plural distinction is important in syntax. Take the basic patterns in (12):

(12) a.   The car is red.
      b.   The cars are red.

If the subject is *the car*, the verb has to be *is* and not *are*, and the opposite is true when the subject is *the cars*. It matters in syntax whether an element is singular or plural because you see its effects, such as the shape of the verb that agrees with the subject. So we need to say that *car* and *cars* both have a feature [N], but that *car* has an additional feature [Singular] and *cars* has a feature [Plural]. Since the rules of English say that every combination of the article *the* and an adjective can be combined with some element [N], it now follows that you can replace *car* by *cars* (and vice versa) in example (10). But only certain nouns can be preceded by an adjective in the absence of an article. Plural nouns can do that without any problem. So, *cars*, carrying [N] plus [Plural], is fine in (11), but *car*, carrying [N] plus [Singular], is not.

To conclude the discussion so far, we have used the substitution test as a tool for distinguishing elements that belong to different categories. As it turns out, the tool is more powerful, as it also leads us to discover non-categorial features that play an important role in syntax, such as the singular–plural distinction. Applying the tool in (9) leads us to this discovery. So let's use our familiar tool, now endowed with even more power, and explore what other features we need in order to understand what syntax cares about.

The [Singular]/[Plural] distinction is not the only way in which nouns can be different from each other. In (13), we discover the relevance of another subfeature:

(13)   a.   *Car is red.
       b.   Blood is red.

Even though both *car* and *blood* carry [N] and [Singular], they cannot be interchanged in every sentence. The reason is that *car* is a so-called count noun, whereas *blood* is not. You can say *one car, two cars,* but you can't say *one blood, two bloods. Blood* is therefore called a mass noun. This is because nouns like *blood* refer to unspecified masses of some stuff, not to individual people or things. Since the mass–count distinction between nouns can be responsible for a difference in grammaticality too, as (13) shows, grammar must also be sensitive to [Mass] and [Count] features on nouns. We therefore conclude that the noun *car* must have three features: [N], [Singular] and [Count], whereas *blood* has [N], [Singular] and [Mass]. We see that nouns exploit two pairs of subfeatures, [Count]/[Mass] and [Singular]/[Plural], which we can put into a structure as in (14).

(14)

```
                              [N]
                 ┌─────────────┴─────────────┐
             [Count]                      [Mass]
          ┌─────┴─────┐              ┌──────┴──────┐
      [Singular]  [Plural]       [Singular]    [Plural]

        car        cars            blood      DOES NOT OCCUR
```

What (14) shows is that there are count and mass nouns, and the former category comes in two flavours, singular count nouns and plural count nouns. Mass nouns, by contrast, come not in two flavours but only in one. As (13b) shows, a mass noun requires the agreeing verbal form to appear in the singular: change *is* to *are* and the result becomes ungrammatical. Mass nouns cannot appear in the plural. The reason is straightforward: in order to be able to appear in the plural, you must be countable and mass nouns are not countable; only count nouns are, and that's how they are defined.

Note that it is possible for some (but not all) mass nouns to become count nouns. An example is *wine*. It can occur as a subject without an article, as in (15a), showing us that it behaves like a mass noun. On the other hand, its co-occurrence with *this* and *those* in (15b)–(15c) shows that you can turn it into a count noun.

(15)   a.   Wine is always good in Spain.
       b.   This wine is always good in Spain.
       c.   Those wines are always good in Spain.

Other mass nouns, like *blood*, do not function as count nouns (you can't say *those bloods*), although one could imagine that, in an environment where bottled quantities of blood are as common as bottles of wine (such as in a hospital or vampire community), opinion as to the grammaticality of *those bloods* may be different. It is impossible, however, to turn a noun carrying the feature [Count] into a noun carrying [Mass], and this explains the ungrammaticality in (13a).

So far, we have used the substitution test to discover which features and subfeatures play a role in syntax. That is quite an achievement for such a simple test. Given this success, we are now in a position to trust the test well enough to drive its logic to its extreme. And if we do, we will come to a surprising conclusion: there exist words that are not expressed. How do we know that? Well, just run all the substitution tests with the different noun types we have now introduced. Consider the following data:

(16) a. I like a car.
      b. I like the cars.
      c. I like cars.
      d. I like blood.

What these examples show us is that *a car, the cars, cars* and *blood* all pass the substitution test: *a car* can appear where *the cars, cars* and *blood* can also appear, etc. This means that they must be categorially similar. Now, what category would that be? According to (16a)–(16b), what is present after *I like* is the sequence of features [D] and [N]. However, according to (16c)–(16d), *I like* can be followed by something carrying just [N]. Now, it could very well be the case that an '*I like*' context (or any so-called verb–object context for that matter) is flexible with respect to what elements may follow it, as long as it contains [N]. But that is too weak. If this were true, the following sentence would be grammatical, contrary to fact:

(17) *I like car.

So more needs to be said. We cannot say that anything carrying [N] is acceptable in '*I like*' contexts. It should be [N] plus something else, and the most obvious candidate for this 'something else' is of course [D]. After all, these are the elements that we see showing up in (16a)–(16b). Here is the point: the logic of the substitution test leads us to conclude that *I like* is combined with the sequence of a [D] and [N] element. Therefore, there must be [D] elements in (16c)–(16d), even though we cannot see them. If *a car, the cars, cars* and *blood* have to be categorially similar, there are only two ways to proceed. Either we say that the articles we see in (16a)–(16b) are not really there, or we say that (16c)–(16d) contain articles although we cannot see them. Now, the first option is more obviously wrong than the second option (it is hard to say that something that you see isn't present), so we adopt the second option. Strictly applying the test in (9) leaves us no other choice.

This means that we accept the existence of articles that are unexpressed, at least in English. ('Unexpressed' means that they are still there in the syntax, but you don't see or hear them.) This leads to the following article system for English: in definite contexts the article *the* is used, and in indefinite contexts the choice depends on the features of the noun. With [Singular]/[Count] nouns *a/an* is used, and in other contexts the unexpressed article ∅ is used. This system is schematised in the following table:

(18) ARTICLES   [Singular][Count][N]   [Plural][Count][N] or
                                                [Mass][N]

      DEFINITE [D]   the car   the cars, the blood
      INDEFINITE [D]   a car   ∅ cars, ∅ blood

The inclusion of unexpressed articles in two specific contexts explains two facts. The first, as we have seen, is that it helps us understand that *cars* and *blood* can substitute for *a car* and *the cars*. The second fact is a prediction that follows from the schema in (18). Once indefinite *cars* and *blood* in (16c)–(16d) have been combined with an unexpressed article, it should be impossible to combine them with an expressed one. After all, we cannot say *the the car*, or *a a car*, strongly suggesting that combining a noun with one article is the maximum. This prediction is correct, as the following data illustrate:

(19) a. *I like a cars.
      b. *I like a blood.

To be honest, the ungrammaticality of (19a) is hardly surprising. If article *a* only combines with singular nouns, then obviously combining it with a plural noun like *cars* is impossible. But *blood* is singular, because it triggers singular agreement in the verb (see (13b)). Therefore, the example in (19b) is ungrammatical in a meaningful way: it correctly follows from the existence of the unstated article which English uses in indefinite contexts with nouns carrying [Mass].

We are nearly done now. There is one class of nouns whose features we have not identified yet. This is the class to which pronouns (elements like *I, you, they, me, him* and *us*) and proper nouns (*John, Mary, Queen Elizabeth*) belong. You might wonder why we want to treat these two together, but it is easy to see that pronouns can be replaced by proper nouns and vice versa:

(20) a. John left.   ↔   He left.
      b. I like Mary.   ↔   I like her.

Note that there are some cases where this doesn't work. For instance, *they* in *They leave* cannot be replaced by *Mary* (as *Mary leave* is ungrammatical), but that shouldn't surprise you by now. Whatever category a pronoun belongs to, this category may have additional subfeatures such as [Singular] and [Plural]. And obviously, one cannot replace singular *Mary* by a plural pronoun *they*.

As their names already reveal, pronouns and proper nouns in some sense behave like nouns. For instance, a mass noun or a plural count noun can easily be replaced by a proper name or a pronoun:

(21) a. I like wine. ↔ I like Mary.
    b. I like cars. ↔ I like her.

But we now should be careful here. We have previously seen that *wine* and *cars* in (21) are not nouns only when they appear in the '*I like*' context, because they can substitute for combinations of a [D] and an [N] category. For this reason, we assumed the existence of unexpressed articles. In fact, we can use pronouns and proper nouns in '*I like*' contexts too, as (21) shows. It stands to reason, therefore, that we analyse pronouns and proper nouns along similar lines: they are preceded by an unexpressed article.

(22) a. I like $[\varnothing]_D$ Mary$_N$.
    b. I like $[\varnothing]_D$ her$_N$.

This is a very suspect analysis, however. With mass nouns and plural count nouns, we saw that they are combined with unexpressed articles in indefinite contexts. Outside of these contexts, however, they could still be combined with an article. *A blood* is ungrammatical (unless you are a doctor or a vampire), but *the blood* is not. And *cars* can be combined with *the* without any problems. Pronouns and proper names, however, cannot be simply combined with any article, as the following data show:

(23) a. Cars are cool.
    a'. The cars are cool.
    b. Water is liquid.
    b'. The water is liquid.

(24) a. *The John is cool.
    a'. *A John is cool.
    b. *The he is cool.
    b'. *A he is cool.

Now, if pronouns and proper nouns can never be combined with any expressed article, in contrast to *blood* and *cars*, it is not very plausible to assume that they can be combined with an unexpressed one. This means that the analysis we adopted for indefinite mass nouns and plural count nouns does not carry over to pronouns and proper nouns.

What other analysis can be pursued, then? Note that the analysis must still be able to account for the relevant substitution options. That is, the data in (21) must still be accounted for. Now, if pronouns and proper names can substitute for combinations of a [D] and an [N] but cannot be combined with a [D] category, this only leaves one option: they carry both an [N] and a [D] feature. Then you can account for both facts at the same time. Pronouns and proper names can substitute for [D]–[N] combinations because they have the relevant features. At the same time, they cannot be combined with articles because they already carry the [D] feature.

Now, you might object and say that it would be weird that some categorial features, such as [D], can be a feature of an element that already carries some other categorial feature, [N]. But why would that be weird? So far, nothing we have said would forbid it. And allowing it actually solves a problem that would be very hard to tackle otherwise. You might even take this a step further. If you don't forbid a particular feature combination (like [D] and [N]), you are in fact predicting that their combination should be possible (unless there are other reasons to rule it out, of course). And so pronouns and proper names nicely confirm this prediction. Pronouns and proper names thus carry both [N] and [D]. In addition, they carry number features, [Singular] or [Plural]. And pronouns can even carry person features ([1st person], [2nd person], [3rd person]) as well (e.g., *I, you, she*).

1.3.2 Subfeatures of Verbs

Applying the tool in (9) helped us in finding more syntactic features than just [N] in the domain of nouns, and made us discover some new facts. Proper nouns and pronouns carry both [N] and [D], and there exists an unpronounced article $\emptyset_D$. But now we should also be able to unravel other features in other domains. We have already seen, for instance, that in the domain of verbs different kinds are identified as well. If our approach is correct, we should also expect various subfeatures here. And indeed, such verbal subfeatures exist as well.

In order to explore what is going on in the verbal domain, let's focus on regular verbs (so not verbs like *to be* or *to have*). Now, verbs do not only carry the feature [V] but also other features that are grammatically important. For instance, the verb *(to) dance* can be used in different forms. It can show agreement with the subject, as the presence of *-s* in (25b) shows, or it can carry a marker for past tense, such as the *-d* in (26).

(25)   a.   I/you/we/they dance   Finite (present)
       b.   he/she/it dances

(26)   I/you/he/we/they danced   Finite (past)

Verbs that are marked for agreement and/or tense are called finite verbs, as indicated above. These contrast with non-finite forms, and we can distinguish three of these:

(27)   to dance   Infinitive

(28)   he has danced   Perfect participle

(29)   he is dancing   Progressive participle

These three verbal forms are not marked for either agreement or tense. You may perhaps be inclined to interpret the *-(e)d* in *danced* in (28) as a past tense marker, but it is not: it indicates that the verb is a participle. The sentence itself is in the present and not the past tense, which is determined by the finite verb *has*, the past tense of which would be *had*. In English, you can clearly show that (28) is a sentence in the present tense because including an adverb referring to the past tense makes the sentence ungrammatical. Note the following contrast:

(30)   a.   *Yesterday, John has danced.
       b.   Yesterday, John danced.

The different shapes that *dance* can appear in show that the feature [V] at most captures their similarities but not their differences. We need more features, and the terms in the right-hand side column of (25)–(29) suggest some names for features. Again, subgroups can be identified within these five distinct forms and these subgroups can be described with the use of particular features. Take for instance (25) and (26). There is something that these forms have in common to the exclusion of the other verbal forms. The forms in (25) and (26) can be combined only with a subject, thereby forming a grammatical sentence: *You dance, He dances* and *He danced* are grammatical sentences in English. You certainly cannot do this with the forms in (27) and (29): *You to dance* and *You dancing* are not grammatical sentences in English.

It may look like you can combine just a subject with the form in (28) (after all, *You danced* is grammatical) but that is coincidental. It so happens that the regular past tense form in English is identical to the regular perfect participle, so you cannot know whether *You danced* is grammatical because you have combined a subject with the past tense form, or with the perfect participle. Here, irregular verbs come to the rescue. Take the verb *to fall*. The past tense form is *fell* and the perfect participle is *fallen*. Although *You fell* is a grammatical sentence, *You fallen* is not. This shows that you cannot combine a subject with a perfect participle to form a grammatical sentence.

Since the forms of *dance* in (25) and (26) can be combined only with a subject, in contrast to the forms in (27), (28) and (29), we need to distinguish these forms by a feature. The label we use is [Finite]. As said, a finite verb is a verb that is marked for tense and/or for agreement, and only finite verbs can be combined with only a subject to create a grammatical sentence. The forms in (25) express present tense (denoting an event happening in the present), whereas the form in (26) expresses past tense, denoting that the event took place in the past. So what we say is that *dance* and *dances* in (25) carry the feature [Present], whereas *danced* in (26) carries the feature [Past]. But for the forms in (25) that is not enough, as this cannot make the distinction between the 3rd person singular and the other forms: *dances* in (25b) must carry an additional feature [3SG] (which stands for 3rd person singular), so that its featural make-up is [V], [Finite], [Present] and [3SG].

So far, we have identified the finite verb forms among the total number of verb forms and shown that these contain forms that carry either the [Past] or the [Present] feature. Within the set of present-tense forms, an additional distinction must be made related to the expression of agreement with the subject. Here, a question arises. We see that the form *dance* can appear with any subject, as long as the subject is not 3rd person singular. But what feature do we assign to finite *dance*? Take a look at the **hierarchical** representation we have established so far.

(31)

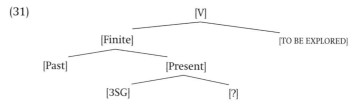

What feature do we put in place of the question mark in (31)? There are two solutions to this problem. The first is to say that this representation is wrong. One could, for instance, say that [Present] splits up into [Singular] and [Plural] and that [Singular] splits up into [1SG], [2SG] and [3SG]. In essence, then, we would replace (31) by (32):

(32)

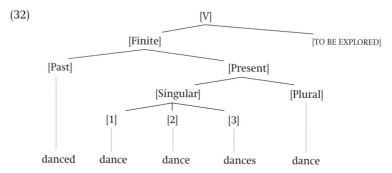

The consequence of this move is that we have to say that there are at least three versions of finite *dance* that accidentally all look the same. In fact, if the singular makes a distinction between [1], [2] and [3] (where [1] and [2] accidentally look the same), there is nothing that excludes making these person distinctions in the plural too, even though in the plural [1], [2] and [3] then accidentally look the same. This is of course a possible claim, and remember that we said something similar for *danced*, which is ambiguous between a finite past tense form and a perfect participle. But saying that two forms accidentally look the same is a more moderate claim than saying that five forms accidentally look the same. Moreover, we saw that in the case of *danced* there was independent evidence from irregular verbs that showed us that the finite past tense form and perfect participle do indeed have to be taken as two distinct forms. There is no independent evidence in English, however, that shows us that for regular verbs five distinct forms must exist. To conclude, we could analyse the finite verb forms along these lines but the justification for it would be very weak.

Here's a second solution. If you were to informally describe what is going on in (25), you would probably say that there is one form for the

3rd person singular (ending in -*s*), and another form for the rest. So, we could say that the forms in the present tense are the following:

(33)   [V], [Finite], [Present], [3SG]   →   *dances*

  Elsewhere: [V], [Finite], [Present]   →   *dance*

Whenever the subject of a sentence is 3rd person singular, *dances* will have to be used. In all other cases, *dance* is used instead. As we will see later on in this book, 'elsewhere' forms show up more often in our analyses and will make it much easier to describe feature systems that play a role in grammar. Then the feature representation looks as follows:

(34)

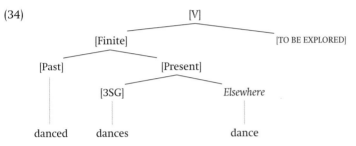

We have now described all finite forms in terms of their features. But what about the forms in (27)–(29)? Again, these forms all share one property: they are not finite forms (as *John to dance* or *John dancing* are not correct English sentences). All these forms, therefore, carry some feature indicating that they are non-finite, so let us call this feature [Non-finite].

Now, if we say that all forms in (27)–(29) carry [Non-finite], we need to say what describes the differences between those forms. The form in (27) can be set apart from the forms in (28)–(29) by noting that the one in (27) is a real infinitive that is combined with what is called an infinitive marker, namely *to* (*to dance, to sleep, to die*). The other forms are participles, verbal forms that, unlike infinitives, do not combine with *to* but, like infinitives, need to be accompanied by some kind of helping verb (or auxiliaries, as they are called), like *have* and *be*, in order to form a full sentence. So we can say that (27) carries a feature [Infinitive] and (28)–(29) a feature [Participle]. Now that we have made that distinction, the only thing left to do is make the distinction between (28) and (29). This difference has to do with the properties of the participle. A perfect participle says that the action described has been completed, whereas a progressive participle says instead that the action described is still going on. Hence, perfectness and progressiveness are properties that play a role in the grammar of English and should thus be recognised as grammatical features as well: [Perfect] and [Progressive]. A perfect participle has to be combined with a form of *have*, whereas a progressive participle has to be combined with a form of *be* (for instance, *he has danced* and *he is dancing*). Doing it the other way around may lead to ungrammatical sentences (**he is danced* and **he has dancing* are out).

In short, different forms of verbs can be described by a small number of features and subfeatures. The entire collection of forms (sometimes called the **paradigm**) can again be depicted in one coherent structure, as we have done in (35).

(35)

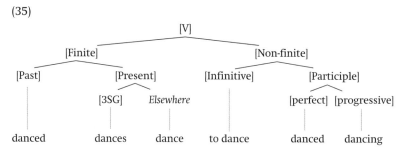

So far, we have been able to characterise all the forms that verbs and nouns can appear in. What we see is that words do not carry just a categorial feature but that within a particular category subcategories can be identified, each characterised by a distinct subfeature, as shown in the trees in (14) and (35).

So, to wrap up, what we have now is a theory of categorial features. The main categorial features [V], [N], [A], [Adv], [P], [C] and [D], together with their subfeatures, allow us to categorise all existing words in English. From now on, when we formulate our syntactic rules, i.e. the rules that allow us to combine words with other words, we only have to refer to a small number of (sub)features.

Exercises

A11   Provide the features and subfeatures of the following verb forms:
  a.   I am <u>giving</u> away the answer.
  b.   He <u>talks</u> too much.
  c.   Elvis <u>has</u> <u>left</u> the building.
  d.   She <u>wanted</u> to <u>know</u> why you <u>have</u> <u>stopped</u> <u>loving</u> her.

A12   What kind of nouns can be combined with *a(n)*? Use the subfeatures from the text and give a few examples.

B13   According to the text there are no nouns that carry both [plural] and [mass]. However, as we have seen it is possible to say things like *Those wines from Spain are excellent*. What explains treating *wines* as a count noun in this case, instead of as a mass noun?

C14   We identified complementisers as a distinct category consisting of words (such as *that, if* and *whether*) that can introduce a clause. This can be evidenced by the substitution test for examples like (i):

  (i)   I didn't know <u>that/if/whether</u> Mary was ill.

At the same time, in many other examples this test fails.

(ii) I wondered whether/if Mary was ill.
(iii) *I wondered that Mary was ill.

(iv) I said that Mary was ill.
(v) *I said whether/if Mary was ill.

What would be the difference between *that* and *if/whether*, such that the facts in (ii)–(iii) and (iv)–(v) follow?

Summary

In this first chapter, we have tried to destroy a myth. The common conception of the utterances that we use in daily life is that they come about by combining words. We have a desire to say something, find the appropriate words and put them in the right order. In a loose sense, 'combining words' is of course exactly what happens, but science is not about loose senses.

As soon as we try to be precise, it turns out that the mental machine responsible for our utterances – yes, we mean syntax – does not care about words at all: it cares about categories. Words are not atoms but consist of features, and some of these features are categorial features. A categorial feature is the property of a word that tells us for instance whether something is a verb or a noun, or whether it belongs to some other category, and it is what syntax is interested in. We have seen, however, that syntax also cares about the subfeatures of a word.

In the second chapter, we are going to destroy a second myth. When we have a desire to say something, we find the appropriate words with certain categorial features and put these in the right order, right? In a loose sense, yes. But once we approach syntax as a science, then 'putting them in the right order' is not even close to what syntax actually does. Curious? The next chapter will explain.

Further Reading

That syntax operates on categories that are determined by their features goes back to the work by Chomsky & Halle (1968) on phonological features. The idea of using features had already been proposed by G.H. Matthews around 1957, as noted in Corbett (1981). That syntactic categories (and therefore syntactic features) are different from semantic categories/features has been proposed by many scholars (see e.g. Katz & Fodor 1963, Edmonds 1976 and Williams 1983). Proposals on how categories should be perceived as feature bundles go back to Chomsky (1970) (see also Chomsky 1995). For an overview of the various syntactic features that can be identified in English and other languages, see for instance Harley & Ritter (2002), Corbett (2006, 2012).

2 Merge

KEY TERMS

Merge
constituent
head
phrase
node
hierarchy
dominate

We have seen that words in a language are not an arbitrary set of items, but that every word belongs to a particular syntactic category, such as 'noun', 'verb', or 'complementiser'. In this chapter, we are going to look at combinations of categories, for instance the combination of an adjective and a noun. We can make a very simple observation here about such a combination: an adjective and a noun together behave just like a noun without an adjective. In other words, the noun is more important than the adjective. Although this observation is simple, the consequences will turn out to be enormous: the most important is that phrases and sentences should be analysed as structures or, to be even more precise, hierarchies. This insight is perhaps the most fundamental in syntactic theory. This chapter will develop this idea and present the most important predictions that it makes. These predictions turn out to be correct and therefore provide strong evidence in favour of this idea.

2.1 Insight: Constituents Are Headed

As established before, nouns can be preceded by one or more adjectives. We can, for instance, say *sausages* and *delicious sausages*. In the latter case we have combined one unit, *delicious*, with another unit, *sausages*, thereby creating a third, bigger, unit: *delicious sausages*. The word linguists use for such units is constituent, so we will use this term from now on.

What can we say about the behaviour of the constituent containing a noun and an adjective? Would it behave like a noun, like an adjective, or like something different? In order to investigate this, let's take the constituent *delicious sausages* and see what grammatical properties it has. In other words, let's see in what kind of syntactic environments this constituent of two words can stand.

First, *delicious sausages* can be combined with another adjective, like *expensive*, giving us *expensive delicious sausages*. Second, we can put the article *the* in front of it: *the delicious sausages*. Third, we can change *delicious sausages* (which is plural) into a singular expression: *delicious sausage*. Fourth, we can have it followed by some prepositional expression, such as *from Italy*, as in *delicious sausages from Italy*. The striking fact here is that all these properties do not just apply to the combination of *delicious* and *sausages*, but also to the word *sausages* itself. First, you can combine *expensive* with *sausages*, just as you can combine it with *delicious sausages*. Second, you can put a determiner in front of it (*the sausages*). Third, you can also change *sausages* into a singular expression: *sausage*. And fourth, you can also add a prepositional expression to *sausages*: *sausages from Italy*.

So *delicious sausages* syntactically behaves just like the noun *sausages*. We can at the same time show that *delicious sausages* does not behave like the adjective *delicious*. An adjective, for instance, can precede a noun, but you cannot put *delicious sausages* in front of a noun. *Delicious sausages cheese* is bad English (as before, indicated by the symbol *). An adjective can be combined with *so* or *too*, giving *so delicious* and *too delicious*. *Delicious sausages*, on the other hand, cannot be combined with these words, suggesting it is not adjectival:

(1)   a.   *so delicious sausages
      b.   *too delicious sausages

Another test is the following. The question *How do they taste?* has to be answered by something adjectival. *Delicious!* would be an appropriate answer, but *Sausages!* would not be. *Delicious sausages!* is also an inappropriate answer to the same question, showing that the combination of the adjective and noun behaves like a noun, not like an adjective.

So *delicious sausages* behaves syntactically just like a noun and not like an adjective. But didn't we say before that what makes a noun a noun (or actually: what makes a word carry a feature [N]) results from its syntactic behaviour? If that is the case, then we must conclude that the combination of an adjective and a noun (or the combination of something with a feature [A] and something with a feature [N]) must also carry the feature [N]. Put differently, a combination of an element with feature [A] and an element with feature [N] inherits the grammatical feature of the noun. The newly created constituent also has the feature [N], indicating that it shares this categorial property with one of its components. This is indicated in (2) by the added [N] feature to the whole constituent:

(2)   [delicious$_{[A]}$ sausages$_{[N]}$]$_{[N]}$

Note that what we are doing here is a variation on the substitution test introduced in chapter 1, based on the following generalisation:

(3)   If two elements X and Y share the same syntactic features, then in every grammatical sentence that contains X you can replace X by Y (and vice versa) and the sentence remains grammatical.

We observed in section 1.2.2 that you can always substitute any element for any other with the same syntactic features; so, for example, *car* for *apple*. Even if this leads to a ridiculous meaning, *John drives an expensive apple* is as grammatical as *John drives an expensive car*. This shows that *car* and *apple* carry the same relevant features and must belong to the same category, noun. Here, we just observed that you can always substitute *delicious sausages* with *sausages*, and this shows the same thing: both carry the same categorial feature, [N]. What we can also do is use a personal pronoun. *They*, we argued in chapter 1, carries the features [D] and [N]. The fact that it carries the feature [N] suffices for *they* to be able to substitute for *delicious sausages*. Remember that we argued, in respect of indefinite plural expressions, that they contain an unexpressed article? Therefore, both *they* and *delicious sausages* contain an [N] and a [D] feature. We can then understand that *They are expensive* is as grammatical as *Delicious sausages are expensive*, and *they* can be interpreted as referring back to *delicious sausages* in the right context: *We both like delicious sausages but they are expensive*. This again shows that *delicious sausages* must be featurally similar to *they*, and is therefore not adjectival.

The observation that the combination of two grammatical categories inherits the feature of one of them is not specific to adjectives and nouns. In fact, this can easily be observed in many other cases. We provide two more examples.

First, when an adjective is combined with an adverb, such as *extremely*, the combination behaves like an adjective: *extremely delicious* can be used in every sentence that contains the adjective *delicious* and the other way round, e.g. *I find these sausages (extremely) delicious*. But in this example you cannot remove *delicious* from *extremely delicious*; the sentence **I find these sausages extremely* is ungrammatical. Again, on the basis of the simple substitution test from chapter 1 we can conclude that the combination of an element of category [Adv] with an element of category [A] inherits the feature [A]. This is indicated in (4) by assigning the feature [A] to the entire combination:

(4) [extremely$_{[Adv]}$ delicious$_{[A]}$]$_{[A]}$

Second, an adverb can also be combined with a verb instead of an adjective. In that event, the verb determines the category of the newly created constituent. Take the combination *often reads* in the sentence *John often reads*. This adverb + verb combination can be replaced by *reads*, giving *John reads*. This suggests that the grammatical properties of *reads* and *often reads* are the same. This is indeed the case. Both *reads* and *often reads* need a subject (such as *John*), can be put in the past tense (*John (often) read*), can be made progressive (*John is (often) reading*), etc. All the properties of verbs that we discovered in chapter 1 also apply to *often reads* (you can check this yourself). By contrast, the adverb *often* cannot replace *often reads*: *John often* is ungrammatical. This shows that *often* has different grammatical properties from *often reads*. So, we can indicate this in the now familiar way: we add [V] to the combination of [Adv] and [V]:

(5) [often$_{[Adv]}$ reads$_{[V]}$]$_{[V]}$

Note, by the way, that it is not because the verb follows the adverb that the verb determines the categorial status of the new constituent. The so-called **linear order** (the order in which the words are pronounced) is irrelevant. The combination *often reads* in the sentence *John often reads* can be replaced by *reads often*, which shows that both *often reads* and *reads often* behave like a verb.

Now we can make a generalisation over all combinations of two constituents: whenever two constituents (both of course carrying some feature) can be combined, then the feature of one of them becomes the feature of the newly created constituent. Such a generalisation captures all the concrete cases that we have seen so far, and many more.

Note that this does not mean that all constituents can simply be combined into larger constituents (*very reads* is bad, for instance). Rather, it says that whenever two constituents can be combined, in other words when the combination is good English, one of the two constituents determines the feature of the newly created constituent. Let's be precise. We say that whenever there is a grammatical combination of two constituents that each carries some feature, let's say [X] and [Y], one of the two determines the feature of the whole, so either [X] or [Y]. This we can formalise as in (6) below:

(6) [[X] [Y]]$_{[X \text{ or } Y]}$

The statement in (6) is a generalisation which sets the agenda for what our syntactic theory must do: it must at least produce the result that for every combination of two syntactic constituents one of the two prevails in determining the properties of the new constituent. What we will do next is provide such a theory.

So far we have only considered the simplest of cases, namely ones in which two words are combined, and then the feature of one of these words determines the feature of the whole. But constituents can be much bigger than units of two words. No matter how big a constituent is, however, there is always one word in it that is responsible for the feature of the entire constituent. Take for instance *expensive delicious sausages*. Just like *delicious sausages, expensive delicious sausages* behaves nominally (that is, like a noun) and not like an adjective. For instance, you can have it be preceded, like any other noun, by the article *the* (*the expensive delicious sausages*), and you cannot modify it by *so* or *too*: **so/too expensive delicious sausages*. So we can say that the constituent *expensive delicious sausages* has a feature [N] too. The exact same thing is true for *expensive delicious sausages from Italy*, etc. In all these cases, there is a one-word feature, *sausages*, that is responsible for the feature, and therefore for the syntactic behaviour, of the entire constituent. We can write down this generalisation as follows.

(7)   Every constituent has a feature that is the same as the feature of one of the words in it.

If you want to formalise this as (6), you can write the following:

(8) $[\,[X]\,[Y]\,[Z]\,\ldots\,]_{[X]\,\text{or}\,[Y]\,\text{or}\,[Z]\,\text{or}\,\ldots}$

Again, this generalisation is true for all types of constituents, not just of nominal ones. In a similar way, we can say that a constituent consisting of a verb and two adverbs rather than one (*often reads quietly*) also carries the feature [V], and a constituent consisting of an adjective and two adverbs (*quite seriously late*) also carries the feature [A].

To conclude, if you look at the simplest syntactic structure, one consisting of two words, then one of these words determines the properties of the new constituent. And if you look at a more complex constituent then, no matter how complex it is, one word in there is always responsible for the behaviour of the entire constituent. What we need now is a mechanism that derives this generalisation. In other words, what we need is a theory.

Exercises

A1   Take a look at the following constituents and determine which word in it is responsible for the syntactic behaviour of the whole constituent, and which categorial feature it therefore carries. Ignore what is in brackets. Justify your answers.
   a.   very happy with this news
   b.   most intelligent women on the planet
   c.   (Tom) probably likes such nonsense.
   d.   rather ridiculously
   e.   men that don't know how to shave
   f.   (Fatima) is probably a Chelsea fan.
   g.   right in the middle

B2 It is possible in English to combine two adverbs, as in *quite seriously* or
really stupidly. These whole constituents obviously behave like adverbs
(how could they behave otherwise?) but one may wonder which of the
two adverbs is here responsible for the feature of the whole constituent.
Do you see a way of determining this?

2.2 Implementation: Operation Merge

The syntactic theory that we now set out to build must, as its prime
effect, cause the generalisations in (6)–(8) to hold. What does such a
theory look like? We will have to provide a technical implementation:
we must engineer a mechanism that has the desired outcome. There are
two reasons why making the step from insight to implementation is so
important.

First of all, it forces us to become extremely precise and concrete
about the workings of syntax, and this is what you generally want to do
in science: a vague theory is not a good theory and is destined to end up
in the graveyard of scientific theories.

Second, there is usually more than one way of turning an insight into
an implementation. And this immediately raises the question as to what
the right implementation is. In other words, we have to choose one
among possible alternatives and send the rest to the aforementioned
graveyard. Yes, science can be a deadly affair.

In this section, we will present one implementation, the mechanism
dubbed Merge. What Merge will do is capture the insight from section
2.1 in a straightforward way. In section 2.3, we will then compare Merge
to other possible implementations and show that Merge makes predictions that these alternatives do not make. And testing these predictions
will point to Merge as the winner.

2.2.1 Syntactic Heads
The Merge mechanism combines two constituents, each consisting of
one or more words, and through this combination it creates a new constituent that carries the feature of one of those constituents as its feature.
The way we express this is by using a hierarchical representation as in (9):

(9)

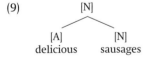

This representation expresses three things. First of all, it expresses
that a constituent with the categorial feature [A] is merged with a constituent carrying the feature [N]. Second, it expresses that Merge gives
us as an output a new constituent and it does so quite literally. We start
out with [A] and [N] and we end up with [A], [N] and another [N]. As a
consequence of Merge, we have three rather than two constituents and

these directly correspond to three separate nodes in the structural representation. The top node, [N], did not exist before *delicious* and *sausages* were combined. Third, the representation in (9) expresses that the whole constituent is an [N] constituent and not an [A] constituent, recognising that the feature of *sausages* determines the feature for this whole construction and not the feature of *delicious*. Merging two constituents thus gives rise to three features: one for *delicious*, one for *sausages* and the one at the top for *delicious sausages* as a whole. Whenever you combine two words, the word that determines the feature of the new constituent is referred to as the head of that constituent. So, *sausages* is the head of *delicious sausages*.

Note that the Merge operation instantaneously captures the generalisation in (6): whenever you merge two constituents the result of this merger inherits the categorial feature of one of them. However, it captures not only these simple cases, but also (8). How? Well, Merge combines two constituents with a feature and not necessarily two single words with a feature. The reason Merge can combine two words is because every word has a feature. But if the result of Merge also has a feature, nothing keeps you from merging this result again with something else (as long as that something else has a feature too).

This means not only that we can merge an adjective with a noun but also that we can merge an adjective with a constituent that is the result of a merger between an adjective and a noun. Since the combination of an [A] and [N] feature creates a constituent with the feature [N], it can effortlessly be combined with another constituent with an [A] feature. The feature of the new constituent is determined as before: when you combine an [A] constituent with an [N] constituent, the latter determines the feature of the new constituent, no matter that this [N] constituent consists of one or several words. This gives us the representation in (10).

(10)

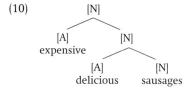

Now the generalisation in (7)/(8) naturally follows. To see this, take the structure in (10). The feature for the entire constituent comes from the feature of one part of it (*delicious sausages*), which in turn inherits the feature from the noun *sausages*, the head of the whole constituent. Therefore, as (7) states, the feature of one word is responsible for the feature of the entire constituent, and the size difference between (9) and (10) is simply irrelevant. We conclude, therefore, that *expensive delicious sausages* is created not by two distinct grammatical operations but by applying one and the same syntactic operation twice (namely, combining constituents with a feature [A] and [N] yields a constituent with feature [N]). In both (9) and (10), *sausages* is the head, responsible for the categorial feature of the entire constituent.

Repeated application of Merge means that *expensive delicious sausages* is internally structured. It does not just consist of three words but it also contains the constituent *delicious sausages*. This means that *expensive delicious sausages* has three layers of '[N]-ness', namely *sausages, delicious sausages* and *expensive delicious sausages*. This will become important later on.

2.2.2 Heads vs. Phrases

In the representation in (10), the feature [N] is used three times, correctly expressing that *sausages, delicious sausages* and *expensive delicious sausages* behave alike. All three of these constituents show 'nounish' behaviour, which explains their carrying the feature [N]. At the same time, we do not wish to say that *delicious sausages* and *expensive delicious sausages* are similar to *sausages* in that they are also nouns. A noun is a word, and obviously *expensive delicious sausages that we ate last summer in Italy* is not just one word but a full constituent consisting of a whole bunch of words, even though this constituent behaves 'nounishly' too. How can we formulate our theory to make sure that a constituent like *delicious sausages* is on the one hand nounish but on the other hand not a noun itself?

What we need to indicate in a structure like (9) is that the two instances of [N] are different. The lower instance of [N] is a single word, the higher instance of [N] is not. Here we introduce a new term: 'phrase'. A phrase is a constituent with a head. If the head is a noun, the phrase is called a noun phrase (or a nominal phrase). Both *expensive delicious sausages* and *delicious sausages* are therefore noun phrases and both contain the same head, namely *sausages*.

The notion of a phrase now allows us to distinguish the different occurrences of [N] in the same representation. For the structure in (9) we can now write (11), where NP stands for Noun Phrase. This makes it clear that the phrase *delicious sausages* and the noun *sausages* are different entities. At the same time, both carry the feature [N], since *sausage* is a noun (N) and *delicious sausages* is an NP, and therefore has the noun as its head.

(11)

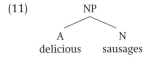

NP
A   N
delicious   sausages

This notation gives us everything we need. We are now able to provide syntactic analyses of the other cases we have discussed. For example, (12) provides the analysis for *very delicious*:

(12)

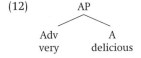

AP
Adv   A
very   delicious

This structure states that *very delicious* behaves like an adjective and that the adjective *delicious* is therefore the head. The entire constituent thus has the feature [A]. In the same way, the merger of a verb and an adverb (in whatever order) yields a VP (Verb Phrase), as shown below. This ensures that the entire constituent has the feature [V] and behaves verbally.

(13)   a.

So, now we can deal with these syntactic representations (often referred to as syntactic 'trees') that consist of a head and some other element. The head and the constituent this head is merged with are sisters to one another, as the node immediately above either of these is in fact the same node: in (11), A and N are sisters of the node NP, and in (12) the node AP is immediately above Adv and A, so Adv and A are sisters too, etc. Let's go one step further and ask the next question that arises: how to represent a structure like (10), which contains two nominal phrases. The most logical way would be the following. There are two nominal phrases, so two NPs.

(14)
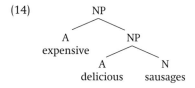

It is quite standard in the syntactic literature, however, to reserve the _P notation for the highest node of the phrase. Lower phrases of the same categorial type, such as the node dominating *delicious sausages*, are marked as intermediate, and the notation used for such levels is ' (said: *bar*). The structure of (14) with this notation is then the following:

(15)
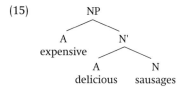

We now have all the notation we need to analyse nominal constituents that are more complicated than the ones in (15), as well as nominal constituents that are simpler than the one in (15). Let us go over both of these.

Suppose you have an even bigger NP: *expensive delicious spicy sausages*. What's the tree like then? According to our theory we have a phrase consisting of three adjectives and one noun, where the noun is the head. If the entire nominal phrase is the NP, and the head is a noun (N), both intermediate phrases (*delicious spicy sausages* and *spicy sausages*) are then N'.

Note, though, that because we reserve the 'P' for the highest instance of some feature, single words can be phrases too. Take, for example, a

constituent that consists of a noun only, e.g. *Mary*. The representation of
the word *Mary* would be as in (16):

(16)   N
       Mary

But suppose that we now merge *Mary* into a syntactic structure, by
combining it with the verb *like*. Then we get the representation in (17):

(17)

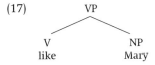

Here, *Mary* is the highest nominal category; the node above it lacks the
feature [N]. We can tell, because the node straight above NP is VP, and VP
is not nominal. Therefore, *Mary* is a phrase, and therefore we call it NP,
although it consists of a single word only. Now, because we want to be
consistent, we should do the same for the representations in (11)–(13),
where the adjective in (11) and the adverbs in (12) and (13) should be
treated as phrases as well. We should therefore add the Ps to the representations in the following way:

(18)

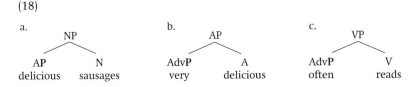

For now, this may look like a notational trick, but we will see later on
that an analysis of phrases that includes single-word phrases has various
advantages.

Recall that we argued in chapter 1 that nominal phrases (like *delicious
sausage*, or *delicious sausages*), proper names (like *Mary*) and pronouns (like
her, *it* and *he*) share the same syntactic behaviour: we can for instance
replace one with the other. For this reason, we concluded that all these
constituents carry a [D] and an [N] feature, even when you don't see the
element with the [D] feature. Now, when you look at the representations
of nominal phrases in this section, you can clearly see their '[N]-ness',
but you may wonder what happened to their '[D]-ness', as there is no [D]
feature (or D node) in sight. We will forget about [D]/D for the moment,
and return to it in section 4.3, where it will be responsible for an important development in the theory.

2.2.3 The Non-Head: Another Generalisation

So far, what we have seen is two core properties of our structure-build-
ing machine called syntax. First, Merge states that if you combine two
constituents, then one of them must either be the head (as in [*delicious* +
sausages$_{head}$]) or contain the head (as in [*expensive* + [*delicious* + *sausages*$_{head}$]]).
Delicious sausages behaves nominally, which means that *sausages* and not

delicious must be the head, and *delicious* is therefore the non-head. *Sausages* remains the head even when another adjective is added to the structure.

Now, what can we say about the constituent that merges with the head, the non-head? Or, to be more precise, what does our theory tell us about what a head can merge with? Take the following tree, where the verb V is the head and the VP is the phrase that V is the head of:

(19)
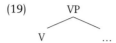

There is no restriction on the length of what can replace the dots because the theory simply does not say anything about it. The theory requires that the VP has a head, which it does, and that is all. We therefore expect that a verb can be combined with an [N] category consisting of a single word, as in *(to) know Mary*. Alternatively, it can be combined with a bunch of words. This is indeed correct. *(To) know Mary* is a correct expression in English, but so is *(to) know beautiful Mary*.

(20)   a.   b.

At the same time, all these constituents that the verb can merge with, regardless of whether it is *Mary, beautiful Mary* or *beautiful Mary from Italy*, have a feature [N]. So the verb can merge with anything that is a nominal phrase, i.e. a phrase with the noun as a head.

Let us try to put this into a precise but very general statement. The phrase that merges with some head is always the highest phrase of that categorial type, which we indicate by using the 'P'. For example, since the verb in (20) heads a phrase of its own, the nominal phrase it merges with must be a full NP. The fact that the non-head is always a maximal phrase (YP, where Y can be any category) can be formalised as in (21):

(21)   A constituent that merges with a syntactic head X is always a
       maximal phrase: $[X\ YP]_{XP}$

YP is a phrase and a phrase, we determined earlier, is a constituent consisting of a number of words. Now, the number of words can be one. This entails that a verb can be combined with an NP consisting of several words, as in (20b), but also with an NP consisting of one word, as in (20a): *know Mary* fits the pattern in (21) as much as *know beautiful Mary* does.

Let us provide a second example, now with different categories. Take the expression *in trees*, as in 'These animals live in trees'. *In trees* is a constituent consisting of two words, the preposition *in* and the noun *trees*. What is the head? If *trees* is the head, we expect *in trees* to appear in every environment in which noun phrases can appear. A noun phrase can, for instance, be combined with the verb *like: I like trees*. If *in trees* is a noun phrase too, we would expect that *I like in trees* is grammatical too. It is not. We would also expect that you could put a determiner in front of it: *the in trees*. You cannot. We conclude therefore that not *trees* but *in* must be the head. In other words, *in trees* is a prepositional phrase, a PP, not an NP.

But if the preposition is the head, we can predict that the non-head does not have to consist of just one word. In fact, we predict that a preposition always merges with an NP that can consist of one word, or of many words. It is easy to establish that this prediction is correct, as there does not seem to be any upper limit on how big the NP can be that merges with the head P to yield a PP:

(22) a. in trees
     b. in the trees
     c. in the most beautiful trees
     d. in the most beautiful trees in the whole of Britain
     e. ...

One issue that may pop up, though, is that, as opposed to NPs, PPs cannot consist of one word, namely the preposition only. *In trees* is a well-formed syntactic constituent, but just *in* is not. Note for instance that a verb can be combined with an NP consisting of just a noun (as in *I love trees*) or with a more complex NP (for instance, *I love these trees*). On the other hand, a verb can be combined with a PP (for instance, *They live in trees*) but not with just a preposition (*They live in*). This does not run against the generalisation, though, as it only states that heads merge with maximal phrases. It follows from the generalisation that if you merge a head with a constituent of which the P is a head, this head merges with the PP. The fact that a PP cannot consist of just a preposition, unlike an NP, which can consist of only a noun, must then have an independent reason, which according to most linguists working on prepositions lies in their meaning (you can't talk about *in* or *on* without specifying in or on what).

We have seen two examples of the pattern in (21) now, one in which X is a verb and one in which X is a preposition. It is quite easy to show that in other cases, where X is, for instance, an N or A, it can combine with a constituent consisting of more than one word too. Wherever *afraid of John* can appear *afraid* can appear as well, showing that *afraid of John* is an adjectival phrase (an AP) in which an A is combined with a PP, and this PP consists of more than one word (here, *of John*). This creates the structure in (23a). In the same vein, a noun like *destruction* can occur in every position where *destruction of Rome* can occur, which shows that we are dealing with an NP in which a noun is combined with a PP, and this PP consists of more than one word. The structure is provided in (23b).

(23) a.
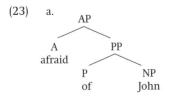

     b.
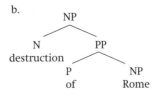

We have now reached the conclusion that any head X obeys the statement in (21), even when this X merges with one single word. It is important to see that this generalisation is a consequence of the Merge mechanism, which puts a clear restriction on what can be a head (one word) but no restriction on the constituent that a head combines with (one or more words).

In our illustration of (21), all examples so far have involved merging a head with something on the right. Would that mean that (21) is only valid with mergers in which the head is on the left? No. There is nothing in (21) that is sensitive to left–right distinctions. The mechanism in (21) holds for every merger involving the head, both on the left and on the right. Let us now look at an example involving the left side of the head. We saw earlier that a noun can be modified by an adjective to yield a nominal phrase, like *delicious sausages*. We also saw back in example (12) that *very delicious* is an adjectival phrase. So we predict that we can also merge a noun like *sausages* with the AP *very delicious*. Of course, this prediction is correct as well: *very delicious sausages* is a grammatical nominal phrase. Its structure looks as follows:

(24)

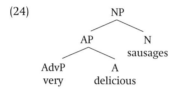

It is also easy to show that two phrases within an NP, each consisting of more than one word, can occur on different sides of the head. Suppose we modify *sausages from Italy* by adding the information that they are very delicious. This would give us the following structure:

(25)

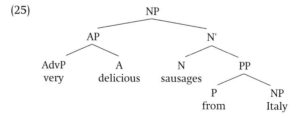

Since it turns out that heads can be combined not with just one phrase consisting of one or more words, but with several, the generalisation in (21) can be broadened to the one in (26):

(26)   Every maximal phrase, XP, contains minimally a head X but can in addition contain one or more phrases: [… (ZP) X (YP) …]$_{XP}$

Whether ZP and YP occur on the right or left of the head does not really matter (and is a topic that we will not deal with much until chapter 9).

To sum up, we have proposed Merge as the operation responsible for the creation of larger constituents out of smaller constituents. This operation requires that every phrase contains minimally a head. Apart from the head, this phrase may contain one or more other phrases and these other phrases can consist of one or several words. This generalisation is valid no matter what type of phrase we are dealing with. It is, in other words, a cross-categorial generalisation. A fundamental property that products of Merge share is that they are **hierarchies**. It is this property that will become important in the next section.

Exercise

A3 Draw the tree structure of the following constituents. You can forget about elements of category D for the time being.
a. really stupidly
b. talk really stupidly
c. beautiful red dress
d. draw syntactic trees
e. really

2.3 Consequences: Testing the Predictions of Merge

We now have a theory of syntactic structure predicting that every syntactic constituent consisting of more than one word has an internal hierarchical structure. The Merge hypothesis predicts that a phrase can consist of two constituents, and each of these constituents can again consist of two constituents, etc. Eventually, you will reach the word level. But how do we know that this is the correct way of looking at syntactic structures?

The best way to test this, and to test hypotheses in general, is to see what kinds of predictions this hypothesis makes. If these predictions are incorrect, the hypothesis must be rejected, or at least modified. For instance, the hypothesis that the earth is flat predicts that you cannot sail around it. Since you can, you know this hypothesis is false.

But what if the predictions are borne out? You might cheer and think your hypothesis is correct (and this happens way too often). But you must be more careful. To come up with an example: suppose you entertain the hypothesis that the sun rotates around the earth (as many people thought for a long time). You might say that this predicts that roughly half of the day you can see the sun and the other half of the day you can't. This is obviously correct, but at the same time we know now that the hypothesis is wrong. In fact, this 'correct prediction' does not tell us anything. The reason is that another hypothesis, the one that says that the earth moves around the sun, makes exactly the same prediction, namely that there are days and nights.

What does this tell us? It tells us that whenever you want to test a particular hypothesis you should not only show that the predictions that one hypothesis makes are correct, but also that the alternative hypotheses do not make these correct predictions. As it turns out, the hypothesis that takes the sun to be the centre of our solar system explains the orbits of other planets better than the hypothesis that the earth is the centre. The behaviour of other planets, then, falsifies the earth-central hypothesis and confirms the sun-central hypothesis.

So if we want to check whether the Merge hypothesis is correct, we need to compare the predictions of this hypothesis with the predictions made by other hypotheses about syntactic structures. Now, what would be an alternative hypothesis to the idea that phrases and sentences are hierarchical structures built up with the operation Merge, the way we saw earlier? This would for instance be a hypothesis stating that sentences are not hierarchical, and that every word in a complex constituent is just a bead on a string; under this hypothesis constituents (and sentences) would lack internal structure beyond individual words. Such a hypothesis would simply say that every word is glued to another word in the phrase. For *expensive delicious sausages*, this would mean that *delicious* is glued to *sausages* and *expensive* is glued to *delicious*. We therefore call this hypothesis the Glue hypothesis. This leads to the following two representations for *expensive delicious sausages*:

(27)

a. *The Merge Hypothesis*   b. *The Glue Hypothesis*

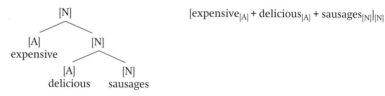

Now we have a very clear difference between the Merge hypothesis and the Glue hypothesis. The Merge hypothesis predicts that every syntactic constituent has an internal hierarchical structure. The Glue hypothesis predicts that syntactic constituents do not have an internal structure beyond the words that are glued together. To give a concrete example, under the Merge hypothesis *delicious sausages* is a constituent within the constituent *expensive delicious sausages*, whereas this is not the case under the Glue hypothesis: under the latter hypothesis there is one big constituent, consisting of identifiable words only. If we want to argue in favour of the Merge hypothesis and against the Glue hypothesis, then, we must provide evidence for the existence of such intermediate constituents as *delicious sausages*.

Now, there are two types of evidence that we can distinguish, not just in this case but in scientific research in general, namely conceptual evidence and empirical evidence. One theory can be considered superior to an alternative theory if it is conceptually simpler, more attractive, more elegant, more beautiful, or requires fewer assumptions. In addition, a theory can be considered superior to an alternative if it can account for more empirical observations: in that event, the theory is empirically superior. Both types of evidence in favour of the Merge hypothesis can be put forward. We will start in section 2.3.1 with empirical evidence for Merge based on the syntactic behaviour of phrases. Then we will continue in section 2.3.2 with showing that Merge is conceptually attractive once you start to compare it to alternative theories.

2.3.1 Empirical Evidence: Constituency Tests

In this and the previous chapter, we have used substitution tests to find out the nature of syntactic units. Nominal constituents, for instance, can be replaced by other nominal constituents, and it does not really matter if the constituents you are using are single words or phrases. It turns out that substitution not only provides us with information about the categorial status of a particular string of words but also tells us that this string of words is a constituent to begin with. Let us start with a straightforward example in which we use pronouns (such as *he, him, her, they,* etc.) to perform the substitution test with. Note that the italicised string in (28a) can be replaced by *her*, as in (28b), where *her* then refers to the Queen of Denmark.

(28)   a.   You know that I met *the Queen of Denmark* frequently.
       b.   You know that I met *her* frequently.
       c.   You know that I met *her*.

At the same time, if we try to replace *the Queen of Denmark frequently* in (28a) by *her*, then it becomes obvious that *her* cannot refer to the entire string that we have replaced. *Her* in (28c) can only refer to *the Queen of Denmark* and not to *the Queen of Denmark frequently*. This makes sense if you think about how we interpret this sentence. *The Queen of Denmark* and *her* refer to a person, so it is no surprise that *her* cannot refer to the combination of a person and an adverb that provides some information about the frequency of the whole event at the same time. But there is more to substitution by pronouns than first meets the eye. Take a look at the following conversation, in which the pronoun *ones* replaces the nominal constituent *sausages*:

(29)   ANDRÉ: Do you like sausages, sir?
       PETER: Oh yes, especially expensive delicious ones!

In this conversation, we interpret *ones* as *sausages*. Now, consider the following two conversations:

(30)   ANDRÉ: Do you like delicious sausages, sir?
       PETER: Oh yes, especially expensive ones!

(31)   ANDRÉ: Do you like expensive delicious sausages, sir?
       PETER: Oh yes, especially Italian ones!

In (30) we interpret *ones* as *delicious sausages*, and in (31) as *expensive delicious sausages*. What you can apparently do is not only replace a whole nominal phrase by a pronoun, but also part of a nominal phrase. Under the Merge hypothesis, a very simple generalisation now emerges: every [N] node in the hierarchical structure can be replaced by the pronoun *ones*. This is indicated in (32):

(32)
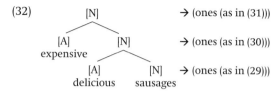

But this simple generalisation is only possible if those [N] nodes exist in the first place. Since under the Glue hypothesis *delicious sausages* is not a constituent, no such simple generalisation is possible. Of course, we could strengthen our point by simply merging more adjectives to the structure. Each additional adjective will create an additional subconstituent, and this subconstituent can in its turn be replaced by *ones*. We therefore have a situation in which the data can easily be captured by the one theory but not by the other.

We conclude on the basis of the data in (28)–(31) that pronouns can be used to replace syntactic constituents and syntactic constituents only. Therefore, we have good reason to believe that the substitution test can be used as a diagnostic for constituency. If so, the test reveals the existence of multi-word constituents within multi-word constituents, just as Merge expects. We should be careful, however, not to take this too hastily as evidence for the Merge hypothesis. What we are in fact saying is the following: *the Queen of Denmark frequently* is not a constituent because we cannot replace it by a pronoun. And the pronoun *her* cannot refer back to *the Queen of Denmark frequently*, because that is not a constituent. In effect, we have a case of **circular reasoning**, because you can only accept the conclusion (which is: based on the substitution test *the Queen of Denmark frequently* is not a constituent) if you also believe the premise, namely that substitution by a pronoun reveals constituency to begin with. What we need, therefore, is some independent evidence that tells us that the substitution test indeed reveals constituency, as we strongly suspect. In other words, we need a second diagnostic.

As we have seen, in our hierarchical representations every node is a structural unit, or building block, and we have reserved the word 'constituent' to refer to these units. Now, each individual word is a constituent but, as we have seen, several words can together form a subconstituent in an even bigger constituent. What we can observe, and this will be our second diagnostic, is that in a lot of cases these subconstituents can be moved to another place in the sentence, for instance to the front. Take the example in (33):

(33)   Harry doesn't usually believe in new leaders.

In this sentence, we can identify *believe in new leaders* as a subconstituent. It can for instance be used as an answer to the question *What is it that*

Harry doesn't usually do? We can observe that it is possible to put this constituent at the beginning of the sentence, as in (34):

(34)   Believe in new leaders, Harry doesn't usually.

So the idea that *believe in new leaders* is a constituent, a group of words belonging together, is underscored by the fact that you can take it and put it somewhere else. It behaves syntactically as a constituent in (34), you could say, by the fact that it can move. We can take this one step further. On the basis of the theory developed in this chapter, we must represent the internal structure of this constituent as follows.

(35)

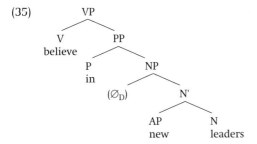

We can observe that within this VP there is a subconstituent of the type PP, namely *in new leaders. In new leaders* is a constituent because there is a node in the tree, namely PP, that dominates *in, new* and *leaders* and nothing else. **Dominate** here means: you can reach *in, new* and *leaders* from the PP node by only going down; you cannot reach *believe* by only going down from the PP node. Therefore, the PP does not dominate *believe.* In the same vein, this PP in turn contains a subconstituent, namely *new leaders.* NP is a node in the tree that dominates only *new* and *leaders* but not *believe* and *in. New leaders*, therefore, is a constituent too. What we can observe is that both the PP and the NP can be fronted (brought to the beginning of the sentence) as well, showing quite clearly that they behave as syntactic units:

(36)   a.   In new leaders, Harry doesn't usually believe.
       b.   New leaders, Harry doesn't usually believe in.

At the same time, *believe in* is not a constituent because there is no node in the tree that only dominates *believe* and *in* but no other words. After all, the only node that dominates both *believe* and *in* is VP but this node also dominates *new* and *leaders.* Similarly, *in new* is not a constituent either. What we can observe is that neither *believe in*, nor *in new*, can be fronted:

(37)   a.   *Believe in, Harry doesn't usually new leaders.
       b.   *In new, Harry doesn't usually believe leaders.

Movement can therefore be seen as a second test for constituency (also known as the movement test for constituency): if you can move an element, it is always a constituent.

Let's now return to the examples in (28) and observe that the movement test shows exactly what the substitution test was intended to show, namely that *the Queen of Denmark* is a constituent but *the Queen of Denmark frequently* is not. Only the former successfully passes the movement test:

(38)   a.   The Queen of Denmark, you know that I met frequently.
       b.   *The Queen of Denmark frequently, you know that I met.

Here, we clearly see that *the Queen of Denmark* behaves as a syntactic unit but *the Queen of Denmark frequently* does not. We conclude that the substitution and movement tests point in the same direction, so that each test for constituency provides independent support for the other. As a consequence, our reasoning is no longer circular.

To sum up, a structural analysis that uses hierarchical representations is able to understand the difference between the sentences in (36), (37) and (38) in an elegant way. Now, compare this to the Glue hypothesis, which states that constituents are linear strings, like beads on a string. In such a theory *believe in* and *in new* are substrings of the entire syntactic unit just as much as *new leaders* and *in new leaders*. It is therefore much harder under such a hypothesis to single out the grammatical sentences as the ones predicted to be grammatical than it is under the Merge hypothesis.

A word of caution, though. Although both tests provide convincing evidence for the existence of hierarchical representations, each single test does not necessarily provide evidence for all the nodes in these representations. Note for instance that in (35) *leaders* is a constituent, and the same is true for *delicious sausages* in (32). Nevertheless, these constituents cannot be fronted.

(39)   a.   *Leaders, Harry doesn't usually believe in new.
       b.   *Delicious sausages I bought expensive.

At the same time, the substitution test does work here, as *ones* can replace *delicious sausages* and *leaders* without any problems: *I especially like expensive ones, Harry doesn't usually believe in new ones*. So one test succeeds and one test fails to show the constituency in these examples. It is also possible that the movement test works but not the substitution test. And *Harry doesn't usually believe in ones* doesn't sound good at all, although the movement test clearly shows that *new leaders* is a syntactic constituent.

What this tells us is that these are one-way tests: if a string of words can be moved or substituted by a pronoun, it is a constituent. If you cannot move a string of words, however, you cannot conclude anything. And the same is true if the substitution test fails. Compare this to the following. If it rains, you get soaked. But if you are soaked, it does not automatically follow that it is raining. Other factors may have caused this, for instance a bucket of water that someone put on the door for you. The same is true for the relation between constituency and constituency tests. A test may fail but for a reason that has nothing to do with constituency. The fact that the tests only work one way is what provides work for syntacticians. One of their tasks is to unravel the restrictions on these processes, and we will do some of this in later chapters (especially chapters 6 and 7). Whatever the outcome of this research will be, though, there are two immediate lessons for now.

One is that, as a student, you should always run both tests: if one works (as with *in new leaders*) or two work (as with *the Queen of Denmark*), bingo. If both fail (as with *the Queen of Denmark frequently*), you have no evidence for constituency.

And second, it is fairly clear that the facts are much better handled by a theory that uses hierarchical representations than one that uses linear strings. The Merge hypothesis starts out with certain predictions (one should in principle be able to move a constituent, or replace it by a pronoun), whereas the Glue hypothesis assumes that there are no internal constituents beyond the individual words, and therefore cannot predict these facts.

2.3.2 Conceptual Evidence: Merge vs. Glue and List

We have just provided an empirical argument in favour of the Merge hypothesis and against the Glue hypothesis. Movement and substitution data can be made to follow directly from the type of products that Merge gives us (hierarchies), whereas it is unclear how to do this with the products of Glue (linear strings). In addition to this empirical argument, we can also provide a conceptual argument in favour of the Merge hypothesis: it allows for a simpler grammar. Note that under the Merge hypothesis we need a rule that says that you can combine an [A] with an [N] category, and that the [N] is then the head of this constituent. This rule you can reiterate by adding another [A] to the [N] that you have just created. Merge gives you the structure in (27a), repeated here as (40a). Note, however, that under the Glue hypothesis we need a second rule. Not only do we need to be able to combine an [A] with an [N], but we also need a rule that allows us to combine an [A] with an [A]. Why? Well, look again at what Glue gives us in (27b), repeated here as (40b).

(40)

a.   *The Merge Hypothesis*   b.   *The Glue Hypothesis*

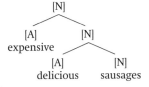

$[\text{expensive}_{[A]} + \text{delicious}_{[A]} + \text{sausages}_{[N]}]_{[N]}$

Here, we have glued three words together to form a string. *Delicious* is glued to *sausages*, and *expensive* is glued to *delicious*. As a result, we get *expensive delicious sausages*. Now, let us look at the precise rules that these two grammars need in order to build *expensive delicious sausages*. The Merge grammar needs a rule allowing merger of [A] and [N]. The Glue grammar needs two rules, one that glues together [A] and [N], and a second that glues together [A] and [A].

(41) a. *The Merge Grammar*   b. *The Glue Grammar*

    Rule 1: Merge ([A], [N]) =   Rule 1: Glue ([A], [N]) = [A+N]

            [N]   Rule 2: Glue ([A], [A]) = [A+A]

       [A]   [N]

So here is the conceptual evidence in favour of the Merge hypothesis. If you ask yourself the question which of these two grammars is simpler, there can be only one answer. The Merge grammar wins, as it only requires one rule to build *expensive delicious sausages* ([A]+[N]), whereas the Glue grammar needs two. In other words, the Merge grammar is a simpler and more elegant grammar. This makes it conceptually more attractive.

But the situation deteriorates quickly for the Glue hypothesis if we consider its predictions. The Glue grammar must contain a rule that combines an [A] with another [A], as we have just seen. This rule not only leads to a more complex grammar, it is actually a rule that we do not want in the first place. The Glue grammar predicts that [A]+[A] constituents are grammatical expressions in English, but they are not. As an answer to the question 'How are your sausages?', you could say 'Expensive!', or you could say 'Delicious!'. But you cannot say 'Expensive delicious!' To exclude such examples, grammars must contain a rule that bans [A]+[A] constituents in English. These rules are added in (42):

(42) a. *The Merge Grammar*   b. *The Glue Grammar*

    Rule 1: Merge ([A], [N]) =   Rule 1: Glue ([A], [N]) = [A+N]

            [N]   Rule 2: Glue ([A], [A]) = [A+A]

       [A]   [N]   Rule 3: *Glue ([A], [A]) = [A+A]

    Rule 2: *Merge ([A], [A])

Note now that this additional rule can be simply added to the Merge grammar but not to the Glue grammar for the simple reason that it would create a contradiction with the already existing Rule 2: Glue ([A], [A]). A grammar cannot contain a rule allowing a particular combination and at the same time forbidding it. On the other hand, the Merge grammar does not have any rules that contradict each other. This means that the combination of the ungrammaticality of *expensive delicious*, and the grammaticality of *expensive delicious sausages*, is evidence in favour of the Merge hypothesis and against the Glue hypothesis, because only the first, unlike the second, hypothesis can capture these facts.

In short, the Glue hypothesis does not give us what we need. This does not automatically mean that the Merge hypothesis is what we need, since we have only considered one alternative. Although it is impossible to go through all the imaginable options, there is at least one alternative we should look at. Let's call it the List hypothesis. It shares with the Glue hypothesis the idea that syntactic structures are not hierarchically structured but are just linear orderings. At the same time, it crucially deviates from the Glue hypothesis in not requiring an [A]+[A] rule, i.e. it is not expected that [A]+[A] combinations are possible. How would that work? Well, the List grammar just lists all the linear strings that are grammatical, as in (43b). It just says that [A A N] is a grammatical string in English. There is no longer any mechanism, such as Merge or Glue, that creates these strings. The strings are just listed. The advantage is that we no longer need a Glue operation that puts an [A] and an [A] together to create *expensive delicious sausages*. And if we want, we can just state that the string [A A] is ungrammatical, thereby mimicking the Rule 2 of the Merge grammar:

(43)   a.   *The Merge Grammar*   b.   *The List Grammar*

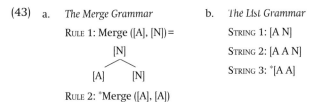

The List hypothesis does better than the Glue hypothesis in that it does not run into the empirical problem we noted, namely how to exclude the ungrammatical 'Expensive delicious!' Conceptually, however, it is easy to see that the List grammar still needs a larger set of statements than the Merge grammar, namely three vs. two. This conceptual problem gets bigger with every [A] that you add. The List grammar needs to add a statement to the effect that [A + A + A + N] is also grammatical, and so is [A + A + A + A + N]. There is no upper limit. And all that time, the Merge grammar can take a nap, as it already covers all these grammatical strings.

Exercises

A4   Determine with the use of tests whether the italicised strings form a constituent.
  a.   Esther bought *three bottles with her credit card*.
  b.   Peter talked *endlessly about his uncle*.
  c.   Peter talked endlessly *about his uncle*.
  d.   Peter talked endlessly about *his uncle*.
  e.   Santa Claus sent *me a new computer*.
  f.   *The creature that really gave me the creeps* was E.T.
  g.   I *read this book* last week.
  h.   I read *this book last week*.

B5   Draw tree structures for the following constituents:
  a.   rely on unclear information
  b.   unreasonably angry about stuff
  c.   above green meadows
  d.   back in France
  e.   talk to me slowly

B6 Fronting always involves constituents. Take the following three sentences:
  (i) (You) believe in change.
  (ii) Change you believe in.
  (iii) In change you believe.
  a. Give the tree structure of sentence (i) without the subject.
  b. Indicate all the constituents in sentence (i), excluding the subject.
  c. Now indicate all the constituents in sentence (ii), excluding the subject. Are there any differences between the constituents in (i) and (ii)?
  d. Try to explain in your own words what a *discontinuous constituent* would be.
  e. Does (iii) contain a discontinuous constituent as well?

B7 The following sentence has two meanings:
  (i) Our neighbour attacked a man with a knife.
  a. State the two meanings that this sentence can express.
  b. Draw two distinct VP structures that correspond to those two meanings in a transparent way.
  c. If you front *a man with a knife*, as in (ii), the sentence all of the sudden has one meaning only. Why is this?
  (ii) A man with a knife, our neighbour attacked.

C8 The following constituent can have two trees. What are those two trees? Justify your answer.
  (i) expensive shoes from Italy

Summary

In this chapter, we have looked at the motor of the syntactic component. It turns out to involve a very basic operation, called Merge, which takes as its input two categories and puts them together. One of these categories subsequently determines the properties of the newly created constituent. Because we can apply Merge endlessly there is no limit to the size of the structures (and the length of the utterances) that we can produce, except that one sometimes has to sleep. The fact that structures that look rather complicated are derived by a very simple mechanism is surprising and a fundamental discovery in the workings of syntax. We have shown that it follows from our conception of Merge that every phrase must have a head, which corresponds to one word. Apart from the obligatory head, a phrase can contain one or more other constituents, and each of them can consist of one or more words. These generalisations hold for all phrases, no matter what categories they belong to. We therefore conclude that we have taken an enormous step in our endeavour to create some order from the chaos. If you look underneath the surface, you have to conclude that syntactic structures are highly organised, and this organisation all follows from one simple operation, Merge. It is for this reason that Merge has achieved the status of a cornerstone in syntactic theory.

Further Reading

Some notion of hierarchy can be found, or read into, traditional grammar, which for instance assumes a subject and a predicate, where the predicate can again be split up into several parts. In theoretical linguistics, the conception of syntactic structures as hierarchies has precursors before Noam Chomsky's work (see Wells 1947 for the notion 'immediate constituent'), but it was Chomsky who, in his (1957) book *Syntactic Structures*, crafted it into a fully-fledged science and developed the detailed tree structure representations that we still use today.

The term 'Merge' was coined in *The Minimalist Program* (Chomsky, 1995) and became the standard tool for structure building within generative linguistics. The text of this chapter is a less formal, simplified exposition of Chomsky's ideas but nevertheless maintains their essentials.

The idea of syntactic structures being flat with little internal structure, represented here as the Glue and List hypotheses, has become popular again in recent years within a framework called Cognitive, or Usage-Based, Linguistics (Langacker 1987, 1991), or Construction Grammar (Goldberg, 1995). One point of discussion is about the extent to which we actually create these hierarchies when we produce or perceive sentences, and psycholinguistic evidence for both sides is currently being put forward. Whatever the outcome of this debate, it will be clear that this book sides with the hierarchical concept, and it presents some pertinent linguistic arguments in favour of it. The arguments suggesting that structures are hierarchical are based on contrasts between grammatical and ungrammatical examples, and these judgements are the result of our linguistic knowledge. It is therefore reasonable to assume that an operation like Merge is central to our linguistic cognition.

Recently David Poeppel's lab claims to have found neurological evidence for the use of hierarchical representations during language processing (see Ding et al. 2015). They found brain activity that can be related to constituents on word, phrasal and sentential levels. The strength of this evidence is currently under investigation.

3 Theta Theory (θ-Theory)

CHAPTER OUTLINE

In the previous chapters we concluded that grammar exploits a Merge operation to combine elements that carry syntactic features. Such a system derives all the sentences that we need to derive but, as we will see, it also derives various sentences that are actually ungrammatical. We can say that Merge overgenerates: it does more than it should do. In the following chapters, we will see what kind of principles constrain Merge in such a way that this **overgeneration** no longer takes place. This chapter focuses on the meaning of the verb and introduces the so-called Theta theory (θ-theory), a theory that explains and predicts how verbal meanings rule out certain syntactic structures that Merge can in principle build.

3.1 Insight: Merge and the Meaning of Verbs and Nouns

In the previous chapter, we saw that we can merge verbs with nouns and that the result still behaves verbally, i.e. it has a feature [V]:

(1)   a. (to) kill Bill / (John) kills Bill

   b.

The reason why we treat *(to) kill Bill* or *kills Bill* as verbal and not nominal is that we can replace *kill(s) Bill* with another verb (e.g. *to walk / walks*), but not with another noun: **to Bill / Bills*.

At the same time, the verb *kill* itself cannot be replaced by every verb. Take the following examples:

(2)   a.   *Mary snores Bill.
   b.   Mary loves Bill.
   c.   *Mary assigns Bill.

As shown in (2), *kill* can only be replaced by the verb *love*, not by *snore* or *assign*. This shows that verbs do not form a homogeneous category but rather come in different kinds. What kinds, then, do we have? For this, we need to look more closely at the differences between the verbs in (2).

The first verb, *to snore*, cannot be combined with the object *Bill*, whereas *to kill* can. The reason for this is that the meaning of *kill* requires the involvement of two parties: a killer and a killee (i.e. the killed one). By contrast, it is virtually impossible to think of snoring as an activity that requires two parties. For a snoring event you need a snorer, and that's it. You cannot snore something or somebody. The verb *to assign*, in a way, forms the mirror image of *to snore*. The reason why you can't say *Mary assigns Bill* is that assigning always requires three parties, as shown in (3):

(3)   Mary assigns Bill an important task

In (3) we have the assigner *Mary, Bill* is the person who is assigned something and *an important task* is what is assigned to Bill by Mary.

Now, what we have here is a semantic constraint that determines what constituents must be merged with verbs. In principle, verbs can merge with nominal constituents but the meaning of the verb constrains how many nominal constituents it can merge with: with only a subject (as in *Mary snores*), with a subject and one object, the so-called **direct object** (as in *Mary kills Bill*), or with a subject and two objects, the direct and the **indirect object** (as in *Mary assigns Bill an important task* or *Mary assigns an important task to Bill*). So it is the meaning of the verb that determines what it can merge with. In particular, its meaning determines the number of constituents that the verb is allowed to merge with. The constituents whose presence in a sentence is required by the meaning of the verb are called **arguments**. *To snore* is a verb that has one argument; *to kill* has two arguments; and *to assign* has three arguments. Verbs that have one argument are called **intransitive verbs**, verbs with two arguments **transitive verbs** and verbs with three arguments **ditransitive verbs**.

What we minimally need to implement in our grammar, then, is a condition that ensures that a sentence contains exactly enough arguments, because this directly affects the grammatical status of the sentence. The next section, implementation, introduces the basics of this theory.

Exercises

A1 How many arguments do the following verbs have?
  a. to fall
  b. to give
  c. to call
  d. to eat
  e. to cry
  f. to send
  g. to marry
  h. to promise

A2 Divide the verbs in A1 into intransitive, transitive and ditransitive verbs.

B3 Does every verb in A1 always take all its arguments?

3.2 Implementation: Theta Theory (θ-Theory)

The insight that the meaning of the verb determines how many elements it may merge with is an important one. The theory that captures how exactly verb meanings do this, and in what way, is known as Theta (θ) theory, where 'Theta' (θ) stands for 'thematic roles', the exact properties that arguments can have. θ-theory tells us what arguments a verb requires, and how many. However, before diving into this, we must first be more precise as to what exactly arguments are, and how you can spot them.

3.2.1 Arguments vs. Adverbials

So far, we have used arguments in a semantic way: they are constituents required by the meaning of the verb. But this book is about syntax. So the question arises as to what kind of syntactic constituents can be arguments. At first sight, this seems an easy question: arguments are nominal constituents, so they carry the categorial feature [N]. In (4), for instance, the verb *said* requires two arguments (one introducing the sayer, and one introducing the thing being said).

(4)   Mary said two words.

Now, the two constituents present (*Mary* and *two words*) are both nominal, in line with the idea that arguments are nominal constituents. But this is too simplistic. Take for instance the sentences in (5).

(5)   a.   Mary said that John was ill.
      b.   That Mary was late said nothing.

In (5a), *said* again needs two arguments, because that is simply a consequence of what that verb means. However, the sentence has only one nominal constituent, *Mary*. The other argument is a *that* clause: *that John was ill*. And this clause conveys what Mary said. But *that John was ill* is not a nominal constituent. For instance, it cannot be combined with an article or be put in the plural:

(6)   a.   *the that John was ill
      b.   *that Mary was lates

Example (5b) shows that we can even imagine sentences with the verb *said* in which the subject is not a nominal constituent. We conclude, then, that arguments of the verb are not always nominal constituents, although of course they can be. Both sentences in (5) contain two arguments, as required by the verb. Therefore, these examples sound completely natural.

These data show that what matters is the presence of enough arguments. It matters much less what the syntactic category is of such an argument: they can be NPs, *that* clauses or even PPs, as in (7).

(7)   Mary relies on John.

Now consider the following example:

(8)   Mary arrived this evening.

Here we have two nominal constituents, *Mary* and *this evening*, but only one of the two can be an argument (namely *Mary*). *To arrive* is an intransitive verb. It requires somebody who arrives and that's it. For this reason, *this evening* can easily be left out of the sentence: *Mary arrived* is a good sentence, too. So what, then, is *this evening*? Well, if the verb requires one argument and the sentence contains two constituents apart from the verb, then they cannot both be an argument. *Mary* must be an argument (she is the one who arrives), so *this evening* cannot be an argument of the verb. The same applies to *the whole night* in (9).

(9)   John snores the whole night.

Constituents that appear in the sentence but can in principle be left out are called adverbials. Adverbials add all sorts of extra information to the sentence but their presence is not dictated by the semantics of the verb: you can easily leave out *this evening* in (8) or *the whole night* in (9), which shows that the verb does not really require their presence: *John snores* is as grammatical as *John snores the whole night*. The sentence without *the whole night* may provide less information, but leaving out *the whole night* does not affect the grammaticality of the sentence at all. Leaving out *John*, however, does: *Snores the whole night* or *Arrived this evening* are bad sentences because obligatory arguments are missing.

Sentences, then, consist minimally of a verb and its arguments, and in addition may include a bunch of constituents that can be classified as adverbials. We have already implicitly introduced one test to distinguish the two. If you want to know whether a particular constituent is an argument or an adverbial, try to establish whether you can leave that constituent out without affecting the grammaticality of the sentence.

A second test that can distinguish between arguments and adverbials is another substitution test. Remember from chapter 1 that we can test whether a particular word is for instance a noun by replacing the word we are testing by a word that we know is a noun. If this is possible, we know that the word we replaced is a noun. We can also use such a substitution strategy to find out what the function is of a particular constituent. If you want to know whether a particular constituent is an adverbial, then try replacing it by a constituent that you know is an adverbial. Now, the prototypical adverbial is an adverb. An adverb like *probably* or *quickly* typically provides additional information to the sentence that is not required by the semantics of the verb. So we start with the sentence *John snores the whole night* and we want to know what the grammatical function is of *the whole night*: is it an argument or an adverbial? We replace *the whole night* by *quickly* or *probably*. The result we obtain, *John snores quickly/probably*, is grammatical. We therefore conclude that *the whole night* is an adverbial. And replacing *the whole night* by a real argument, such as *Mary*, does not work. As we saw, *John snores Mary* is out. Actually, the fact that an adverbial can always be replaced by an adverb (and thus has the same syntactic behaviour as an adverb) is the reason why it is called an adverbial.

Note that what we observed for arguments is also true for adverbials: they come in different categorial flavours. Earlier we saw that the argument of a verb can appear as (be realised by) a nominal or prepositional constituent, or by a *that* clause. We have now seen that adverbials can be realised by adverbs (like *probably*) or nominal constituents (like *the whole night*), but this does not exhaust the possibilities. It is quite easy to think up examples in which the adverbial is realised by a prepositional constituent, or a clause (such as a *when* or *if* clause):

(10)   a.   John snores **on Sundays**.
       b.   John snores **when/if he is asleep**.

Now that we have a better understanding of what an argument is or is not, and introduced tests to tell the two apart, let us turn to the grammatical condition that has the desired effect of excluding those sentences that are ungrammatical because of the argument requirements of the verb.

3.2.2 The Theta Criterion (θ-Criterion)

What we can conclude so far is that a verb determines how many arguments it must be combined with. The formal way to express this is to say that every verb assigns, depending on its meaning, a number of so-called thematic roles, abbreviated to theta (θ)-roles: an intransitive verb assigns one θ-role, a transitive verb two θ-roles, etc. Now, the most straightforward formulation of such a rule would be to say that every θ-role of a verb must be assigned to an argument. So (11a) is good, because *love* assigns two θ-roles and the sentence contains two arguments. Example (11b), on the other hand, is bad, as the sentence contains only one argument.

(11) a. Mary loves John.
      b. *Mary loves

We can state, then, that (11b) is ungrammatical because one of the verb's θ-roles cannot be assigned. This is not yet precise enough, however.

We all agree that (11b) is a bad sentence. But why couldn't it mean 'Mary loves herself'? *Love* assigns two θ-roles, and we could imagine that both θ-roles were assigned to *Mary*. However, it seems that *Mary* cannot receive more than one θ-role. So, if a verb assigns two θ-roles, it must assign these to two *different* arguments. The formal way of saying this is that every θ-role must be assigned to a unique argument.

But we're not there yet. So far, our implementation tells us that every verb must properly assign its θ-roles to unique arguments. But that does not tell us why a sentence like (12) is bad (where *Mary Bill* is not the name of one person).

(12) *John loves Mary Bill.

Here, the verb can assign its two θ-roles unproblematically. After all, it has a choice of three. But this choice actually ruins the sentence. No matter how you assign the θ-roles, one argument always ends up without one. So, it is necessary, but not sufficient, to say that every θ-role must be assigned to a unique argument. The reverse must also hold: every argument must receive a θ-role. Since in (12) one of the nominal constituents cannot be assigned a θ-role, it cannot be interpreted as an argument. The only option left, then, is to try to interpret the nominal constituent without a θ-role as an adverbial. But then we run into trouble. Adverbials introduce information about the time when, place where or manner in which a particular event took place, and none of *John, Mary* or *Bill* has the proper meaning for this. So one of the three nominal constituents can be interpreted neither as an argument nor as an adverbial. For this reason, the sentence is bad.

The two conditions together form the so-called Theta Criterion (θ-criterion), the implementation of the idea that the meaning of a verb constrains the number of arguments it can be merged with.

(13) THE θ-CRITERION
      Every θ-role must be assigned to a unique argument and every argument must receive a θ-role.

The θ-criterion is the most important pillar of θ-theory. It correctly allows example (11a) to be ruled in: here the number of θ-roles neatly matches the number of available constituents that can function as arguments. Examples (11b) and (12) are correctly ruled out because these sentences contain not enough or too many arguments.

Before we go on, one caveat must be mentioned. Not every verb comes with a fixed number of arguments. The verb *to eat* is a good example of a verb that sometimes has one and sometimes two arguments (14). The verb *to give* comes at least with two arguments, but can also have three (15).

(14) a. Anna is eating.
      b. Anna is eating a sandwich.

(15) a. Edith gave a book.
      b. Edith gave Peter a book.

The verb *to assign* is of this type too. We showed with example (3) that it requires three parties, but since then you have become quite used to statements like 'this verb assigns two θ-roles'. As you can see, the indirect object is often left out.

Do these examples falsify the θ-criterion? If you say that *to eat* is a transitive verb, and *to give* a ditransitive verb, then one argument is missing in the (a) examples in (14) and (15). But if instead you say that *to eat* is an intransitive and *to give* a transitive verb, as shown by the (a) examples, then the (b) examples all of a sudden become problematic, as they then contain an argument too many. It is not possible to put this right by saying that *a sandwich* or *Peter* are adverbials that introduce additional information. If they were constituents that could function as adverbials, then it is not so clear why they can't do just that in the following examples:

(16) a. *John snored a sandwich.
      b. *John snored Peter.

There is a way out, however. Nowhere was it stated that verbs always assign a fixed number of θ-roles. Nor would anything forbid certain verbs to assign θ-roles optionally, rather than obligatorily. We could therefore say that *to eat* sometimes assigns one θ-role and sometimes two, and that *to give* always assigns two θ-roles and optionally a third one. This way, all the sentences in (14) and (15) are ruled in, given the θ-criterion in (13), and we can keep it in its present formulation.

The only question might then be what allows a verb like *to eat* or *to give* to optionally assign a particular θ-role, and why can transitive verbs like *to announce* or *to state* not do the same? The examples in (17) sound bad, in contrast to (14a) and (15a).

(17) a. *John announced.
      b. *John stated.

It is not that easy to understand what the underlying differences are that set verbs like *to eat* or *to give* apart from *to announce* or *to state*. In both

(14a) and (15a), the argument that has been left out can still be understood: if you eat, you eat something, and if you give something, you give something to somebody. But the same could be said about the examples in (17): *to state* and *to announce* always involve stating something or announcing something. To a certain extent, the fact that some verbs assign optional theta-roles and others do not is accidental, an arbitrary property of those verbs. Such arbitrary properties, especially when it comes to word meaning (also known as **lexical semantics**), show up quite frequently in language. For instance, why would it be *I believe in her* and *I'm counting on him* instead of the other way round (**I'm believing on her* or **I'm counting in him*)? There is nothing 'inny' about believing or 'onny' about counting. The correct preposition required by *believe* and *count* is also an arbitrary property, no different from the optionality or obligatoriness of the second θ-role of *to eat* or *to state*. So we may not know what exactly underlies the difference between *eat/give* on the one hand and *announce/state* on the other, but that there are such differences is no surprise.

3.2.3 θ-Roles and the θ-Hierarchy

So far we have only discussed the number of θ-roles a verb can assign, not what different kinds of θ-roles there can be. It actually turns out that there is only a limited number of θ-roles.

Let us start with (18):

(18) a. The detective interrogates the suspect.
  b. Mary kicks the ball.

In (18a) *the detective* is the one undertaking some action (in this case the act of interrogating the suspect). For this reason we call *the detective* the **agent**. Since θ-roles are generally written in capitals (to distinguish them from other usages), we say that *the detective* has the AGENT role. *The suspect*, by contrast, is a person undergoing an action. For this reason we say that *the suspect* is a PATIENT. PATIENT roles are restricted to animate or human beings. Therefore, *the ball* in (18b) cannot be a PATIENT. It is a so-called THEME. Mary in (18b) is still the AGENT. For this reason, the sentence in (19) strikes us as funny:

(19) The detective interrogates the ball.

The verb *interrogates* needs a living entity to undergo the interrogation and a ball cannot take on this role. However, a lot is possible in cartoons, as we have seen. If a sentence is acceptable in a cartoon, it shows that the weirdness is not grammatical or syntactic: the difference between a PATIENT and a THEME is purely semantic. Note that if the meaning of a verb allows for both living and non-living entities, such a verb may assign both a PATIENT and THEME role, depending on the semantic properties of the respective arguments. *To love* is a good example:

(20) a. Mary   loves   the children
      AGENT   PATIENT

  b. Mary   loves   classical music
      AGENT   THEME

Note, though, that an AGENT can be either a living or a non-living entity. Both subjects in (21) are AGENTs:

(21)   a.   The thief destroyed their happiness.
       b.   The fire destroyed their happiness.

Quite often, when a verb assigns three θ-roles, a RECIPIENT role (sometimes also called a BENEFICIARY role) is involved. *Peter* in (22) is one, with *Edith* being the AGENT and *a book* the THEME that is undergoing the action.

(22)   Edith gave Peter a book.

A final θ-role that is often used is GOAL. Consider the following sentence:

(23)   John sent his purchase to a foreign country.

Now, *a foreign country* here looks like a RECIPIENT. However, just as in the case of PATIENT and THEME, RECIPIENTs and GOALs behave differently with respect to whether the argument can be animate or inanimate. RECIPIENTs, as receivers in general, are typically animate entities, but you can send something *to* anything, a human being or a post office. Look at the following pairs:

(24)   a.   John sent Mary a letter.
       b.   John sent a letter to Mary.

(25)   a.   *John sent a foreign country his purchase.
       b.   John sent his purchase to a foreign country.

Whereas it is quite easy to turn a RECIPIENT into a GOAL, as you can see in (24), it is generally much harder to turn a GOAL into a RECIPIENT, as (25) illustrates. This follows if there is a restriction on what can be a RECIPIENT (i.e. it has to be animate), whereas no such restriction holds for GOALs. And this shows that we really have two different θ-roles here.

The claim that RECIPIENTs are always animate might be at odds with sentences like the ones in (26) (which therefore may look like counterexamples):

(26)   a.   The Prime Minister sent Australia a letter of complaint.
       b.   The Nazis gave London something to worry about.

But this is only apparently the case. The way we interpret these sentences is not with Australia and London as locations but as representing national authorities, and these are human beings. Such examples, then, actually underscore the same point: a RECIPIENT must be animate.

So far, we have discussed transitive and ditransitive verbs, where things look quite clear: there are AGENTs, PATIENTs/THEMEs and, in the case of ditransitives, also RECIPIENTs or GOALs. Intransitive verbs look less clear at first sight. What are the θ-roles that the arguments of intransitive verbs may have? For many intransitive verbs the argument, always a subject, is an AGENT. *John* is a sleeper in (27a), a snorer in (27b) and a walker in (27c).

(27) a. John sleeps.
     b. John snores.
     c. John walks.

It might be tempting, then, to say on the basis of these examples that all arguments of intransitive verbs are AGENTs. But, alas, this is not true. There are many intransitive verbs for which this does not hold. Take the following examples:

(28) a. Bill fell.
     b. Carl died.
     c. The glass broke.

Falling, dying and breaking involve particular actions, but you can't say that Bill undertook the action of falling. Bill could have done something that caused him to fall, but he was not *actively* involved in the falling action itself. He rather underwent it. The same is true for *dying*: Carl can die while unconscious, unable to be actively involved with the dying process (in fact somebody else may even have murdered Carl). And the glass presumably broke because somebody dropped it on the ground. It is not the glass itself doing it. So the subjects in (28) cannot be AGENTs because they are entities undergoing rather than performing the actions they are involved in. A helpful test for diagnosing whether an argument is an AGENT is the so-called *-er test*. The suffix *-er* can be attached to a verb creating a noun that refers to an AGENT. For this reason, it can only attach to verbs that assign an AGENT role. A *baker* is somebody who bakes, and a *lover* someone who loves. But you cannot say for Bill in (28a) that he is a *faller*, and the glass in (28c) is certainly not a *breaker*. Since you have to be an AGENT to pass this test, *Bill, Carl* and *the glass* cannot be AGENTs in (28).

But what are they then? Well, just as there is a test for AGENTs, there are tests for PATIENTs/THEMEs. Take *the ball* and *the book* in (18b) and (22). You can say 'what happened to the ball was that Mary kicked it' or 'what happened to the book was that Edith gave it to Peter'. You can also say: 'what happened to Bill is that he fell', 'what happened to Carl is that he died' and 'what happened to the glass is that it broke'. This makes their roles strikingly similar to those of *the ball* in (18b) and *a book* in (22). The test, then, makes us arrive at the same conclusion we had already reached: *Bill* and *Carl* must be PATIENTs in (28a)/(28b), and *the glass* must be a THEME in (28c).

Let's take stock. For the verbs used in this section, we can provide the following list, where the brackets indicate an optional θ-role:

(29) *to snore, to sleep*   AGENT
     to break   AGENT, THEME
     to fall   AGENT, PATIENT/THEME
     to love   AGENT, PATIENT/THEME
     to kick   AGENT, PATIENT/THEME
     to eat   AGENT (, PATIENT/THEME)
     to give, to send   AGENT (, RECIPIENT), PATIENT/THEME or
                        AGENT, PATIENT/THEME (, GOAL)

What this shows is that the number of θ-roles is quite limited. This list of possible θ-roles may not be 100% complete, and syntacticians have argued the case for a few more, but not a lot. For our purposes, however, the list we now have suffices.

To sum up so far, we have built our θ-theory on two pillars: (i) the θ-criterion and (ii) the observation that the roles performed by arguments in the sentence can be captured by a relatively small list.

Before we close this section, we would like to mention a third pillar. There appears to be a clear restriction on what kind of argument (subject, direct object, indirect object) may receive which θ-role. Take a look at the examples in (30). These all involve a transitive verb, so each sentence contains two arguments. The subject is interpreted as an AGENT and the object as either a PATIENT or a THEME.

(30) a. Mary loves John.
      b. John kicks the ball.
      c. Laurent eats a sandwich.

As it turns out, this is a fixed pattern: whenever the verb requires the presence of an AGENT and a PATIENT/THEME, it is always the subject that carries the AGENT role, never the object. There are simply no sentences in which the subject is the PATIENT or THEME and the object is the AGENT.

Now, one way of capturing this pattern would be to say that subjects are AGENTs and objects are PATIENTs or THEMEs. But this cannot be right. We have already seen that there are subjects that are not AGENTs, and a PATIENT or a THEME does not always have to be an object. Think, for instance, of *to fall*. The only thing we can say is that if there is an object and if there is a subject, and if a verb assigns both an AGENT role and a PATIENT/THEME role, then the subject is the AGENT and the object is the PATIENT/THEME. But this does not follow from anything; it is just restating the facts.

How do we make sense of this? So far, we can say that if multiple θ-roles are assigned, they are always assigned in a specific order. For instance, the order of the AGENT and PATIENT/THEME roles is always fixed. We formalise it like this:

(31)   AGENT > PATIENT/THEME

An order like (31) represents a hierarchy. It means that some θ-roles take preference over others. Therefore (31) describes a θ-**hierarchy**. This hierarchy makes it possible to account for the fact that subjects always receive the leftmost θ-role in the hierarchy in cases where the verb assigns two of the roles mentioned in (31). This does not mean that a subject always has to be an AGENT, but only that the AGENT role is what it takes on if another θ-role is assigned by the verb as well. If there is only one θ-role to assign, the subject just gets that θ-role. If the one role assigned by the verb is an AGENT, then of course the subject will be an AGENT. This gives us the example *John snores*. If the only role that a verb assigns is a PATIENT role, however, the subject will just as happily take on this role. This gives us *Bill fell*.

We can now even extend this hierarchy to other θ-roles. A verb like *to give*, when it assigns three θ-roles, also always does so in a particular order:

(32) a. John   gave   Mary   the book.
        AGENT   RECIPIENT   THEME

     b. *John   gave   the book   Mary.
        AGENT   THEME   RECIPIENT

Note that (32a) respects the hierarchical order between AGENT and PATIENT/THEME. Again, the AGENT is the subject and the THEME the direct object. In fact, (32b) also respects this order but something has gone wrong here: the RECIPIENT cannot appear at the end. We can rule in (32a) and at the same time rule out (32b) by simply including RECIPIENT in the θ-hierarchy as follows:

(33) AGENT > RECIPIENT > PATIENT/THEME

Now, interestingly, the hierarchy in (33) also applies to transitive verbs. Basically, (33) says that if you have more than one θ-role, their internal order is AGENT > RECIPIENT > PATIENT/THEME. If there is no RECIPIENT, the order is simply AGENT > THEME. But this also predicts that if there is no AGENT but just a RECIPIENT and a PATIENT/THEME, the RECIPIENT should be the subject. And, indeed, this is true. The following data confirm this:

(34) a. John   received/got   a book.
        RECIPIENT   THEME

     b. *A book   received/got   John.
        THEME   RECIPIENT

Now, one might object, though, and argue that (33) is not always correct. After all, (32) could be rephrased as (35), with the indirect object following the direct object:

(35) John   gave   the book   to Mary.
    AGENT   THEME   RECIPIENT

But remember that we noted earlier that *to Mary* is not a RECIPIENT but rather a GOAL. Whereas RECIPIENT arguments precede PATIENT/THEME arguments, GOAL arguments follow the PATIENT/THEME. This is shown below:

(36) a. John   gave   the book   to her.
        AGENT   THEME   GOAL

     b. John   gave   her   the book.
        AGENT   RECIPIENT   THEME

This means that we can include the GOAL in our hierarchy of θ-roles and replace (35) by (37):

(37) AGENT > RECIPIENT > PATIENT/THEME > GOAL

To conclude, all θ-roles introduced so far stand in a particular hierarchical order, an important linguistic discovery: AGENTs are higher than RECIPIENTs; RECIPIENTs higher than PATIENT/THEMEs; and PATIENTs/THEMEs higher than GOALs.

3.2.4 Interim Summary

So far we have seen that every argument needs a unique θ-role and every θ-role needs a unique argument. In addition, we have seen that θ-roles stand in a particular hierarchical order. These two components together capture all possible configurations of verbs and arguments that we can find.

For intransitive verbs, it is simple: the verb assigns only one θ-role, so the subject receives that θ-role, as in (38). Nothing more needs to be said. In the case of transitive verbs, the verb assigns two θ-roles, and the subject receives the highest θ-role and the object the lowest one, as in (39). And in the case of ditransitive verbs, if a RECIPIENT is present, the subject takes the highest role, then comes the indirect object with the RECIPIENT role and finally the object that takes the PATIENT/THEME-role; if a GOAL rather than a RECIPIENT is present, the direct object is next in line and gets the PATIENT/THEME-role, and the PP to the right of it receives the GOAL argument, as in (40).

(38)   Intransitive verbs

    a. John   snored.
         AGENT

    b. John   fell.
         PATIENT

(39)   Transitive verbs

    a. John   loves   Mary.
         AGENT   PATIENT

    b. John   kicked   the ball.
         AGENT   THEME

(40)   Ditransitive verbs

    a. John   gave   Mary   the book.
         AGENT   RECIPIENT THEME

    b. John   gave   the book to her.
         AGENT   THEME   GOAL

These are the simple cases. In the next section, we will look at more complicated phenomena, and we will show that θ-theory can actually be used to understand these more complicated phenomena: they involve more fine-grained predictions confirming our theory.

Exercises

A4 Are the underlined constituents arguments or adverbials? Justify your answers.
   a. John cooked <u>a meal.</u>
   b. John read <u>a book.</u>
   c. John read <u>about mice.</u>
   d. John read <u>in the kitchen.</u>
   e. I want to know <u>when he'll leave.</u>
   f. Mary sleeps <u>in the dark.</u>
   g. Mary listens <u>to the radio.</u>
   h. Peter ate <u>every cookie.</u>
   i. Peter ate <u>every morning.</u>

A5 What are the θ-roles of each of the arguments in the following sentences?
   a. John broke his leg.
   b. I assigned the exercise to Mary.
   c. Mary finally surrendered.
   d. Mary finally arrived.
   e. Ivan gave the secret report to the KGB.
   f. I never promised you a rose garden.
   g. The door opened.
   h. Mary gave Ali a lecture.

B6 Some PPs are arguments, some are adverbials. The distinction is sometimes difficult to make. Take a and b (in their most straightforward readings). How do we know that *on the calculator* is an adverbial and *on Mary* is an argument?
   a. He counts on the calculator.
   b. He counts on Mary.

B7 NPs and PPs can be both adverbials and arguments. But how about adverbs? Can there be adverbs that are arguments?

C8 The text says that there may be other θ-roles than AGENT, RECIPIENT, PATIENT/THEME and GOAL. Some syntacticians also distinguish EXPERIENCER and SOURCE θ-roles, for instance in sentences like:
   a. John feared the wolf.
   b. Mary sensed a strange atmosphere.

This means that in such sentences *John* and *Mary* are not AGENTs and *the wolf* and *a strange atmosphere* cannot be THEMEs/PATIENTs. Can you put forward some arguments that would favour these claims? Also reconsider the AGENT role that we have assigned to the subject of *to love* in (39a).

3.3 Consequences: Missing Arguments – Passives, Ergatives and PRO

In this section, we will first look at so-called passive constructions and see that θ-theory accounts for several of their crucial properties. Then we will look at two constructions that are even more complex, involving the verbs *to seem* and *to hope*. We will see that θ-theory again shows us that there are words that are never expressed.

3.3.1 Passives and Ergatives

Most of the sentences that we have seen so far have been active sentences. Active sentences contrast with passive sentences. The passive counterparts of the active sentences in (39), for instance, are as follows:

(41)　a.　Mary is loved (by John).
　　　 b.　The ball was kicked (by John).

In a passive sentence, the original subject disappears (and may come back in the so-called by phrase) and the original object takes over the position of the subject. The original object, at the same time, retains its θ-role. *Mary* and *the ball* are still PATIENT/THEME in both (39) and (41). What is going on here?

Let's first look at what we can already say on the basis of the examples we have seen so far. The first conclusion we can draw is that every sentence must contain a subject. Objects appear only with active transitive verbs, and indirect objects only with active ditransitive verbs. If a verb has only one argument, this argument is the subject. This is the case with intransitive verbs, but, as we see now, it also applies to passive transitive verbs. We can thus formulate the following principle:

(42)　Every sentence has a subject.

The principle in (42) is almost exceptionless. Only two kinds of constructions appear to run counter to it. As for the first, take a look at (43) and (44).

(43)　Doctor:　　So how's John?
　　　 Jeanette:　He's fine…
　　　 Doctor:　　Does he get enough rest?
　　　 Jeanette:　Oh yes. Snores the whole night.

(44)　Mary:　　Have you been to Paris recently?
　　　 Bill:　　 Haven't been there in ages.

In these examples the subject appears to be missing (*Snores the whole night; Haven't been there in ages*). At the same time, we know what the subject is: *John* in (43), *I* in (44). Not only does the context tell us so, the verb also has the additional *-s* marker in (43) that reveals to us that there is a 3rd-person singular subject, whereas in (44) the verb agrees with *I*.

In particular cases, when the choice of the subject is already clear from the context, the subject may be left unexpressed. This phenomenon is called **subject drop**. Note that this does not mean that the subject is absent: if it were absent, the verb could never agree with it. But if the subject is present (albeit unexpressed), the examples in (43) and (44) do not run counter to the principle in (42).

The second construction that might be problematic for (42) are so-called **imperative clauses**:

(45) a. Give me the keys!
      b. Sit down!

But imperatives too have an understood, and unexpressed, subject. In an imperative, a subject may always be included:

(46) a. You give me the keys!
      b. Everybody sit down!

So, imperatives do not run counter to (42) either. They involve subject drop. These cases already prove (42) right. But there is even more evidence for it. There is one type of example that very clearly shows the need for a sentence to have a subject no matter what. This type involves *weather* verbs:

(47) a. It's raining.
      b. It's snowing.

These verbs allow one subject only, namely *it*. Replacing *it* by another subject simply leads to ungrammaticality:

(48) *She/the sky rains.

The reason why (48) is bad is that nobody or nothing can rain, nor can somebody or something be rained. *To rain* simply does not assign any thematic role. This is also why you cannot ask 'What snows?' Consequently, a sentence with the verb *to rain* should lack any argument. But a sentence without any argument leads to a violation of (42), which tells us that every sentence must have a subject. A sentence with a *weather* verb, then, must meet two requirements: (i) it cannot contain an argument and (ii) it must have a subject. In order to meet both requirements, a dummy subject (or an expletive subject, in formal terms) is inserted. Such an expletive subject can be seen as the simplest subject possible (*it*), and as an element that is not a real argument. Since this element does not count as an argument, it can satisfy the principle in (42) without violating the θ-criterion.

Now let's go back to passive constructions. What is it that makes a passive verb a passive? It turns out that it is only one thing: it assigns one fewer θ-role. And, if a transitive verb assigns one fewer θ-role, it has one argument left, just like any other intransitive verb. This argument, then, must be the subject, given (42). But how do we know which θ-role disappears? Why is it in the examples in (41) that the AGENT role disappears, and not the PATIENT or THEME role?

Again, our θ-hierarchy is of service: whenever, in a particular English construction, a verb assigns one fewer θ-role, the θ-role that disappears is always the highest one. In (41), neither *to love* nor *to kick* any longer assigns an AGENT role but, given that the verbs still assign PATIENT or THEME roles, these roles are taken on by the subject in these passive constructions.

The mechanism we are applying works perfectly for passives of ditransitives as well. Take the following examples:

(49) a. Mary was given the books.
      b. *The books were given Mary.

(50) a. The books were given to Mary.
      b. *Mary was given the books to.

To give assigns three θ-roles. If you turn it into a passive, it only assigns two. Given the θ-hierarchy, the AGENT role no longer gets assigned. Now, we saw that *to give* assigns either a RECIPIENT role (higher than the THEME role) or a GOAL role (lower than the THEME role) to the person that receives something. In the first case, the subject of the passive sentence becomes a RECIPIENT, and the object remains a THEME. This gives us the example in (49a). The reverse (a subject THEME and a RECIPIENT object) is predicted to be bad, and that is indeed the case, as (49b) shows. But in the second case, in which *to give* assigns a GOAL instead of a RECIPIENT role, the subject will be the THEME, which is the second-highest θ-role, after the AGENT (as there is no RECIPIENT now). Therefore *the books* must be the subject in the passive (50), and not *Mary*.

One might wonder why sometimes the THEME can be the subject in passives without a GOAL or RECIPIENT present. Take, for instance, (51), where this is the case.

(51) The books were given.

If only one argument remains unrealised (absent) in a passive construction, this sentence must have an active counterpart with only two arguments (e.g. *Mary gave the books*). We saw earlier that the third θ-role of *to give* is optional. When this role is absent, *to give* behaves like a transitive verb, with an AGENT and a THEME. Consequently, the AGENT role disappears in the passive construction, and the subject thus takes on a THEME role.

The type of θ-role carried by a subject or object, both in active and passive sentences, thus follows directly from the θ-hierarchy. But we can make correct predictions for more than just passive constructions. Additional evidence comes from certain other verbs, traditionally known as **ergative verbs**. Such verbs can sometimes be transitive and sometimes intransitive. Good examples are verbs like *to melt, to sink*, and *to cook*:

(52) a. The butter melts.
      b. Bill melts the butter.

(53) a. The ship sank.
      b. The pirates sank the ship.

(54) a. The potatoes are cooking.
      b. John is cooking the potatoes.

Ergative verbs are verbs that can function without the highest θ-role, i.e. they only optionally assign the AGENT role. In the (b) examples, both an AGENT and a THEME are present. But in the (a) examples, there is only the THEME. As in a passive construction, the highest θ-role has disappeared and the object has become the subject of the intransitive counterpart, completely as predicted. Hence, our θ-hierarchy turns out to be very helpful: it not only tells us what the order of arguments is, but also which arguments can be removed and which ones cannot.

3.3.2 Unexpressed Subjects

Now that we have significant confirmation for our theory, let us see what other things in English grammar it can reveal. A good theory, as we will see now, can help us discover things that otherwise we would never see. In this section, we will look at one such thing that would otherwise remain unobserved. The starting point is the following pair of sentences:

(55) a. John hopes to win the race.
      b. John seems to win the race.

These sentences are complex in the sense that they contain two main verbs: *hopes/seems* and *to win*. (These sentences sound more natural if the embedded clause contains an adverbial like *always*, as in *John seems to always win the race*, but we omit this here for the sake of clarity.) Every main verb implies the existence of what we have referred to as a **clause**. This means that both of these examples can be analysed as consisting of two clauses, with one embedded in the other. In other words, the entire string is a **main clause**, and part of the main clause is an **embedded clause**. This is indicated by bracketing in (56):

(56) a. [main clause John hopes [embedded clause to win the race]]
      b. [main clause John seems [embedded clause to win the race]]

We will use the term **sentence** as an alternative for main clause, which is a unit centred around a verb that can stand on its own. So *John hopes/seems to win the race* is a sentence and a (main) clause. *To win the race*, on the other hand, is only an (embedded) clause, not a sentence, and it needs to be part of something bigger to survive.

Looking at the similar bracketing in (56a) and (56b), you might be inclined to think that their underlying structures would be the same. However, according to our θ-theory this cannot be the case. Why? Well, let's look more closely. *John* in (55a) is clearly a 'hoper', but *John* in (55b) is not a 'seemer'. To the extent that *seems* assigns a θ-role, it only has one. You can conclude this on the basis of asking yourself the question 'What seems (to be the case)?', or 'What is seemingly the case?' The answer

would be something like 'for John to win the race'. We conclude therefore that *John … to win the race* is θ-assigned by *seems* and that this θ-role is
not an AGENT but rather something like a THEME.

Interestingly, there is a paraphrase of example (55b) that leads to the
same conclusion, namely the one in (57).

(57)   It seems that John wins the race.

The subject of the main clause is the expletive subject *it* (as in the
case with *weather* verbs), which cannot be assigned a θ-role, and the
only role that *seems* assigns goes to the embedded clause *that John wins
the race*. Note that a difference between (55b) and (57) is that in the former the θ-role is assigned to a group of words that does not form a unit,
John … to win the race, where *John* is separated from *to win the race* by the
verb *seems*. This is an interesting, and, as it will turn out, very important, property but we will ignore it for now. The importance of this for
our theory will be revealed in chapter 6, so be patient.

But if *John* in (55b) is not assigned a θ-role by *seems*, which verb is responsible for the θ-role of *John*? *John* is an argument and therefore it must be
assigned a θ-role. There is only one candidate left: the other verb in the
sentence, *to win*. In a construction like (55b), then, *John* plays some kind of
double role. It is the subject of the verb *seem*, but it receives a θ-role from
to win (a verb that assigns both an AGENT and a THEME role). Even though
this might look a little strange, it is not in violation of anything we have
said so far: the claim in (42) says that every sentence must have a subject,
and this is satisfied by (55b). And θ-theory demands that every argument
receives a θ-role, and that every θ-role of the verb is assigned to a different argument, and these requirements are satisfied as well. *Seems* assigns
a θ-role to *John … to win the race*, and *to win* assigns its θ-roles to *John* and
the race, respectively. So, our θ-theory actually predicts that such constructions are possible. Schematically, θ-role assignment then looks as follows:

(58)

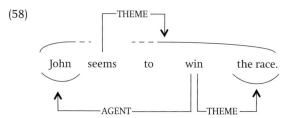

The grammaticality of (55b) should not surprise us, because none of
the rules of our θ-theory has been violated.

But how about (55a), *John hopes to win the race*? Again, *to win* must assign
two thematic roles. But *hopes* must do that as well. *To hope* is a clear example
of a verb that assigns two θ-roles: it needs a hoper and a thing that is hoped
for. If both *hopes* and *to win* assign two θ-roles each, and every argument
may only receive one θ-role (as we established earlier), then the maths
is very simple: we need four arguments in (55a). But we can count only

three: *John, to win the race* and *the race*. Just go through it: *hope* assigns its AGENT role to *John* and the THEME role to *to win the race*. *To win* assigns its THEME role to *the race*, but then the question is, to what argument can it assign its AGENT role? *John* already has a θ-role, so a problem arises.

Now, there are two conclusions we can draw from this: either our theory is right and a fourth argument is present but we can't hear it (as we saw with subject drop in the previous subsection), or our theory is wrong and a single argument, in this case *John*, can in fact receive two θ-roles (the AGENT role from *hopes* and the AGENT role from *to win*). Obviously the first hypothesis may look a bit crazy (although we have already noted something similar), but we can at least try to see how it would work by establishing what kinds of predictions it makes. We can then compare them with the predictions of the theory stating that (55a) contains only three arguments, with one of them carrying two θ-roles.

Let's start with the former option. If there is a fourth argument present, it would probably be some kind of pronoun, since (55a) has a meaning that is almost identical to (59), where the subscript indices ($_i$) indicate that *he* refers back to *John* and not to some other guy:

(59)   John$_i$ hopes that he$_i$ wins the race.

So, applying θ-theory forces us to assume that (55a) has an underlying structure that looks like (60), with some unexpressed pronoun, known as PRO, referring to John:

(60)   John$_i$ hopes PRO$_i$ to win the race.

Schematically, the θ-role assignment looks as follows:

(61)

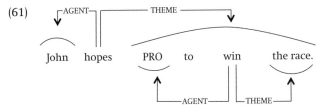

As we can see, this organisation fits well with θ-theory: every θ-role is assigned and no argument receives more than one role.

Now, let us consider the alternative option, namely that θ-theory's prediction is wrong and that there can be no such thing as PRO. This would mean that the structure of (55a) is identical to the structure in (55b), the only difference being that *John* has two θ-roles in the *hope* construction. Syntactically, (55a) and (55b) are the same and in neither example does the embedded *to* clause contain any unexpressed material.

So, which option is right? At first sight, you might say that the latter approach wins because it does not have to postulate an abstract, unexpressed element. However, this analysis then has to accept that arguments can carry two θ-roles. This would open a Pandora's box, and even some very basic facts will no longer follow from our theory. Remember the example in (11b), repeated here:

(62)   *Mary loves

If arguments can receive two θ-roles, (62) should be fine, with *Mary* receiving both an AGENT and PATIENT role. The sentence would then mean 'Mary loves herself.' But the sentence is clearly bad, and certainly cannot be read that way. This shows that it is not possible to assign two θ-roles to the same argument.

We therefore maintain the assumption, explicit in θ-theory, that arguments can only receive one θ-role, because not making that assumption creates a lot of problems. As a consequence, we are forced to conclude that there can be an empty argument, PRO: it is syntactically present, and so it can receive a θ-role, but we do not express it. This means that the structures of the examples in (55a) and (55b) have to be different, as we have argued.

The analytical difference between the *hope* and the *seem* constructions, forced upon us by θ-theory, now gives rise to an interesting prediction. We have argued that *hope* assigns a θ-role to its subject, whereas *seem* does not. This leads to the expectation that the subject in a *seem* sentence can remain without a θ-role, whereas this should be impossible in a *hope* sentence. The following examples show that this prediction is borne out:

(63)   a.   It seems that John wins the race.
       b.   *It hopes that John wins the race.

Both examples contain an expletive subject *it*. This does not create a problem for *seem* in (63a). After all, *seem* does not assign a θ-role to its subject. At the same time, a sentence should have a subject, so *it* is present to make sure that this requirement is met. Inserting *it* does lead to a problem in (63b), however. *Hope* needs to assign a θ-role to its subject but *it* is just an expletive subject. Inserting *it* leads to ungrammaticality because the AGENT role of *hopes* has not been assigned, in violation of θ-theory. The fact that *seem* constructions are fine with an expletive subject but *hope* constructions are not is not just an arbitrary fact of English, but something we now actually understand. It is a consequence of θ-theory and something that directly follows from our hypotheses.

However, there is one question left: if an empty pronoun, PRO, exists, doesn't this predict that the example in (62) is grammatical? After all, we can represent it as in (64), with an empty object.

(64)   *Mary loves PRO.

This sentence should mean 'Mary loves her', or perhaps even 'Mary loves herself.' Allowing an empty pronoun to take on the role of an argument makes it possible to create (64) but this example has to be ruled out. In fact, the following examples have to be ruled out as well:

(65) a. *PRO loves John.
      b. *PRO loves PRO.

How can we use PRO in such a way that we do not all of a sudden create a lot of ungrammatical sentences? It must be the case that there are restrictions on the occurrence of PRO. There is an important difference between these ungrammatical examples and the one in (55a). In the *hope* sentence, PRO appears in the non-finite clause: [PRO *to win the race*]. To be more precise, PRO is the subject of the non-finite clause. In the examples in (64) and (65), on the other hand, we have put PRO in either subject or object position, and these clauses are all finite. What restriction(s) on PRO do we need in order to obtain the desired outcome? Basing ourselves on the examples we have seen, we can say that PRO can only be the subject of a non-finite clause (and leave the explanation for why that would be until later). This, then, has the desired consequence of ruling in (55a) and ruling out examples such as (62), (64) and (65): the latter do not contain a non-finite clause.

Exercises

A9   Make the following sentences passive. Explain what happens to the θ-roles present in the active sentences.
     a. Mohammed buys a house.
     b. John wins a prize.
     c. John receives a prize.
     d. I never promised you a pay rise.
     e. I am sending the document to London.

A10 Take the following sentences:
     a. John happens to win the race.
     b. John wants to win the race.
     c. John tries to win the race.
     d. John appears to win the race.
     e. John expects to win the race.

     Which of these sentences behave like *seem* constructions, and which behave like *hope* constructions?

C11 Normally, changing an active sentence into a passive sentence changes the θ-role of the subject. In *Mary loved John*, the subject *Mary* is the AGENT, but in *John was loved*, the subject *John* is the PATIENT. Intransitive ergative verbs form an exception to this rule; in both a and b *the potatoes* are the THEME:
     a. The potatoes cook.
     b. The potatoes are cooked.

     Why do we not see a change in θ-role when changing an active intransitive ergative into a passive?

Summary

In this chapter we started out with the observation that verbs need arguments. We then looked in more detail into the relation between verbs and arguments and concluded that arguments need to be distinguished from adverbials, which are elements whose presence is not required by a verb. From there we took the next step and showed that a general principle holds. This principle is known as the θ-criterion, and it states that a verb needs to assign all its so-called θ-roles (roles like AGENT, PATIENT, THEME, RECIPIENT and GOAL) and that every argument in a sentence needs to be assigned a unique θ-role.

Moreover, we saw that the θ-roles that a verb assigns always follow a general hierarchy that takes AGENT to be a higher role than RECIPIENT, RECIPIENT to be a higher role than PATIENT and THEME roles, and PATIENT and THEME to be higher roles than GOAL. In the third section, we saw that this theory, known as θ-theory, makes a number of correct predictions. For instance, once we know what the θ-roles of a verb are, we can predict for every construction – active, passive or ergative – what roles their subjects and direct and indirect objects receive.

Finally, we saw that two seemingly identical constructions (*seem* constructions and *hope* constructions) are actually fundamentally different in exactly the way that θ-theory predicts. θ-theory led us to hypothesise that *hope* constructions, opposite to *seem* constructions, contain an extra silent (that is, an unexpressed) pronoun, known as PRO.

We have now made serious progress in solving the problem that the previous chapter left us with. Merge overgenerates: it can create a lot of sentences that are ungrammatical. We therefore concluded that Merge needs to be constrained. θ-theory is the first serious constraint. A lot of sentences that Merge can create are now filtered out because they violate θ-theory and therefore cannot be properly interpreted. Since we are not at the end of the book yet, you may suspect that θ-theory is probably not the only constraint, and that the next chapters will introduce some examples that are still incorrectly predicted to be ungrammatical, even with the addition of θ-theory. Your suspicion would be correct.

Further Reading

θ-roles were introduced by Gruber (1965, 1967) and Fillmore (1968). The θ-criterion stems from Chomsky (1981). θ-hierarchies have been proposed by Jackendoff (1972), Larson (1988), Baker (1989) and Grimshaw (1990), the latter containing a good overview of the discussion.

Expletive subjects have been discussed by many linguists. Milsark (1974), Lasnik (1992) and Moro (1997) are good examples. PRO was introduced in Chomsky (1981). Currently a debate is under way about whether the theory can somehow do without PRO, with Hornstein (1999) and Boeckx & Hornstein (2004) arguing that it can and Landau (2003) and Bobaljik & Landau (2009) arguing that it cannot. To a large extent, this discussion centres around the syntax of Icelandic and Brazilian Portuguese. Not every debate can be settled by just looking at English.

The grammaticality condition we mentioned in (42) – that every sentence have a subject – is known as the Extended Projection Principle (EPP). Originally put forward by Chomsky (1981), it has returned in various guises in the theory.

4 Case Theory

CHAPTER OUTLINE

In chapter 2, we saw that the Merge operation, elegant as it is, can still create both grammatical and ungrammatical structures. We therefore concluded that we need constraints that filter out these ungrammatical structures. θ-theory was the first serious constraint we introduced. The nature of this constraint is semantic: we saw the number of arguments present in the syntax must match the semantics of the verb. Sentences like *Edith assigns* or *John loves Mary Paul* (where Mary and Paul are two different people) are now correctly filtered out. It is quite easy to see, however, that more work needs to be done. Let us give you a very simple example. The sentence *Him calls she* is ungrammatical, despite the fact that the verb can assign both its θ-roles to the arguments that are present (i.e. the AGENT role to *him* and the PATIENT role to *she*). In terms of the meaning, then, nothing is wrong, but something is not quite right with the form of the sentence. This chapter will explore in detail how to make this explicit, and how syntax will ensure that the structures it creates have the right form. This second filter on the Merge operation is called Case theory. We will see that the Case theory presented in this chapter has far-reaching consequences for the syntax of English sentences.

4.1 Insight: Case as a Filter on Syntactic Structures

Although θ-theory is a necessary filter on constructions created by the Merge operation, at least three problems emerge if we say that θ-theory forms the only constraint on Merge.

The first problem concerns θ-mismatches, examples in which the number of arguments does not match up with the number of θ-roles that the verb needs to assign. It turns out that an unassigned θ-role is not as bad as an argument without a θ-role. For instance, transitive verbs that are used intransitively can be quite bad (as expected by θ-theory), but sometimes they can survive. *Edith assigns* could be said in a situation in which the manager, on asking who assigns tasks to new employees, is told that it is Edith who does the assignments. The same holds for the verb *to kill*. The sentence *Peter kills* is degraded (halfway between grammatical and ungrammatical) owing to the θ-criterion: the PATIENT role is not assigned. But if Peter were a professional hitman, one could say that *Peter kills for a living*. It is perhaps not perfect but given the right context certainly tolerable (the sentence, that is, not the profession). On the other hand, sentences like *John loves Mary three little kittens* or *Bill kills the policeman her* are always bad. There are no ways to contextually repair a transitive verb with three arguments. In short: one argument too few can still be OK if the context allows for it; an argument too many is always bad. But this does not follow from θ-theory, which expects both sentence types to be equally bad. This contrast, therefore, is in need of an explanation.

But this is not the only problem we have. If it were, we could just decide to modify θ-theory to capture these facts. However, there are more examples showing that the θ-criterion is not the only filter on Merge, and that more filters are needed. In the last chapter, for instance, we ended with the discovery of a silent pronoun, PRO, which was made necessary by the fact that *hope* constructions otherwise miss an argument. Remember this representation?

(1)

As pointed out in the discussion on *hope* constructions, though, PRO cannot replace just any pronoun. The **distribution** (or use) of PRO is much more restricted, and we hypothesised that it can only function as the subject of an embedded, non-finite clause. Otherwise, a sentence like (2) would be grammatical, contrary to fact.

(2)   *John loves PRO.

Again, this does not follow from θ-theory itself; θ-theory allows PRO to receive a θ-role (an AGENT in (1), for instance). But then why not in (2)?

Finally, we observe a third problem, related to the following examples:

(3)   a.   He visited her.
      b.   *Him visited she.
      c.   *He visited she.
      d.   *Him visited her.

From the perspective of the grammar that we are building, all the sentences in (3) are predicted to be grammatical. The verb *visited* assigns two θ-roles; an AGENT expressing the person responsible for the visit and a PATIENT expressing the person being visited. The presence of two constituents in the sentence, *he/him* and *she/her*, should be enough to meet the requirements of the verb: *him* could be assigned the AGENT role and *she* the PATIENT role in (3b) for instance. Nevertheless, this sentence is downright ungrammatical. And the same, in essence, applies to (3c)–(3d). Why is this?

For this last problem at least, the source of the error is easy to spot. The AGENT is *him* in (3b), but it should be *he*. It simply appears in the wrong form. The same is true for the PATIENT: *she* should be *her*. The technical term that is used to distinguish the different forms of these pronouns is case. *He* and *she* are **nominative** case forms, and *him* and *her* are **accusative** case forms. What makes (3) ungrammatical, therefore, is that the AGENT and PATIENT appear in the wrong case form. Something must be added to the grammar such that sentences like (3b)–(3d) are correctly ruled out, and this additional statement must refer to case. Now, what could that statement be?

One approach we could take is to add information about case forms to θ-theory. We could say, for instance, that an AGENT has to appear in the nominative form and a PATIENT in the accusative form. The consequence is then that (3b)–(3d) are immediately excluded by θ-theory: after all, the AGENT does not appear in the nominative form and/or the PATIENT does not appear in the accusative form. It would be great if this were all there was to it. But this potential, tiny enrichment of θ-theory does not capture all the facts we need to capture. In fact, it turns out to be blatantly wrong. The reason is that the AGENT–PATIENT distinction and the nominative–accusative distinction are completely independent of one another.

To see this, take a look at the following examples, and assume that they are describing the same situation: there is a masculine person visiting a feminine person.

(4)   a.   He visited her.
      b.   *Her was visited.
      c.   She was visited.

Example (4a) is grammatical, with the AGENT appearing in the nominative form and the PATIENT in the accusative form, as required by this hypothesis. But then the ungrammaticality of (4b) is completely surprising. Here we have a sentence with only one argument present, *her*, and it refers to the person being visited, just as in (4a). This means that *her* is the PATIENT in both (4a) and (4b). Now, if a PATIENT must appear in the accusative case form, (4b) should be fully grammatical, but it is not. Instead, as shown in (4c), the PATIENT requires nominative case here. From this, we can conclude that PATIENTs are sometimes nominative and sometimes accusative, and that nominative case is not reserved for AGENTs only.

This does not yet show that the AGENT–PATIENT distinction and the nominative–accusative distinction are fully independent, though. It could still be the case that every accusative must be a PATIENT (but not the other way round), or it could be that every AGENT must be a nominative (and not the other way round). However, these hypotheses can be easily falsified too. Take a look at the example in (5):

(5)   I caused [him to quit his job].

The verb *caused* assigns two θ-roles: one to someone who acts as the causer and one to something that is being caused. Now, *him to quit his job* is the THEME expressing what is being caused. This clause, in turn, contains a verb (namely *quit*) that assigns two θ-roles itself: *him* is the AGENT and *his job* the THEME. Therefore, (5) is an example that contains an AGENT, namely *him*, that appears in the accusative form. If *him* were replaced by nominative *he*, the sentence would be bad:

(6)   *I caused [he to quit his job].

Since the AGENT appears in the nominative form in (4a) and in the accusative form in (5), it cannot be true simply that an AGENT has to appear in a particular form either; and the examples above show as well that an accusative can sometimes be a PATIENT (or THEME), and sometimes an AGENT too. However you look at it, there is simply no one-to-one correspondence between case-forms and θ-roles.

We have seen that case plays a significant role in English grammar and that the case forms required cannot be linked directly to θ-roles. In other words, case plays a role of its own in the grammar. This is the crucial insight that linguists have obtained studying data such as the examples above. What we therefore need is a Case theory, a filter that can distinguish between the grammatical and ungrammatical sentences in (3)–(6). This chapter will develop such a theory.

A very attractive feature of the Case theory that we will develop is that it will solve not only the problems concerning the different case forms, but also the first two problems we mentioned (the problem that an argument too many is much worse than an argument too few, and the problem that PRO has a much more restricted distribution than θ-theory would predict). In addition, it will turn out that Case theory puts restrictions on where nominal arguments can occur. Since these restrictions look the same for nominal arguments that show case distinctions (namely, pronouns) and nominal arguments that do not (such as *John, the car,* or *people,* which will always look the same, whether they occur as a subject or object), we will conclude that Case theory puts restrictions on nominal arguments *in general*, irrespective of whether they are pronouns or not. Case plays a role even if you do not see it. But before you can appreciate this insight, we first have to go through the basics.

Exercises

A1   Use the pronouns in the following sentence pairs to argue that there is no one-to-one correspondence between specific θ-roles and specific case assignments.
- a.   (i)   Fred praised her a lot.
       (ii) Fred gave her a compliment.
- b.   (i)   Give him the double espresso.
       (ii) Give the double espresso to him.
- c.   (i)   Ahmed expected her.
       (ii) Ahmed expected her to leave.
- d.   (i)   I left.
       (ii) Daisy wanted me to leave.
- e.   (i)   The manager of the local zoo fired her.
       (ii) She was fired by the manager of the local zoo.

B2   Use the pronouns in the following sentence pairs to argue that there is no one-to-one correspondence between specific grammatical functions (subject of a main clause, subject of an embedded clause, direct object, indirect object) and specific cases.
- a.   (i)   I left.
       (ii) Daisy wanted me to leave.
- b.   (i)   They expected to earn a lot of money.
       (ii) Annie expected them to earn a lot of money.
- c.   (i)   Ahmed expected her.
       (ii) Ahmed expected her to leave.
- d.   (i)   Show him the exit.
       (ii) Show him to Sharon.

4.2 Implementation: Case-Assigning Heads

We observed in the previous section that pronouns need to appear in a particular case form and that a sentence becomes ungrammatical if a wrong case form is chosen. For this reason, *he* cannot appear where *him* can appear, and vice versa. The same is true for *she* and *her*, *me* and *I*, etc. What we need, then, is a theory that determines which case forms can appear in which positions, and this theory needs to be as explicit as possible about the mechanisms that ensure the proper distinction between grammatical and ungrammatical sentences.

Now, if nominative case forms can only appear in particular syntactic positions, and the same is true for accusative case forms, then a particular syntactic environment must somehow be responsible for the case form that can be used there. The question is then how to formalise this: what are the relevant mechanisms? As a starting point, we will borrow an idea from chapter 3. Remember that, in order to account for the number of arguments in the sentence, we assumed that these arguments were related to one head in the sentence, namely the verb. We said that this verb 'assigns' θ-roles to constituents in the sentence so that the number of θ-roles of a verb determines the number of arguments required.

The core mechanism we adopted in θ-theory, then, was one of assignment: a verb 'assigns' a θ-role to a particular constituent. Now that we have started talking about another property, namely case, let us make the assumption that the mechanism responsible for the right case forms appearing in the right positions is exactly the same. Why invent something new if we don't have to? We hypothesise, therefore, that case is a property of a nominal constituent that is also assigned to this constituent by a particular syntactic head. This syntactic head will then determine which case forms can show up in its environment. Since nominative and accusative case forms show up in different positions, it must be true that different syntactic heads are responsible for different cases. Our job therefore is to identify those syntactic heads that assign nominative and accusative case.

We will build up Case theory in two steps. First, we will identify the heads responsible for accusative case assignment (section 4.2.1). In section 4.2.2, we will look at the exact environment in which nominative case forms can appear. As we will see, looking closely into nominative case assignment has the favourable consequence that it leads to an understanding of what the structure of an English clause must look like. Earlier, we talked about the structure of NPs, PPs, APs and VPs. Now the time has come to look at sentential structures. As it will turn out, sentential structures faithfully comply with the theory of Merge introduced in chapter 2. Section 4.3 will show what further predictions this idea makes.

4.2.1 Verbs and Prepositions as Accusative Case Assigners

How is accusative case assigned? As a starting point, consider the following two examples:

(7) a. Children love him.
     b. children's love of him

The example in (7a) is a sentence, with *love* as a verb. The example in (7b), on the other hand, is a noun phrase, with *love* as a noun. Run the substitution test if you don't believe us. Both examples express something very similar. Semantically, *children* and *him* fulfil the same functions in (7a) and (7b). Despite these similarities, there are two notable differences. There is an *'s* attached to *children* only in the second example, and the preposition *of* precedes *him* only in the second example (where it cannot be left out). Let us focus on this preposition *of* (and come back to *'s* later, in section 4.3). You may wonder what *of* is doing there, as it does not seem to carry any meaning; it does not express possession, for instance, which *of* sometimes does. It is just there. You could note this as an arbitrary fact of English. 'If you have a noun followed by another noun, just put a preposition in between.' Instead, syntacticians have turned the presence of this little preposition into one of the pillars of Case theory. Why have they done this, and how?

Follow this train of thought. In (7a), we see that the verb *love* can be combined with a nominal expression in the accusative form. Let's therefore assume that *love* assigns accusative case to its direct object. In other words, we take it that the direct object in (7a) appears in the accusative form as a direct consequence of it being merged with *love*. Since the verb assigns accusative case and not nominative case, a sentence like *Children love he* (with *he* as the object) is ungrammatical. Let's now turn to (7b) and make the following assumption: whereas there is one case that verbs can assign (accusative case), nouns cannot assign any case at all, neither nominative nor accusative. This explains, then, why *children's love him* is ungrammatical: *him* needs accusative case but the noun *love*, in contrast to the verb *love*, has no case to assign. If this is correct, we can explain why *of* must be inserted in (7b): although it does not contribute any meaning, this preposition ensures that the object gets accusative case. Whereas a verb (V) can merge with an NP, and assign accusative case to it, a noun (N) cannot merge with an NP and assign accusative case to it. Therefore, N needs to combine with a PP instead. It is within this PP that the NP gets assigned accusative case, namely by P.

According to the hypothesis, then, *both* verbs and prepositions can assign accusative case, but nouns cannot. The contrast between the two examples in (7), essentially the presence of the preposition in the second example, provides our initial content to Case theory, as we have now identified two syntactic heads that can act as case assigners (namely, V and P). In addition, we know which case they can assign (namely, accusative). Now, let us see why this would make sense. After all, it is just an analysis of the data in (7). Is there any reason to think it is the right one?

Let us first evaluate one important ingredient of this analysis, namely the idea that prepositions are case assigners. This assumption is justified. Although Modern English does not show many case distinctions (there remains just the nominative–accusative distinction for pronouns), Old English was much richer: it also had genitive and dative cases. Now, the interesting observation is that the case that you see in a noun following a preposition depends on this preposition: *andlang(es)* ('along') is followed by a genitive noun, *innan* ('in') is followed by a dative noun and *þurh* ('through') is followed by an accusative noun. No preposition ever takes a nominative complement.

(8) a. I go through the gate   (*through* + accusative case)
         ic gā þurh **þæt**(ACC) **geat**(ACC)

     b. I go within the monastery   (*within* + dative case)
         ic gā innan **þǽm**(DAT) **mynstre**(DAT)

     c. I go along the street   (*along* + genitive case)
         ic gā andlang(es) **þǽre**(GEN) **strǽte**(GEN)

Similar observations can be made for Modern German and many other languages. If prepositions are responsible for the case forms of the nominal constituents that follow them, they must of course be able to assign case. Although prepositions in Modern English can no longer assign dative or genitive case, their ability to assign accusative case has been maintained. In fact, in virtually all languages that show different cases and have prepositions, these prepositions place specific case requirements on the following NPs, indicating that prepositions do indeed assign case.

An observation that aligns very well with the proposal that, besides prepositions, verbs assign accusative case has to do with the fact that an accusative object in English has to appear very close to the verb. Take a look at the following data:

(9) a. John very often believes him.
    b. *John believes very often him.
    c. John believes him very often.

The grammatical sentences are the ones in which the verb and object appear next to each other. What makes (9b) ungrammatical is that the AdvP *very often* intervenes between the verb and the object. In these examples, the object of the verb *believes* is an NP. Note now what happens when the object is a PP:

(10) a. John very often believes in him.
     b. John believes very often in him.
     c. John believes in him very often
     d. *John believes in very often him.

The first three sentences are grammatical and the fact that an AdvP (*very often*) intervenes between the verb and the PP does not seem to matter in (10b). In contrast, no AdvP may intervene between a preposition and its sister (recall from section 2.2.2 that two nodes are sisters if they are immediately dominated by the same node). Why would the choice between *believe* + NP and *believe* + PP make such a difference? From the perspective of Case theory, this difference between (9b) and (10b) can be easily understood. *Him* needs to be case-assigned and the intervening AdvP makes this impossible in (9b). The same problem does not arise for *him* in (10b), because *him* gets its accusative case from the preposition *in*. In other words, there is a case-relation between the verb and the pronoun *him* in (9), and apparently this case-relation cannot be established when an AdvP intervenes. In (10), on the other hand, the case-relation is between the pronoun and the preposition and for this reason the PP can be separated from the verb. At the same time, putting the AdvP in between the preposition and the NP would disrupt the case assignment relation between them, as it does between a verb and an NP, and this make the sentence bad (as in (10d)) for exactly the same reason as (9b) is bad.

To sum up so far, the idea that verbs and prepositions are responsible for case assignment can be independently verified by looking at language varieties that have more cases in their grammars than just nominative and accusative. In addition, we saw that when a pronoun receives case from a preposition, it is part of a constituent that can drift away from the verb a bit. When a pronoun gets its case from the verb, it has to be next to it.

So far, we have only looked at pronouns. Here you can really see and hear the different cases (e.g. *she* vs. *her*). It is not true, however, that all nominal expressions show these case distinctions. Take *John*. This nominal expression can be a subject, an object or part of a PP, as the examples in (11) show:

(11)   a.   John believes me.
       b.   I believe John.
       c.   I believe in John.

Whereas a pronoun in a subject position looks different from a pronoun that appears as an object or as part of a PP, *John* looks the same wherever it occurs. Must we conclude, then, that *John* is a nominal argument that does not require a particular case, in contrast to pronouns? The same would then be true for all non-pronominal nouns, such as *kitchen, houseboat*, and *friends*.

But this would be to draw the wrong conclusion. The reason is that, syntactically, *John* behaves exactly like a pronoun when you look at where it may appear in a sentence. We saw a moment ago that a pronoun in an accusative case-relation with a verb has to appear adjacent to the verb, whereas it can be further away from the verb if it is case-assigned by a preposition. Now, exactly the same is true for *John*, as we can conclude from the following data:

(12)   a.   Children love John.
       b.   Children's love *(of) John.

(13)   a.   I very often believe John.
       b.   *I believe very often John.
       c.   I believe John very often.

(14)   a.   I very often believe in John.
       b.   I believe very often in John.
       c.   I believe in John very often.
       d.   *I believe in very often John.

In (12b) *John* needs the preposition *of*, just as did the pronoun *him* in (7b); this preposition cannot be left out. In (13) and (14) it is shown that *John* cannot be separated from the verb, but there is no problem with putting an AdvP between the verb and the PP of which *John* is a part. At the same time, this AdvP may not appear between the preposition and *John*. So what was true for the pronoun *him* is also true for *John*. Therefore, if the distribution of *him* (i.e. the positions in a sentence where *him* may appear) follows from Case theory, this must also be the case for *John*. We must conclude, then, that *John* also enters into an accusative case relationship with either the verb or a preposition. What makes (13b) ungrammatical is exactly the same as what made (9b) ungrammatical: *John* cannot be case-assigned by the verb.

The generalisation we have come to is the following: a nominal argument that is not a subject needs to be assigned accusative case by either a verb or a preposition. This requirement restricts the positions in which nominal arguments can occur, because they are dependent on these heads for case assignment. The fact that case seems to play a role in the grammar, and that we need to refer to this notion to account for the (un-)grammaticality of sentences, is something we derive from the positions in which for instance *he* and *him* can occur: *he* appears where *him* cannot, and vice versa. It is, however, not true that all nominal arguments overtly show the case that is assigned to them. *John* looks the same irrespective of the position it is in. But *John* cannot appear just anywhere, as we have seen. It cannot escape accusative case assignment, even though it never actually shows up in an accusative case form. And the same applies to every other nominal expression.

Now, it may seem weird to assume that a nominal argument can have either accusative or nominative case without you being able to see it, but this is simply an automatic consequence of the hypothesis that aims to explain the distribution of nominal arguments following a verb or a preposition. If a verb or a preposition sometimes assigns case to its nominal sister, it always does so. This means that we must accept the idea that case is sometimes visible but can sometimes be invisible too. Case is not necessarily a concrete property of nouns (something that you can easily see), but rather an abstract property of nouns (a property that is always there, irrespective of whether you can see it or not). The idea that case is something more abstract, and not just some formal property that shows up only on pronouns, may be a bit hard to swallow, but when you think about it, such abstraction is really nothing new. Several properties relevant to the syntax that we have already seen are abstract. Take, for instance, categorial features like [N] and [V]. We argued in chapter 1 that there is no reliable way of relating these features to the sound or meaning properties of a word. This means that they are abstract. The same is true for θ-roles. Remember that we argued in chapter 3 that a verb like *kill* assigns a PATIENT role to its object. It is not true, however, that this property 'PATIENT' is visible in the object in any way. PATIENT Mary and AGENT Mary (as in *Peter saw Mary* and *Mary walked*, respectively) look exactly the same. Case theory now leads to a similar conclusion: verbs and prepositions assign a property that is not necessarily visible.

θ-theory and Case theory together show something similar, and important, about syntactic theorising. What we are learning at the moment is that grammars are all about dependent relationships between constituents, and syntax is that part of the grammar where these so-called **syntactic dependencies** are established. Syntacticians try to figure out which dependencies syntax cares about, which constituents are involved and what kind of properties or features are relevant in these dependencies. Sometimes the nature of these dependencies is directly visible (such as nominative and accusative case on pronouns) but often we have to deduce them from the data in a more abstract way. That's how we got to categorial features and θ-roles. We have no photographic, audio or X-ray data providing evidence in favour of their existence, at least not in English, but having these properties surely gives us a much firmer handle on the data. Abstractions over data are the hallmark of science. They are the tools that scholars use to try to make more sense of the world around them. But as in any good science, syntacticians cannot just postulate abstractions for the heck of it. Each abstraction has to be carefully justified and its status in the theory depends on the extent to which it is able to create order out of the chaos.

We have also seen how our syntactic reasoning sometimes can lead to the postulation of empty constituents. Think of the unexpressed determiner introduced in chapter 1, or PRO introduced in chapter 3. This comment about abstraction is to put you in the mood for the next section, which is going to introduce a syntactic head that you do not always see or hear directly. And this head will be responsible for nominative case assignment. But don't get worried. There is going to be lots of evidence for its existence.

4.2.2 The Nominative Case Assigner: A Functional Head

In the previous section we established which syntactic heads are responsible for accusative case assignment, namely V and P. We haven't looked at nominative case yet. But one thing is clear, already: under the assumption that cases are assigned by syntactic heads, nominative case must also be assigned by a head. The only question is which one.

It is immediately clear that there is not a lot of choice. Take the following example:

(15)   They bother me.

This sentence contains two nominal arguments that had to be assigned case, nominative *they* and accusative *me*. The accusative case of *me* is assigned by *bother*. There seems to be only one possible answer to the question as to which head is responsible for nominative case assignment to *they*, because there is only one head in this sentence that can possibly be a case assigner, namely the verb *bother*. There is simply nothing else here that could assign nominative case to *they*.

But this is where the mystery begins. The verb *bother*, the head of the VP, cannot be responsible for nominative case assignment. Why is that? As a first indication, note that the subject does not have to appear close to the head of the VP (*bother*), unlike the object:

(16)   They obviously never bother me.

More importantly, we can show that *bother*, or any other verb, must be the wrong head. Take a look at the following examples:

(17)   a.   John saw [them arrest me].
       b.   *John saw [they arrest me].

(18)   a.   I wanted [them to arrest me].
       b.   *I wanted [they to arrest me].

As already noted in section 4.1, it is not the case that subjects always appear in the nominative case. You may recall from the previous chapter that both finite and non-finite clauses have subjects (remember, for instance, that PRO is a subject of the embedded non-finite clause like … *to win the race* in *John hopes PRO to win the race*). Now, we know that embedded subjects do not always carry nominative case. *Them* and *they* in the examples above function as AGENT subjects of the embedded clause. The only grammatical sentences in (17) and (18) are in fact those in which the subject of the embedded clause appears in the accusative case, so *arrest* and *to arrest* cannot be said to assign nominative case here. If we conclude on the basis of (15) that a verb assigns nominative case to its subject, then why does it not do so in (17) and (18)? Given these conflicting data, we must conclude that there is no specific case relation between the verb (*to*) *arrest* or (*to*) *bother* and the subject. But if there isn't, then we are back to our main question: what assigns nominative case to the subject in (15), if not the verb?

There is one property that the verb has in (15) and that the embedded verbs in (17) and (18) lack. The verb in (15) is a finite verb, whereas the verbs in (17) and (18) are infinitives and therefore non-finite (look again at section 1.3.2 if the distinction between finite and non-finite is not 100% clear to you). Could it be, then, that nominative case marking is only possible if the sentence contains a finite verb? This may look like a plausible hypothesis. And, as with every hypothesis, we must consider whether its predictions are correct. So, let's test it. If nominative case assignment depends on finiteness, then any non-finite verb should be unable to assign nominative case, not only infinitives, but also participles. We have identified two participles so far: progressive participles (e.g. *leaving, killing*) and perfect participles (e.g. *left, killed*). It is quite easy to think up examples of a clause with just a subject and a participle. And as you can see below, in these sentences the subject indeed has to appear in the accusative form again, and nominative forms lead to ungrammaticality, parallel to structures with infinitives:

(19)   a.   I saw [her leave the building].
       b.   *I saw [she leave the building].

(20)   a.   I saw [her kill the tiger].
       b.   *I saw [she kill the tiger].

(21)   a.   I saw [her leaving the building].
       b.   *I saw [she leaving the building].

(22)   a.   I saw [her killing the tiger].
       b.   *I saw [she leaving the tiger].

(23)   a.   They found [her left by a tiger].
       b.   *They found [she left by a tiger].

(24) a. They found [her killed by a tiger].
      b. *They found [she killed by a tiger].

This shows that our prediction is borne out and that we are on the right track. Being verbal does not make you assign nominative case, whereas finiteness does.

This conclusion is confirmed by examples of the following type:

(25) a. He may leave soon.
      b. She can accept the decision.
      c. He must understand the impact of this.

As you can see, these examples all contain a nominative subject, so there must be a head responsible for this. Now, each example has an infinitive verb in it (*leave, accept* and *understand* respectively), which cannot be the source of this nominative case. Each infinitive is preceded by another verb. The question, therefore, is whether we can argue that *may, can* and *must* are finite forms. If this is true, we can simply say that *may, can* and *must* assign nominative case in (25). But the fact that *may, can* and *must* are finite may not be obvious at first. Note that the subject is a 3rd person, and this usually means that the verb must agree with it and carry the marker *-s*. But *may, can* and *must* never carry an *-s*, which means that they are never marked for agreement. Are they marked for tense, then, the other hallmark of finite verbs? The fact that you cannot insert the adverb *yesterday* in any of these examples suggests that these are indeed present-tense forms.

(26) a. *He may leave yesterday.
      b. *She can accept the decision yesterday.
      c. *He must understand the impact of this yesterday.

But there is even stronger evidence that shows us that *may, can* and *must* are finite forms: they simply do not have non-finite counterparts. There is no infinitive form of these verbs, and they never combine with a *to* infinitive marker. This can be observed in the following examples:

(27) a. *I expected [her to may leave soon].
      b. *I expected [her to can do this].
      c. *I expected [her to must leave soon].

In addition, there are no participial forms of these verbs either:

(28) a. *I regret musting (to) leave early.
      b. *I have canned (to) leave early.
      c. *He has mayed (to) leave for Paris.

We therefore conclude that verbs like *can, may* and *must* are indeed finite verbs. In fact, they are verbs that have a finite form only. For this reason, they have been taken as a distinct class of verbs. *Leave, accept* and *understand* are called **lexical verbs**, and they have finite and non-finite forms. Verbs like *may, can* and *must* are called **modal auxiliaries** (to separate them from non-modal auxiliaries, such as *has* in *Mary has walked* or *is* in *Fred is sleeping*). You use these verbs to indicate how possible, probable or necessary you think the event described by the sentence is. Modal auxiliaries in English are inherently finite. It therefore comes as no surprise that their presence in a sentence allows for the presence of a nominative subject as well. Being finite, modal auxiliaries can assign nominative case.

Just as a small aside, the fact that nominative case assignment requires a finite verb in the clause explains why the (b) examples in (17)–(23) are ungrammatical. Note that this does not yet explain why the (a) examples are grammatical: although we understand why the embedded subjects cannot appear in a nominative form, we still have to explain why they can appear in an accusative form. You may suspect that the verb in the main clause is responsible for this. You would be right, but we will leave the details until the end of chapter 7. We will continue here with more pressing matters. If nominative case assignment depends on finiteness, we have to determine what this means structurally. Which syntactic head is responsible for nominative case assignment?

As a step towards an answer, we will start with a more down-to-earth question: what does the tree of a sentence look like when it contains a modal auxiliary and a lexical verb? Let us start with a trivial observation. Suppose you have a verb *eat* and an NP object *sausages*: you can merge them and get the structure as in (29a). Alternatively, if you have the verb *buy*, you can merge *buy* with *sausages* and derive the structure in (29b):

(29) a.

These VPs can be part of the sentence *I eat sausages* or *I buy sausages*. What is impossible, however, is to say something like *(I like to) eat buy sausages*, or *(I like to) buy eat sausages*. If you combine a V with an NP, the V position can only be filled by one verb. If you try to fit in two verbs, the result is ungrammatical: **I buy eat sausages*. This means that all lexical verbs are in competition with one another. They can all potentially fill the V slot, but once that slot is filled by one verb, other verbs are excluded from that position. What we say is that these lexical verbs are in **complementary distribution** with one another. Where one occurs, the others can no longer occur.

As said, the observation is rather trivial, and basically just states that you can only have one lexical verb in a single VP. But complementary distribution effects are very useful for a syntactician. If two words cannot co-occur together, this may mean that they strive to occupy the same position. But if two words can peacefully co-occur in a clause, it means that they are in a different position. Therefore, complementary distribution effects may inform us about the underlying structure of the string of words we are analysing. Take the sentences in (25). What we see here is that it is entirely unproblematic to have a modal auxiliary and a lexical verb in the same sentence. Following our reasoning, we must conclude that modal verbs and lexical verbs occupy different positions: they are not in complementary distribution. At the same time, we can observe that all modal auxiliaries are in complementary distribution with one another. There can be only one modal auxiliary in a clause, as the following examples show:

(30)   a.   *He must can do better than this.
       b.   *She will must do her homework.
       c.   *He should will take care of his mother.

This means that there must be one position that all modals want to be in but once it is occupied by one of them, the other modal auxiliaries can no longer occur there. At the same time, this position must be distinct from the position that lexical verbs are in. Taking these observations together, we arrive at the following abstract structure, in which we call the position that the modal auxiliaries want to occupy X, while waiting for a better term:

(31)

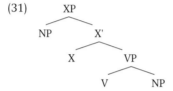

What (31) tell us is that lexical verbs aim to be in V and all modal auxiliaries aim to be in X, and that V and X are distinct syntactic heads, so that no complementary distribution effects between lexical verbs and modal auxiliaries are expected. This is schematically what a sentence with a modal auxiliary would look like. X is the syntactic head in which modal auxiliaries reside.

Now, before going on, note that there is nothing strange about the structure in (31). It is perfectly in line with the Merge theory that we introduced in chapter 2. There is a phrase, XP, of which one constituent can be identified as the head, namely the modal auxiliary in X. This word in X is combined with two other phrases, NP and VP, and both these phrases can either consist of one word (as in *He may leave*) or more words (as in *The man may leave his house soon*). The structure of sentences with a modal auxiliary is fundamentally similar to the structure of an NP or PP. Nothing new has to be said.

Nothing new, however, is not the same as nothing more. We have to at least be a bit more precise about what X is. To determine this, we must first establish what elements can appear in that position. We have already identified modal auxiliaries as X elements, but these are not the only possible X elements. It is also possible to combine a verb with other finite auxiliaries, such as finite forms of *have* and *be*:

(32)   a.   Elvis has left the building.
       b.   Bono is rehearsing with his band.
       c.   Beyoncé was reviewed quite favourably.

It must be the case, then, that all these elements (modal auxiliaries, other finite auxiliaries such as finite forms of *have* and *be*) want to be in X. And again, they are in complementary distribution with the modal auxiliaries, as there can only be one finite auxiliary in every clause:

(33)   a.   *Elvis must has left the building.
        b.   *Bono is may rehearsing with his band.
        c.   *Beyoncé was has reviewed quite favourably.

There is additional evidence for this conclusion that there is a single, separate position in the structure for all finite auxiliaries. All these finite auxiliaries can appear to the left of the negation marker *not*:

(34)   a.   Bono must not rehearse with his band.
        b.   Beyoncé was not reviewed quite favourably.
        c.   Elvis may not leave the building.

No lexical verb, on the other hand, can do such a thing. This is immediately clear for (35b), which is simply ungrammatical, but it is also true of (35a). This is ungrammatical without a continuation like '… *but carrots*', in which case what is negated is *sausages* and not the entire sentence.

(35)   a.   *John loves not sausages.
        b.   *Mary walks not.

We can readily account for this difference with the structure in (31), because auxiliaries are structurally higher than verbs. Under the assumption that *not* sits somewhere between X and VP, the contrast follows immediately:

(36)

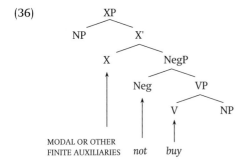

The different orderings with respect to negation neatly confirm an analysis that posits an X and a V position, each associated with different heads. What all elements that can occur in X have in common is that they are marked for finiteness. Modals, we have seen, are inherently finite, and so are finite forms of the auxiliaries *have* and *be*. And as we saw in chapter 1, all these finite verbs carry the feature [Finite].

So, let's summarise. X is a position that can only be filled by elements that carry the feature [Finite]. The most straightforward thing to say is that X is nothing but [Finite]-ness. It is the position that introduces finiteness into the sentence: X is Finiteness (abbreviated as Fin), and XP is FinP. Fin', then, is the intermediate Fin category in the structure, on a par with N', V', etc.

(37)

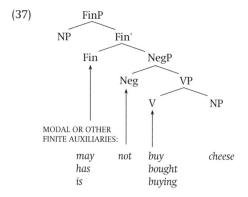

Extra evidence for the hypothesis that the position identified is associated with finiteness comes from sentences that are non-finite, or infinitival. Such sentences contain not a finite verb, but an infinitival marker *to*. We have already seen that it is possible for a *to* infinitive marker to appear between the subject and the lexical verb (see (18a)). Here is another example:

(38)   I wanted [them to convince me].

And finite auxiliaries and *to* are again in complementary distribution, as you can see in the following examples:

(39)   a.   *Bono has to rehearsing with his band.
        b.   *Beyoncé must to reviewed quite favourably.
        c.   *Elvis may to leave the building.

Now, what modals, auxiliaries and the *to* marker have in common is that they are marked for finiteness. A clause with a modal or a form like *has* or *was* is always finite. A clause with a *to* marker is always non-finite. In this respect, modal and other auxiliaries and the *to* marker differ from infinitives or participles, as the latter can appear both in finite and non-finite clauses:

(40)   Finite clauses
        a.   Mary must leave the house.
        b.   Mary is leaving the house.
        c.   Mary has left the house.

(41)   Non-finite clauses
        a.   to leave the house
        b.   to be leaving the house
        c.   to have left the house

So, modal and other auxiliaries and *to* markers are specifically marked for finiteness, either positively or negatively. Other verbs are not inherently marked for finiteness. This enables us say that those elements that are marked for finiteness appear in X, and those elements that are not marked for finiteness cannot appear in X.

This further corroborates the hypothesis that XP must be a Finiteness Phrase (abbreviated to FiniteP or FinP), and the idea that it is headed by words that are positively or negatively marked for finiteness. In other words, FinP is occupied by words that carry either the feature [Finite] or the feature [Non-finite]. Now we can take the next step. If Fin is occupied by the feature [Finite], FinP can contain a nominative subject. Therefore, *he is walking* is fine. If *to* carrying [Non-finite] occurs in it instead, a nominative subject cannot occur there. Therefore *he to leave* is a bad sentence. So it is neither finiteness, nor the presence of Fin in the structure, that is responsible for nominative case assignment, but the feature [Finite] (in contrast to [Non-finite]) in the head of FinP:

(42) a.

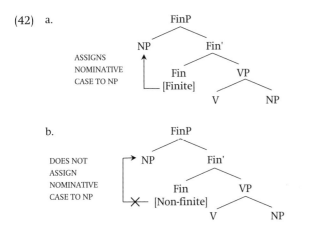

b.

Let us finally turn to the answer to the big question that is still in the air: what about a simple sentence without a modal, an auxiliary or *to*? What is the analysis for an example like (43)?

(43) John loves sausages.

This sentence contains a finite verb. What makes this verb visibly finite is the fact that it is marked by the agreement -*s*. Now, if elements expressing finiteness belong in the Fin position, and -*s* expresses finiteness, why don't we bite the bullet and assume the structure in (44)?

(44)

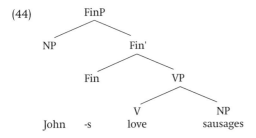

Here, we are actually splitting up the word *loves* into *love* and -*s* and saying that they are generated in two distinct positions. Since -*s* is an affix and needs a verb to survive, we need some mechanism that will ensure that the -*s* is pronounced with the verb. Let us not bother about this mechanism for the moment. That -*s* and *love* are pronounced as one word is a matter of morphology (the part of grammar where words are created; chapter 8 will specifically look at this relation between morphology and syntax). Let's just ask ourselves if there are any reasons to assume that the structure in (44) is correct. We just gave you a conceptual argument: strictly speaking it is only the -*s* that makes the sentence in (44) finite, so this is the element that should reside in Fin. We will now give you two empirical arguments (see section 2.3 for the difference between conceptual and empirical arguments).

The first is based on a prediction that we immediately make under this hypothesis. If the 3rd person singular -*s* is an element that wants to be in Fin, then we expect it to be in complementary distribution with all the elements that also want to be in Fin. And this is exactly what we see. Modals, finite forms of auxiliaries *have* and *be* and the *to* infinitive marker never co-occur with a lexical verb marked for -*s*, as the following data show, and this complementary distribution effect is what our hypothesis expects if -*s* competes with these heads:

(45)   a.   *John may loves sausages.
      b.   *John has loves sausages.
      c.   *(I wanted) John to loves sausages.

The second empirical argument is based on sentences with a negation in it. If we try to make the sentence in (44) negative, then no matter where we put the negation, the sentence is ungrammatical:

(46)   a.   *John not loves sausages.
      b.   *John loves not sausages.

Why would this be? Well, consider the structure of a clause that contains the affix -*s*, as well as a negation marker.

(47)

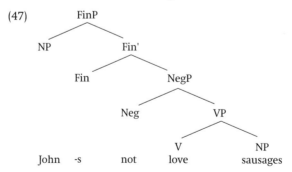

As before, the -*s* is generated in Fin, whereas the verbal stem *love* is generated in V. This -*s* has to be pronounced as part of V, so that we get *loves*. Now here is an idea. Suppose that -*s* and *love* cannot come together because there is a syntactic head intervening, namely Neg. This blocks the -*s* from becoming part of *love*. As a consequence, -*s* is dangling in its Fin position but it needs an element that it can become a part of. English grammar has found the following solution (which we will flesh out in more detail in chapter 8): instead of using -*s* as the Fin head, it uses an empty, almost meaningless auxiliary, so as not to change the meaning of the non-negative sentence beyond the inclusion of the negation. This auxiliary is *do*, and in the 3rd person singular the form is *does*. With this auxiliary projecting FinP, the structure looks as follows:

(48)

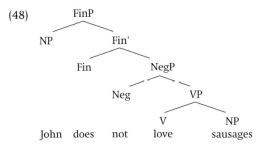

John does not love sausages

Irrespective of the further details, we can now already make our point. Because -*s* and the verbal stem cannot come together, due to the interfering negation, another finite element must be used instead. In the current example, *does* is used. As a consequence, this finite head shows up exactly in the position where we hypothesised that finiteness originates: in Fin, preceding the negation. This is our evidence that ties -*s* to the Fin position. It is in the absence of negation that -*s* and the verbal stem can come together effortlessly, and in these examples it is simply harder to tell where -*s* originates. It is only in the presence of negation that we can clearly see where finiteness is located, as a consequence of the blocking effect induced by negation. In other words, the hypothesis that -*s* originates in Fin gives us a handle on the ungrammaticality of (46). If on the other hand we hypothesised that *love* and -*s* are together generated as the head of VP, there is no reason why you could not say *John not loves sausages*, because the blocking story would simply no longer work. And then the ungrammaticality of the examples in (46) would remain a mystery.

4.2.3 The Case Filter
So far our Case theory successfully accounts for the positions that nominal arguments can appear in, under the assumption that each of them needs to be assigned either nominative or accusative case. The rule we imposed, therefore, is that every nominal argument must receive case; a sentence with a nominal argument that cannot be case-assigned is ungrammatical. This rule is called the Case filter:

(49)   THE CASE FILTER
Every nominal argument must be assigned either nominative or accusative case.

Nominative case is assigned by the head of FinP if that carries the feature [Finite]; accusative case is assigned by the head of VP (i.e. the feature [V]) or the head of PP (i.e. the feature [P]). A sentence in which not every nominal argument has been assigned case is ungrammatical, as it violates the Case filter. This filter applies not only to pronouns (where you hear the difference), but also to other nouns (where you don't hear it).

Very interestingly, our Case theory accounts not only for the distribution of nominative and accusative forms, but also solves the other problems we mentioned. First, recall from section 4.1 that an argument too many is worse than an argument too few. Even though neither are perfect, the (a) examples in (50) and (51) are better than the (b) examples (which we indicate by using a question mark rather than an asterisk).

(50) a. ?John loves.
       b. *John loves Mary three little kittens.

(51) a. ?Bill kills.
       b. *Bill kills the policeman her.

This now follows directly from Case theory. In (50a) and (51a), only the θ-criterion is violated, as in each case one θ-role remains unassigned. In (50b) and (51b), however, both the θ-criterion and the Case filter have been violated: *three little kittens* and *her* do not receive a θ-role and in addition cannot be assigned nominative or accusative case, which makes the sentences they are in extra bad.

And, finally, we can now explain the distribution of PRO. We saw before that PRO can only be inserted in a very particular position, namely as the subject of an embedded non-finite clause like (52):

(52) John hopes PRO to kiss Mary.

We are now able to identify this position: it is the position of the subject in FinP, where the head carries [Non-finite]:

(53)

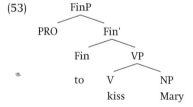

What we see is that PRO can only appear in a position in which it cannot be assigned any case. Apparently, PRO is special in two ways: it is never expressed and it cannot receive any case. These two properties are probably not coincidental, but syntacticians differ as to how to express their relation. Does Case theory only hold for NPs that you can express? Or do we need a special third case, besides nominative and accusative case, that a non-finite head can only assign to PRO? Whatever the outcome of this debate, for now it is important to establish that the occurrence of PRO is restricted to those subject positions to which no nominative or accusative case is assigned; it can never appear in a position where either accusative or nominative case is assigned.

Let's finalise our conclusions in the following table.

(54)   Case theory – summary:

Merge with:	Case assigned:	Examples:
[V], [P]	accusative	*him, her, me, Mary, the man*
[Finite]	nominative	*he, she, I, Mary, the man*
[Non-finite]	no case	*PRO*

Even though our reasoning has been quite complex and abstract at points, this is what Case theory basically amounts to: three assumptions, listed in the table above, that together correctly predict the distribution of nominal phrases in English.

Exercises

A3   Explain the ungrammaticality of the following sentences in theoretical, not 'observational', terms. To see what we mean by this, look at the sentence in (i):

(i)   *Him visits Mary and Martin.

Example (i) is ungrammatical because *he* should be *him* (which is why it is observationally ungrammatical), but how does the theory now account for this? We would say that *him* is in the subject position in FinP where it can only receive nominative case, not accusative case. Okay, you're next:

a.   *The police ended up looking for he.
b.   *I have loved always them.
c.   *I would think that Evelene will must try to get more sleep.
d.   *We may never appreciates good health.
e.   *Him tried to be on time.
f.   *Of he tried to be on time.
g.   *I implored she to look after her health.
h.   *The president arrived not, although we expected her.
i.   *Kareema may to want to spend more time with her aunt.
j.   *Eleanor probably not loves the latest Bond movie.

A4   Draw the tree structures for the following examples. For one last time, you can ignore elements of category D.

a.   Bono is probably rehearsing new songs.
b.   Harriet may not leave soon.
c.   Claudine has married Patrick.
d.   Amateurs should not bother with this.
e.   Effie always talks about furniture.
f.   Hans does not speak German fluently.
g.   The new banks invested in new property.
h.   Friends of mine have not seen Mira for ages.
i.   Jean expects to kiss Marie.
j.   Marie expects Jean to kiss her.

B5   In section 4.2.2, we argued that the 3rd-person singular agreement marker *-s* cannot function as the head of FinP in the presence of negation. Show that this analysis can be fully extended to the past tense marker *-ed*. Show that it creates the same problem in the same environment, and that the same solution can be used to circumvent the problem.

4.3 Consequences: Functional Projections

The Case theory developed in this chapter is one in which two cases, nominative and accusative, are assigned by distinct heads: accusative case is assigned by V or P, whereas nominative case is assigned by a finite Fin, the head of FinP. The properties of nominative case assignment led us to believe that finiteness is the source of nominative case, and that there is a VP-external, abstract head, namely Fin, where nominative case is located. We subsequently provided the syntactic evidence for this claim. The hypothesis that VP is dominated by FinP led to an increased understanding of the structure of a clause, but the impact of this discovery was much greater than this. The idea that there are functional heads that can project their own phrase, thereby creating a so-called **functional projection**, turned out to be a powerful one, and it led to an increased understanding of other constructions. In this section we will look at two of these. First, we will have another look at nominal phrases, and discover that their structure can be better understood if we include a functional head (section 4.3.1). After that, in 4.3.2, we will look at embedded clauses and show that their structure can be readily understood if we include a second functional head.

4.3.1 Going from NP to DP

The search for the source of nominative case assignment has led us to hypothesise that there is a category, Fin, that is the syntactic head of a phrase, FinP, dominating VP. Whenever this head contains a finite element, nominative case can be assigned to the subject in FinP. This leads to the structure in (55):

(55)

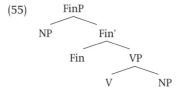

We subsequently argued that the existence of Fin can be independently verified by observing that there is a class of morphemes that all strive to be in the position of Fin. This makes sense because Fin is a syntactic head position and head positions cannot contain more than one item. The complementary distribution of finite heads underscores the existence of Fin. Fin is therefore more than just something we need to explain nominative case assignment. It is actually a syntactic position that can be independently justified.

Looking at the structure in (44), repeated below, we can see that the tree consists of a VP and a FinP.

(56)

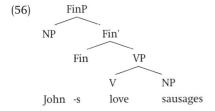

John -s love sausages

The VP is a projection of some verb; the FinP is a projection of a more abstract head that can contain different lexical items, as long as they are marked for finiteness. Remember from chapter 1 that we can separate categories into open and closed classes. Verbs form an open class, and every day new verbs are added to this class. The group of finiteness markers, on the other hand, we can characterise as a closed class. After all, the English language does not increase the number of elements that can appear in Fin every day. Another difference is that verbs have a clear meaning: they generally refer to events or states in the real world. Characterising what finiteness means, on the other hand, is less easy. Finite verbs comprise tense and agreement; non-finite verbs are tenseless, so you could say that finite verbs place the event or state denoted by the verb in a context. It tells us for instance whether this event is taking place now, or took place in the past. Non-finite verbs do not put such events or states directly in a context: *to eat cake is nice* does not tell us when the cake eating takes place. Note that in addition, finite verbs provide information about the number and person of the subject. Verbs have been called lexical because of the clear lexical meaning that they carry. Finiteness markers have been called functional, because they embed the lexical information provided by the VP into some context. The functional projection FinP also literally embeds the lexical projection in the syntax because, as you can observe in the tree structure, VP is dominated by FinP.

The conclusion that the tree structure of a clause consists of a lexical domain embedded under a functional domain turns out to be a tremendous eye opener in syntactic theory. It allows us to look at syntactic structures from this new perspective, and understand things we hadn't previously thought of. Take the following case. We merge a noun with an article and end up with the following structure.

(57)

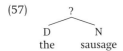

the sausage

As indicated by the question mark, you may wonder what kind of categorial feature this merger carries. Do we have an NP or a DP? You may conclude that it has to be an NP because *the sausage* refers to *sausage* and not to *the: sausage* is simply more important than *the*. So far, this is our tentative assumption.

This assumption, however, is wrong for two reasons. First, if *the sausage* were nominal, empirically we'd expect *the sausage* to be able to combine with *expensive*, because we established earlier that an [N] category can be combined with an [A] category. We therefore expect *expensive the sausage* to be grammatical, contrary to fact. Second, the fact that *sausage* carries more meaning, or at least more obviously so, is a semantic observation. But we are doing syntax here. The meaning of *the* is indeed harder to pinpoint because it is a functional element. It says that we are talking about a known sausage, one that we have been talking about earlier. Otherwise we would not have used the definite article *the* but the **indefinite article** *a*. But if *the* is a functional element, we can push for the same analysis that we ended up with for clauses, namely one in which a lexical domain is embedded under a functional domain. By doing this, we provide a conceptual argument for a DP analysis: it allows an elegant parallel with the structure of sentences.

(58)

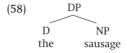

Empirically, this analysis immediately excludes *expensive the sausage* because this would involve merging an [A] category with a [D] category, not with an [N] category.

More corroborating evidence for the DP analysis comes from complementary distribution effects. As was the case with Fin, D is a functional head that can host different types of determiners. In chapter 1 we said that an article, like *the* or *a(n)*, is called a determiner (hence the feature [D]). The reason for using this category is that there are many other elements that compete for the same position as articles. Of all these elements, only one at a time is allowed, as illustrated by the following data:

(59) a. this sausage
      b. that sausage
      c. some sausage
      d. no sausage
      e. her sausage

(60) a. *the this sausage
      b. *that the sausage
      c. *a some sausage
      d. *no some sausage
      e. *the her sausage

The elements in (59)–(60) that compete for the same position go under different names. *The* and *a* are articles, but *this* and *that* are demonstrative pronouns (just like *these* and *those*, which precede plural nouns). The element *her* in (59e) is called a possessive pronoun and belongs to a group that includes *my, his, your* and *their*. *No* is the negative counterpart of *a*, and is therefore called a negative indefinite pronoun. All these different elements compete for the same position and therefore carry the same categorial feature, [D]. 'Determiner', therefore, is the umbrella term for all these elements, just as Fin is the umbrella term for modals, finite forms of *have* and *be*, the *to* infinitive marker, and the affixes -s and -ed. The examples in (59) show that different types of determiners can be combined with *sausage*, and (60) shows that combining more than one leads to ungrammaticality. What justified the existence of the Fin position is exactly what justifies the existence of a D position.

The complementary distribution effect can be extended to include possessive constructions in which the possessor is not expressed by a possessive pronoun (like *my* or *their*) but contains lexical information, such as in *John's car*. Note that it is impossible to combine *John's* with some other determiner:

(61) a. *John's the car
      b. *John's his car
      c. *John's that car

You may for a minute be inclined to analyse *John's* as one word, sitting in the D position, but this is untenable. Note that instead of just *John* we could have a more extensive phrase denoting the possessor, as illustrated below:

(62) a. [the neighbour]'s car
      b. [the hard-working police officer]'s car
      c. [my favourite but not so bright uncle]'s car

Clearly, these possessor phrases cannot be squeezed into the head position of the DP, which is supposed to host at most one word. But the possessive morpheme *'s* could very well occupy the D position, because it is smaller than a word. It would thereby resemble 3SG -s, which we argued occupies the Fin position. Then, it would be this D head *'s* that causes the complementary distribution effects with other D heads. The phrase denoting the possessor can then be put in the DP, much as the subject of a clause can be put in a FinP headed by for instance 3SG -s. This gives us the structure in (63), which is the standard analysis for possessive constructions in English.

(63)

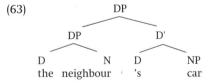

A final argument for the DP analysis that we will mention has to do with reordering possibilities of prenominal modifiers. Note that, at least to a certain extent, you can change the word order of adjectives that precede the noun. *The red plastic bag* is as acceptable a nominal phrase as is *the plastic red bag*. The latter can for instance be used in a conversation about red bags where you want to say something specific about the red bag that is made of plastic. Note, however, that it is impossible to include *the* in any reorderings:

(64) a. *red the plastic bag
      b. *red plastic the bag

Consider the NP and the DP analysis of this phrase:

(65) a.   b.

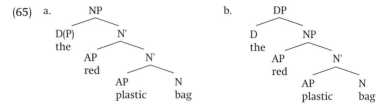

In (65a), the article *the* functions as one of the prenominal modifiers of the noun, like *red* and *plastic*. Under the NP analysis, the fact that *red* and *plastic* can be reordered but not *the* has to follow from an additional rule. You would have to add a statement to your grammar that excludes *the* from undergoing reordering with one of the adjectives. Such a statement is not necessary if you adopt the DP analysis in (65b). The article *the* is the head of a functional projection that dominates the NP containing *red, plastic* and *bag*. It therefore cannot be treated as syntactically on a par with *red* and *plastic*. In short, then, the ungrammaticality of the examples in (64) follows automatically.

Now, there is something very attractive about this DP hypothesis, and for this we need to go back to what we did in chapter 1. There, we said that every noun combines with a determiner, even in cases like (*John likes*) *water* or (*John likes*) *cars*. We argued that in such cases there is an unexpressed article (i.e. an unexpressed determiner) present: (*John likes*) $\varnothing_D$ *water* or (*John likes*) $\varnothing_D$ *cars*. And if every nominal constituent contains a determiner at its beginning, every nominal constituent is a DP. What we then arrive at is an even closer comparison to what happens in the verbal and nominal domain: in the nominal domain every NP is 'roofed' by a DP, and in the verbal domain every VP is 'roofed' by a FinP. We also showed in chapter 1 that a nominal phrase can be replaced by a pronoun or proper name. If a nominal phrase is analysed as a DP, then we have to ensure that pronouns and proper names are analysed in such a way that we can understand their ability to substitute for a nominal phrase. So yes, indeed, pronouns and proper names are DPs too. Here is how we will represent them:

(66) a. DP   b. DP
          Mary   She

If the Case filter requires that all nominal arguments are assigned either nominative or accusative case, and nominal phrases are DPs, we must assume that case features are assigned to DPs rather than to NPs. We will assume this to be so from now on.

But there is even more. Apart from saying that functional elements head particular functional phrases, those functional phrases also look kind of similar. Take the FinP in (67) and compare it with the two DPs in (68).

(67)

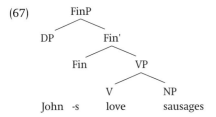

(68)

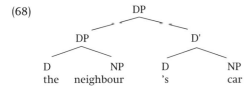

What we see is that both Fin and D first merge with a (lexical) phrase (VP and NP respectively), and then the result of this merger (Fin' / D') merges again with another phrase: Fin' with a DP, yielding FinP; D' with another DP, yielding a full DP. This pattern, in which a functional phrase contains a head and two phrases, is a pattern that we will see several more times. For this reason, syntacticians have devised names for the two phrases that a functional phrase contains. The first phrase that a head merges with is called a com-plement, and the second one, the one that merges with the result of this first merger, is called the specifier. The following diagram illustrates this:

(69)

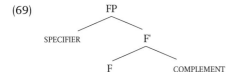

In (67) the VP is the complement of Fin, and the subject *John* is its speci-fier. In (68), the NP *car* is the complement of the D headed by *'s*, and *the neighbour* its specifier.

Now, you may wonder why we should bother with this. There does not seem to be any real difference between complements and specifiers. In both cases an element with some particular feature ([Fin]/[D]) merges with another constituent and becomes the head of it. However, there is a clear difference: the complement of a head always follows it, whereas the specifier precedes it. That suggests that there is some kind of a dif-ference between the two. This legitimises making the distinction, even though we will postpone dealing with this left–right asymmetry until chapter 9. So far, the notions *complement* and *specifier* are nothing but descriptive tools, names for particular positions. However, it turns out that these descriptive tools are very useful, as they allow us to refer to particular positions.

4.3.2 Extending the Clausal Structure: CPs

We have been able to show that functional elements can yield functional projections of their own. We saw this for FinP, and we saw that the same mechanism allows us to diagnose DPs.

Now we will introduce a third kind of functional head, which appears in sentences with two lexical verbs. So far, we have given you the tools to structurally analyse a simplex sentence containing only one main verb. But what do we do when a sentence contains more than one? Let us look at the following examples:

(70)   a. I think that Adrian has always liked yellow chairs.
        b. I wonder if Adrian has always liked yellow chairs.

These are complex sentences in that each contains two lexical verbs (*think/wonder* and *like*), so they must be analysed as main clauses that contain embedded clauses:

(71)   a. [$_{main\ clause}$ I think [$_{embedded\ clause}$ that Adrian has always liked yellow chairs].]
        b. [$_{main\ clause}$ I wonder [$_{embedded\ clause}$ if Adrian has always liked yellow chairs].]

Let us pose two questions: (i) what is the structure of the embedded clause, and (ii) how is the embedded clause embedded in the main clause? As for the first question, note that the embedded clauses are introduced by a complementiser preceding the subject *Adrian: that* and *if* respectively. It will be obvious that complementisers form a closed class in English, so we can analyse them as functional heads. From there, it is a small step towards using these heads to project their own phrases, traditionally called complementiser phrases, or CPs. The CP then extends the functional domain of VP with one extra layer and determines that the clause it heads is an embedded clause.

(72)

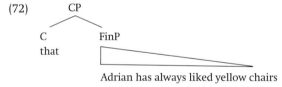

Adrian has always liked yellow chairs

As for the second question, it is important to realise that the embedded clauses function as THEME arguments of the lexical verb of the main clause. That Adrian has always liked yellow chairs is what I think, and whether Adrian likes yellow chairs is what I ask. The CP therefore has to be generated as the complement of the main clause V, as would any other direct object. This gives the structure in (73).

(73)

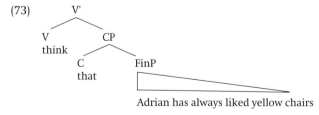

Adrian has always liked yellow chairs

The C position (the head of the CP) is not only the position that encodes clauses for embedding; it is also the position that encodes the type of embedded clause. A *that* clause is an embedded **declarative clause**: it follows verbs such as *say* or *think* that declare something. By contrast, *if* clauses, which follow verbs such as *ask* or *wonder*, introduce embedded **interrogative clauses**. Complementisers not only turn a FinP into an embedded clause, but also play an important role in determining the **clause type**.

The addition of CP to the clausal structure may look like a reasonable but not very exciting little piece of syntactic structure, but do not underestimate it. It will be back in chapter 6, and there it will stand a better chance of wowing you. Oh, and it will be another functional phrase where the terms 'complement' and 'specifier' turn out to be very useful.

Exercises

B6 Draw the tree structures for the following examples. State for each functional projection (FinP, CP or DP) what the specifier and complement is (if present).
  a. the love of his life
  b. a mother's love for her child
  c. these incredibly ridiculous jokes
  d. an argument against this new theory of syntax
  e. the prospect of the children's return
  f. Paola has asserted that she will not comply with their wishes.
  g. He did not ask to stay.
  h. He never asked if he could stay.
  i. That Harry actually speaks Japanese surprised us.
  j. To indict him would confuse the entire population.

C7 It was observed that prenominal modifiers can be reordered with respect to one another, whereas determiners do not engage in these reorderings. The reordering of adjectives is restricted, however: sometimes, reordering gives a funny, or even ungrammatical, result if you evaluate the ensuing word order without any context. See what reordering possibilities and restrictions you can find for the following examples. Combine the following nouns with the modifiers provided and see what reordering possibilities and restrictions you find.
  (i)   NOUN: sausages   +   MODIFIERS: Italian, tasty, expensive
  (ii) NOUN: vases   +   MODIFIERS: red, three, horrible
  (iii) NOUN: sauce   +   MODIFIERS: excellent, meaty, sweet
  (iv) NOUN: boys   +   MODIFIERS: Dutch, naughty, several
  (v)   NOUN: chair   +   MODIFIERS: comfortable, wooden, classy

C8 Take a look again at the following two sentences from section 4.2.1.
  (i)   Children love him.
  (ii) children's love of him
  We argued that the function of the preposition *of* was to ensure that *him* can be assigned accusative case. What do we need to say if we also want to account for the second obvious difference between (i) and (ii), the presence of 's in (ii)? Also take another look at the tree in (63).

C9 We argued above that pronouns and proper names are DPs too, and provided the analyses in (66). For a pronoun, you could easily see that it is just a functional element, and that therefore the functional projection DP suffices. A proper noun like *Mary*, however, also has lexical content, which makes it similar to *table* or *happiness*. Suppose that for proper names we maintain the idea proposed in chapter 1, namely that they carry both an [N] and a [D] feature at the same time. Show how the following data can be used in defence of this idea. Then draw the trees of the italicised sentences.

(i)   We will never be able to carry this washing machine upstairs. *We need Michael!*

(ii) We will never be able to carry this washing machine upstairs. *We need a Michael!*

(iii) The Michael I used to know was a nice person.

Summary

Whereas the previous chapter dealt with the needs of verbs, this chapter dealt with the needs of nominal arguments (that we now know are DPs). We established that these DPs need to be assigned an appropriate case, and these particular cases are assigned by designated syntactic heads. V and P assign accusative case, and Fin assigns nominative case. The dependencies between case-assigning heads and case-requiring DPs give us the syntax of nominal phrases. Since nouns that do not visibly show a particular case are also restricted in their distribution, we concluded that *all* DPs need case, not just the ones that show case distinctions (that is, pronouns). Another far-reaching conclusion is that syntactic structures have a lexical and functional domain. Our search for the relevant case assigners has led to an increased understanding of the structure underlying clauses and nominal phrases. We found that NPs can be part of a DP, and VPs can be part of a FinP, which can in turn be part of a CP. The next chapters will dive more deeply into the behaviour and needs of these functional projections, especially FinP and CP.

Remember that we closed the previous chapter with the suspicion that Merge plus θ-theory would probably not be enough to rule out all ungrammatical examples of English? But would Merge plus the θ-theory and Case theory filters together now suffice? We saw that with these two filters, we have come to a much better understanding of the underlying syntax of English sentences, and closer to our goal of ruling out ungrammatical sentences. However, it turns out that Merge plus the θ-theory and Case theory filters is still not enough. Alongside θ-roles and case, we need to look into a third phenomenon that plays a central role in English syntax, agreement. What it is and how it works, we will see in the next chapter. Stay tuned.

Further Reading

The idea that nominal arguments need to be case-assigned by dedicated heads is due to Jean-Roger Vergnaud. He expressed his ideas in a personal letter to Chomsky in 1977, published as Vergnaud (2008), which Chomsky took over and developed in Chomsky (1980).

The idea that the structure of a clause consists of a lexical core embedded within projections of functional categories is due to Chomsky (1986a). The standard name for the lower projection is IP ('Inflection Phrase'), but in recent years TP ('Tense Phrase') has become more common. We have used FinP because the empirical justification for this projection most naturally leads to the conclusion that this phrase is projected by finiteness markers (tense *or* agreement markers). In the recent literature, FinP as a label is used for a functional projection that partly has the same functionality as CP. We deviate from this usage in this book.

Since Pollock (1989), scholars have vividly explored the hypothesis that the FinP (or TP or IP) projection must be split up into several others. Pollock initially proposed a TP and an AgrP ('Agreement Phrase') but we have seen many varieties of this idea in the last two decades (see Cinque 1999 for a fully-fledged version). A similar approach has been undertaken for CP (see for instance Rizzi 1997). In order to account for the syntax of English, we have found little use for these extended conceptions of the clausal spine and therefore kept it simple (siding with scholars who have argued that one needs to adopt as much structure for a particular language as this language provides evidence for, such as Iatridou 1990, van Gelderen 1993, Ackema, Neeleman & Weerman 1993, Koeneman 2000 and Zeijlstra 2008).

The DP analysis of nominal phrases is due to Abney (1987).

5 Agreement and Uninterpretable Features

In the previous chapter we encountered a particular syntactic dependency: *case*. Even though sentences containing constituents with the wrong case marking would be semantically good, syntax does not allow them. In this chapter we will see that case is not the only kind of syntactic dependency that can be identified. There are more constructions that, from a semantic perspective, would be good, but that syntax does not like. For instance, sentences like **I walks* (instead of *I walk*) or **She walk* (instead of *She walks*) are bad. Other examples are sentences like **John hopes that Mary loves himself* (instead of *John hopes that Mary loves him*), or **I love me* (instead *of I love myself*). These sentences are clearly ungrammatical, even though it is not that hard to figure out what they could mean. The big question that arises is whether all these syntactic dependencies are different in nature, or underlyingly the same. The latter would be the best outcome, since in that event there is only one mechanism in syntax that we need to understand rather than several. Indeed it turns out that all these syntactic dependencies are the result of a single mechanism: *agreement*.

5.1 Insight: Agreement Reflects Syntactic Dependencies

The previous two chapters introduced two main constraints on what you can create with the Merge operation: θ-theory and Case theory. θ-theory is essentially a semantic constraint; verbal categories that merge with too few or too many arguments yield degraded sentences, since the meaning of the verb dictates how many arguments it should merge with. θ-theory has an effect on syntax, since it partly determines the structural size, but it is not a syntactic constraint. Case theory, by contrast, is a syntactic constraint. Sentences that are perfect from a semantic point of view (*She loves I* instead of *She loves me*) are ruled out by the syntax. Every DP should be assigned case, and particular structural positions are responsible for particular case assignments.

A question that may now arise is whether there are more syntactic dependencies than just those involving case assignment. The answer is yes. Consider the following sentences:

(1)   a.   *John love her.
      b.   *I loves him.

θ-theory has no problem with these sentences, as the two θ-roles of *love* are readily assigned to distinct constituents. Case theory is satisfied too, because the direct objects, *her* and *him*, are assigned accusative and both subjects, *John* and *I*, bear nominative case (although you can't see that for *John* in this example). The problem, of course, is the missing *-s* on the verb in (1a) (it should be *John loves her*), and the *-s* that is present in (1b) (it should be *I love him*). The failure of the verb to agree with the subject of the sentence is what causes the ungrammaticality. In English, this *-s* is the only overt agreement marker and it shows up only if the subject is a 3rd-person singular subject; no other subject triggers the presence of the marker *-s* on the verb. English thus exhibits a second syntactic dependency: agreement between subjects and verbs. This becomes especially clear when we provide the complete agreement paradigm, the overview of possible subjects and the corresponding verb forms.

(2)   to speak

	Singular			Plural	
1st	I	speak	1st	we	speak
2nd	you	speak	2nd	you	speak
3rd	he/she/it	speak-**s**	3rd	they	speak

English is not the only language that exhibits subject–verb agreement. Many languages do so, including most members of the Germanic language family. In contemporary English, agreement is not very strongly present. It only affects 3rd-person singular subjects. However, in previous stages of the language subject–verb agreement was much richer. For instance, Middle English (as spoken in the Midlands in the Middle Ages) had the following paradigm:

(3) to speak

Singular			Plural		
1st	I	speak-**e**	1st	we	speak-**en**
2nd	thou	speak-**es(t)**	2nd	ye	speak-**en**
3rd	he/she/hit	speak-**eth**	3rd	they	speak-**en**

As we will see, there are two facts related to agreement that are important for us: (i) agreement markers appear obligatorily and (ii) at the same time agreement markers turn out to be semantically inactive (i.e. they are meaningless). We will discuss these two facts in more detail later on, but let's start by giving you a first impression.

First, whenever the subject is 3rd person singular, the verb must be marked for 3rd person singular too, using the agreement marker *-s* or, in the case of irregular verbs, another specific 3rd-person singular form of the verb, such as *is* for *to be* or *has* for *to have*. Leaving out the agreement marker yields ungrammaticality. *John love her* is simply ungrammatical. It must be *John loves her*. The same holds for *John are ill*, rather than *John is ill*. This shows that agreement markers must be obligatorily present.

Second, the meaning of the verbal form *love-s* in *John loves her* is the same as the meaning of the form *love* in *You love her*. The fact that these two sentences have different meanings is simply due to the different subjects and not to the different agreement endings on the verb. How do we know that? After all, you could argue that the two sentences differ in meaning because of two differences, rather than one. We know this because different varieties of English have different agreement paradigms, but this does not affect the meaning of sentences. In some American varieties, for instance, *John love her* is grammatical. These speakers drop the *-s* in 3rd-person contexts. Nevertheless, *John love her* for these speakers means exactly the same as *John loves her* for speakers that use the paradigm in (2). If the *-s* in the grammar of the latter group of speakers meant something, we should be able to identify this meaning. But we can't. Similarly, some other varieties may use the *-s* in 1st-person singular contexts, which means that *I loves him* is grammatical for speakers of that variety. Again, there is no difference in meaning between Standard English *I love her* and *I loves her* in such a variety of English. In fact, the same reasoning applies to Modern English vs. Middle English: *I speak-e* meant the same for a Middle English speaker as *I speak* does for a Modern English speaker. The conclusion, therefore, is that agreement endings on the verb do not add any meaning to the sentence in general and are semantically void. This means that sentences with an agreement error are *syntactically*, not *semantically* ill-formed.

We have just established that agreement constitutes a syntactic dependency. Whereas case assignment constitutes a dependency between a case assigner and a nominal category, agreement constitutes a dependency between a subject and a finite verb. This chapter will show that more syntactic dependencies can be identified, for instance between subjects and reflexives (i.e. elements like *myself* or *herself*). The central insight that this chapter offers is the following. All these syntactic dependencies are variations on the same theme. Agreement involves the presence of two similar features in the same clause, and one of these is semantically inactive. We will see that the same applies to both case and reflexives. This simply turns out to be the hallmark of syntactic dependencies in general. What looks like a bunch of different types of constructions on the surface are uniform underneath. Syntax is a machine that encodes dependencies of different types but it always uses the same simple mechanism. The purpose of this chapter, therefore, is not just to understand subject–verb agreement, but to unify all syntactic dependencies discussed so far.

Exercises

A1 This chapter provides the paradigm for the regular verb *to speak*.
  a. Now give the paradigms of two irregular verbs: *to be* and the modal auxiliary *must*.
  b. What are the most striking differences with respect to the regular paradigm? And what are the similarities?

A2 The paradigms so far were all about the present tense.
  a. Now, provide the paradigm for the simple past tense of the regular verb *to walk*.
  b. What is the major difference between the regular present- and past-tense paradigms?

B3 To what extent does the absence of person and number agreement markers in the past tense form evidence for the claim that these markers are semantically inactive (in other words: they are meaningless)?

5.2 Implementation: Agreement as Feature Dependency

In this section, we will argue for and develop the hypothesis that features in syntax come in two types, interpretable ones and uninterpretable ones. We will then show how this characterisation of a syntactic dependency captures both subject–verb agreement and case.

5.2.1 Interpretable and Uninterpretable Features

The hallmark of the first two chapters of this book was that syntax looks at the features of a word rather than at the words themselves when it creates sentences. It is not the case that the sentence *John walks* is good English because there is a rule allowing the word *John* to be merged with the word *walks*, but rather because a DP with a 3rd-person singular feature is merged with a finite verb that also carries a 3rd-person singular feature.

The idea that syntax operates on the features carried by words and phrases is essentially correct, but what the agreement facts above show is that not every feature behaves in the same way. Person (1st, 2nd, 3rd) and number (singular, plural) features on a noun behave very differently from person and number features on a verb. A 3rd-person singular feature on a noun is semantically active, whereas a 3rd-person singular feature on a verb is not. One of the arguments was that in dialects that lack (3rd-person singular) agreement, the combination of subject and verb still means the same thing.

(4)   a.   John loves her.   Standard English
       b.   John love her.   Non-standard English

This strongly suggests that the -s in *loves* does not cause an extra semantic effect: it is semantically void. But let us try to be clever and see what we could possibly say in order to argue the opposite, namely that agreement markers do contribute to how we interpret sentences, despite appearances. There are two ways we could go.

One way would be to assume that -s and *John* together form the subject and because of this both their features matter for semantics; therefore, their features should be the same. But this cannot be correct. Suppose that a non-native speaker of Standard English were to say something like (5) to a native speaker of Standard English. What would the latter understand the former to be saying?

(5)   I   walk-s
       [1SG]   [3SG]

In fact, (5) does not even have to be uttered by a non-native speaker of English. A native speaker who lives in rural Somerset or Dorset could utter (5) rather than *I walk*, as this is the way you can speak in West Country English. The same question arises: how would a native speaker of English who is not from that area understand this West Country English speaker? The speaker of Standard English would presume that s/he meant 'I walk', and not, for instance, 'He walks' or 'I walk and he walks'. But why would that be? If both features ([1st] and [3rd]) were semantically active, then the other intended meanings should equally well emerge. But if person and number features are semantically active only on the subject, it follows immediately that we take the sentence to be about a 1st-person singular subject and not a 3rd-person singular subject. This example therefore shows that the person and number features on a noun contribute more to the meaning of the sentence than the person and number features on a verb.

Another way of supporting the idea that all elements, including the so-called agreement markers, contribute to the semantics would be to assume that the entire VP has person and/or number properties. Suppose we have the sentence *Harry is lifting a piano*. We could say that both the subject and the verb (or the VP) are singular because there is only one AGENT (Harry) and there is also one piano-lifting event. In other words, the *-s* would indicate not that there is only one AGENT but that there is only one piano-lifting event. But this cannot be correct either. Take, for instance, (6).

(6)   The girls are lifting a piano now.

The most salient reading of (6) is the one in which a group of girls are jointly lifting one piano (and not a reading where the girls each lift a piano). This shows that there is only one, singular lifting event going on, despite the fact that the finite auxiliary is marked for 3rd person plural rather than singular (*are* instead of *is*). So, if plural marking on the verb were semantically active in the way we are hypothesising, the standard meaning of (6) would be impossible to get to, contrary to fact. The reverse holds for (7): here we have singular *is* (and not plural *are*), but the sentence naturally conveys the reading that each girl carries her own umbrella.

(7)   Every girl is carrying an umbrella.

Conclusion: there is no way to argue that agreement markers contribute to the semantics, however clever we try to be. They are indeed really semantically inactive. This conclusion has serious repercussions for our hypothesis that syntax operates on features. Again, take (4a), repeated as (8):

(8)   John   love   -s   her.
       [3SG]   [3SG]

As you can see, there are two elements that have a [3SG] feature, but only one of the two is semantically active, namely the one on *John*. This means that the two features are essentially different. Whereas the first is a feature that will be interpretable as such, the second one is semantically uninterpretable. When you interpret the meaning of this sentence, you simply ignore the *-s* on *love*, exactly as you ignore the *-s* when a foreigner utters (5). For this reason, we call such features **uninterpretable features**, and we indicate this with a small 'u':

(9)   John   love   -s   her.
       [3SG]   [u3SG]

The [3SG] feature on *John* does contribute to the meaning of the sentence because this sentence is a statement about a single individual, and not about several individuals. The [3SG] feature on *John* is therefore called an **interpretable feature**. Even though people sometimes indicate this with a small 'i' ([i3SG]), we will not use this extra symbol, and just adopt the convention of writing [3SG] (without the small 'i'). What is crucial is that every feature is either interpretable or uninterpretable.

The fact that uninterpretable features can be ignored by the semantics, however, does not mean that they are inconsequential for the syntax. After all, uninterpretable features have the power to make a sentence completely ungrammatical. Since syntacticians deal with the syntactic (un)well-formedness of phrases and sentences, they must provide a description of what has gone wrong in a sentence like (10) from the perspective of a speaker of Standard English:

(10)   *I loves her.

The description is actually quite straightforward: what has gone wrong in (10) but not in (9) is that the former contains an uninterpretable feature, [u3SG] in the absence of an interpretable [3SG] feature in the same clause. What we can say, then, is that ungrammaticality arises if an uninterpretable feature appears without an interpretable counterpart. Formally, we can state this as follows:

(11)   Any clause in which some element carries an uninterpretable feature [uF] requires the presence of a matching interpretable feature [F]; otherwise the clause is ungrammatical.

The statement in (11) is one of the guiding principles of grammar and determines how syntactic dependencies are formed in general. We first show exactly how this principle applies to subject–verb agreement. Then we will show that it underlies not only subject–verb agreement, but also case assignment. Finally, we will address in more detail where exactly in the tree structure that we have developed for English these interpretable and uninterpretable features should sit.

5.2.2 Person and Number Agreement in English

Now let us look in detail at the workings of subject–verb agreement in English. In chapter 4, we identified the position of the agreement marker as the head of a functional phrase FinP. The agreement marker -s, for instance, is hosted in the head of FinP and attaches later to the verb *love*.

(12)

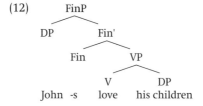

Being the head of FinP, the morpheme -s must carry the feature [Finite], which we abbreviate to [Fin]. This [Fin] feature must be interpretable. This follows directly from the fact that finite and non-finite expressions have a different meaning. The examples below differ in their semantics:

(13)   a.   (for Mary) to be leaving
         b.   (Mary) is leaving.

Only (13b) states that something is indeed happening right now. (13a) talks about leaving in general, but leaves it open as to whether it happens or not, and if it does, when it happens. Therefore, -s carries [Fin] and not [uFin]. Finiteness pertains to the head of the clause, Fin, as either being positively or negatively marked for tense and/or agreement, as we established in chapters 1 and 4. However, whereas agreement is uninterpretable on the Fin head, tense is not. We can clearly tell whether a clause makes a statement about the present or the past, or not, and this information is obligatorily expressed by the tense information provided by Fin. Therefore, we interpret finiteness as being marked or not for tense. [Fin], the feature that signals a positive marking for being tensed, must therefore always carry a tense subfeature like [Present] or [Past], which we indicate as: [Fin: Present] and [Fin: Past] respectively. The sentence in (13b) is in the present tense (since the event of Mary leaving is taking place right now), so it contains a feature [Fin: Present]. Note that we do not use a subfeature [Future] as a specification for [Fin]. The reason is that [Present] and [Past] are expressed in a similar way in English. A lexical verb can appear in the present or past tense: *I walk* vs. *I walked*. Future, however, cannot be expressed in the same way. There is no verb form of *walk* that would do that. Instead, English uses the modal auxiliary *will* to express that something will happen in the future, or a construction with *am/is/are going to*. Future tense, then, is not expressed by specifying the Fin head as [Fin: Future] but by using specific auxiliaries.

Taking [Present] and [Past] to be not features that are independent from [Fin], but subfeatures of it, has the advantage that it reduces the number of possible feature combinations. It guarantees us, for instance, that an element not carrying [Fin] cannot be marked for past or present tense either. This allows for the existence of the infinitival marker *to*, which carries [Non-fin(ite)] rather than [Fin], and cannot be marked for [Present] or [Past]. Note that an elegant consequence is that we now also rule out heads that are marked for [Fin] but not for [Past] or [Present], or vice versa, and these heads indeed seem not to exist in English. If you are a Fin head, you can be either present (*am*) or past (*was*). But if you are a non-finite head, *to*, you lack a specification for tense.

As for agreement, we have already established above that the *-s* carries the feature [u3SG], which agrees with the subject. Now, you may be inclined to treat agreement as consisting of two features rather than one: an uninterpretable person and an uninterpretable number feature, [u3] and [uSG], respectively. At the same time, it is clear that the person and number features always agree with the subject in tandem. They are together part of one marker: *-s*. For this reason, syntacticians usually assume that person and number features together form one feature that has several values, or subfeatures. Such features are called φ-features (pronounced 'phi-features', after the Greek letter 'phi'). A φ-feature is a feature that has a person and number subfeature (for instance, 3rd person singular, or 1st person plural).

A φ-feature is always either interpretable or uninterpretable. Nouns carry interpretable φ-features, verbs carry uninterpretable φ-features. So *John* in (12) carries an interpretable φ-feature, and this feature carries two subfeatures: [φ: 3, SG]. The affix *-s* carries an uninterpretable φ-feature that has the same subfeatures: [uφ: 3, SG]. The relevant features and their places in the structure are given in (14):

(14)

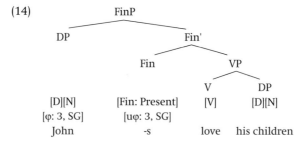

Now, the grammaticality of (14) is in accordance with the principle in (11): every feature [uF] has a matching feature [F] in the same clause. The representation of an ungrammatical counterpart of (14) is given in (15). The ungrammaticality of this sentence follows from (11) as well: [uφ: 3, SG] on -*s* lacks a matching feature [φ: 3, SG].

(15)   *

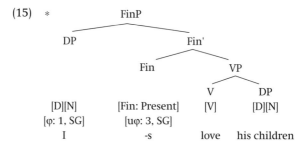

In order to rescue the sentence, either the subject should carry [φ: 3, SG], as in (14), or Fin should host an element that carries [uφ: 1, SG], which is the unpronounced agreement marker -*ø*, as in (16).

(16)

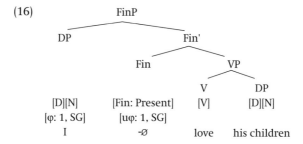

Although (11) does a good job in distinguishing between grammatical and ungrammatical agreement patterns, it does not yet fully explain the data. Why, for instance, would sentence (17) be ungrammatical?

(17)   *

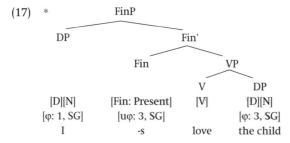

This sentence contains an agreement marker *-s* carrying [uφ: 3, SG], and a DP, *the child*, carrying [φ: 3, SG]. According to (11), there is no reason why this sentence should be bad. At the same time it is. Intuitively, the answer is clear: only subjects, not objects, control agreement on the verb. In other words, uninterpretable φ-features in Fin can only agree with interpretable φ-features on subjects, not on objects. But so far, this does not follow from anything. This means that (11) as it stands is not precise enough, and we must incorporate some property that distinguishes subjects from objects.

What we also observe is that the constituents introducing the interpretable and uninterpretable φ-features of the relevant syntactic dependency (the subject and the agreement marker *-s*, respectively) both sit in the same phrase: [uφ: 3, SG] sits in the head of FinP and [φ: 1, SG] sits in the specifier of FinP. Therefore, as a first attempt, let us adapt our principle to the formulation in (18), which allows us to correctly make the difference between (14) and (17):

(18) An uninterpretable feature [uF] requires the presence of a matching interpretable feature [F] within the same phrase, not in any lower phrase.

How well does this adaptation do? The principle in (18) looks empirically correct for all the data described so far. To be sure, example (17) is bad because the only interpretable [φ: 3, SG] feature present is carried by a constituent that is not present on the head, complement or specifier of FinP; it resides inside the lower VP. Therefore, the uninterpretable [uφ: 3, SG] feature on Fin cannot see [φ: 3, SG], in accordance with (18). Despite this positive result, we may want to explore further why agreement is restricted in this way: what is behind (18)? Before we dive into this, we will first take an in-depth look at nominative and accusative case from the perspective of interpretable and uninterpretable features, and see whether the principle in (18) is also active there.

5.2.3 Case Agreement in English

It is quite clear that agreement markers need some other element to agree with. But the principle in (18) applies to other syntactic dependencies than agreement relations. Take for instance nominative case assignment. We can say that nominative constituents have the following property: they can survive only if they are assigned nominative case by an element in the head of FinP that carries the feature [Fin: Present/ Past]. This explains why the occurrence of nominative constituents is restricted to finite clauses. At the same time, we do not wish to say that nominative subjects carry the feature [Fin: Present/Past] themselves. Finite elements introduce tense properties into the clause, and can agree with the subject. A nominative subject never introduces present or past tense features into the clause. This, then, creates a bit of a paradox: nominative subjects are restricted to finite clauses (suggesting that they are marked for finiteness) but do not introduce the semantics that we associate with finiteness (suggesting that they lack such marking). Nominative subjects, then, require the feature [Fin] so as to explain why their occurrence is restricted to finite clauses (recall that *I want they to arrest me* is bad). Yet they do not themselves carry [Fin].

The way we described agreement dependencies in the previous section, however, provides an elegant solution. The agreement marker *-s* does not carry the feature [φ: 3, SG], but needs a constituent with the feature [φ: 3, SG] in the same phrase. Therefore we said that *-s* carries [uφ: 3, SG]. Does this start to ring a bell? We can use exactly the same trick to deal with nominatives. We can simply say that nominative subjects carry [uFin]. Since the finiteness feature on a nominative subject is uninterpretable, it needs to agree with an element carrying a [Fin] feature in the same phrase. This ensures that nominative subjects can only appear in finite clauses without having to say that nominative subjects are finite elements themselves. At the same time, it allows us to encode the dependency between a nominative subject and the finite head that it is dependent on for its nominative case. Note that we are not saying here: nominatives carry [uFin: Present/Past]. There is nothing in a nominative constituent that specifies a restriction to past- or present-tense contexts; it is only restricted to finite contexts.

So even though nominative case does not look like an agreement marker, at a slightly more abstract level it behaves in an exactly similar manner. We can therefore change our tree in (14) into the one in (19), where we have used *he* as a subject to clearly show that the subject is nominative. All uninterpretable features obey our principle in (18): both [uφ: 3, SG] and [uFin] reside in the FinP, and their interpretable counterparts (that is, [φ: 3, SG] on *he* and [Fin: Present] on *-s*) as well. Its grammaticality, then, follows as a direct consequence. To make clear that the present- and past-tense subfeatures on the [Fin] feature in the Fin head do not play a role in nominative case assignment, we do not include them in the tree. *He* has only [uFin], so it suffices to say that *-s* carries [Fin] (though nothing would be wrong if you said here that *-s* carries [Fin: Present]).

(19)

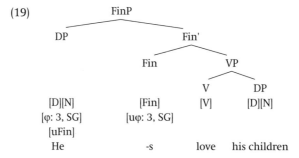

Let us take a moment to evaluate what we are doing here. Whereas in chapter 4 we talked about nominative case as a feature that was assigned to the subject by a Fin head, we have now encoded the case relationship between these elements in terms of an agreement relation between an element carrying [Fin] and an element carrying [uFin]. Nominative case is what [uFin] 'sounds' like, much like -*s* is the 'sound' of a [u3SG] feature. Now, what is the added benefit of doing it this way, i.e. encoding case agreement with the use of [Fin] and [uFin]? Why don't we simply stick to the old idea that a Fin head assigns a nominative case to the subject? Well, the benefit is that we no longer need to allude to a special Case theory to account for the effects of nominative case assignment. The principle in (18) now accounts for both nominative case assignment and subject–verb agreement in exactly the same way. In other words, we have *unified* nominative case assignment and subject–verb agreement to one mechanism: agreement between [F] and [uF]. Only the content of F is different. Nominative case and φ-feature agreement appear to be different dependencies on the surface, as they involve different features, but underlyingly they work in exactly the same way.

But if we really want to get rid of Case theory and formulate a more general theory of syntactic agreement relations, we have so far only done half the job. In addition to the assignment of nominative case, we have also discussed that of accusative case by verbs and prepositions. The obvious goal, therefore, is to see whether accusative case assignment can be reformulated as an agreement relation too.

Consider the following ungrammatical sentence:

(20)   *Him loves his child.

Before we say anything about this, let us briefly re-establish what accusatives are. We have seen that accusatives show up in the vicinity of verbs and prepositions, much as nominatives show up in the vicinity of a finite head. For this reason, we identified verbs and prepositions as potential accusative case assigners. Let us now draw a parallel between nominative and accusative case assignment and see what we have to say for accusatives.

We reanalysed nominative case assignment as a relation between two constituents that carry the same categorial feature. The Fin head, by definition, carries an interpretable [Fin] feature, and the nominative subject that is dependent on this head carries the [uFin] counterpart. If accusatives are dependent on the presence of a V or P, then this logically leads to the following analysis: accusative case is nothing but an uninterpretable feature reflecting the category that it is dependent on: [uV] or [uP]. Since accusatives carry this feature, they need to appear in the same phrase as V and P, the carriers of [V] and [P], respectively. The result of this is that case assignment in general is now reanalysed as agreement between constituents carrying interpretable or uninterpretable categorial features. Nominative case is the reflection of a [Fin]–[uFin] agreement relation and structurally this relation is one between a head and a specifier. Accusative case is the reflection of either a [V]–[uV] or [P]–[uP] agreement relation, and structurally this is a relation between a head and a complement. Both a specifier–head and a head–complement relation are relations within the same phrase. This is perfectly in line with the principle in (18), which demands of [F] and [uF] that they sit in the same phrase. Since case effects are now expressed as an interpretable–uninterpretable feature match under the same structural conditions, identical to what we observed with person/number agreement on finite verbs, we no longer need to refer to a special Case theory. Case is nothing but a form of agreement.

Let us now return to what we set out to explain: the ungrammaticality of (20). The structure is given in (21).

(21)   *

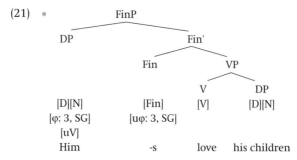

Him is an accusative form, so it carries [uV]. Since *him* is the specifier of FinP, *him* requires a constituent carrying [V] in the head of FinP. As no [V] feature is present on Fin (there is only [V] in a lower phrase), the sentence is ungrammatical, as it violates (18).

So we can now explain the following minimal pair:

(22)   a.   He loves his children.
     b.   *Him loves his children.

But this accounts for only half of the case examples that we discussed in chapter 4. The other half involved minimal pairs like (23), in which the object cannot be a nominative, but must be an accusative.

(23)   a.   Mary loves me.
     b.   *Mary loves I.

Nothing new, however, has to be said to account for this contrast either. If accusative case is what [uV] (or [uP]) 'sounds' like, the example in (23b) is readily excluded. The tree in (24) is fully in accordance with (18).

(24)

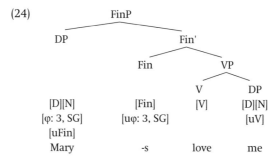

The representation in (25), however, is not. Here, the [uFin] feature of the DP *I* is not in the same phrase that contains [Fin]. The only element carrying [Fin] is the *-s* which heads the FinP, and this element is not contained in the VP.

(25)   *

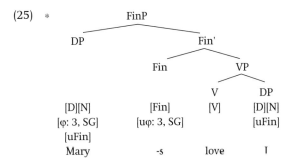

To conclude, it is not only nominatives but also accusatives that can be fully captured by the mechanism in (18), initially developed for subject–verb agreement. This shows that the two syntactic dependencies described so far fall under the same heading. That the proposed mechanism can replace case assignment can of course be seen as extra support for dealing with agreement in terms of uninterpretable and interpretable features.

All the syntactic dependencies seen so far are the result of one single agreement mechanism. The question arises, however, as to whether there are more syntactic dependencies present in the grammar of English, and to what extent they can be reduced to agreement properties as well. This is what we will investigate in the next section, in which we introduce a new type of syntactic dependency, known as **binding**.

Exercises

A4   For the following sentences, indicate what are the interpretable and uninterpretable φ-features:
   a.   John likes the students.
   b.   Mary seems unhappy about the syntax exercises.
   c.   I have always wanted to hear her sing.
   d.   Nobody knows the trouble I see.
   e.   People don't know why you walked away.
   f.   A group of students is leaving the building.

A5   Now do the same things for all case features, both interpretable and uninterpretable, in sentences a–f of A4.

A6   Draw the trees for the following two sentences, and indicate all the relevant features.
   a.   John talked to me.
   b.   They don't know the answer.

B7   Certain words in English can have both singular and plural agreement, such as the word *committee*:
   a.   The committee is meeting tonight.
   b.   The committee are meeting tonight.

   What does this tell us about the φ-features of *the committee*?

B8   Clearly *John* and *Mary* both carry the feature [φ: 3, SG]. Nevertheless, the agreement on the verb is not [uφ: 3, SG] when the subject is *John and Mary*:
- a. *John and Mary sings.
- b. John and Mary sing.

Does this create a problem for agreement theory?

C9   In this chapter, it was said that accusatives always carry [uV] or [uP]. But there is a third type of accusative, as you can see below:
(i) Mary's book was interesting.

Which noun in the sentence above cannot have the feature [uV] or [uP]? Can this noun have the feature [uFin]? If not, what kind of feature should it have?

5.3 Consequences: Binding, C-Command and Agreement

If we want to have a maximally general theory of syntactic dependencies, one that correctly captures all syntactic dependencies with the same mechanism, we must be sure that we have looked at all of them. In this section, we will introduce an example of yet another dependency: binding. Binding involves the phenomenon in which two constituents in a clause refer to one and the same element. It turns out that binding involves various syntactic constraints, and we will try to investigate whether these can be described by the same agreement mechanism that we explored before. The conclusion will be that this can in principle be done (except for one particular problem that we will solve later), but only by revising the relation between uninterpretable and interpretable features that we proposed in (18).

5.3.1 Binding
Take the following sentences:

(26)   a. I like myself.
        b. Mary sees herself in the mirror.
        c. Peter and Bill excused themselves.

What do these sentences mean? In all these cases, a second DP (*myself, herself, themselves*) refers back to an earlier DP (*I, Mary, Peter and Bill*, respectively). The meaning of this second DP is determined by an earlier element and not by the DP itself (or by the context of the conversation). You would not know who *herself* refers to were it not for *Mary* being mentioned in the same sentence.

If one element depends for its interpretation on another element in the same sentence, we say that it is bound by it: *herself* is thus 'bound' by *Mary*, or *Mary* 'binds' *herself*. For this reason, the phenomenon discussed in this section is by convention referred to as 'binding'. We will argue in this section that binding is a syntactic dependency, much like the others we have seen. An automatic consequence of establishing this dependency in syntax is that the two DPs are interpreted as referring to the same entity (person or thing). The semantic implication of binding, then, is coreference. The way coreference relations are expressed is usually with the help of indices, added to DPs as subscripts. We illustrate this in (27) below for the examples in (26).

(27) a. I_i like myself$_i$.
b. Mary$_i$ sees herself$_i$ in the mirror.
c. [Peter and Bill]$_i$ excused themselves$_i$.

The fact that *I* and *myself* have the index 'i' indicates that *I* and *myself* corefer: they refer to the same individual walking around in the real world. An expression ending in *-self/-selves* is called a **reflexive** (or a reflexive pronoun), and the element that it depends upon (or to put it more formally: the element that is binding it) is called the **antecedent**. The fact that reflexives are dependent on another DP for their interpretation makes them similar to **non-reflexive pronouns**, such as *him, her* or *them*. In (28), it is shown that these non-reflexive pronouns can be bound too. Note that (28b) contains two binding relations in one sentence. *They* binds *them*, and *John* binds *he*. We use 'i' and 'j' to distinguish the two relations.

(28) a. John$_i$ told Mary$_j$ that she$_j$ can call him$_i$ at 7.
b. They$_i$ didn't tell John$_j$ that he$_j$ had misrepresented them$_i$.

At the same time, however, there are significant differences between reflexives and non-reflexive pronouns when it comes to binding. The ways in which syntactic dependencies involving these two types of elements are established are significantly different. We will discuss the two most important here.

First, reflexives must always be bound; non-reflexive pronouns do not have to be bound. For instance, the following sentences are acceptable.

(29) a. Mary called me.
b. They said I was wrong.
c. I can't believe he did that.
d. You are not allowed to smoke here.

In all these examples, the non-reflexive pronouns (*me, they, I, he* and *you*) are not bound by any other expression in the sentence. The non-reflexive pronoun *he* in (29c), for instance, may of course refer to some person that we talked about before we uttered (29c), but at the level of this sentence *he* is unbound, or free. This is the case for all the pronouns in (29).

In fact, sometimes you even have a choice. With possessive non-reflexive pronouns in particular this can become very clear:

(30) Every boy who knows his house can direct you to it.

The sentence in (30) has two interpretations: one in which each boy can direct you to the house where that boy himself lives, and one in which there is a particular person, say Bill, whose house is known to all the boys present. In the former case, *every boy* binds *his*, because the way we interpret *his* is determined by *every boy*. In the latter case, however, *his* is free within the sentence and refers to someone that must have been mentioned before (30) was uttered, for instance Bill. In that case, *every boy* does not determine how we interpret *his* and therefore does not bind the possessive pronoun. This ambiguity is represented by the different indices as in (31): *his* can either be bound and share the index 'i' with *every boy*, or *his* is unbound and has index 'j', indicating that it refers to somebody not mentioned in this sentence.

(31)   [Every boy]$_i$ who knows his$_{i/j}$ house can direct you to it.

Reflexives, on the other hand, must always be bound. The examples in (32) are unacceptable because the reflexives are not bound by another DP:

(32)   a.   *You like myself.
     b.   *John sees herself in the mirror.
     c.   *Peter knows each other.

And the following example does not give rise to the same ambiguity that we saw arising with the non-reflexive possessive pronoun *his* (compare example (31)).

(33)   [Every boy]$_i$ who likes himself$_{i/*j}$ can be perceived as arrogant.

The interpretation of (33) cannot be that there is one male individual such that every boy likes that individual. So we see that reflexives and non-reflexive pronouns differ in the obligatoriness of being bound.

The second difference between non-reflexive pronouns and reflexives concerns the domain of binding. Consider the following two sentences:

(34)   a.   John said that Peter thought that Harry blamed himself.
     b.   John said that Peter thought that Harry blamed him.

How do we interpret *himself* in (34a)? There is only one option: the person who gets the blame is Harry. In other words, *himself* must be bound by *Harry* and cannot be bound by either *Peter* or *John*. Let us compare this to how we interpret *him* in (34b). There are three options: the person who gets the blame is either Peter, John, or some person not mentioned in the sentence. The sentence cannot mean, however, that Harry gets the blame. In other words, *him* can be bound by *Peter* or *John*, but not by *Harry*. We can conclude, therefore, that the binding possibilities for reflexives and non-reflexive pronouns are in perfect complementary distribution here (remember the term from chapter 4): in a position where a reflexive can appear, the corresponding non-reflexive pronoun cannot appear, and vice versa. Crucially, the reflexive in (34a) can only be bound by a close, or nearby, antecedent. The non-reflexive pronoun in (34b), on the other hand, can be bound by any antecedent *except for the close one*. The requirement that non-reflexive pronouns must remain unbound by a close antecedent can also be shown by the simple sentences in (35): the non-reflexive pronouns may not be bound by the subject, and as a consequence they cannot corefer with the subjects.

(35)   a.   *I_i like me_i.
       b.   *$Mary_i$ sees her_i in the mirror.
       c.   *[Peter and Bill]$_i$ excused $them_i$.

To account for the different behaviour of reflexives and non-reflexive pronouns, we have come up with the following two generalisations:

(36)   a.   A reflexive must be bound by a nearby antecedent.
       b.   A non-reflexive pronoun cannot be bound by a nearby antecedent.

These two generalisations are often referred to as Principle A and Principle B of the Binding theory. Principle A is a condition on reflexives, stating that they must be bound by some nearby element, and Principle B is a condition on non-reflexive pronouns that states that they cannot be bound by something nearby, and can therefore only be bound over a greater distance. Before we try to arrive at an explanation of these principles, however, we should first say more about what exactly counts as nearby.

5.3.2 C-Command

In the previous section, we saw that in simple sentences, i.e. sentences consisting of a single clause, reflexives must be bound and non-reflexive pronouns must be free:

(37)   a. I_i like $myself_i$.
       a'   *I_i like me_i.
       b. $Mary_i$ sees $herself_i$ in the mirror.
       b'. *$Mary_i$ sees her_i in the mirror.
       c.   [Peter and Bill]$_i$ excused $themselves_i$.
       c'. *[Peter and Bill]$_i$ excused $them_i$.

In addition, reflexives cannot be bound by antecedents outside the clause:

(38)   a. $John_k$ said that $Peter_j$ thought that $Harry_i$ blamed $himself_{i/*j/*k/*m}$.
       b. $John_k$ said that $Peter_j$ thought that $Harry_i$ blamed $him_{*i/j/k/m}$.

Himself must be bound by *Harry* and as a consequence it must corefer with it, as indicated by the index 'i'. It cannot be bound by *Peter* or *John*, and the impossibility of coreference with $Peter_j$ or $John_k$ is indicated by the starred indices 'j' and 'k'. Nor can *himself* refer to somebody not mentioned in this sentence, as indicated by the starred index 'm'. As you can see in (38b), the possibilities for non-reflexive *him* are the exact opposite. This allows us to hypothesise that the domain within which Principles A and B must hold is to be defined as a FinP and everything that is below FinP. We use the term 'dominate' for this, introduced in chapter 2. Remember that a particular node A dominates another node B if you can reach B from A just by going down. Now, intuitively, we can say that a reflexive must find an antecedent within the closest FinP it is dominated by. Note, though, that the binding domains are restricted to finite FinPs. A reflexive in a non-finite clause can be bound by an antecedent outside of this clause:

(39) a. John$_i$ wants [$_{FinP}$ himself$_i$ to succeed].
      b. We$_i$ expected [$_{FinP}$ ourselves$_i$ to do better next time].

Now we can redefine the binding principles as follows:

(40) a. PRINCIPLE A
          A reflexive must be bound within the closest finite FinP
          dominating it.
      b. PRINCIPLE B
          A non-reflexive pronoun cannot be bound within the closest
          finite FinP dominating it.

Note that under these formulations the possible and impossible interpretations for the sentences in (34)/(38) follow automatically:

(41) a. [$_{FinP}$ John said [$_{CP}$ that [$_{FinP}$ Peter thought [$_{CP}$ that [$_{FinP}$ Harry blamed
          himself]]]]].
      b. [$_{FinP}$ John said [$_{CP}$ that [$_{FinP}$ Peter thought [$_{CP}$ that [$_{FinP}$ Harry blamed
          him]]]]].

Himself needs an antecedent that is dominated by the closest FinP that
dominates it, which is the FinP of the deepest embedded clause *Harry
blamed himself*. This restricts the number of possible antecedents to one,
namely *Harry*. *Him*, on the other hand, is by definition free within the
closest finite FinP dominating it. This means that only *Peter* and *John*
can be antecedents, because they are not dominated by the lowest FinP.
Harry is dominated by the lowest finite FinP that also dominates *him*.
Therefore, *Harry* cannot bind *him*.

Despite this increased precision, our binding principles are unfortunately not yet precise enough in their current formulation. Why not?
Well, take a look at the following sentences:

(42) a. *The book about the president$_i$ upset himself$_i$.
      b. *John$_j$'s sister likes himself$_j$.
      c. *Admiring Mary$_k$ suits herself$_k$.

All these sentences are ungrammatical, but would be predicted to be
grammatical under (40a). It is therefore clear that more needs to be said.
Let us therefore compare the grammatical (37a) with the ungrammatical
(42b). In both cases the VP is more or less the same (*like myself* vs. *likes himself*). The main difference lies in the complexity of the subjects: a single
subject *I* vs. a complex subject *John's sister*. And this difference must make
all the difference. Let us zoom in by providing the structures:

(43)

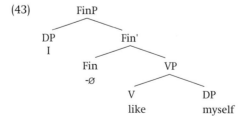

(44)

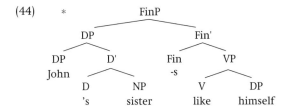

In (43), the antecedent *I* is directly dominated by the FinP: if you go one step up from DP *I*, you are already in FinP. But in (44) it takes two steps from DP *John* to reach FinP. Since (43) is grammatical and (44) is not, and they do not differ in other relevant grammatical aspects, this must be the key difference. A reflexive can be bound by an antecedent if there is a node in the tree structure dominating the reflexive that is only one step away from the antecedent. The node FinP in (43) dominates *myself*, as there is a direct line going from FinP to the reflexive, and from FinP it is only one step to reach the DP *I*. You can also characterise the relationship from the viewpoint of the antecedent, of course. From the DP *I*, you can reach the reflexive by going only one step up and then down again. This relation (one up, then down) is known as the **c-command** and is one of the most important relations in syntax. Let's therefore be very precise about it.

(45)   C-COMMAND
       A c-commands B if and only if the node that immediately
       dominates A also dominates B, and A does not dominate B.

The two structures below illustrate the difference:

(46)   a.   A C-COMMANDS B:

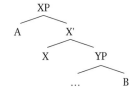

       b.   A DOES NOT C-COMMAND B:

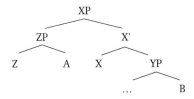

In (46a), XP is one step above A: XP thus immediately dominates A. XP also dominates B, so A c-commands B. In (46b), it takes more than one step to reach XP from A, so XP does not immediately dominate A, and therefore A cannot c-command B. In the same vein, you can establish that in (46a) A c-commands X, and X c-commands B, but that B does not c-command X, and that X does not c-command A. Informally, then, A c-commands B if you can reach B from A by going one node up, and down the other way as many nodes as you like.

Now we can understand the differences between the sentences in (37a)/(43) and those in (42b)/(44) in these structural terms. Given c-command, (43) is a grammatical structure because *I* c-commands *myself*. The structure in (44) is not grammatical because the only antecedent that matches in features with *himself* (which is *John*) does not c-command the reflexive. Now, if the number of steps from DP *John* to a node that dominates the reflexive is already too many in a structure like (44), you can readily imagine that the number of steps needed from DP *the president* in an example like (42a) is really far too many. We leave you to establish the exact structure of that sentence.

Note that c-command is purely structural. It does not care about the nature of the nodes (X, X' or XP) it has to look at. It only cares about the number of structural steps between two elements. This predicts that you can also have binding within for instance a DP, as long as the antecedent c-commands the reflexive. This prediction is indeed borne out. Look at (47) and (48):

(47)   John likes Mary$_i$'s ideas about herself$_i$.

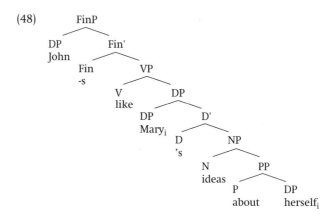

In (47) and (48) *Mary* c-commands *herself*, so binding of *herself* by *Mary* is possible.

So, now we can state the binding principles in their definitive forms.

(49)   a.   PRINCIPLE A
            A reflexive must be bound by a c-commanding antecedent that is dominated by the closest finite FinP that also dominates this reflexive.
       b.   PRINCIPLE B
            A non-reflexive pronoun may not be bound by a c-commanding antecedent that is dominated by the closest finite FinP that also dominates this non-reflexive pronoun.

Antecedents that bind reflexives must (i) always c-command these reflexives, and (ii) be directly dominated by the same FinP as the reflexive. This seems essentially correct. And now that we have established the principles that together describe the facts in a technically precise way, we can wonder why they are the way they are. And more specifically, how does binding relate to the other syntactic dependencies we have seen?

5.3.3 Binding and Agreement

So now let's see why there should be such a thing as Binding theory, and moreover whether it is similar to or different from Case or Agreement theory. Since it contains two principles (A and B), explaining Binding theory reduces to explaining them both. Let's start with Principle B.

Principle B is not just an arbitrary principle. In a way, it is the mirror image of Principle A. Basically, Principle B says that in all cases where Principle A forbids you to use a reflexive you can use a corresponding non-reflexive pronoun instead (that is, a non-reflexive pronoun with similar person and number values). And wherever Principle A allows you to use a reflexive, using a non-reflexive pronoun is not an option. This allows us to rephrase Principle B as follows:

(50) PRINCIPLE B

If you have a choice between using a reflexive and a corresponding non-reflexive pronoun to express the same meaning, you must use the reflexive.

Note that there is nothing new in (50): it only restates what we have already observed. The question is how we can explain Principle B as formulated here. Well, let's think a bit more about reflexives. They are essentially special pronouns, pronouns that are much more specified than other, non-reflexive pronouns. Whereas non-reflexive pronouns can be bound from a distance and do not even have to be bound at all, reflexives must be bound under very precise and restricted circumstances. So we can think of a reflexive like *myself* as a more restricted version of the corresponding non-reflexive pronoun *me*. We might even take it one step further and say that *myself* is a special form of *me*, for instance by saying that it is like *me* but with an extra feature [Reflexive].

Now, it is a well-known fact about language that special forms have a special status. As an example, take irregular forms such as *left* (instead of *leaved*) or *feet* (instead of *foots*). There are two ways to talk about the bad forms *leaved* and *foots. You can say that they are forbidden in general, but that would be kind of strange, since the rule for past tense is that in principle you add *-ed* to the verbal stem (or just a *-d*, as in *lie–lied*, and *lay–laid*). Why all of a sudden have a rule that says that you may not add *-ed* to *leave*? And the same applies to plurals: you add *-s* to the singular form. Alternatively, you can say that every verb (including *leave*) can receive a past tense by adding *-ed*, but if there exists a more specific past-tense form of the verb, such as *left*, you must use that specific form. And every singular noun can become a plural by adding *-s* (including *foot*) but, again, if there is a more specific form to express the plural, such as *feet*, you must use that form. Then the fact that you must always use the specific form comes from a very general principle, namely the one in (51):

(51)   THE 'ELSEWHERE' PRINCIPLE
       Whenever there is competition in grammar between a
       more specific and a more general form to express the same
       meaning, the more specific one wins if no grammatical rules
       are violated.

Given this 'Elsewhere' principle (to be discussed in more detail in chapter 8), Principle B as formulated in (50) receives a clear explanation. If you have a choice between the two, that is, if Principle A is not violated, you must use the more specific, reflexive form (*myself, himself*). Only when the more specific, reflexive form is forbidden (owing to Principle A) can the corresponding 'elsewhere' form (a non-reflexive pronoun like *me* or *him*) be used. In this way, then, the combination of Principle A and (51) gives us all the effects that we previously described by referring to Principle B. In other words, we don't need Principle B. Principle A plus the 'Elsewhere' principle do all the work.

With Principle B out of the way, let's now turn to Principle A. This principle is a syntactic dependency: any sentence that violates Principle A is simply ungrammatical. The cartoon test from chapter 1 is of no help: there is no imaginary situation possible in which the sentences in (42) all of a sudden become possible. Now, the first part of this chapter introduced a theory of syntactic dependencies that reduced the two kinds of syntactic dependencies we had considered so far (agreement and case) to one principle: every uninterpretable feature requires the presence of an interpretable feature in the same phrase. [F] and [uF] need to be in either a specifier–head or head–complement relation. In the best of all possible worlds, we should try to apply this mechanism to the binding theory as well. There are actually good reasons for doing this.

A reflexive cannot be interpreted on its own. It needs an antecedent in the same clause to be properly interpreted, and this antecedent refers to the same individual or entity as the reflexive that it binds. The sentence in (52a) is ungrammatical because the reflexive has no antecedent. There is no way of interpreting this reflexive pronoun. The sentence in (52b), on the other hand, contains a non-reflexive pronoun. Although we do not know from this sentence alone who *her* refers to exactly, the sentence is still grammatical, showing that *her* can be interpreted on its own in a way that *herself* cannot.

(52)   a.   *I love herself.
       b.   I love her.

But if reflexives do not have an interpretation of their own, they do not have a 'real meaning' of their own. And if reflexives lack an inherent meaning, this can be captured by saying that they carry not interpretable, but uninterpretable features. If reflexives carry uninterpretable features, they need to enter a relation with a constituent that carries corresponding interpretable features. Otherwise, they cannot survive.

The semantics of reflexives thus suggests that they form a relation with their antecedents that is not fundamentally different from other syntactic dependencies, as the dependency of a reflexive and its antecedent can again be described in terms of interpretable and uninterpretable features. The antecedent of a reflexive carries interpretable φ-features, whereas the reflexive itself carries uninterpretable φ-features. This idea is supported by the fact that the antecedent of the reflexive needs to be dominated by the closest FinP that also dominates the reflexive. This means that the antecedent and the reflexive form a syntactic dependency within the same clause, just as we saw with case or subject–verb agreement.

Let us explore the consequences of this hypothesis and see what it gives us. Its immediate first gift, of course, is that binding can now be cast in the same terms as case and subject–verb agreement. This way we have reduced a third and important syntactic dependency to the mechanism that underlies agreement as well. A reflexive like *myself* has an uninterpretable 1st-person singular feature ([uφ: 1, SG]) and a reflexive like *themselves* has an uninterpretable 3rd-person plural feature ([uφ: 3, PL]). The hypothesis predicts that sentences containing these reflexives can be grammatical only if there are elements in the same clause that contain the matching interpretable features (*I* carrying [φ: 1, SG] or *they* carrying [φ: 3, PL]). And that is indeed what we see. It appears, therefore, that the feature mechanism that we have employed to capture case and agreement dependencies can also capture Principle A of the Binding theory. So at least the approach seems promising. However, there is one problem. The problem concerns the relation between interpretable and uninterpretable features that we proposed in (18) and that we repeat below.

(53) An uninterpretable feature [uF] requires the presence of a matching interpretable feature [F] within the same phrase, not in any lower phrase.

According to (53), both the interpretable and the uninterpretable element must be *in* the same phrase, which means that [F] and [uF] need to be either in a specifier–head or head–complement relation. This was needed to account for the fact that an object could never agree with a finite verb: **I loves the child* is bad. The constituent agreeing with the Fin head, we therefore assumed, needed to be in the specifier of FinP (spec-FinP). In the same vein, an accusative needs to be *in* the same phrase as a V or P, so that an accusative subject leads to ungrammaticality: **Him loves her*. Now, if we want to say that the mechanism in (53) is also behind Principle A of the Binding theory, our attempt fails miserably, because the antecedent and the reflexive can be further apart than a case assigner and a case-assigned constituent. After all, we are talking about a dependency between a subject and an object in the case of sentences like *Dan loves himself*. And the subject sits in spec-FinP, whereas the object is the complement of V. Should we therefore give up on the idea that all these syntactic dependencies (agreement, case and binding) are regulated by the same mechanism?

Well, not yet. Instead of modelling binding on case and subject–verb agreement, we could in fact try to do the opposite: model case and subject agreement on binding. How would that work?

In the previous subsection we derived a new syntactic relation, c-command. Could c-command replace the 'within the same phrase' requirement in (18)/(53)? Let's give it a try:

(54)   An uninterpretable feature [uF] must be c-commanded by a matching interpretable feature [F] in the same finite clause; otherwise the structure is ungrammatical.

In its current formulation, (54) is in full compliance with Principle A of the Binding theory: a reflexive in direct object position with an uninterpretable φ-feature is bound within the finite clause (FinP) it sits in by the c-commanding subject carrying an interpretable φ-feature. This should come as no surprise, since we used Principle A to drive the change in formulation. The real question is whether (54) can also deal with the other two syntactic dependencies: subject agreement and case. Let's look at a tree in (55) which contains all the relevant relations, and see how well the proposal in (54) fares.

(55)

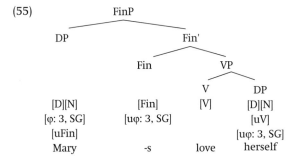

There are four syntactic dependencies at work in this tree: (i) a case relation between the subject *Mary* and Fin, (ii) an agreement relation between the subject *Mary* and Fin, (iii) a case relation between V and the object *herself*, and (iv) a binding relation between *Mary* and *herself*. These dependencies all involve feature matching, so let us restate the dependencies in those terms: (i) [Fin] on *-s* and [uFin] on *Mary*, (ii) [φ: 3, SG] on *Mary* and [uφ: 3, SG] on *-s*, (iii) [V] on *love* and [uV] on *herself*, and (iv) [φ: 3, SG] on *Mary* and [uφ: 3, SG] on *herself*.

The structural requirement on syntactic dependencies, inspired by reflexive binding, has now become the requirement that uninterpretable features be c-commanded by their interpretable counterparts in the same finite clause. Now, dependencies (ii) and (iii) adhere to (54) in a straightforward manner. With respect to (ii), note that [φ: 3, SG] on *Mary* c-commands [uφ: 3, SG] on *-s*. And with respect to (iii), note that [V] on *love* c-commands [uV] on *herself*. Also realise that it is clear why there can be no agreement relation between Fin and an object (which was the original reason to formulate the requirement that the matching interpretable and uninterpretable feature should be in the same phrase). The ungrammatical *I loves the child is correctly excluded by the new formulation in (54). To see this, look at the structure in (56) below:

(56) *

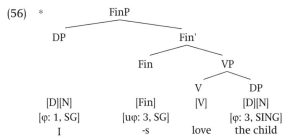

Note that [uφ: 3, SG] on -s is not c-commanded by [φ: 3, SG] on the child. Rather, it is the other way round: the uninterpretable φ-feature on -s c-commands the interpretable φ-feature on the object. This inverse c-command relation entails a violation of (54), so that (56) is correctly predicted to be ungrammatical.

We have almost succeeded in unifying our three syntactic dependencies (agreement, case and binding). Almost because, as you may have noticed, we have skipped over dependency (i) in the discussion of (55), the case relation between the nominative subject and Fin. As you can see in (55), [uFin] on Mary c-commands [Fin] on Fin, so we have an uninterpretable feature c-commanding an interpretable one rather than the other way round, as (54) requires. The fact that [Fin] on Fin does not c-command [uFin] on Mary is predicted to make this example ungrammatical, contrary to fact. So we're stuck here, and we have to make a choice.

One option is to give up (54) and go back to (53). This comes down to admitting that we have failed in our attempt to unify the three syntactic dependencies, and we conclude that binding simply works differently from case and agreement. That would of course be a pity, because the goal of a syntactician, as indeed of any scientist, is to formulate the simplest theory. And a theory with two types of syntactic dependencies is not as simple as a theory with just one.

The other option is to maintain (54) and continue our attempt at unification. This requires that we should look at the case relation between a nominative subject and the Fin head in more detail to see if we may have missed something. As you can already guess, we are indeed not going to give up (54) and will rather search for the missing ingredient. It turns out that there is one phenomenon, which we will introduce in the next chapter, that makes it possible to reconcile everything. So all we can do now is to ask you to be patient. Assume for the time being that (54) is correct and that the one problem we have encountered is going to be solved. In fact, the solution will be such that a number of syntactic phenomena that we have already seen will receive a more substantial analysis as well. In other words, it will definitely be worth the wait.

Earlier, we saw that Principle B could be left out of the theory because other, more general principles explained what Principle B was trying to explain. It turned out to be unnecessary. We are in almost the same position with Principle A, because its effects follow from the more general feature-checking mechanism in (54). So, once we can solve this problem with the nominative case features, we can establish that all syntactic dependencies, including Principle A, follow from the need of uninterpretable features to be c-commanded by matching interpretable features in the same clause.

Exercises

A10   Indicate all the binding relations in the sentences below. Use subscripts $(_{i, j, *i, *j})$ to indicate possible or impossible coreference relations.
   a.   John thinks about rewarding himself.
   b.   John thinks about rewarding him.
   c.   Everybody knows what he is up to.
   d.   I'll show everybody to themselves in the mirror.
   e.   She has always known that she was right.
   f.   Peter is anxious to learn whether Mary loves him.

A11   Draw the tree of the following sentence: *Mary's brother has always hated himself.* Also say for every word which other words it c-commands.

A12   Explain the ungrammaticality of the following sentences:
   a.   *Susi's old grandfather hurt herself.
   b.   *John bought a picture that looks like himself.
   c.   *We know myself.
   d.   *She sat next to herself.

B13   All reflexives in English are accusatives: *myself, himself, themselves*. Why are there no nominative reflexives in English (words that would sound like *Iself, heself*, or *theyselves*)?

C14   It seems that a reflexive object in a non-finite clause can be bound by an antecedent outside that clause, but is this really correct? Take the following sentence:

   John wanted to shave himself.

   Must it really be the case that *John* binds *himself* here? If your answer is 'no' (which it should be), what binds *himself*? And what are the consequences of this fact?

Summary   This chapter has shown that all syntactic dependencies reduce to one and the same agreement mechanism. This holds for plain agreement phenomena (such as subject–verb agreement), case phenomena (both nominative case and accusative case assignment), and even binding phenomena. For this reason we have argued that the ideal theory of syntax adheres to the following rule:

(57)   An uninterpretable feature [uF] must be c-commanded by a matching interpretable feature [F] in the same finite clause; otherwise the structure is ungrammatical.

Another way of formulating (57) is by saying that an uninterpretable feature must be checked off by a c-commanding matching interpretable feature in the same clause. Syntacticians therefore often speak about **feature checking**. The principle in (57) unifies all syntactic dependencies, but there is one question left. If nominative case reflects the presence of a feature [uFin], how can it meet the requirement in (57)? After all, the matching interpretable feature [Fin] resides in the head of FinP, where it is c-commanded by, and not c-commanding, the nominative (the [uFin] feature on the subject). It is as if we had to say that the nominative subject starts out below the FinP, for instance in the VP, and only later ends up in the FinP. The nominative case feature would then first be c-commanded by the feature [Fin] in the Fin head, and later the nominative subject moves to a position from where it would c-command the feature [uφ] in the Fin head. Of course, this sounds crazy. Unless the idea that words and constituents can move around in a sentence turns out not to be so crazy after all and is in fact something that can be independently verified. Excited about that idea? Turn the page …

Further Reading

The definition of agreement as a systematic covariance between a semantic or formal property of one element and a formal property of another goes back to Steele (1978) and the phenomenon is extensively discussed in Corbett (2006). The analysis of agreement in terms of uninterpretable features goes back to Chomsky (1995). Treating case features as uninterpretable features has been proposed by Pesetsky & Torrego (2004, 2007).

The Binding theory, with its Principles A and B, goes back to Chomsky (1981, 1986b). Other prominent approaches to binding are Reinhart & Reuland (1993). Reuland (2001, 2011), as well as Kratzer (2009) and Rooryck & vanden Wyngaerd (2011), treat binding in the same way as agreement. See also Büring (2005) for discussion and overview.

The notion of c-command was originally proposed in Reinhart (1976) and the idea that feature checking takes place under c-command was proposed in Chomsky (2000, 2001). That agreement is the core driver of syntactic operations stems back to Chomsky (1995) and is further elaborated in Chomsky (2000, 2001). There is some controversy about the direction of agreement, whether it operates in a downward fashion (Chomsky 2000, 2001, Bošković 2007, Preminger 2013) or in an upward fashion (Bjorkman 2011, Wurmbrand 2012, Zeijlstra 2012).

6 Movement and Remerge

CHAPTER OUTLINE

We saw in the previous chapter that every syntactic dependency reflects a relation between an interpretable and uninterpretable feature of the same type. In this way, we were able to generalise over case assignment, agreement relations and binding phenomena. However, we were not at that stage able to provide a uniform analysis for [F]–[uF] agreement, since nominative case agreement did not really fit in: the [uFin] feature on the subject in spec-FinP c-commands the [Fin] feature on the Fin head (and not the other way around), whereas other dependencies show the opposite c-command relationship. We have seen that an attempt to simplify the system usually leads to new insights. We will therefore hypothesise that we have not yet been able to account for agreement in a uniform way because we are still missing something. This chapter introduces this missing piece of the puzzle, which is a topic in its own right. It involves the recognition that constituents sometimes appear in positions in which we do not interpret them. They seem to move around. Syntactic movement, we will show, is not a new property of syntax. Rather, it follows immediately from the building procedure we already have: Merge. The existence of movement phenomena is therefore a prediction, and a confirmed one, made by the Merge hypothesis.

6.1 Insight: Constituents Can Move

So far, we have created structures by binary application of Merge. What does this mean? It means that you take two constituents and put them together. And if you want to build something bigger, you take a new constituent and add that to the structure you previously created. So if you have a sentence like *Adrian has always liked this yellow chair*, you take *yellow* and *chair* and merge them, and you merge the result *yellow chair* with *this*. Then you merge the DP *this yellow chair* with *liked*; this result you merge with *always*, you then take *has* and merge it with what you have. Finally, you merge that product with *Adrian* and you get *Adrian has always liked this yellow chair*. We have seen that some more detail can and should be added to this process (remember the distinction between heads and phrases), but this is basically what structure building by means of Merge comes down to. Subsequently, we spent three chapters making sure that this building process did not put together constituents randomly. θ-theory (a semantic constraint), Case theory, subject–verb agreement and binding (syntactic constraints) determine to a significant extent which of the outputs of syntax is actually grammatical. By invoking these constraints, we can account for the fact that not every product of Merge leads to good English.

There is one observation, however, that we have not yet discussed in detail, namely the fact that sometimes constituents do not appear in the location we expect them to be in. Take *yellow chair*, the direct object of the sentence above. This constituent receives a θ-role and accusative case from the verb *liked*. Now, we have seen previously that in order for a nominal constituent to receive accusative case it has to appear next to the verb. For this reason, the following sentence is ungrammatical:

(1)   *Adrian has liked always this yellow chair.

Now here is a puzzle: if *this yellow chair* has to be next to the verb, then why is the following sentence grammatical?

(2)   This yellow chair, Adrian has always liked.

In fact, constructions of this type have been discussed earlier, in chapter 2, where we used them to prove that a string like *this yellow chair* is a syntactic constituent: the fact that you can put *this yellow chair* at the beginning of the sentence shows us just that.

The puzzle introduced by (2) can quite easily be made more perplexing. Just take a look at the following example:

(3)   This yellow chair, I never said that John has always liked.

Here, the distance between *this yellow chair* and its case assigner *liked* is even greater than in (2), but it does not affect the grammaticality of the sentence. How is this possible if *this yellow chair* needs accusative case? Shall we increase the distance? Here we go:

(4)   This yellow chair, I don't think I ever said that John has always liked.

Now, these are probably not sentences you would use every day. You would be more likely to use examples in which *this yellow chair* appears at the end of the clause, exactly in the position where it receives accusative case, but the ones with *this yellow chair* at the beginning are not ungrammatical. It is simply a fact that you can utter such sentences. There is actually another construction in which putting the direct object at the beginning of the sentence is the normal pattern, whereas leaving it at the end is unusual. All you have to do is exchange *this* for *which*:

(5)   Which yellow chair has Adrian always liked?

This sentence is a question, a very natural sentence type. It asks of the hearer which yellow chair it is that Adrian has always liked. If the question pertains to information expressed by the direct object of the sentence, the direct object appears at the beginning of the sentence, with a question word (here, *which*).

Now, it is possible to leave *which yellow chair* at the end, as in (6).

(6)   Adrian has always liked which yellow chair?

You will immediately recognise this sentence as a special question, however, not a very natural one. It is not the usual way to ask an open question. The example in (6) either expresses that you did not hear which yellow chair the person talking to you said that Adrian has always liked, or it expresses surprise about the fact that Adrian, of all possible chairs, apparently prefers this yellow one. The only real way of asking a question would be as in (5), with *which yellow chair* at a distance from its accusative case assigner. Again, we can increase the distance more and more:

(7)   a.   Which yellow chair did you say that Adrian has always liked?
       b.   Which yellow chair do you think that I said that Adrian has always liked?

So here is the paradox: we have good reason to assume that accusative case dependencies operate strictly locally (i.e. with nothing intervening between the verb and the object), but in questions this local relation is not present. We could of course make an exception for questions, or we can think of a different solution. One such is already implicit in the way we talked about these types of constructions in chapter 2, and the solution is as simple as it is elegant: these sentence-initial constituents have undergone **movement**. In fact, that was already the word we used in chapter 2: if you can *move* a group of words to the beginning of the sentence, these words must form a constituent together. Now, let us take this notion very seriously and interpret movement quite literally. The direct object is first merged with the most deeply embedded verb *liked*, early on in the building process, and that is where it enters into an accusative case relation with the verb. Subsequently, as the last step in the building process, it is syntactically merged again (let's call it *re*-merged) into the sentence-initial position. Movement, then, is a process by which a particular constituent appears in two syntactic positions.

Schematically, it looks like (8) (with angle brackets placed around constituents that have moved):

(8)   This yellow chair, Adrian has always liked <this yellow chair>.

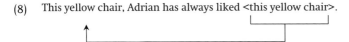

Movement may initially sound like a way out of our paradox and of rescuing our Case theory, since now we can maintain that case is assigned by *like* to its sister, as predicted. Note, however, that the issue at hand is much broader. There are various reasons for thinking that constituents indeed move around in these constructions. Take for instance θ-theory. Note that in every sentence in which *this yellow chair* or *which yellow chair* appears at the beginning of the sentence, we always interpret it as an argument of the most deeply embedded lexical verb. In (7b), for instance, *which yellow chair* is not an argument of *think* or *said*: it expresses the thing that Adrian likes; it is the 'likee'. We can even use the following paraphrase to bring this out:

(9)   Which yellow chair is such that you think that I said Adrian has
       always liked this yellow chair?

We must conclude, therefore, that in these constructions the constituent in sentence-first position is furthest away from the verb that it gets its θ-role from. In essence, then, these constructions are not only a puzzle for Case theory but are also striking from the point of view of θ-theory. Once we have movement, however, this fact can be naturally accounted for. *Which/this yellow chair* is merged with *liked* initially, receives the THEME role from it, and subsequently moves to sentence-initial position. Movement solves more puzzles than just the case paradox.

And if you're not yet convinced, here is a third fact that is completely puzzling unless you accept movement. As you recall from the previous chapter, reflexives like *herself* must be c-commanded by an antecedent in the same clause. Now, notice that in the following sentence *Mary* does not c-command *herself*.

(10)   Which pictures of herself do you think that Mary posted?

Nevertheless, (10) is fully grammatical. This fact follows without further ado if we assume what we were ready to assume anyway: *which pictures of herself* starts out in a position below *Mary*, so that *herself* can properly locate its antecedent, and is subsequently moved to sentence-initial position.

(11)

Which pictures of herself do you think that Mary posted <which pictures of herself>?

Let us now look in a bit more detail at what movement is in a technical sense. The operation that allows us to build structures is Merge. If we have constituents W and X and put them together, we get a mini-tree. In this tree, one of the two functions is the head, say W. As a consequence, the other constituent functions as a phrase, XP, within the WP headed by W, since it is the highest projection of X. This structure, obtained after one application of Merge, is illustrated in (12):

(12)   *Before Merge*   *After Merge*

From here, we can merge another constituent, say Y, and if it is just one word it can in principle become the head of the next projection, creating (13):

(13)

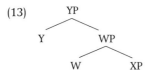

And so on. Now, here is the point. Suppose you want to create a bigger structure by extending the one in (13). You can do this by taking a new constituent, for instance, some Z, and merging it with YP. This would give you (14):

(14)

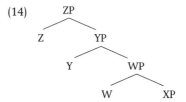

There is nothing about the Merge operation, though, that tells you that you should take a *new* constituent if you want to extend the structure. Merge merely states that you can put two constituents together and that one of them determines the properties of the whole new structure. Instead of merging something new, like Z, into the structure, nothing forbids you to merge YP with something that is already part of the structure, for instance XP. If we merge XP again now, we obtain the following structure:

(15)

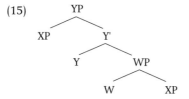

This tree expresses that the structure contains an XP but that this XP occurs in two places: it is first merged below WP, as a sister of W, and later becomes the specifier of Y. This is basically what movement is: **Remerge**. Technically, movement is nothing new. It is simply another outcome of a Merge operation, with the only difference being that the constituent you merge has already previously been merged. In the next section, we will show how this idea of Remerge can be applied to concrete constructions.

Exercises

A1   Indicate for each italicised constituent (i) which θ-role it receives from which syntactic head and (ii) what kind of case relation it is engaged in with which syntactic head:
   a.   *What* did Harold think that his grandmother had bought?
   b.   *Which known criminal* did the police conclude took my wallet?
   c.   *Whom* did Leon call while he was watching TV?
   d.   *What* did nobody expect that he would give to his students?
   e.   *Which miracle* do you think Aysa still believes in?
   f.   *Which portrait* Rembrandt painted himself was hard to determine.
   g.   *What on earth* are you talking about?
   h.   *Where* did Leah believe that he left his keys?

A2   Turn the following sentences into questions by replacing the italicised words with **Wh-question** words and fronting them. If this turns out to be impossible, try to explain why. You do not have to draw tree structures.
   a.   Jesse was waiting for *Celine* in vain.
   b.   I thought you would never believe *the things that I said to you.*
   c.   She will say that I have always despised *my uncle's* nephew.
   d.   Will we meet *the Johnsons today*?
   e.   Will we meet the Johnsons *in Rome*?

6.2 Implementation: Movement as Remerge

That constituents exhibit movement effects, i.e. that they can be merged more than once in the structure, turns out to be a tremendous insight. A lot of phenomena will start to make a lot more sense now that we have realised that a constituent is not always **base-generated** in the position that we see it in but has sometimes been moved there, away from its base position. To take a straightforward example, consider again the sentence in (5), repeated below.

(16)   Which yellow chair <u>has</u> Adrian always liked?

Here we see that the auxiliary *has* precedes the subject. Why should this be? We saw in section 4.2.2 that *has* is base-generated as the head of FinP. Since the subject is the specifier of FinP, it always sits in a higher position than the head of FinP. For this reason, we expect the subject to precede *has*. This generally holds true, but not for questions. How, then, do we account for the fact that *has* precedes the subject in (5) and (16)? By syntactic movement (or, to be more precise, Remerge). And this is just one instance of movement. We will now take a look at a number of them, firstly at how Remerge is specifically implemented in questions (6.2.1); then we will look at some other examples of movement (6.2.2).

6.2.1 *Wh*-Movement and Auxiliary Movement

Take as a starting point the sentence in (5), repeated here as (17):

(17)   Which yellow chair has Adrian always liked?

We observed in the previous section (6.1) that we can analyse the word order in this sentence as a consequence of two movements: *which yellow chair* has moved from the end to the beginning of the sentence, and the auxiliary *has* has moved from a position following the subject to one preceding the subject. This is all very well, but we would love to draw the tree structure. And nothing we have said so far can accommodate these word orders. We have analysed clauses as FinPs, with the highest constituent being the subject. In (17), however, we see two constituents preceding the subject, and these must – in hierarchical tree-speak – be higher than FinP. So how do we proceed from here? To accommodate the constituents that move in a question, let us first reconsider how we accommodated constituents without movement. Let us return to FinP.

FinP results from (i) the presence of some head with the feature Fin that merges with the VP, and (ii) the subsequent merger of Fin' with the subject DP, creating spec-FinP. What we end up with is a FinP that contains a head (*has*), and two other constituents that are phrasal, namely its complement, VP (*always liked this yellow chair*), and its specifier, the DP (*Adrian*):

(18)

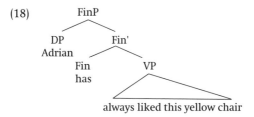

Now, what is the piece of structure that we need above FinP? The first step towards a concrete analysis is the realisation that, in abstract, the pattern that we see strikes us as completely familiar. The closest position to the subject in (17) is taken by the auxiliary *has*, and *has* is one word. In fact, it has to be a position that can host at most one word, because you can easily show that in questions only one auxiliary can precede the subject that belongs to the same clause (in these examples *has, will* and *must*, respectively):

(19)   a.   Which yellow chair has John been trying to find?
         a'. *Which yellow chair has been John trying to find?
         b.   Which yellow chair will John be trying to find?
         b'. *Which yellow chair will be John trying to find?
         c.   Which yellow chair must John have tried to find?
         c'   *Which yellow chair must have John tried to find?

In other words, the first structural position preceding the subject is to be identified as a head position, and can be filled by one word at most. This is not the case for the second position preceding the subject; *which yellow chair* is obviously a phrase. This second position to the left of the subject (and therefore the first position to the left of the auxiliary) must be phrasal and therefore may consist of more than one word. Taking these two observations together, we conclude that there must be structure above FinP, and this structure again offers room for a head and a specifier. What this boils down to, then, is that in questions there is exactly one additional functional projection above FinP (let's call it XP for now, so as to show that we are not yet sure about the nature of this projection) to which both *has* and *which yellow chair* move. We can schematise this as in (20):

(20)

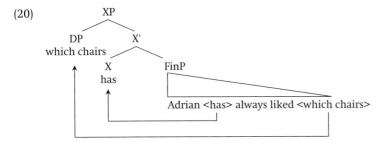

The hallmark of this analysis is that it uses the same kind of structural configuration that we have already seen many times before. The proposal we put forward in (20), then, does not introduce anything new. It simply follows from the building procedures we adopted from the start: it is a result of previous analytical steps and therefore fits into the expected pattern. The fact that in a question the *Wh*-phrase has to precede the auxiliary (and not the other way round) and the fact that in non-questions the subject has to precede the auxiliary (and not the other way round) are essentially one and the same fact. They follow from the way the internal structure of XP and FinP is organised. And this organisation, in turn, follows from Merge: a phrase minimally contains a head but can also contain other constituents and these other constituents are phrasal and can therefore consist of more than one word. This is the pattern we see for FinP and XP.

Now that we have schematically analysed the structure of an English *Wh*-question, we have to fill in the details. There are two issues to be addressed. One is about the nature of XP. What kind of a projection is it? And, second, we need to know why auxiliaries and *Wh*-phrases move in English. Obviously, it would be advantageous if we could relate the latter question to the former. Let us attempt a hypothesis, and see what it gives us: the nature of the projection determines the reason for the remerger of particular constituents.

Let us first determine the nature of XP and remind ourselves of the fact that we already have seen an instance in which a clause consists of more than just a FinP. Take a look at (21) and focus on the embedded clause:

(21)   I don't think <u>that Adrian has always liked yellow chairs</u>.

An embedded finite clause in English is introduced by a complementiser (here *that*, but often unexpressed), and this complementiser marks the left-hand side of the clause that it is a part of. It sits in a head position that has to be structurally higher than FinP, because the complementiser precedes the subject of the embedded clause. In chapter 4, we analysed this projection simply as a CP, a complementiser phrase, of which the head, C, merges with FinP. This CP can subsequently be merged with a verb and function as the argument of this verb.

(22)

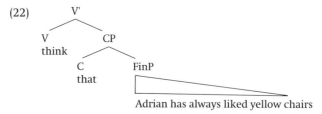

The complementiser *that* has a feature, [C], and this feature projects into a CP, in the same way that the features [Fin] and [D] can project. This is, however, not the only feature that complementiser *that* is endowed with. This becomes obvious when we contrast *that* with another complementiser, namely *if*, as in (23):

(23)   I asked <u>if Adrian had always liked yellow chairs</u>.

Both *that* and *if* are complementisers, but they differ from each other in the sense that *if* introduces an embedded question and *that* introduces an embedded declarative (and not a question). This means that alongside a feature [C] the complementiser *if* must have an additional subfeature [C: Question], whereas *that* has the subfeature [C: Declarative]. The similarity between *that* and *if* is that both introduce embedded clauses and have the feature [C]; they only differ in the subfeatures of [C]. The distinction therefore is that *if* introduces embedded questions, whereas *that* introduces embedded non-questions.

We can in fact unify these two complementiser functions by saying that what they do is introduce special clause types. *If* introduces an embedded question and *that* introduces an embedded declarative. The term Complementiser Phrase, the original abbreviation for CP, is therefore actually a misnomer: it is a Clause-type Phrase, whose features can mark a clause for being embedded (which makes these heads complementisers) and for being questions or declaratives. But if there can be a functional head in an embedded clause responsible for introducing different clause types like questions, then we expect the existence of clause-typing heads in non-embedded clauses as well. This in fact would hand us the content for the XP that we postulated in (20). Put differently, the X heading the XP in (20) can now be identified as exactly that type of element: it introduces a question that is not an embedded question. The clause-type feature C has two subfeatures here: [C: Non-embedded, Question].

(24)

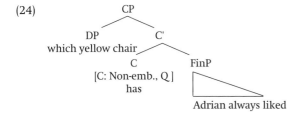

The C head in which *has* resides is the element that turns the sentence into a question. This might look a little counter-intuitive, as you would be inclined to think it is the presence of the specifier (namely *which yellow chair*) rather than the head of the CP that turns the sentence into a question. However, it is not the case that every question contains a *Wh*-phrase. There are also yes/no questions like (25):

(25)   Has Adrian always liked this yellow chair?

This sentence does not contain a question word. Yet, it is a question. This is good evidence for the hypothesis that the [Question] subfeature must be present on the C head.

Let us be very precise about what we mean with this last statement. The constituent sitting in the C position in (24) is *has*. We cannot say, however, that the word *has* itself contains the feature [C: Non-embedded, Question]. If that were the case, we would incorrectly predict that every sentence with the word *has* in it is a question, which is clearly not the case. What we need to do, then, is reconcile the fact that the sentence is turned into a question by a subfeature of C in the head of the CP with the fact that the element in the head position of the CP, namely *has*, lacks a C feature itself. We have good reason to believe that there is a head introducing the [C: Question] feature but there is no visible constituent that actually carries this feature. We will therefore do what we have done before: if there is syntactic evidence for a constituent but we don't see it, we assume that this constituent is syntactically present but not visible or, better, unexpressed. In the present case, this constituent is the head of the CP. Before movement of the auxiliary, the structure of a main-clause question must be as in (26), with an unexpressed clause-typing C head with two subfeatures: [C: Non-embedded, Question]. It is this head that projects the CP.

(26)

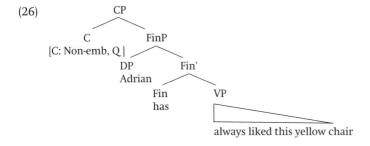

This feature [C: Non-embedded, Question] is responsible for the fact that we interpret (25) as a question. But if you were to utter (26), what you get is (27) and not (25):

(27)   Adrian has always liked this yellow chair.

As you can see, the word order in (27) is identical to the word order of a declarative. As a consequence, there is no way of telling that we are underlyingly dealing with a CP, and not just with a FinP. In order to distinguish a yes/no question from a declarative non-question, something must indicate the underlying presence of the C head. The solution that English employs is to make the C position visible by moving the auxiliary. The way to implement this is to say that the head of the CP is an unexpressed clause-typing head to which the auxiliary attaches. Then we can explain why a moved auxiliary gives rise to a question without having to say that the auxiliary itself is the question marker of the sentence. Moving the auxiliary into the C head is just the way of making the C head visible.

What we have done so far is explain the nature of the projection dominating FinP as a functional projection that is used for clause-typing: it is a CP. The fact that a fronted auxiliary leads to a yes/no question without this auxiliary carrying any question-related feature itself was taken to reveal the existence of an abstract C head to which the auxiliary moves. The upside of assuming the existence of such an invisible element that carries a C feature with the relevant subfeatures ([C: Non-embedded, Question]) is that it gets us two facts: (i) we understand what contributes the relevant features to the structure such that we get the correct interpretation, namely that of a (non-embedded) question; and (ii) we understand why an auxiliary has to move there, namely, to make the presence of this position visible. The downside of assuming something abstract is of course that you have to assume something that you cannot directly see. The more reasons you have for thinking that this abstract C head indeed exists, the better it is of course. With this in mind, let us demonstrate that the analysis makes an interesting prediction, to which we now turn.

If there is a covert element that can project a CP, we expect this element to be in complementary distribution with other elements that can also project a CP. Remember that we explained the existence of Fin in exactly these terms: different elements of category Fin can be merged with VP to project FinP (such as modal auxiliaries, finite forms of auxiliaries *to be* and *to have*, and the *to* infinitive marker), but only one of these elements can be used in one particular clause. Similar reasoning was used to motivate the D position: no more than one D element can be the head of a DP. Now, in an embedded clause, CP has to be introduced by a complementiser like *that* or *if*, because these heads mark the clause as being embedded. This means that the unexpressed element that we use in main-clause yes/no questions, namely [C: Non-embedded, Question], cannot be used in embedded clauses, simply because *if* is used instead. Since unexpressed C carries the subfeatures [C: Non-embedded, Question], it is useless in embedded clauses because it has the wrong subfeature, namely [C: Non-embedded, Question], not [C: Embedded, Question]. *If* carries [C: Embedded, Question] and is therefore used in embedded questions instead. Now here is the point: this predicts that auxiliary movement across the subject can never take place in embedded clauses. Why not? Well, the element triggering the auxiliary to move is the abstract C, and this head simply cannot appear in embedded questions, only in non-embedded questions. So we expect that subject–auxiliary inversion is possible in main clauses (in fact, it is obligatory), but impossible in embedded clauses. The theory predicts that auxiliaries always follow the subject in embedded clauses, just like lexical verbs. And this is indeed what happens in (Standard) English. Although the auxiliary must move across the subject in main-clause yes/no questions (25), it cannot move across the subject in embedded questions, as shown below:

(28) a. *I wonder has Adrian always liked this yellow chair?
      b. *I wonder which yellow chair has Adrian always liked?

In short, the complementary distribution of *if* (which is [C: Embedded, Question]) and the hypothesised null element [C: Non-embedded, Question] correctly predicts some very basic word-order facts of English embedded clauses. This means that we have been able to provide independent evidence for the existence of the unexpressed C element. In other words, it now does more than what it was initially invented for, thereby strengthening the proposed analysis.

Now, the final question to be addressed here is where the *Wh*-phrase moves to. The answer to this question, however, is very straightforward. The *Wh*-phrase *which yellow chair* is remerged and becomes the specifier of CP. This leads to the following representation for (17). Again, we put angle brackets around the base positions of Fin (*has*) and DP (*which yellow chair*) to indicate that these are positions that these constituents have moved out of.

(29)

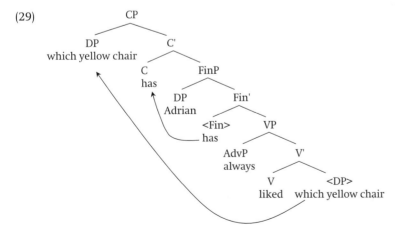

This is indeed the structure of an English *Wh*-question. It involves two syntactic Remerge operations, which means that two constituents, *has*

and *which yellow chairs*, have been merged twice in the structure. *Has* has been base-generated as the head of FinP and *which yellow chairs* inside the VP. Both end up in a functional projection CP directly above FinP. The idea that constituents can be merged more than once, which is what constitutes movement, is often indicated in the literature by arrows, as in (29).

6.2.2 Another Example of Movement: Raising

Let us now go back to the two ostensibly similar sentences that we discussed in chapter 3, repeated here in (30).

(30)   a.   John seems to win the race.
       b.   John hopes to win the race.

What we saw for these examples was that in (30a) *John* does not receive a θ-role from the verb *seem*. After all, *seem* allows a dummy, expletive element as its subject, showing us that it does not assign a θ-role to its subject (as shown in (31a)). In (30b), on the other hand, *John* does receive an AGENT role from the verb *hope*. That *hope*, in contrast to *seem*, does assign a θ-role to its subject explains why it cannot take an expletive subject (31b):

(31)   a.   It seems that John wins the race.
       b.   *It hopes that John wins the race.

Since *John* needs to receive a θ-role in (30a), we concluded that it must receive an AGENT role from the embedded verb *win*. But if *hopes* does assign a θ-role to *John*, the verb in the embedded clause, *win*, must assign its AGENT role to a different argument. Remember that an argument cannot carry more than one θ-role. We took this to mean that the *hope* construction includes an unexpressed pronoun, PRO, in the embedded infinitival clause. Schematically, this contrast looks as follows.

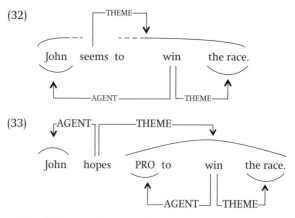

(32)

(33)

The difference between *hope* and *seem*, in a nutshell, is that only *hope* assigns an AGENT role, and the ungrammaticality of (31b) demonstrates this.

There is something that feels not quite right about the analysis of the *seem* construction, though, and that we (quite deliberately, of course) glossed over in chapter 3. If you compare (30a) with (31a), there is another noticeable difference. *Seem* is a verb that assigns only a THEME role. What is the constituent that receives this θ-role? For (31a), this is straightforward: the embedded clause *that John wins the race*. For (30a), we must say that this θ-role goes to *John … to win the race*, where part of the argument follows the verb *seems*, but part of it (namely *John*) precedes the verb. After all, what seems to be at issue is John winning the race. In essence, then, *seems* assigns its one θ-role to a constituent that is broken up. Now, this is perhaps not problematic, but the fact that the *seem* construction is the only construction in which we see this happening makes it a bit fishy.

But there is more fishiness to come. Let us consider the trees of these two constructions. We know that the *to* infinitive marker resides in Fin, and we know that PRO is an empty subject in spec-FinP, present in a *hope* construction but not in a *seem* construction. This leads to the following trees.

(34)

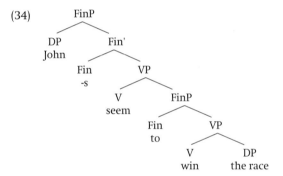

(35)

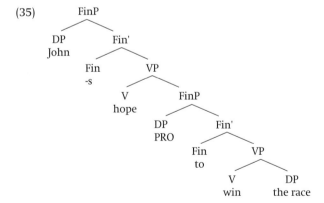

If we make this direct comparison, we see that in the *hope* construction both subjects, *John* and PRO, receive their θ-role in the FinP that directly dominates them: John receives the AGENT role from *hope* and PRO receives the AGENT role from *win*. In the *seem* construction, on the other hand, the position in which *John* receives the AGENT role in

(34) is far removed from the verb that assigns this θ-role (namely, *win*). In fact, it receives the AGENT role from a verb in a different, embedded clause. Now, if you think about it, this is quite strange. If it were possible to assign a θ-role to an argument in a different clause, we would expect sentences to be more ambiguous than they actually are. A sentence like (36) could have an interpretation in which *Mary* is the kisser and *John* the sayer. After all, nothing would forbid θ-role assigners assigning a θ-role outside the clause they appear in:

(36)   Mary said that John kissed Bill.

Clearly, (36) cannot have this meaning. The easiest way to rule this out is by assuming that a verb can only assign θ-roles to constituents within the same clause. That should not surprise us in the least, since so far all dependencies, both syntactic and semantic, have been established clause-internally (where a clause is everything that is contained by a FinP). So let us take this to be a principle of θ-role assignment.

(37)   All θ-roles must be assigned clause-internally.

Note that we already assumed constraint (37) implicitly when we talked about movement of *which yellow chair* from the embedded object position to the front of the sentence. Those too were examples in which (37) seemed to have been violated, but that was before we had the idea that constituents can be remerged.

Obviously, something like (37) has consequences for our analysis of the *seem* construction too, but the solution can now be exactly the same. Much like *which yellow chair* in the previous section, *John* in the *seem* construction is not in the position in which we interpret it. We interpret *John* as part of the embedded clause, and the example in (31a) clearly shows this. We now know what is going on in (30): *John* has been remerged. It is merged in the embedded clause, where it receives the AGENT role from *win*, but it is subsequently remerged in the position we see it in. The structure in (34) should therefore be replaced by the one in (38):

(38)

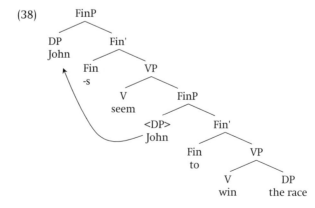

This analysis solves the two problems we raised at the outset. First of all, *John* now sits in the same clause as its θ-assigner, namely the embedded FinP. And second, we can now say that *seem* assigns its THEME role to the FinP it is merged with (*John to win the race*), and *John* is of course included in that constituent, just as it is in example (31a). The fact that *John* shows up in a position preceding *seems* is the result of subsequent remerger of *John* higher in the structure. This remerger, however, does not undo the clause-bound nature of θ-role assignment required by (37). It only makes it harder to see it.

To wrap up, both the *seem* and the *hope* construction in (30) have an embedded infinitival clause but the nature of the embedded subject is different. The *seem* construction has a subject that is later remerged in the main clause. This means that *John* at the beginning is a subject that has undergone movement, or raising, from the embedded clause. For this reason, the *seem* construction is known as the **subject-raising construction**. The *hope* construction, on the other hand, has an empty subject in the infinitival clause, and the interpretation of this empty subject is determined, or 'controlled', by an argument in the finite clause (here, PRO is controlled by the main clause subject *John*). For this reason, the *hope* construction is generally known as a **control construction**. Note, finally, that both the non-finite clause in the subject-raising construction and the non-finite clause in the control construction have a subject. This means that every embedded clause, whether finite or non-finite, has a subject. In embedded finite clauses this is obvious (an embedded clause like ... *that/if Suzanne repaired the car* has a clear subject: *Suzanne*); in embedded non-finite clauses where you don't see the subject, it is either PRO, or a subject like *John* that has moved out of the embedded clause into a higher clause.

In the next section, we will present an additional argument for subject raising: it solves the problem that formed the cliff-hanger of chapter 5. Remember that we almost unified all syntactic dependencies, but not quite? We will now take the last step. In addition, we will show that the constraint on θ-role assignment formulated in (37) is not strict enough and that the domain in which θ-role assignment takes place is even smaller than FinP.

Exercises

A3   Draw the tree structures for the following examples and clearly indicate the movements.
    a.   Would Karl know the answer to this question?
    b.   Are you talking to me?
    c.   Whom did you meet?
    d.   In whose apartment do you live?
    e.   Which bad movie did you watch quite often?
    f.   Which member of the family did they not confide in?

B4   Okay, let's take this up a notch. Do the same for the examples below. Note that each sentence now contains two lexical main verbs. This means that (i) you minimally need two FinPs, one embedded in the other, and (ii) that whenever a FinP has no overt subject, you must try to establish whether the subject has moved into the higher clause (raising) or is PRO (control). This involves finding out whether the main clause verb is a verb that assigns a θ-role to its subject. If so, it is a control verb. If not, it is a raising verb.
  a.   Did Esther's boyfriend appear to care for her?
  b.   Whom did he happen to look after?
  c.   In which country have you always wanted to live?
  d.   Which colour do you expect to hate?

C5   We have seen two diagnostics that inform us about the position that a verbal head sits in. If it follows negation, it sits in the V position (as do lexical verbs). If it precedes negation, it minimally sits in the Fin position (as do modal auxiliaries and finite forms of *be, have* and dummy *do*). If it also precedes the subject, it means it has moved all the way up to C. Consider the following data (from Shakespeare's *Hamlet*) from Early Modern English and try to characterise in what way this grammar differed from the grammar of Modern English.
  (i)   Looks it not like the king?
  (ii)   In what particular thought to work I know not …
  (iii) Did you not speak to it?
  (iv)   How comes it? Do they grow rusty?
  (v)   Man delights not me.
  (vi)   What say you?
  (vii) For nature, crescent, does not grow alone …
  (viii) Then saw you not his face?
  (ix)   And can you, by no drift of circumstance, get from him why he puts on this confusion …
  (x)   We think not so, my lord.
  (xi)   … but wherefore I know not.
  (xii) … this brain of mine hunts not the trail of policy …

6.3 Consequences: The VP-Internal Subject Hypothesis

Let's take stock. So far we have seen that elements in a sentence can be remerged, i.e. they can move from one position in the structure to another. Now, you may recall from the end of chapter 5 (see 5.2.3) that we had one problem left in our attempt to unify all syntactic dependencies. The problem was as follows. If we adopt the condition on uninterpretable features requiring that all uninterpretable features must be c-commanded by their matching interpretable counterparts for feature checking to take place, nominative case agreement could not be accounted for. Let us first repeat the exact condition on uninterpretable features in (39) and see it at work in example (40), which contains all syntactic dependencies that we have discussed (subject–verb agreement, nominative case agreement, accusative case agreement and binding (i.e. agreement between a reflexive and an antecedent)).

(39)   An uninterpretable feature [uF] must be c-commanded by a matching interpretable feature [F] in the same clause; otherwise the sentence is ungrammatical.

(40)   Mary loves herself.

The structure for (40) looks as follows:

(41)

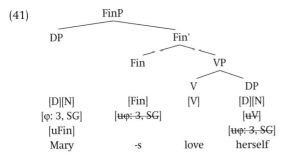

All uninterpretable features in (41) that fulfil the requirement in (40) have been marked by means of strikethrough, a convention we will use from now on. Those features have been checked. The only unchecked feature in (41) is [uFin] on *Mary*, as this feature is not c-commanded by any [Fin] feature. It is the other way round: [uFin] c-commands [Fin], in violation of (39).

We saw in the previous section (6.2.2) that a subject in FinP is not always base-generated in that position but can be remerged there. In a subject-raising construction, the main clause subject gets its θ-role in the embedded infinitival clause before it is remerged as the subject in the main clause. Now, if FinP is a position in which subjects can be remerged, rather than merged for the first time (that is, base-generated), there is an imminent solution to our problem. We could hypothesise that the structure for (40) is actually as in (42), where the subject starts out as the specifier of VP and subsequently moves to spec-FinP.

(42)

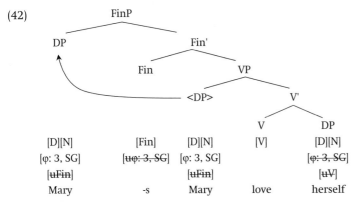

In this structure, *Mary* occurs in two positions, and one of these positions is inside the VP. The [Fin] feature on Fin now c-commands the [uFin] feature on *Mary* in VP, perfectly in line with (39). Therefore, feature checking can proceed once Fin is merged with VP. What happens after this merger of Fin is that *Mary* is remerged into the structure again, as part of the FinP, where it checks the [uφ: 3, SG] feature on Fin. Since *Mary* now carries an already checked [uFin] feature, this remerger is completely innocent. Consequently, every instance of feature checking can take place in accordance with our condition on syntactic dependencies. And this, in turn, means that these dependencies have a uniform character: *whatever the nature of the dependency, the interpretable feature always c-commands its uninterpretable counterpart.* Problem solved.

Now, before you start dancing on the table to celebrate this achievement, you should remain level-headed for a little bit longer. What we have shown so far is that you *can* unify all syntactic dependencies, and the way to do this is by assuming that nominative subjects start out in a position lower in the tree than where they ultimately end up. But we have not yet shown that you *must* assume that the nominative subject starts out in this lower position. It is conceptually attractive to do this, as it allows a unification of the format in which the syntax encodes dependencies, but you need additional arguments in favour of this hypothesis, which is known as the **VP-Internal Subject Hypothesis (VISH)**, to show that it makes sense to do this, independently from the fact that it solves our problem. To this end, we will now show that at least four arguments, three empirical and one theoretical, can be provided to lend further support to VISH.

The first argument pertains to *there* constructions. In English (and in many other languages), indefinite subjects, such as *a man*, can generally be combined with a so-called expletive subject *there*:

(43)   There is a man walking in the street.

The *there* construction is used when we want to ensure that the subject does not receive a specific interpretation. The example in (44) without *there* is still grammatical, but has a different meaning. The most natural meaning of (44) is that there is a specific man on the street, for instance John, whereas (43) lacks this reading.

(44)   A man is walking in the street.

The question that is relevant for us syntacticians is, what is the syntax of constructions such as that in (43)? In a way, there are two subjects present: *there* is an expletive subject sitting in the classical subject position (inside FinP) and a real subject appears lower in the structure. Since the real subject is not in the usual subject position, syntacticians refer to this as the **associated subject**, or **logical subject**. Now, the question is what position this associated subject occupies in the syntactic structure. For the view that says that all subjects are base-generated in FinP, these *there* constructions come as a bit of a surprise. But VISH has an elegant way of dealing with them. Under that hypothesis, the associated subject simply occupies the position in which it is base-generated, namely spec-VP:

(45)

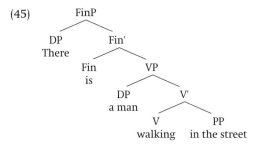

Why does *a man* not undergo raising to FinP, as in (42)? Well, because that position is already taken by *there*. Expletive constructions, then, provide straightforward evidence for VISH because we can see a subject surface in exactly that position in which VISH says it is base-generated in the first place.

A second piece of evidence comes from so-called **floating quantifiers**. Take a look at the following sentences:

(46) a. All the teachers are dancing on the table.
　　　b. The teachers are all dancing on the table.
　　　c. *The teachers are dancing all on the table.

(47) a. Both Harold and Maude are sitting in the garden.
　　　b. Harold and Maude are both sitting in the garden.
　　　c. *Harold and Maude are sitting both in the garden.

The (a) and (b) sentences in (46)–(47) are grammatical and basically have the same meaning, whereas the (c) examples are ungrammatical. What does this tell us? It tells us that *all* and *both* are not regular adverbs. If they were, they should have a distribution similar to for instance *wildly*. But they don't. The pattern in (48) is quite different:

(48) a. ?Wildly the teachers are dancing on the table.
　　　b. The teachers are wildly dancing on the table.
　　　c. The teachers are dancing wildly on the table.

Wildly is fine in (48c), in a position where *all* and *both* are bad, as shown in (46c) and (47c). In addition, *all* and *both* are perfectly fine as part of the subject, whereas *wildly* in (48a) is at best a fronted adverb, and definitely not part of the subject. The following examples confirm this:

(49) a. Who was dancing on the table? All the teachers.
　　　b. Who was sitting in the garden? Both Harold and Maude.
　　　c. Who was dancing on the table? *Wildly the teachers.

So what are *all* and *both*, then? Since they are modifiers of the subject, they should be part it. But how do they then end up more to the right, following the auxiliary, as in (46b) and (47b)? Again, for the view that subjects start out in FinP this is very hard to explain. But under VISH, we can make sense of the data in the following way. The entire subjects *all the teachers/both Harold and Maude* start out in VP:

(50) a. [_VP all the teachers dancing]
      b. [_VP both Harold and Maude sitting]

Then Fin is merged:

(51) a. [_Fin' are [_VP all the teachers dancing]]
      b   [_Fin' are [_VP both Harold and Maude sitting]]

At this point, two options arise: either the entire subject moves out of the VP and into spec-FinP, or only the part without *all*/*both*, as shown below (where the angle brackets again show the base-generated position of the moved elements):

(52) a. [_FinP all the teachers [_Fin' are [_VP <all the teachers> dancing]]]
      b. [_FinP the teachers [_Fin' are [_VP all <the teachers> dancing]]]

(53) a. [_FinP both Harold and Maude [_Fin' are [_VP <both Harold and Maude> sitting]]]
      b. [_FinP Harold and Maude [_Fin' are [_VP both <Harold and Maude> sitting]]]

In the (b) examples, then, these quantifiers are left behind by the moving subject: hence the name floating quantifiers. Structurally, this can be analysed as follows: *all* and *both* are quantifiers heading a projection at the top of DP. Note that we cannot treat *all* and *both* as D heads because they can co-occur with *the* (as in *both the boys* and *all the boys*). For this reason, syntacticians have assumed that they head another projection, dubbed QP (Quantifier Phrase), that dominates DP. Given such an analysis, the choice, then, is between moving the entire QP and moving only the DP.

(54) a.   b.

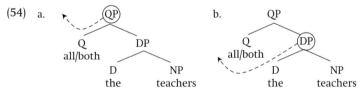

This captures all the facts. The examples in (46c) and (47c) are ungrammatical because *all* and *both* sit in a position to the right of the verb, which is not a position for subjects. And if subjects cannot sit there, *all* and *both* cannot either, because they are part of the subject.

If elements like *all* and *both* can be left behind by a moving subject, we can use floating quantifiers to check our earlier claims regarding the subject-raising construction. If in *seem* constructions subjects start out in the embedded clause and are remerged in the higher clause, a floating quantifier should be possible in any earlier position of the moved subject, and nowhere else. This is indeed the case, as shown below (where curly brackets denote possible positions for the floating quantifier).

(55) a. [_FinP {All} the teachers [_VP {all} seem [_FinP {all} to [_VP {all} dance {*all} on the table]]]]
      b. [_FinP {Both} Harold and Maude [_VP {both} seem [_FinP {both} to [_VP {both} sit {*both} in the garden]]]]

As the examples in (55) show, floating quantifiers only show up in subject positions, i.e. spec-VP and spec-FinP. They can appear between the subject and the raising verb *seem* (the subject position in the main clause VP), between the raising verb *seem* and *to* (the subject position in the embedded FinP, and between *to* and the infinitival verb (the subject position in the embedded VP). This last option is often discouraged by prescriptive grammars that suggest it is better to keep *to* and the infinitive together, but many speakers accept such 'split infinitives', meaning that the grammar we are building must allow it. And it does, because *all* occupies a regular subject position. They cannot, however, show up to the right of the infinitival verb because there is no subject position there. Therefore, floating quantifiers not only provide evidence for VISH but also provide extra evidence for the analysis of raising constructions.

A third argument for the hypothesis that a subject starts out in the VP comes from idioms. Take a look at the following examples:

(56) a. John/the baker/the queen/three of his uncles [kicked the bucket]
      b. John/the baker/the queen/three of his uncles [hit the nail on the head]
      c. John/the baker/the queen/three of his uncles [had cold feet]

The fragment in square brackets has a literal and an idiomatic meaning. Example (56a), for instance, can literally mean that the subject kicked a bucket but can also mean that the subject died. The idiomatic meaning of (56b) is 'to identify something exactly', and that of (56c) is 'to lack the courage to do or finish something'. Here, we are interested in these idiomatic meanings. What you can observe is that the verb and the object together can have a meaning that does not directly follow from the meaning of its parts. Note that this idiomatic meaning is fixed: if you replace *the bucket* by *the broom* in (56a), for instance, the sentence is no longer about dying. But note that the subject is not fixed: [*kick the bucket*] can be combined with any subject. These idioms can therefore be characterised as follows:

(57) DP + [$_{VP}$ kicked the bucket] → 'DP died'

An interesting observation is that it is very hard to find idioms in English in which the subject and the verb together create an idiomatic meaning and the object is variable. Let us therefore make one up. Imagine that 'The shadow hit X' is an idiom that means 'X died' ('The shadow hit Bill' would then mean 'Bill died'). Then we would have an idiom with the following format:

(58) [The shadow hit] DP. → 'DP died.'

What appears to be the case is that idioms with this format do not really exist, and the question is why. One obvious difference is that the verb and object together form a constituent, whereas the subject and the verb do not. After all, any phrase that will include both the subject and the verb, such as FinP, will automatically include the object. By way of hypothesis, we can formulate the following generalisation for idioms:

(59)　THE IDIOM GENERALISATION
　　　　Only fixed constituents can receive an idiomatic interpretation.

VP idioms with the format of (57) are in line with (59), whereas the format in (58) is ruled out. Once the subject is fixed, the object has to be fixed too, according to (59). Note that indeed such idioms exist. Consider the following examples:

(60)　a.　The shit hit the fan. (= 'Trouble started.')
　　　　b.　All hell broke loose. (= 'Everything went wrong.')

In these examples, the idiomatic meaning comes about by combining exactly these subjects, exactly these verbs and exactly these objects. Since all the constituents are fixed, we can call these FinP idioms, to distinguish them from VP idioms. But now a problem arises. These FinP idioms can contain a variable element in the Fin position, illustrated here for the idioms in (60):

(61)　a.　The shit *has* hit the fan.
　　　　b.　The shit *will* hit the fan.
　　　　c.　The shit *must* hit the fan.

(62)　a.　All hell *has* broken loose.
　　　　b.　All hell *will* break loose.
　　　　c.　All hell *must* break loose.

All of these examples are grammatical, although these FinP idioms have different constituents realising the Fin head (*has, will* and *must*, respectively). Therefore, they violate (59). And this, in turn, makes it hard to see why the examples in (61)–(62) are productive, in contrast to the idiom format in (58). To put it differently, if Fin can be flexible, why can't the subject be as well?

Here, the VP-internal subject hypothesis again comes to the rescue. Under the assumption that subjects start out within the VP, *the shit* in examples like (61)–(62) forms part of the VP before it is remerged in spec-FinP. The idiomatic meaning then ensues from a VP in which subject, verb and object are fixed, and this is perfectly in line with (59). These are not FinP idioms, therefore, but simply VP idioms. The only difference between (56) and (61)–(62) is that, in addition to the verb and object, the subject contributes to the idiomatic meaning. Since the Fin head is external to VP, it does not contribute to the idiomatic meaning, and this gives rise to the variation in (61)–(62). Note, by the way, that nothing excludes idioms in which everything is fixed, even the tense and modal properties. And such idioms indeed exist. Some examples are given below:

(63)　a.　Curiosity killed/*has killed/*will kill/*must kill the cat. (= 'Being too curious can be dangerous.')
　　　　b.　Elvis has left/*will leave/*is leaving the building. (= 'It's all over now.')

In this way, the syntactic constraints on idioms provide a third piece of evidence for VISH.

So much for the empirical arguments. These nicely favour VISH over the alternative hypothesis that takes the position within FinP to be the base position of the subject. But VISH also makes a theoretical claim. It basically states that not only direct and indirect objects of a verb start out in the VP, but also subjects. Now, we know that verbs must assign θ-roles to all of their arguments. These arguments cannot be just anywhere in the sentence. In the previous section (6.2.2), we saw that θ-roles must be assigned to arguments that are minimally in the same clause as the verb. VISH makes this claim even more precise by stating that V assigns all its θ-roles inside its own projection, namely the VP. Conceptually, that is an attractive idea, since it allows us to better understand how θ-role assignment works. There is now a clear link between the source of the θ-roles (V) and where they can be assigned (within the largest constituent of which this source is the head, the VP). Under the alternative hypothesis, this relation is only indirect: the source of the θ-roles is V, but the domain of θ-role assignment would be the entire clause in which V appears. This anomaly is eliminated once we adopt VISH. To see this, take a very simple, and perhaps the most classical, example from the syntax literature, *John loves Mary*. The θ-roles are nicely assigned within the VP:

(64)

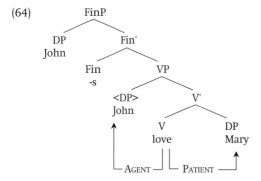

Exercises

A6   You know the drill. Some trees please, but now with subjects always starting out in VP. Indicate with arrows the instances of movement that are taking place.
   a.   All the kids were hiding in that shed.
   b.   The kids were all hiding in that shed.
   c.   The kids all hid in that shed.
   d.   The kids seemed all to hide in that shed.
   e.   The kids seemed to all hide in that shed.

B7 We have seen that a raising verb like *seem* does not assign a θ-role to its subject. Its subject has either become the subject by moving out of a lower clause (as in (i)), or it is an expletive subject (as in (ii)):
(i) John seems <John> to win the race.
(ii) It seems that John wins the race.
    At the same time, we have seen how the VP-internal subject hypothesis makes it possible to move the VP-subjects of idioms into a higher subject position. We now make a prediction: if any subject can be the subject of a raising verb, raising verbs should be able to have a subject that is part of an idiom. Control verbs should not allow this because they need to assign a θ-role to their subjects. Test this prediction using several raising and control verbs, and with several idioms.

C8 We have seen that expletive *there* can occupy spec-FinP, with the logical subject then appearing lower in the structure. We therefore expect that expletive *there* can undergo movement into the main clause in a raising construction but not in a control construction. Test this prediction and explain why the difference arises.

C9 Some more arborial fun. Draw the trees of the following examples. You now have to combine VISH with a diagnosis of the main-clause verb as being either a raising or control verb. To establish what kind of verb you are dealing with, use the tests that you have seen before but use also the expletive test introduced in the previous question.
a. I tend to eat slowly.
b. Did Josh try to contact you?
c. Whom are they going to hire?
d. These girls happened to expect to all go to Greece for the summer.

Summary

Certain constituents appear in a syntactic position in which they could not have originated: they must have moved. The operation that is responsible for this is not a new syntactic tool, though. The possibility of moving constituents follows directly from Merge. After all, there is nothing that would forbid merging a constituent that is part of a structure for a second time.

The idea that constituents can move (i.e. remerge) solves a whole range of problems in syntactic theory. For one, it allows us to keep case and θ-relations between assigners and assignees really tight. It also provides a straightforward analysis for *seem* constructions and allows us to understand how the subject of the main clause can be removed from the THEME argument of *seem* that it is a part of. Moreover, it allows us to have a fully unified account of feature checking that can deal with nominative and accusative case agreement, subject–verb agreement and binding in exactly the same terms.

However, one question that remains open is why elements must remerge. For head movement (like movement of an auxiliary into the head of CP in an interrogative sentence), there might be a clear explanation: it makes visible the otherwise unexpressed head of the CP, the head that, in turn, renders the sentence interrogative. But for other cases things are less clear. Why, for instance, must *Wh*-constituents like *which yellow chair* move to CP? And why must subjects move to FinP? Why can't we say *Is Mary sleeping* with the declarative meaning 'Mary is sleeping'? And why can't we leave the subject in VP and move something else to FinP? In other words, why is *Probably is Mary sleeping* ungrammatical? Apparently, movement is constrained but it is not yet clear what it is constrained by. In the next chapter, we tell you what this constraint is. And by now you should know us well enough to think that this constraint is probably not going to be a new one, but one that we have already.

Further Reading

The insight that constituents can appear in a displaced position has been part of generative syntax from the start, when movement operations were referred to as transformations (see Harris, 1951, Chomsky 1957). The analysis of raising constructions was developed by Rosenbaum (1967), Postal (1970, 1974), Jackendoff (1972) and Chomsky (1973), among others. The claim that subjects are generated inside the VP arose in the mid 80s in works like Kitagawa (1986), Contreras (1987) and Sportiche (1988). See also Koopman & Sportiche (1991).

Movement is studied widely and many distinct discussions about it can be found in the literature. One discussion is about whether it exists. Some scholars (see for instance Pollard & Sag 1994) propose the analysis of displacement in terms of feature passing: the displaced constituent has not moved but its features are related to the position in which it is interpreted. The question here is how to empirically distinguish proposals that at heart are quite similar.

Unifying Movement and Agreement

CHAPTER OUTLINE

We have seen that words or constituents can remerge. Remerge, also known as movement, explains a lot of things. Thanks to Remerge we are able to understand that a constituent can appear in a position far removed from the case and θ-role assigner on which it depends. And, by assuming that subjects start out in the VP and are subsequently remerged, we are able to treat all syntactic dependencies on a par, including the previously problematic nominative case relation between a subject and Fin. But what we don't yet understand is why elements must remerge. Why do subjects remerge into FinP, and *Wh*-phrases into CP? In this chapter we address this question, and we will conclude that the same feature-checking mechanism that we have already used to characterise syntactic dependencies provides us with the trigger for such instances of Remerge.

7.1 Insight: Agreement Triggers Remerge

In the previous chapter, we established that constituents – heads and phrases alike – can be remerged into the structure we build, thereby giving rise to the effect that we know as movement. By adopting this notion of Remerge we were able to understand a number of phenomena that would otherwise remain rather mysterious. In addition, it allowed us to maintain generalisations that would otherwise be lost, such as our unified characterisation of syntactic dependencies in terms of [F]–[uF] feature checking.

The fact that we can analyse certain phenomena as involving Remerge, however, does nothing to explain why these instances of Remerge actually take place. Take two significant Remerge operations that we have considered: (i) Remerge of a *Wh*-constituent to a clause-initial position and (ii) Remerge of the subject from VP to FinP.

(1)   a.   Which yellow chair has Adrian always liked <which yellow chair>?
      b.   The teachers are all <the teachers> dancing on the table.

Assuming that Remerge has taken place in (1a) allowed us to maintain our restrictions on case agreement, and to assume that θ-role assignment is strictly local, and always takes place within the VP. These reasons also accounted for remerger of the subject in (1a) from spec-VP to spec-FinP, and for the presence of the floating quantifier *all* between the auxiliary and main verb. We should realise, however, that the constraints that we formulated, and that accounted for the base positions of the remerged constituents, would also be satisfied by not remerging *which yellow chair* and *the teachers* at all and by leaving them in their base positions. *Which yellow chair* would already be case assigned in the object position of *liked* even if it was not subsequently remerged. Both *which yellow chair* and *the teachers* would receive a θ-role in their base positions. And the quantifier *all* would not have to float around if *the teachers* had not decided to undergo Remerge. Even though we have good reasons to believe that these two constituents have moved, we do not yet understand why they had to do so. And move they must, because if we leave them in their base positions, these sentences are ungrammatical: (2a) is an ungrammatical *Wh*-question, and (2b) is an ungrammatical declarative.

(2)   a.   *Has Adrian always liked which yellow chair?
      b.   *Are all the teachers dancing on the table (is what Mercedes declared).

This very strongly suggests that when constituents can undergo a particular Remerge operation they in fact must do so: Remerge is not optional. In *Wh*-questions, the *Wh*-constituent must remerge, as well as the auxiliary. In every yes/no question, the auxiliary remerges. And subjects always remerge as spec-FinP (unless there is already an expletive subject present). This means that for every instance of movement there must be a reason why this movement takes place. As soon as we see the rationale for these movements we understand why not moving what apparently should be moved automatically results in ungrammaticality. Question: what is the trigger for movement?

To get a first impression of what the answer to this question looks like, let us review those cases for which we did in fact supply a trigger. Section 6.2.1 provided two such cases: (i) Fin movement into the C head (like the movement of *did* in (3)), and (ii) subject movement from VP to FinP, as in (4).

(3) $[_{CP}$ Whom did-C $[_{FinP}$ you <did > $[_{VP}$ see <who>]]]

(4) $[_{FinP}$ Mary has $[_{VP}$ <Mary> loved John for a long time]]

For (3), we said that moving *did* into the C head makes the C head visible. For (4), we proposed a different trigger: in the lower position, *Mary* can check its nominative case feature [uFin] against the c-commanding Fin head, but [uφ: 3, SG] on Fin cannot be checked by *Mary* in its base position. By moving *Mary* to spec-FinP, [uφ: 3, SG] on Fin can be checked by [φ: 3, SG] on *Mary*.

What does this tell us? Well, it tells us that we have two clearly distinct triggers: (i) invisible heads trigger visible movement (to make them visible) and (ii) the necessity to check off features that would remain unchecked triggers movement. Now, let us evaluate these triggers in a bit more detail. It turns out that (ii) is a much better trigger than (i). In fact, it is quite easy to show that (i) does not work that well. If an invisible head in general triggers movement, we must expect that no head can ever remain empty. This prediction is wrong, and the best case to illustrate this with is the following:

(5)   I wonder $[_{CP}$ whom C $[_{FinP}$ Bill has met <whom>]]

The example in (5) contains an embedded question. Structurally, this question is a CP. When this CP contains a *Wh*-constituent, the head of C remains empty. And it has to remain empty. When we move the auxiliary in Fin to the C head, with the noble intention of making this invisible head visible, the result is ungrammatical:

(6)   *I wonder $[_{CP}$ whom $[_{FinP}$ has Bill <has> met <whom>]]

It would therefore be wrong to argue that making the C head visible triggers Fin-to-C movement. Otherwise (6) should be good and (5) bad. We conclude that one of the triggers for movement that we proposed doesn't really work, so that leaves us with the other: movement takes place to bring an interpretable feature into a position from which it can c-command its uninterpretable counterpart. The strategy to pursue is then to try and analyse all cases of movement along these lines.

Actually, this is not just a new goal that we now set for ourselves but a prediction that follows from previous analyses. We concluded in chapter 5 that Merge is constrained by agreement (that is, the need to check uninterpretable features). We concluded in chapter 6 that movement is Remerge, and Remerge is basically Merge. Combining these two conclusions, we now expect (and not just desire) that movement too is constrained by agreement. Chapter 7 must therefore test this prediction. The central insight it offers is ... well, you can already guess: movement is indeed constrained by agreement, too. Movement creates syntactic dependencies and these work like any other syntactic dependency we have seen so far. If so, then movement is not a complication, some extra phenomenon that requires some additional theorising, but something that neatly fits into the theory we already have. As a consequence, we arrive at our maximally simple theory.

Exercises

A1 Which constituents have undergone Remerge in the following sentences?
   a. Whose car did she steal?
   b. Which movies does John seem to watch?
   c. Why are you still all staying at home?
   d. The shit appears to hit the fan every Monday morning.

A2 How do we know that the constituents in the sentences above have undergone Remerge? In other words, how do we know that these elements have not been merged directly in the position in which you see them?

B3 Which of the Remerge steps in the sentences in A1 can we understand as being needed to check off uninterpretable features?

7.2 Implementation: Triggering Remerge

How do we start? We know, as the examples in (2) show, that if you do not remerge a particular constituent that should undergo Remerge, the sentence becomes ungrammatical. At the end of section 7.1, we were left with only one analysis for syntactic ill-formedness. If a sentence is syntactically bad, there must be at least one uninterpretable feature that remains unchecked. What we will do in this chapter, therefore, is the following. We will try to see whether a sentence in which some required instance of Remerge does not take place is bad for exactly the same reason, namely because a particular uninterpretable feature remains unchecked. We will start out with one case of Remerge, namely remerger of the subject from VP into FinP, where this is quite straightforwardly the case: without remerging the subject, the [uφ] feature on the head of FinP can never be checked. Then we will show that very similar patterns underlie remerger of *Wh*-elements into the CP. It is the similarity between subject movement and *Wh*-movement that is going to make the case for a uniform trigger: Remerge takes care of the checking of uninterpretable features.

7.2.1 Subject Movement into FinP

In the previous chapter we saw that subjects start out inside VP and sub-sequently remerge into spec-FinP. The structure of a simple sentence like *Mary sleeps* is then as follows:

(7)

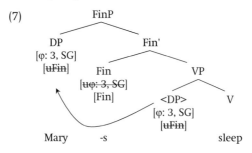

The reason why *Mary* must start out below Fin is two-fold. First of all, it is in the VP-internal position that *Mary* gets its θ-role, as we estab-lished in the previous chapter. Second, if *Mary* is merged directly in the position in FinP where you hear it, its [uFin] feature (which is our char-acterisation of nominative case) can never be checked against the [Fin] feature in the head of FinP. The interpretable feature has to c-command the uninterpretable counterpart, and not the other way around. In its original position within the VP, however, *Mary*'s [uFin] feature can be checked against [Fin] on Fin under c-command. But why could *Mary* not stay inside VP and be happy there? The reason is the presence of the [uφ: 3, SG] feature on Fin. If *Mary* stayed inside the VP, [uφ: 3, SG] would remain unchecked, and then the sentence would be ungrammatical. In order to make the sentence grammatical, then, some element carry-ing [φ: 3, SG] must remerge to a position from where it c-commands the [uφ: 3, SG] on *-s*. The constituent carrying this interpretable feature, of course, is *Mary*.

We have now identified the trigger for movement of the subject from spec-VP to spec-FinP: it takes place to ensure that an uninterpretable feature on Fin (namely [uφ: 3, SG]) can be checked by an interpretable feature carried by the remerged subject. This indeed allows us to under-stand the ungrammaticality of (2b). Without the subject remerging into FinP, there is an unchecked feature in the syntactic structure.

What we basically say is that Remerge here is triggered, and the trig-ger is some uninterpretable feature. Some constituent is remerged into the structure, so that it can check the uninterpretable feature that threatens to make the sentence ungrammatical. The remerged con-stituent carrying the corresponding interpretable feature enters into a dependency relation with that uninterpretable feature, established under c-command, so that checking can proceed. Now, this may look like a simple analysis, but the consequences are huge. What it boils down to is that the dependency between the trigger of Remerge and the remerged element can be analysed as a syntactic dependency like any other, at least for subject movement. It is defined in exactly the same terms that we have already used to characterise case agreement, person/number agreement between subject and finite verb, and binding.

Movement, then, would be nothing but a second instance of Merge, and it takes place to establish the appropriate relation between [F] and [uF]. The question is of course whether this trigger can be defined only for subject movement or also for other instances of movement. What we need to do now is check whether this is indeed all there is to it. If this conception of movement is indeed correct, it should work like this in general, and not just for movement of the subject into FinP. We therefore have to revisit all the instances of movement we have encountered so far and see if we can make this work. If we succeed, it would mean that movement as a syntactic phenomenon actually comes for free: we do not have to extend our theory to give it a proper place. The theory that we have already developed simply predicts Remerge to take place in exactly the way it does.

Before we try to unify distinct instances of movement, however, we have to look at movement to FinP in a bit more detail to ensure that our theory only endorses remerger into FinP of constituents that we want to be able to move there, and nothing more. So far, we have been able to explain subject movement as an agreement requirement that triggers Remerge. But why is it that only subjects may remerge into FinP? Recall from the previous chapter that other elements, such as PPs or (other) adverbials, cannot remerge into FinP. The sentences in (8) are clearly out.

(8)   a.   *Often has Mary kissed Eve.
      b.   *In the garden kisses Mary Eve.

This again follows straightforwardly from the proposed analysis. The feature that puts the sentence in danger of becoming ungrammatical, [uφ: 3, SG], is a very specific feature. Therefore, it is not just any constituent that can be remerged into spec-FinP. The remerged constituent must be one that carries the interpretable counterpart of this feature. Now, whereas *Mary* carries [φ: 3, SG], *often* surely does not. There is no point moving it to FinP because it does not do any work there, and the ungrammaticality of (8a) demonstrates this. Example (8b) is slightly more complicated because obviously *the garden* carries the feature [φ: 3, SG]. Why, then, can *in the garden* not take care of feature checking here, and take on the job that *Mary* likes to fulfil? The reason is c-command. Remember that the interpretable feature must c-command the uninterpretable one. Whereas the DP *the garden* is marked for [φ: 3, SG], the PP *in the garden* is not; it contains at most a constituent that carries this feature:

(9)   *

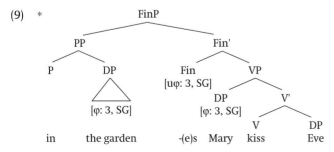

Now, in its position inside the PP, the DP only c-commands the preposition; it cannot c-command out of the PP. Although it carries the appropriate feature for checking the uninterpretable feature on Fin, the appropriate structural configuration is absent. As a consequence, (8b) is ungrammatical for the same reason as (8a): there is an unchecked uninterpretable feature on Fin.

Next, let us consider an example in which two constituents have similar features, for instance a sentence with a 3rd-person subject and a 3rd-person object. This raises the question why an object cannot remerge into FinP. Consider the following sentence:

(10)   *Her has she kissed <her>.

Here, the object *her* has remerged into FinP, making the example ungrammatical. But why would it be bad? *Her* has the same interpretable feature that *she* has, namely [φ: 3, SG]. In principle, then, it could check the [uφ: 3, SG] of *has*. The tree would look as in (11).

(11)

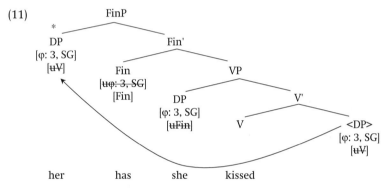

All uninterpretable features in (11) have been checked. The reason why the structure is still bad is that the grammar made the wrong choice here. The feature [uφ: 3, SG] on *has* in Fin requires that it is c-commanded by a DP that carries [φ: 3, SG], and there are two candidates. Why would the grammar prefer *she* over *her*? Well, with good reason. *She* is closer to Fin than is *her*. Hence, if Fin contains an uninterpretable feature and therefore requires some DP with an interpretable version of the same feature to move into the specifier of FinP, why not just take the closest one? For this reason, *her* is ignored and *she* is the preferred candidate. The example in (10) is ungrammatical because there is a constituent sitting in between the trigger and *her* that also carries the appropriate [φ] feature. In that event, the grammar chooses the first constituent that Fin sees when it is looking down into the structure that it c-commands. Once it finds *she*, the grammar simply stops looking further. This restriction of feature checking is known as the **Minimal Search**, which can be formulated as follows:

(12)   MINIMAL SEARCH
       When you need to remerge a constituent with some interpretable feature [F] to check off some uninterpretable feature [uF] on some other constituent, search for the closest constituent with [F] that is c-commanded by the element with [uF].

Although the desire to exploit minimal searches sounds like a promising way of letting the grammar decide between given options, how do we know this is the right way of handling this situation? To answer that question, we must ask ourselves what predictions it makes. Now, Minimal Search makes two straightforward predictions.

First of all, note that the condition in (12) refers to features, and not to subfeatures. This is important for understanding ungrammatical sentences containing subjects and objects with different subfeatures. Take the following sentence:

(13) *Them have Mary loved <them>.

Here you may wonder what rules out (13). After all, *have* and *them* both have 3rd-person plural features, and not 3rd-person singular features. Why can't we move *them* into FinP to have [uφ: 3, PL] on Fin checked? The answer again comes from Minimal Search. It tells us to take the closest constituent with [F] that is c-commanded by the element with [uF] and move it. F in our case is φ. But the closest interpretable φ-feature c-commanded by Fin is on *Mary*, not on *them*. And since Mary carries [φ: 3, SG] it can never check off the uninterpretable φ-feature on Fin: It has the right feature but the wrong subfeatures.

A second prediction that Minimal Search makes is that it does not categorically forbid the remerging of an object into FinP: it is just that the subject, being closer, is the preferred candidate to undergo Remerge. The object would be a perfect constituent for checking the uninterpretable [φ] feature on Fin, *whenever there is no subject present*. In fact, we predict that in such an event the object even *has to* remerge. So the question is whether such examples can be found. Well, yes, because this basically is what characterises a passive construction. Here is why.

Recall from the previous chapter that θ-roles are determined in a very local way. That is, a verb like *love* assigns the PATIENT role to its sister and the AGENT role to the sister of V':

(14)

Now let us look at the passive verb, *(be) loved*. Given the resemblance with (14), we should say that *Mary*, in *Mary is loved*, must also be the sister of V:

(15)
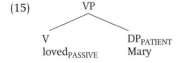

Only in this position can *Mary* receive the PATIENT role of *love*. Now, passive verbs do not assign any AGENT role. After all, if you turn an active sentence into a passive one, the AGENT of the active sentence disappears as an argument (it can at most show up as part of an adverbial *by* phrase). Although *Mary* functions as the grammatical subject in (15), it is the **logical object** of *loved* in the sense that it carries the PATIENT role of *loved*. This also means that the VP headed by the passive verb *loved* in (15) is complete. So the next step in the formation of *Mary is loved* is to Merge Fin:

(16)

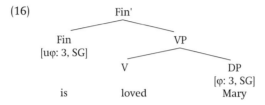

Since Fin carries [uφ: 3, SG], it must be c-commanded by some DP carrying [φ: 3, SG]. Obviously, there is only one candidate present: the object *Mary*. Therefore, *Mary* is triggered to be remerged in spec-FinP, resulting in the grammatical tree in (17).

(17)

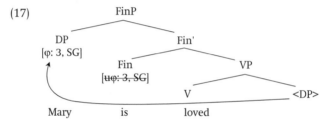

Feature checking can now take care of the uninterpretable feature on Fin.

In short, passive constructions are constructions in which there is no 'logical subject' and only a 'logical object'. The grammatical object of the active sentence therefore becomes the grammatical subject of the passive sentence. What happens is exactly what we predicted should happen: the object remerges to FinP when there is no intervening subject with similar features.

In this section we have shown that movement of the subject can be straightforwardly analysed as a way of ensuring that feature checking can proceed. In other words, subject movement behaves like any other syntactic dependency. Now, let us see if we can do the same for *Wh*-movement.

7.2.2 *Wh*-Movement

What we have just done is establish why a subject remerges into FinP. The idea was that the head of Fin carries a feature [uφ] that can only be checked by moving the highest DP that is c-commanded by this Fin head to a position from where this DP can c-command the Fin head. Subject movement is indeed triggered by the need to check uninterpretable φ-features. Together with Minimal Search this makes exactly the right predictions. With this in mind, let us look at the other example of movement that we have examined so far: *Wh*-movement. Why is it that *which yellow chair* in the example below must remerge into CP?

(18)   Which yellow chair has Adrian always liked <which yellow chair>?

Now, the first logical step is to see whether the explanation we have already developed for subject movement can do this job. Only if *Wh*-movement turns out not to be an instance of remerger triggered by feature-checking requirements must it be explained in other terms. So, how far can we get in trying to understand *Wh*-movement as being feature-driven? Well, quite far, actually.

If we want to understand *Wh*-movement, the *Wh*-constituent that remerges into a position c-commanding the head of the CP should check off some feature that would otherwise remain unchecked. In other words, the C head in main-clause interrogatives, which already carries the feature [C: Non-embedded, Question], should have an additional feature that can be checked off by *Wh*-constituents, and by no other elements. A non-*Wh*-constituent can never check off this feature, as the sentence in (19) is simply not a question.

(19)   *Mary have I seen.

What, then, is the feature that is shared by all *Wh*-constituents and by no other element? The name says it all: that feature is [Wh]. Recall from the first chapter that elements with the same distribution must have the same feature. This tells us that *Wh*-constituents must all have a feature that is not shared by other constituents, and that is the feature [Wh]. Given this logic, the C head in main-clause interrogatives, which already carries the feature [C: Non-embedded, Question], must also have a feature [uWh], triggering some *Wh*-constituent to remerge as its specifier, so that it can c-command this [uWh] feature on C.

Now let us look at the entire picture. Suppose we merge the C head with its full specification, [C: Non-emb(edded), Q(uestion)] and [uWh], with a FinP. C, being unexpressed, needs the auxiliary to remerge into it. This is the stage of the derivation that we see in (20):

(20)

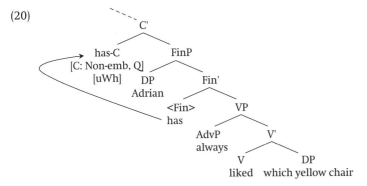

Now, this C head carries one uninterpretable feature, [uWh]. Therefore, this feature needs to be checked against a constituent with the feature [Wh]. The sentence contains such a constituent: *which yellow*

chair. One plus one is two, so *which yellow chair* remerges and becomes spec-CP, as shown in (21), and the grammaticality of the sentence is assured.

(21)

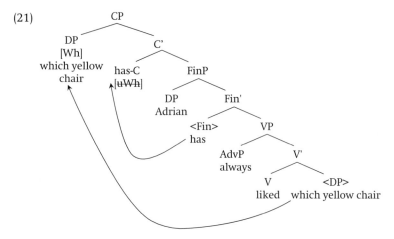

However, there are two problems that need to be addressed. First of all, it now looks as if the only feature that needs to be satisfied in a *Wh*-question is the [uWh] feature on C. But this cannot be the whole story. It would predict that a *Wh*-constituent is fine in its base position and only needs to remerge if there is a C head present that introduces the [uWh] feature. If we take out the C head altogether, and consequently the [uWh] feature, the *Wh*-constituent is predicted to be acceptable in its base position. But that is obviously not the case. Example (22) is fully ungrammatical (ignore the heavily stressed variant *Adrian has always liked WHICH YELLOW CHAIR?*).

(22)   *Adrian has always liked which yellow chair?

But note that (22) is ungrammatical no matter how we interpret it. We cannot interpret it as a question, because there is no C head introducing the [Q] subfeature. But nor can we interpret this sentence as a non-question. Apparently, *Wh*-constituents can only occur in questions, in clauses containing a C head with a [C: Q] feature. If they do not occur in such an environment, they cause the sentence to become ungrammatical, and (22) demonstrates this. We should wonder how our analysis can capture this fact. Well, there is a straightforward way of doing that. If *Wh*-constituents can only occur in questions, they must carry a [Q] feature. However, they cannot carry an interpretable [Q] feature. If they did, example (22) would be interpretable as a *Wh*-question, contrary to fact. This leaves exactly one option: *Wh*-constituents must carry an uninterpretable version of that feature, namely [uQ]. The presence of this feature on these constituents marks their dependence on a [Q] feature that is interpretable, and this is exactly the right result. *Wh*-constituents can only survive if the clause they are in contains a C head carrying an interpretable [Q] subfeature. We take it, therefore, that *Wh*-constituents carry not only [Wh] but also [uQ].

Now the facts are correctly accounted for. If *which yellow chair* carries a feature [uQ], the ungrammaticality of (22) directly follows. This uninterpretable feature is not checked. It can only be checked if the clause contains a head that carries a [Q] (sub)feature, the interpretable counterpart of [uQ], and it is C that has to introduce it. Once C is included in the syntactic representation, [uQ] on *which yellow chair* gets checked against the [Q] subfeature on this C head ([C: Q]) that it is c-commanded by. As we have seen, the C head also introduces the [uWh] feature, and for this feature to be checked *which yellow chair* must remerge as spec-CP.

Yes, we know there is a lot going on. What you should realise, though, is that you have seen exactly this pattern before, namely in the previous section. There is a full parallel with subject–verb agreement. There, the head of FinP checks off an uninterpretable feature on the subject in VP, namely [uFin(ite)], and the subject subsequently remerges as spec-FinP to check off an uninterpretable [uφ] feature on the Fin head itself. Likewise, the head of CP checks off an uninterpretable [uQ] feature on the *Wh*-element before movement and the *Wh*-phrase subsequently remerges as spec-FinP to check off an uninterpretable [uWh] feature on the C head itself. In both cases, there is a double feature-checking relation between some VP-external, functional head and some XP in the VP, and the nature of the features is such that one checking relation happens without the XP moving, but the other checking relation crucially requires the XP to remerge. The situation before Remerge is schematically shown in (23):

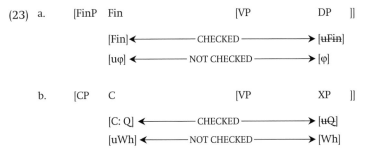

(23) a.   [FinP Fin   [VP   DP   ]]
                [Fin]◄─────── CHECKED ────────►[uFin]
                [uφ] ◄─────── NOT CHECKED ─────►[φ]

     b.   [CP   C   [VP   XP   ]]
                [C: Q] ◄─────── CHECKED ────────►[uQ]
                [uWh] ◄─────── NOT CHECKED ──────►[Wh]

As you can see, [uφ] and [uWh] remain unchecked. It is only after movement of the [φ]- or [Wh]-carrying XP that the second checking relation can be established. This is depicted in (24):

(24)

a.   [FinP   DP   Fin   [VP   DP   ]]
                              [Fin] ◄──── CHECKED ─────► [uFin]
           [φ] ◄─ CHECKED ──► [uφ]

b.   [CP   XP   C   [VP   XP   ]]
                              [C: Q] ◄────── CHECKED ──────► [Q]
           [Wh] ◄─ CHECKED ──► [uWh]

Note, by the way, that the XP is labelled DP in (23)–(24) because only nominal constituents carry [uFin], the feature that represents nominative case. The XP is still labelled XP in (23b) because constituents of different categories can carry a [Wh] feature: DPs can do so but note that adverbs like *where* and *how* must also remerge to clause-initial position.

What we have shown, in short, is that *Wh*-movement and subject movement are two manifestations of exactly the same phenomenon. The proposed analysis does it justice because we have shown that the way feature checking proceeds is quite similar. Only the content of the features involved is different.

Despite this attractive uniformity, there is one property of questions in English that does not seem to be uniform. We have argued that questions can be syntactically characterised as structures that contain an abstract, functional C head which contains at least two features, [C: Q] and [uWh] (let's ignore [Non-embedded] for the moment). The consequence of [uWh] is movement of a *Wh*-constituent to CP, so that feature checking can proceed in the way illustrated in (24b). There is one question type, however, that does not immediately fit this analysis, namely yes/no questions. An example is given in (25):

(25) Has Adrian always liked yellow chairs?

If all questions have the same C head, then all questions need a constituent carrying a [Wh] feature in clause-initial position, preceding the auxiliary that lexicalises this C head. When we look at the example in (25), there is none to be seen. There are two ways we can go from here.

One option is to say that in yes/no questions there is a different C head, namely one that only carries a [C: Q] feature but no [uWh] feature. However, it would be unclear what would be the justification for such a second abstract C head with a different specification, apart from providing an account for (25) being grammatical. One would have to assume that yes/no questions are really a different syntactic type of question from *Wh*-questions. But so far, no additional, independent fact supports such an analysis.

Another option is to stick to the analysis with one C head, specified as [C: Q] and [uWh]. In that event, there must be a constituent carrying a [Wh] feature present in (25), although we cannot see it. This analysis, with a covert *Wh*-constituent, is given in (26).

(26) [$_{CP}$ *Wh*$_{Y/N}$ has-C [$_{FinP}$ Adrian seen any yellow chairs]]?

Again, the only reason for postulating the abstract element, this time an empty *Wh*-constituent, is to account for the grammaticality of (25), and at first sight there does not seem to be any independent support for this. But perhaps there is. The fact that the empty *Wh*-element always remains unexpressed may be one that holds for main clauses only. In embedded clauses, there is a *Wh*-constituent that shows up specifically in yes/no questions. The example we have in mind is *whether*:

(27) Mary wonders whether John cheats on her.

Essentially, then, the unexpressed *Wh*-constituent that we are looking for may be an unexpressed *whether*. Saying it clearly leads to an ungrammatical result:

(28)   *Whether does it rain? (Intended meaning: does it rain?)

The ungrammaticality of (28), however, may be nothing but an arbitrary fact of Modern English. In older versions of English, for instance, *whether* could be used in main clauses, as the following example shows for Old English.

(29)   Hwæðer wæs Iohannes fulluht þe   of heofonum þe of mannum
       Whether was John's   baptism that of heavens   or of man
       'Was the Baptism of John done by heaven or by man?'

It may even be understandable why speakers of English at some point decided to not pronounce *whether* in main clauses any more. If you have a clause with a finite auxiliary in first position, as in (25), you can also understand this clause as a yes/no question, despite the fact that *whether* is not expressed. It is as if having a finite verb in the C position allows you to reconstruct the presence of an unexpressed element in first position. In fact, this reasoning now makes a prediction. If *whether* is an XP sitting in CP and is not expressed because the head of C is overtly realised, then the same must be true for embedded clauses. This indeed seems to be the case. An embedded yes/no question can be recognised by the presence either of complementiser *if*, as in (30a), or of *whether*, as in (30b). But whenever *if* is pronounced, *whether* cannot be, as can be seen in (30c):

(30)   a.   Mary may wonder if John cheats on her.
       b.   Mary may wonder whether John cheats on her.
       c.   *Mary may wonder whether if John cheats on her.

We now have a parallel between main and embedded yes/no questions: it is the pronouncement of the head of CP (in the form of either a finite auxiliary or *if*) that suppresses the pronouncement of *whether*.

In short, there may be reasons to assume that Modern English contains an unexpressed *whether* in main clauses. Assuming so allows us to make a very elegant generalisation. So far, we could say that in every *Wh*-question, the finite auxiliary was the second constituent, i.e. everything preceding the finite auxiliary was one constituent. Yes/no questions would be constructions in which an auxiliary is the first constituent. By assuming that in yes/no questions auxiliaries are preceded by an unexpressed *whether*, we can say by way of generalisation that in all questions the finite auxiliary is in second position, syntactically speaking. This uniformity is brought about by one and the same syntactic head, C. *Wh*-questions and yes/no questions, then, underlyingly have the same structure.

7.2.3 Unifying Head and XP Movement

So far we have established two types of movement: in chapter 6, we discussed head movement that involved remerging a lower head into a higher head position if that higher head position would otherwise remain unexpressed. In this chapter, we have discussed movement of subjects and *Wh*-constituents, both phrasal elements, which involved remerger with the purpose of checking uninterpretable (sub)features that otherwise would cause the sentence to remain ungrammatical. All in all, then, it looks as if we have two types of movement (**head movement** and **phrasal movement**), each triggered for a different reason.

(31) HEAD MOVEMENT

A head remerges into a higher head that would otherwise remain empty (such as the head of CP in questions).

(32) PHRASAL MOVEMENT

Some phrasal constituent (i.e. some XP) remerges to a higher position so that it can check off some uninterpretable feature that would otherwise remain unchecked.

Now, if you are a serious syntactician, this outcome does not make you feel ecstatic. What you would like, of course, is for these two types of movement to be more similar in nature. This means that head movement should be more like phrasal movement, or the other way around.

As stated at the end of section 7.1, we will try to make all movement follow from agreement and feature checking. This means that our analysis of head movement, and not that of phrasal movement, has to be adapted. This sounds like a good choice anyway for the following reason. It is not really clear that head movement takes place to realise an otherwise covert C head; this because in main clauses the C head always needs to be filled, but in embedded clauses this is not the case, as we discussed in section 7.1 (example (5)).

(33) a. What will she buy?
      b. [CP What will [FinP she <will> [VP <she> buy]]]

(34) a. I wonder what she will buy.
      b. [FinP I wonder [CP what [FinP she will [VP <she> buy]]]]

In (33), the C head is filled by *will*, evidenced by the fact that *will* precedes *she*. In (34), there is a CP, which hosts *what*, but this CP does not contain *will* in its head position; *will* is still to the right of *she* and can thus not have remerged into the head of the CP. We argued earlier (in section 6.2.1) that movement from the Fin head into the C head in embedded clauses is blocked because the C position is filled by a complementiser. This complementiser, however, does not have to be visible, as is clear in (34). If this is in principle possible, it becomes unclear why C in a main clause has to be overtly expressed.

To conclude, it seems problematic to state that head movement is triggered by the need to overtly realise a head position, as it would falsely predict that the C head in an embedded clause must be overtly realised too. But what, then, triggers head movement in main-clause questions? Two options: either we introduce a new mechanism as the trigger for head movement, or we try to derive it in a way that is already familiar to us. And since you know us well enough by now, we can continue straightaway with the second option. And this entails feature checking.

Let us zoom in on the two CPs in (33) and (34), respectively.

(35)   a.   b.

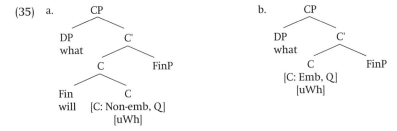

What we see is that in (33)/(35a) the main clause features [C: Non-embedded, Q] and [uWh] merges with *will*, and together with *will* constitutes the head of the CP. In (34)/(35b), the embedded clause feature [C: Embedded, Q] and [uWh] does not merge with *will*, but directly constitutes the head of the CP. So the feature [C: Non-embedded, Q], must have a property that triggers *will* (or any other head of FinP for that matter) to remerge with it, which the feature [C: Embedded, Q] lacks. What would that property be? It would be a property that says that the feature [C: Non-embedded, Q] cannot survive without a sister carrying [Fin]. Given our definition of c-command (one up, and as many as you like down), it follows that sister nodes always c-command each other. In (35a), *will* with the feature [Fin] c-commands the feature [C: Non-embedded, Q], [uWh] and vice versa. We can therefore say that [Fin] c-commands whatever feature on C caused the Fin head to move in the first place. This in turn makes it easy to identify what feature on C this has to be: [uFin].

Therefore, the only difference between (35a) and (35b) (and between the main clause in (33) and the embedded clause in (34)) is that in the former case the feature on the head of CP carries [uFin] and triggers head movement, but in the latter case C lacks [uFin] and does not trigger head movement:

(36)   a.   b.

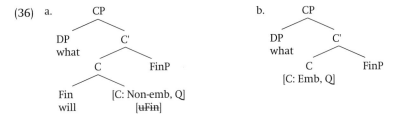

But now be aware that we have actually taken a really big step forward. We saw in the previous sections that phrasal movement must be analysed as triggered by feature checking. We know from the introduction to this chapter that head movement cannot be triggered by the need to make invisible heads visible. This forced us to analyse head movement along the same lines as phrasal movement, being triggered by the checking requirements of uninterpretable features. We have just shown that this can indeed be done. At this stage, the next logical step is to assume that every instance of movement, head movement and phrasal movement alike, is triggered by the need for an uninterpretable feature to be checked by some lower interpretable feature that, in turn, must remerge into a higher position. And if that is the case, all instances of movement are thus the result of the same feature-checking mechanism that is behind any other syntactic dependency as well, and we can reformulate the two types of movement in (31) and (32) into one formulation:

(37)   MOVEMENT
       A constituent (i.e. some head X, or some phrase XP) remerges to
       a higher position so that it can check off some uninterpretable
       feature that would otherwise remain unchecked.

So, we can take every instance of movement to be triggered by feature checking, just like any other syntactic dependency that we have seen. Consequently, we can summarise the contents of the last seven chapters in the following single sentence: *a syntactic structure is just the result of Merge (which includes Remerge), and is grammatical if all uninterpretable features have been checked off.*

Exercises

A4   Show the trees for the following cases of subject movement (you can
       leave the internal structure of DPs unanalysed):
       a.   Arno is leaving the building.
       b.   Mary was given a book.
       c.   Paul and Bill have loved each other.
       d.   Where did Bill go?

A5   Explain the reason for the ungrammaticality of the following sentences
       a.   *A letter was sent Mary.
       b.   *You has killed Mary.
       c.   *Him have I killed.
       d.   *Where has left Mary.

A6   Draw the trees for the following sentences including all instances of
       Remerge (ignore everything in brackets):
       a.   What did you do wrong?
       b.   When will they leave the place?
       c.   Whom did she talk to yesterday?
       d.   (I wonder) why she likes him.
       e.   (I didn't know) what they remembered.

A7   Include all relevant features involved in *Wh*-movement in the trees you
       draw for A6.

B8   Take the following sentence:
             *Them have she seen <them>
       Why is this sentence ungrammatical? After all, *them* has [φ: 3, PL] and the
       [uφ] feature of *have* can be checked by [φ: 3, PL] and not by [φ: 3, SG],
       which is what *she* carries. Why isn't *them* then the closest matching feature?

B9   In the following sentences two *Wh*-constituents are present, but only one of them has undergone remerger.
  (i)   Who do you think bought what?
  (ii)   *What do you think who bought?
 a.   Why does only one *Wh*-constituent need to undergo remerger in (i)?
 b.   Why does remerger of the *Wh*-constituent *What* in (ii) lead to an ungrammatical sentence?

C10   Both the covert *Wh*$_{Y/N}$-constituent and overt *whether* have a [Wh] feature. This checks off C's [uWh] in the sentences below.
  (i)   Did she leave?
  (ii)   I wonder whether she left.
 a.   But do they also have a feature [uQ]? Justify your answer.

Now take the following sentence:
  (iii)   I'm going to leave him, whether he cheated on me or not.
 b.   Does this sentence support the answer you gave to the previous question, or not?
 c.   Draw the tree that results from the answer to question b for the sentence *Must you go?*

7.3 Consequences: Layered VPs

Syntax uses the Merge operation to create syntactic structures in which dependent elements can engage in feature checking. We have seen that these dependencies are surprisingly uniform in that they all involve an interpretable feature c-commanding an uninterpretable feature: the dependent is structurally lower than the constituent it depends upon. We have also seen that movement, or Remerge, creates syntactic structures in which certain dependencies can follow this general schema: it is by moving [F] to a position higher than [uF] that feature checking can proceed as usual. Thereby, movement obtains a natural place in the overall theory.

In lots of ways, we have kept life easy for ourselves, and there are many phenomena and constructions in natural language, including English, that syntacticians are trying to fit into the general theory, but that we have not been able to discuss up till now in this introductory textbook. In this section, however, we will deal with two of them, and both are rather central to the English language. The reason we deal with them here is that we now have all the ingredients to tackle the issues raised by them. In section 7.3.1, we will look at ditransitive constructions, also known as **double object constructions**. First, we will note what the problem is that this construction type raises for Merge, Case theory and binding. Then we will show that, given the theory we have developed so far, there is really only one solution to the problem, and this solution opens up a new avenue to explore. The discussion of this construction therefore highlights again why it is so good to have a theory: it directs your analysis, even in your approach to new constructions. In section 7.3.2, finally, we will look at so-called exceptional case-marking constructions. These are constructions, already introduced in section 4.2.2, with an accusative case dependency that crosses a clause boundary. Contrary to what you may think at first view, they do not pose a problem for the theory, and they can be used to confirm particular analytical choices that we made earlier.

7.3.1 Zooming in on the VP: Double Object Constructions

What do we do when the sentence contains not one argument (a subject), not two arguments (a subject and a direct object) but three (a subject, an indirect object and a direct object)? Simply put, how do we draw the tree structure of *They give Mary flowers*? And does the theory we have developed run as smoothly as before once we have to analyse this more complex construction? Well, yes and no. Structurally, we have to make an adjustment, because it will turn out that the structure of the VP is more complex than we previously thought. This structure, however, can be robustly defended. And once we have it in place, the syntax works as beautifully as before.

Let us see what is at stake. We have committed ourselves to the Merge operation, which creates strictly binary branching tree structures (it is always two elements that merge together, not three or more). This means that a VP-structure like (38) cannot even be considered.

(38)
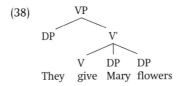

If we stick to binary branching, we must create either (39a) or (39b) in order to get the word order right:

(39)
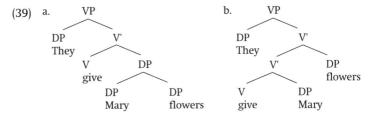

Two remarks are in order. First of all, creating a binary branching tree for a ditransitive VP is easy, and we now have two options we can choose from. Second, neither of these options is something we should embrace. For (39a), the reason is obvious: the verb has merged with one argument only here (*Mary flowers*), consisting of two subparts. After all, the sister of the verb is always one argument. But that is not how we understand a ditransitive construction. *Mary* and *flowers* are different arguments. Moreover, it predicts that *Mary flowers* is a constituent and can be remerged, contrary to fact: *Mary flowers they give*, or *Mary flowers was given*.

For (39b) the reason is obvious too. Because in English there is no morphological contrast beyond subject and object forms (nominative versus accusative), both the indirect and the direct object carry accusative case and must therefore enter into a case agreement relation with the verb. It is clear that in (39b) the [V] feature on V c-commands the [uV] feature on its sister *Mary*, but it does not c-command the same feature on *flowers*. In short, *flowers* cannot enter into a case relation with V.

But there are more reasons why the structure in (39b) does not solve our problem. Remember that there is a structural restriction on reflexives like *himself* and *themselves*: they should be c-commanded by their antecedents (see section 5.3.1). Now, it is fairly easy to construct a ditransitive sentence in which the direct object is a reflexive that refers back to the indirect object, such as example (40a). It is also fairly easy to construct an example in which a possessive pronoun is ambiguous and can receive two interpretations, as in (40b): *her* can refer to a specific female (either the teacher or someone not mentioned in the sentence) or it can trigger a bound reading (Audrey gets Audrey's favourite toy, Marilyn gets Marilyn's favourite toy, etc.). For this second interpretation to obtain, *her* must be bound by the indirect object.

(40)   a.   John showed her herself (in the mirror).
      b.   The teacher gave every girl her favourite toy.

Now, if *herself* in (40a) and *her* in (40b) have to be bound by the indirect object in these examples, then the indirect object should c-command these constituents. In the structure in (39b), this is simply not the case, because the direct object c-commands the indirect object, not the other way around. In order to reach the direct object from the indirect object, you have to go two steps up and not one, as required by c-command.

In order to account for examples like (40), we need a representation in which the indirect object is higher than the direct one. The idea that the indirect object is structurally higher (since the indirect object must c-command the direct object) is also very plausible from the perspective of θ-theory. Remember from chapter 3 that the θ-role RECIPIENT is higher on the θ-hierarchy than the PATIENT role. If that is the case, then the constituent receiving the RECIPIENT role must also be structurally higher than the one that gets assigned the PATIENT role.

The fact that the RECIPIENT is higher than the PATIENT is furthermore confirmed by the following. Recall from the section 7.2.1 that it is always the highest DP that remerges to FinP. In active sentences, this is the subject in VP. In passive sentences, there is no subject in VP, and the object in VP is remerged to FinP instead. Now, let's see what happens if you passivise a double object construction:

(41)   a.   Mary is given flowers.
      b.   *Flowers are given Mary.

Apparently the original indirect object (*Mary*) and not the original direct object (*flowers*) becomes the subject. This means, given the earlier established Minimal Search operation, that *Mary* and not *flowers* must be the closest DP that is c-commanded by the head of FinP. But this is not compatible with (39b).

We conclude, therefore, that the structure in (39b) does not meet the following demands: (i) in ditransitive constructions, the verb must c-command the direct object; and (ii) the indirect object must c-command the direct object. For the sake of clarity, we illustrate the relevant c-command relations in (39b) with the tree in (42). As you can see, there is no arrow pointing from V *give* to DP *flowers*, and no arrow pointing from DP *Mary* to DP *flowers*:

(42)
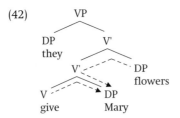

So how then should we analyse the structure of a ditransitive verb with two objects, so-called **double object constructions**? What we need is a structure in which (i) the indirect object c-commands direct object and not vice versa (for binding reasons), and (ii) the verb c-commands the direct object (to check its accusative case feature).

Let us move towards such an analysis. Suppose that we start out as follows.

(43)
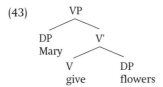

This structure gets three things right and two things wrong. What it gets right is that the indirect object now c-commands the direct object, so that we can straightforwardly account for the binding data in (40) and the fact that only *Mary* can become the subject of a passive construction. It also ensures that DP *flowers* can enter into a case agreement relation with V, because V c-commands this DP, whereas it failed to do so in (39b).

The structure also faces two problems, however. First of all, now the other DP, *Mary*, is not c-commanded by the verb, so that the [uV] feature on *Mary* cannot be checked by the [V] feature on the verb. Moreover, it gets the word order wrong. If we utter the structure in (43), we get: *(They) Mary give flowers* and not *They give Mary flowers*. Now, both of these problems would disappear in one fell swoop if we could ensure that the verb *give* ended up to the left side of the indirect object *Mary*, in a position from which it could c-command *Mary*. This can be achieved by something we have already seen before: Remerge. We take the head of the VP and remerge it out of its projection. This would create (44):

(44)
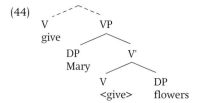

After remerger of *give*, we get the right word order, and *give* is in a position from where its [V] feature c-commands the [uV] features of both *Mary* and *flowers*. At the same time, both objects are as close to the verb as they can get in a binary branching structure.

The only question we need to address is what position the verb remerges *to*. Just as auxiliary verbs can remerge to an empty head position in English questions, a position we called C, here too (in declaratives) we must assume that verbs can remerge to an empty position. This position is generally known as *v* (say: 'little v'). Similarly to what we proposed for head movement into the C position, if *v* carries a feature [uV] it follows immediately that the verb has to remerge into *v*. Now, the presence of [uV] on *v* may seem a bit of an ad hoc solution (it looks as if we postulate it to make our theory work), but actually this can be very well argued: *v*P can only exist if it dominates a VP, and by assuming that *v* carries [uV] we get that requirement for free. What we have generally been referring to as 'the verb phrase', then, can actually be the combination of two phrases, VP and *v*P. The full representation of a ditransitive 'verb phrase' is given below:

(45)
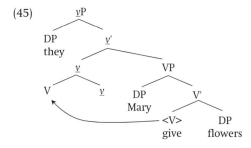

Note that the subject *they* is now base-generated in *v*P before it is remerged into FinP, and not in VP. This difference will become important in a minute. Also note that moving V to *v* creates a complex head (see (36a) for a parallel analysis of Fin to C movement). Although the lower *v* node does not c-command *Mary* and *flowers*, the higher *v* node of course does, so that the [uv] features on these nominal constituents can be checked off, as required.

What we have seen so far is that our general restriction on syntactic dependencies, applied to case and binding, and the necessity to build binary branching structures conspire to provide the analysis in (45) for ditransitive constructions. A consequence of this is that we have an additional head in our clausal structure besides V, Fin and C, namely _v_. As usual, progress comes with new questions. Although _v_ really comes to our rescue here, you may wonder what it actually is, apart from the head that helps us out. If its only purpose is to save our theory from going haywire when confronted with ditransitive constructions, then its use is rather restricted, and the solution it offers is dubious. Syntacticians, therefore, have tried to see whether there is more, independent, evidence for _v_, and have found it to play a much more prominent role in the overall syntactic structure. For this reason, let us look at _v_'s function in more detail.

Take a look again at the structure in (45). We just observed that in its position after movement the verb _give_, carrying [V], is able to check the accusative feature [uV] on the direct and indirect object, because it c-commands these objects. Alternatively, we could assume that the case relation of an object is not with V but with _v_. After all, _v_ also has both objects in its c-command domain. The reason for the verb to remerge into _v_ does not have to be to bring the verb itself into the right position for case relations, because remerger of the verb (V to _v_ movement) is already independently triggered by feature checking.

In fact, assuming that _v_ rather than V is involved in accusative case relations solves a big problem. Look at the following sentences:

(46)   a.   ?Mary kisses.
       b.   *Mary snores Mark.

The sentence in (46b) is much worse than the one in (46a). The reason is that (46a) only violates the θ-criterion: there is one argument missing. (46b) is worse, because it not only violates the θ-criterion (there is an argument too many now), but also, as we have seen in chapter 4, because the verb _snore_ cannot check off an accusative feature. Only transitive verbs can assign accusative case. But why is that? If an accusative case feature is analysed as [uV], it is kind of mysterious why _snore_ cannot assign accusative case. After all, _snore_ is a verb and thus carries [V]. But if accusative is assigned by _v_, then the possibility of an accusative case relation depends on the presence of this _v_ head in the overall structure. Now, suppose we say that _v_ only appears in transitive constructions (i.e. with verbs that have more than one argument), and that we reinterpret [uV] as [u_v_]. Then we can understand why (46b) is worse than (46a). In addition to violating the θ-criterion, _Mark_ violates Case theory: in the absence of _v_, the [u_v_] feature on _Mark_ fails to be checked.

There is not much, then, that holds us back from relieving V of its case duties and bestowing them on _v_. In fact, it may give us a handle on the distinction between (46a) and (46b). But the latter advantage is as real as the assumption it is based on: the hypothesis that _v_ only pops up in transitive (or ditransitive) constructions. The question is therefore if we can account for this hypothesis. Is there any independent support for it? Well, yes. We have seen one construction in which accusative case is lost, namely the passive of an active sentence. The active construction in

(47a) has a nominative and accusative pronoun in it, whereas the passive version in (47b) only has a nominative pronoun:

(47) a. She observed him.
  b. He was observed.

Now interestingly, there are two differences between these two examples. It is not just the accusative case form that goes missing in (47b) but also the AGENT of the verb *observe*. In short, a passive construction can be defined as a construction in which the accusative case and the agentive subject that are present in the active counterpart *both* disappear. In a transitive construction, you could say, assigning accusative and having an agentive subject go hand in hand. This link between the missing accusative case and missing AGENT in a passive construction is known as **Burzio's Generalisation**, named after the Italian linguist, Luigi Burzio, who described it.

Okay, so if you passivise a transitive construction, then both the AGENT and the accusative case disappear. Fine, but what does this bring us? Remember that we wanted to explore the idea that accusative case agreement is a relation between an object and *v*. Now, also observe that in a structure like (45) the subject is base-generated in spec-*v*P, not in spec-VP. Once we take these two observations together, we end up with a very simple way of accounting for the difference between an active and a passive construction: the difference between (47a) and (47b) is that in the passive construction *v* is simply not generated. One consequence of an absent *v* is that no accusative case can be realised because an object cannot undergo accusative case agreement with a missing *v* head. The second consequence is that the agentive subject of the active sentence can no longer appear because the position it would start out in is absent as well. We can therefore distinguish the 'verb phrase' of an active and a corresponding passive construction in the following way:

(48) a. Active constructions: b. Passive constructions:

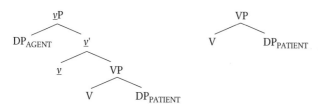

Once FinP is added to (48a), the DP$_{AGENT}$ will be remerged into spec-FinP to c-command the uninterpretable φ-feature on Fin. And once FinP is added to the structure in (48b), DP$_{PATIENT}$ will do the honours. This derives the fact that an active sentence has an AGENT subject and a PATIENT object, whereas a passive sentence only has a PATIENT subject. Since *v* is the head that introduces the AGENT, it is *v* that makes a transitive construction transitive. But if *v* only shows up in transitive constructions, it can only be in transitive constructions that accusative case is checked off.

To sum up so far, a passive construction is a construction in which AGENT and accusative case disappear. The $\underline{v}$ head does a good job in accounting for these two properties because we can relate both of them to the absence of this head from the structure in a passive construction. This means that we have succeeded in providing more content to the syntactic head that we were forced to postulate in order to account for the properties of ditransitive constructions, most notably our desire to put the indirect object in a position from which it can c-command the direct object. In short, then, we have turned $\underline{v}$ into a multi-purpose head that provides insights into several central characteristics of English syntax.

Even more is to be gained. If $\underline{v}$ is a 'transitiviser', the element that is responsible for the syntax of verbs with more than one argument, we predict that it should in principle be possible to make an intransitive verb transitive by adding $\underline{v}$ to the structure. This is a direct prediction that the $\underline{v}$ hypothesis makes. And if this prediction is correct, the hypothesis will be strongly confirmed. The following pairs of sentences do exactly that:

(49) a. Harry boiled the water.
       b. The water boils.

(50) a. The enemy sank our pink boat.
       b. Our pink boat sank.

(51) a. Kirsten eventually closed the door.
       b. The door eventually closed.

In the (b) examples, we observe that the verbs *boil*, *sink* and *close* take one argument. This argument is a THEME. After all, water does not bring about its own boiling, a ship does not sink itself (at least not in (50b)), and the door needs someone or something that causes it to close. In the (a) examples an AGENT is all of a sudden there, and the THEME arguments of the (b) examples now appear as accusative case-bearing objects. Verbs that can display such a pattern are known as ergative verbs. These ergative alternations, then, show the opposite of the active–passive alternation: we start with a verb with one argument, and end up with two arguments. You can already fill in our analysis. Indeed, the (a) examples come about by stacking a $\underline{v}$P on top of the VP already present. The two trees for (49) are drawn below.

(52)

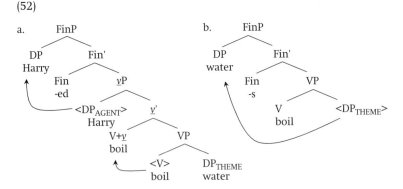

Generalising over active–passive and ergative alternations, then, we can say that _v_P is a property of a construction in which there is more than one argument present. Ergative and passive constructions both bring out the close link between an AGENT and the presence/absence of accusative case. Therefore, any theory that can relate the two in a direct way is a successful theory. The theory we presented is of that type, because the absence of the AGENT argument and the absence of accusative case are accounted for by the absence of a projection, namely _v_P, thereby capturing the link in a very direct way.

7.3.2 Exceptional Case Marking

We have already argued in section 4.2.2 that nominative case, being [uFin], is checked by a functional head, namely Fin, that carries the feature [Fin]. If a clause is non-finite, which means there is no finite verb in it, then a nominative subject cannot occur. This accounts for the fact that nominative forms cannot appear in non-finite contexts, something we noted before:

(53) a. *I saw [she kissing my boyfriend].
      b. *I expected [he to buy that house].
      c. *The police officer made [he tell the truth].
      d. *They had [she pay extra].

The verbs _kissing, buy, tell_ and _pay_ are all non-finite forms. _Kissing_ is non-finite because it is not marked for tense or agreement. _Buy_ is in addition preceded by the infinitival marker _to. Tell_ and _pay_ lack the _-s_ that a 3rd-person singular subject would trigger. The offending constituents in these examples are the subjects of the embedded clauses because they appear in the nominative form in the absence of a [Fin] feature.

Although Case theory correctly captures the ungrammaticality of these examples, how come that they become grammatical if we put in accusative subjects, as in (54)?

(54) a. I saw [her kissing my boyfriend].
      b. I expected [him to buy that house].
      c. The police officer made [him tell the truth].
      d. They had [her come and clean the house].

Given our theory, there can be only one answer: there has to be a head that enters into an accusative case relation with these embedded subjects. Now, in the previous section, we argued that accusative case relations hold between nominal objects and _v_. And _v_, we argued in addition, is only present in clauses with minimally two arguments (that is, in transitive constructions). In each of these examples, there are two verbs present. One sits in the embedded clause (_kissing, buy, tell_ and _pay_), whereas the other verb is the one that selects these embedded clauses as an argument (_saw, expected, made_ and _had_). All verbs present are transitive, so there won't be a lack of _v_ heads. For each sentence, then, we need to determine which _v_ is responsible for the accusative case on the embedded subject: the main clause _v_ or the _v_ in the embedded clause?

The choice is easy because we have a theory, and the theory does not give us much choice. Take the example in (54b). Here, *that house* receives accusative case in the embedded clause, so it must be the *v* that merges with the VP headed by *buy* that enters into a case relation with the object. This *v* head also c-commands *that house*, as required. However, the same *v* head does not c-command *him* in FinP. We conclude, therefore, that the *v* head in the embedded clause cannot be taking care of the accusative case on *him* and that it must be the *v* head in the main clause, the one associated with *expect*. What is 'exceptional' about this so-called exceptional case marking construction is that the *v* head of the main clause enters into a case relation with a nominal constituent in the embedded clause. Usually, *v* enters into a case relation with a nominal constituent within the same clause. The grammar, however, could not care less about this. The main clause *v* is present because *expect* is a transitive verb and it c-commands *him*, the subject in the embedded non-finite clause. And we can independently see that a clause with *expect* in it allows for an object with accusative case. After all, (55) is grammatical:

(55)   I expect him.

The difference between 'regular' and 'exceptional' accusative case agreement boils down to a difference in the syntactic position of the dependent constituent, which can be schematised as follows.

(56)

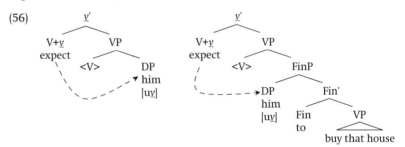

From the perspective of the rules that are active in both these dependency relations, the exceptionality is rather underwhelming: in both cases, the [u*v*] feature is c-commanded by *v*. And that is all that matters.

We therefore conclude that exceptional case marking constructions are constructions in which a main clause *v* checks the [u*v*] feature of the subject in the embedded clause. Our theory predicts that it has to be the main clause *v* that does this because it is the only *v* in the main clause that c-commands the embedded subject. Independent confirmation for this analysis can be obtained. Recall that *v* is only present if the verb in the clause is transitive, i.e. if it takes two arguments. What we can do, therefore, is put a non-transitive verb in the embedded clause, thereby taking away the *v* head from the embedded clause. If the subject of the embedded clause does not enter into a case relation with the embedded *v*, this should be perfectly harmless, and have no effect on the grammaticality of the construction. The following examples confirm that this prediction is correct:

(57) a. I expect [him to snore].
    b. I see [her walking].
    c. The police officer will make [him sweat].

A central property of exceptional case marking constructions is that we see a dependency relation across a clause boundary. There is a FinP embedded in another FinP, and the v in the higher FinP enters into a relation with the subject of the embedded FinP. Now, we have seen reasons to believe that FinP acts as a domain within which a dependency must be established. It is impossible, for instance, to have subject–verb agreement between a main-clause verb and an embedded subject, or between a main-clause subject and an embedded verb (*John say that they is stupid). We also saw that a reflexive must be c-commanded by an antecedent within the same FinP. Is it not problematic, you may wonder, to have a case relation across a clause boundary? Well, no. We have also seen that the domain within which these dependencies hold is not just any FinP but a finite FinP. If so, then a case relation across a non-finite clause boundary should be as unproblematic as a binding relation. And we know that the latter is true, because we have already seen the relevant examples in section 5.3.2, repeated here:

(58) a. John$_i$ wants [$_{FinP}$ himself$_i$ to succeed].
    b. We$_i$ expected [$_{FinP}$ ourselves$_i$ to do better next time].

These examples show that an embedded subject can enter into a dependency relation with a main-clause subject without any problems.

All in all, then, exceptional case marking constructions can be analysed within the theoretical framework we have adopted, and nothing needs to be added.

Exercises

A11   Provide the trees for the following examples, and include all relevant features.
    a. The girls have sent each other letters.
    b. I offered him a drink.
    c. Mary was sent flowers.
    d. Snow is falling.

B12   Explain the ungrammaticality of the following sentences:
    a. *It seems John to sing.
    b. *I want they to leave.

C13   Not every verb can participate in an exceptional case marking construction. To be (surprising), for instance, cannot.
    a. Why is this?
         Sentences like (i) are therefore ungrammatical.
         (i) *It would be surprising him to leave.
         (ii) It would be surprising for him to leave.
    b. Why is sentence (ii) grammatical?

C14   Originally, *Burzio's Generalisation* linked the presence of an accusative to the presence of an AGENT. Nowadays, people assume rather that it links the presence of accusative to the presence of a higher θ-role. Which of the following sentences forms evidence for this more recent version of the generalisation?
      (i)   Bill cooked potatoes.
      (ii) Mary was given the bill.
      (iii) Mary saw them playing together.

7.4 Taking Stock

Now, where do we stand? In the past five chapters we have developed a theory that reduces everything syntactic to two mechanisms: Merge and feature checking. Once you have your words with all their interpretable and uninterpretable features present, you can start building your sentence. And once all uninterpretable features are checked, syntax is done and happy. Ideally, the meaning of the sentence should still make sense, but for syntax this is not essential. A completely nonsensical sentence can still be grammatical, as the following example from the founding father of syntactic theory, Noam Chomsky, shows.

(59)   Colourless green ideas sleep furiously.

What's next? Well, so far we have looked at syntax proper. We have determined what makes a grammatical sentence grammatical. And we have seen that once syntax is done, semantics jumps in and assigns a meaning to the sentence. But semantics is not the only component that plays a role after syntax is done. After all, a sentence must also be uttered. And that is not a trivial thing. We saw for instance that in a sentence like *Mary often works hard*, the verb *work* is in VP, but the affix *-s* is in FinP. Still, they are spoken as one word. How does that work?

So, we can already ask three questions:

(i)   How do sentences receive their meaning?
(ii) How do sentences get uttered?
(iii) How are complex words formed?

We can visualise what we have done, and what we have not yet done, by means of the following grammatical model, the so-called 'inverted Y-model' (60) which you may remember from the introduction:

(60)

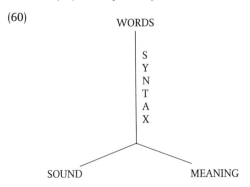

We have shown in these first seven chapters how syntax uses elements from our mental lexicon – the words in a language with their features – to create structures. In the next three chapters, we will look at how the product of syntax receives sound and meaning, thereby addressing the three questions mentioned above. We will deal with them in reverse order. In chapter 8, we will look at the relation between syntax and morphology, the study of word formation. In chapter 9, we will look at the relation between syntax and phonology, the study of pronunciation. And, finally, in chapter 10, we will look at the relation between syntax and semantics, the study of meaning.

Further Reading

The insight that uninterpretable features trigger movement goes back to Chomsky (1995) (and returns in various incarnations). For an overview of the discussion of the various types of movement and their triggers, we refer to Koopman & Sportiche (1991) for subject movement, to Postal (1986), Jaeggli (1986) and Baker, Johnson & Roberts (1989) for passive constructions, to Chomksy (1977), Cheng (1991) and Richards (1997) for *Wh*-movement (including its cross-linguistic manifestations), and to Koopman (1984), Travis (1984), Pollock (1989), Bobaljik (1995), Koeneman (2000), Roberts (2010) and references in those works for verb movement. The idea that movement is constrained by Minimal Search goes back to Chomsky (1995) as well, and builds on insights by Rizzi (1990).

The introduction of layered VPs comes from Larson (1988), and the introduction of v comes from Kratzer (1996) and is also introduced in Chomsky (1995). Burzio's Generalisation was formulated in Burzio (1986). A recent collection of papers on v is D'Alessandro, Franco & Gallego (forthcoming).

Example (29) comes from van Gelderen (2009).

8 Syntax and Morphology

CHAPTER OUTLINE

KEY TERMS

grammatical modules

terminal nodes

spell-out rules

morpho-phonological forms

under-specification

markedness

(un)bound morpheme

M-merger

impoverishment

In this chapter, we will look at the interaction between syntax and morphology. You may wonder why this is of interest, because this is not immediately obvious. Syntax gives us a syntactic tree with words dangling from it. These have to be expressed in a particular order, but that is the job for phonology (to be explored in chapter 9), not morphology. So is there anything intriguing about the relationship between the tree and the dangling words that requires our attention? Morphology would be of little interest to a syntactician if the rules of morphology (the science of word structure) operated fully independently from the rules of syntax (the science of sentence structure). One could say that morphology produces words, syntax subsequently uses these words, and that is all there is to it. Reality, however, turns out to be much more complex. Instead of saying that morphology provides the elements that syntax uses, some observations force us to say the exact opposite: syntax provides the input that morphology uses to create words. This in turn suggests that morphology is not a mere delivery service for syntax but that it becomes active after the syntactic representation has been built. Since the relationship between syntax and morphology is more complex than initially envisaged, it makes sense to study the processes that take place at the interface between these two components of grammar. This is exactly what this chapter will do.

8.1 Insight: Morphology and Syntax are Different Grammatical Modules

The relationship between syntax and morphology is not always transparent; this justifies its study. This may sound like a completely new concept, but in fact you have already seen concrete cases of mismatches between syntax and morphology. Let us look at three of these.

The first involves the syntactic location of the tense and agreement properties that are part and parcel of finite clauses. Remember that we had reasons to think that these properties reside in a syntactic position that we called Fin, the head of the FinP. This is a position outside of VP, so that the proposed tree structure for the sentence *He treasures his health* looks as in (1):

(1)

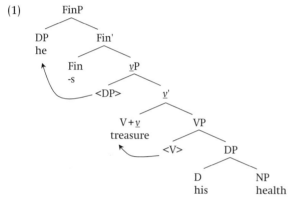

What we have here is a tree in which one word is distributed over two syntactic positions. Two pieces of morphology that are part of the finite verb *treasures* appear in different syntactic heads: the *-s* sits in the Fin position, whereas *treasure* sits in the V position. What is a unit when we utter this sentence is not a unit in the tree. If we were to faithfully utter this tree, it would come out as *He s treasure his health*. This shows us that the word *treasures* must be created by some operation after the syntactic structure has generated the tree in (1).

As a second example of a syntax–morphology mismatch (that is, a case in which the syntactic structure does not fully match with what we morphologically see), consider the same sentence but now with a 1st-person singular subject, *I*. In this case, the Fin head would contain an uninterpretable feature with two subfeatures, one for number and one for person: [uφ: 1, SG]. This is in contrast with the feature that sits in the Fin position in (1), which is [uφ: 3, SG], owing to the presence of *he*. The contrast between these different syntactic subfeatures on Fin is reflected by the overt morphology. After all, a 3SG subject triggers an *-s* on the finite verb, whereas a 1SG subject triggers *-ø*: *he treasure-s* vs. *I treasure-ø*. We therefore say that [uφ: 3, SG] morphologically corresponds to *-s*, whereas [uφ: 1, SG] morphologically corresponds to *-ø*. Note, however, that *-ø* does not only correspond to [uφ: 1, SG]. It also corresponds to [uφ: 2, SG], [uφ: 1, PL], [uφ: 2, PL], and [uφ: 3, PL]. After all, the null form shows up in five out of six person/number contexts. What this means is that the syntactic features do not match up with the morphological paradigm. The morphology seriously *underrepresents* the underlying syntactic structure. As far as subject–verb agreement is concerned, you could say that morphology does a lousy job, since it does not properly reflect what syntax distinguishes.

A third mismatch is introduced by irregular verbs (already briefly discussed in chapter 5). If the tense and agreement features reside in Fin, it makes sense to say that *-s* and *-ed* reside in Fin as well. After all, *-s* and *-ed* are the morphological forms that correspond to these features. This, of course, raises the aforementioned problem of how *-s* and *-ed* end up on the verbal stem, but the problem is significantly greater. Suppose that we have the example in (2), which contains the irregular verb *ran*.

(2)   He ran a health check.

It is difficult to see how our analysis can be upheld here. If finite verbs can be morphologically divided into a verbal stem and a finite element (either tense or agreement), then how would that work for *ran*? After all, you do not say *runned*. No part of *ran* is purely verbal and no part of *ran* is purely Fin-like. It almost looks as if the head of FinP and the head of VP are filled by one and the same word that cannot be split up into smaller morphemes (unlike *treasured*). But that again shows that the morphological form of a word does not always transparently reflect the syntactic structure.

What these three mismatches show is that morphology has a will of its own. It wants *-s* and *-ed* spelled out onto a verbal stem, even though these morphemes are associated syntactically with a designated position separated from the verbal stem. And morphology does not always transparently spell out what the syntactic tree encodes.

It is observations like these that have prompted scholars to adopt a separation between syntax and morphology. They are two independent modules of the same grammar, and each has its own wishes and desires. If syntax cared deeply about morphology, it would generate tense and agreement features in the same position as the verbal stem to begin with. And if morphology cared about syntax a bit more, it would faithfully show which features are present in the syntax. This is apparently not the case. But although syntax and morphology seem to follow their own rules, these two **grammatical modules** obviously have to work together. At the end of the day, they are part of the same grammar and this grammar is able to produce utterances that we find grammatical. This means that the grammar has found ways of doing what it needs to do while keeping happy all the modules involved, at least relatively speaking. The next section will show how this separation can be implemented in a way that does not lead to a completely chaotic and unworkable grammar.

Exercises

A1   Features that are present in the syntax are not always overtly reflected by English morphology, and we have seen that verbal agreement is a clear example of just that. Try to think of other featural distinctions present in the syntax that morphology does not spell out. The inspiration for where to look can be found in the first seven chapters of this book.

B2   Have a look at the present- and past-tense paradigms of the verb *to be* in English and state for each paradigm which features or feature combinations are not morphologically distinguished. What are the similarities, and what the differences?

8.2 Implementation: The Interaction between Syntax and Morphology

We saw in the previous section that we need a separation between syntax and morphology, and the question is how precisely we should implement this separation. What does separation entail? In order to give substance to this separation, we do not really have to invent anything. We can make use of an assumption that we have used all along, and just make it work harder. This assumption is that syntax manipulates features, and nothing more. Remember that we found in chapter 1 that syntax puts together not words but categories. It is not so much interested in the words *eat* and *sausages*. It is primarily interested in the fact that *eat* is of category V and *sausages* of category N, and it is these categorial labels that allow syntax to merge *eat* with *sausages*. Now, these labels V and N represent abstract features. After all, you can't tell from the appearance of *eat* and *sausages* that one is a V and the other an N.

Given our earlier line of argument, let us push this idea to its limit and conclude that syntax can see only features, not the way in which these features are expressed. It simply does not care about this. Strictly speaking, then, it makes no sense to say that *-s* and *-ed* sit in the Fin head. It is the syntactic features [uφ: 3, SG] and [Fin: Past] that sit there, and these features are expressed (or: realised) as *-s* and *-ed*. Now, if syntax is the module that creates structures that are consequently expressed and interpreted (as stated in section 7.4), then it is a small step to take 'consequently' to mean 'sequentially': first syntax builds these structures with abstract features, and it is only after this has happened that the grammar starts caring about how they sound and what they mean. In other words, morphology *follows* syntax. This means that, just like semantics, morphology is a module that interprets syntactic structures. Whereas semantics applies to the abstract syntactic structure and assigns meaning to it (more about this in chapter 10), morphology applies to the syntactic structure and provides it with utterable forms. It for instance makes sure that [uφ: 3, SG] comes out as *-s*, and [Fin: Past] as *-ed* (where appropriate, e.g. in regular non-modal verbs). In section 8.2.1, we will look in more detail at how morphology interprets syntactic structures, and how it goes about inserting the correct forms.

8.2.1 Features and Spell-Out Rules

If morphology is the module that interprets syntactic structures and provides concrete, utterable forms, it must be able to do at least two things: it must have access to the **terminal nodes** of the syntactic representation (the positions in which syntactic features are merged), and it must have access to the **spell-out rules** (sometimes also called *realisation rules*) for concrete forms that it can insert.

Let us consider again the tree structure in (1) and see how this works. The tree structure contains seven terminal nodes : DP, Fin, <DP>, [V+*v*], <V>, D and NP. Two of these, however, refer to constituents that have moved, <DP> and <V>. Since we always 'hear' moving constituents in their final position, we can assume that morphology spells out moved constituents in the position they have moved to, and not in their base or intermediate positions. We can therefore ignore <DP> and <V>. This leaves five terminal nodes to consider and morphology therefore needs to make five choices. Consider the first choice it has to make, namely which pronoun to insert. Now, the tree structure that morphology sees is a bit more detailed than the one in (1). In a more elaborate version, the top part of (1) would look as in (3), where there is no longer a pronoun *he* or an affix *-s* present in the structure, but only the features that underlie them: [φ: 3, SG, Masculine] and [uFin] instead of *he*, and [uφ: 3, SG] and [Fin: Present] instead of *-s*.

(3)

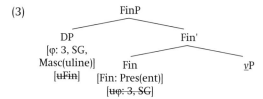

Morphology, then, has to have access to the concrete spell-out forms from which it then has to pick the right ones for insertion into the DP and Fin positions, namely *he* and *-s*. How does it do that? Take a look at (4), which represents a tiny part of the mental knowledge of a speaker of English:

(4) **Pronouns (Singular):**

[φ: 1, SG], [uFin]	↔	*I*
[φ: 1, SG], [u*v*]	↔	*me*
[φ: 2]	↔	*you*
[φ: 3, SG, Masc(uline)], [uFin]	↔	*he*
[φ: 3, SG, Masc], [u*v*]	↔	*him*
[φ: 3, SG, Fem(inine)], [uFin]	↔	*she*
[φ: 3, SG, Fem], [u*v*]	↔	*her*
[φ: 3, SG]	↔	*it*

Agreement:

[Fin: Pres], [uφ: 3, SG]	↔	*-s*
[Fin: Pres], [uφ]	↔	*-ø*

Tense:

[Fin: Past]	↔	*-ed*

These are the morphological spell-out rules that morphology uses to link abstract features to concrete, utterable forms. The right side of the arrow provides the **morpho-phonological form** that morphology can insert, and the left side of the arrow indicates which bundle of syntactic features would trigger that insertion. These bundles of features on the left side are called the morphemes, and these coincide with the terminal nodes of the syntactic tree.

Let us see how the rules in (4) work. The morpho-phonological form *I* is inserted whenever the syntactic terminal node contains the syntactic features [φ: 1, SG], [uFin], *she* when the node contains [φ: 3, SG, Fem], [uFin], etc. Obviously, *I* cannot be inserted in the DP position in (3) for the simple reason that the person feature provided by the syntax is not compatible with the person feature that *I* spells out: *I* is associated with 1st person, not with 3rd person. For the same reason, *you* cannot be inserted: *you* is associated with 2nd person. *Him* cannot be inserted either; although it spells out the right person feature for this particular syntactic context, namely 3rd person, *him* is an accusative form, so it spells out [u̲v̲] rather than [uFin].

It is not the case that the features associated with a particular morpho-phonological form should always form a complete match with the features provided by the syntax. Take the sentence *You treasure your health.* The top of the syntactic structure looks as follows:

(5)

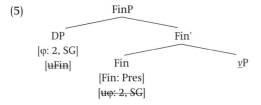

Here, the subject position is characterised as 2nd person singular and, as usual, it is a nominative position. This means that the subject contains a (checked) [uFin] feature. Now, when we inspect the spell-out rules in (4), there is no morpho-phonological form that is associated with [φ: 2, SG], [uFin]. The form *you* is only associated with [φ: 2]. This, of course, is exactly how it should be. First of all, *you* can be used both in the singular and plural: *You treasure yourself* and *You treasure yourselves* are both grammatical. This means that the morpho-phonological form *you* is *underspecified* for number: it is specified for person, as it is associated with 2nd person, but it is not associated with number, and this is in contrast to other forms that are part of the same paradigm; hence the term underspecification. In addition, *you* can be used in all subject and object positions (*I treasure you, you treasure me*), which is impossible to do with *they* or *he* (*I like he/they*). This means that the form *you* is also underspecified for case, and is not associated with either [uFin] or [uV]. Whereas in the syntactic tree the constituent in spec-FinP is fully specified for person, number and case (that is to say, all these features are present), there is no morpho-phonological form available that is equally specified. *You* is therefore not a perfect match for insertion in the DP position of the tree in (5), but it is the best match available, since all the other φ-forms give rise to a feature clash. Inserting *I*, for instance, is impossible as it is specified for 1st person, and this clashes with the 2nd-person feature present in the syntactic tree. To put it differently, the presence of [φ: 2, SG] blocks the form *I* from being inserted. We conclude, therefore, that lack of a perfect match is not a problem, as long as no feature clashes arise. The morpho-phonological form that is inserted in a particular syntactic position cannot be associated with a feature that clashes with the syntactic position that it tries to realise (that is, for example, *you* cannot be inserted in a [φ: 3, SG] context). However, in the absence of a form that is associated with all of the features present in a particular syntactic position, morphology can without any problem insert a form that is only associated with some of these features. Given the rules in (4), *you* is simply the only form compatible with the features that the syntax provides in (5).

Of course, we could alternatively extend the number of spell-out rules and assume that English grammar contains four *you* forms, each with a full specification for person, number and case. That, however, would introduce a lot of redundancy (i.e. superfluousness) and would basically constitute an unnecessarily forceful attempt to keep the relation between syntax and morphology transparent. It would perhaps be an ideal analysis from the syntactic point of view, but a cumbersome analysis from the morphological point of view. And since we are dealing with the concrete forms that are introduced by the morphology, it makes more sense to opt for the analysis that is morphologically optimal.

To sum up the discussion so far, we have established that morphology inserts morpho-phonological forms that are feature-compatible with the syntactic context in which they are inserted. Sometimes there is a complete overlap between the syntactic features and the features associated with the inserted form, but sometimes this overlap is only partial (as with the insertion of *you*).

Now we understand how insertion works for the DP slot in (5), in which *you* has to be inserted. But for the DP slot in (3), where *he* has to be inserted, we are not quite there yet, because there is one detail we have to add. There are two forms, and not just one, that we can insert in the DP slot. One of them is *he*, but note that *it* is also feature-compatible with the syntactic context. It is associated with [φ: 3, SG], which constitutes part of the feature specification of spec-FinP in (3), i.e. [φ: 3, SG; Masc], [uFin]. Since we established earlier that partial realisation of syntactic features is not a problem, why then can we not freely insert *it* as an alternative to *he*? We were easy-going with *you* before, but that now gets us into trouble here.

One solution would be to say that *it* must have a mismatching feature. We could for instance state that *he* is masculine, *she* is feminine and *it* is neuter. Therefore, it has the wrong gender feature for insertion in DP in (3). This, however, is not a very plausible solution. Although *he* obviously refers to masculine entities, and *she* to feminine entities, it is far less clear that *it* refers to entities with a neuter gender. In fact, we have seen that it is very unclear that *it* always refers to something. In an example like (6a), *it* functions as an expletive subject and has no referential powers at all. And in (6b), *it* is an expletive subject related to the logical subject *that Edith will buy a new clock*. Do we really want to say that the embedded clause *that Edith will buy a new clock* has neuter gender?

(6) a. It rains too much in Holland.
     b. It seems that Edith will buy a new clock.

It makes more sense to say that *it* is underspecified for gender. *It*, then, can take on the role of expletive subject precisely because it has *no* gender. But if it is unmarked for gender, there is nothing that can block its insertion in the DP position in (3).

Let us turn to another potential solution. The problem is that *he* and *it* are in competition for insertion in the DP slot, and we obviously want *he* to win in this case. The solution is as simple as it is intuitive. Although *it* has features that match the DP position in (3), *he* has more features that do so. The morpho-phonological form *it* partially realises the syntactic features, whereas *he* does so fully. The reason is that *he* is not underspecified for gender and case, because *he* is associated with [Masc] and [uFin], respectively. You could say that *it* is an 'elsewhere' form for 3SG contexts: whenever *he* or *she* cannot be inserted, *it* is inserted instead. But once *he* or *she* can be inserted, insertion of *it* is blocked by the availability of a more specific form. As in life, always go for the best match. The principle that gives us this result is the 'Elsewhere' principle. We have already seen this principle at work in subsection 5.3.3, when we introduced it to explain Principle B of the Binding theory. The 'Elsewhere' principle is reintroduced and slightly reformulated here as (7):

(7) THE 'ELSEWHERE' PRINCIPLE
     Whenever there is competition in grammar between a more
     specific and a more general form, the more specific one wins if no
     grammatical rules are violated.

This principle is also active in the process that inserts the right morpho-phonological form in the Fin position. It tells us that for all possibilities for the head of FinP in (3), *-s* is the only one that can realise it. Insertion of *-ed* is blocked because the [Fin: Past] feature it is associated with clashes with the [Fin: Pres] feature provided by the syntax. It is also not possible to insert *he*, because *he* is, for instance, associated with the wrong kind of φ-feature, namely an interpretable one. In addition, *he* is triggered by a φ-feature with a subfeature [Masc], and Fin does not contain that. The agreement forms -s and -ø, however, have no clashing features and are both candidates for insertion. Insertion of -s wins out over insertion of -ø in this case because the latter is again an 'elsewhere' form, inserted in all present-tense contexts in which -s is not. Since -ø is underspecified for person and number features, -s is inserted instead because in this context it more faithfully spells out the features provided by the syntax: [uφ: 3, SG].

There is one attractive consequence of having the 'Elsewhere' principle, namely that it allows us to simplify the spell-out rules considerably. If a form can be blocked from insertion because there is a more specific form available, then we can reduce the number of features on the less specific forms in (4). Take the φ-subfeature [SG] (singular). The form *I* is associated with this feature, so as to restrict its occurrence to singular contexts. However, since the spell-out rules also contain the form *we*, and this form is specified as [Plural], this form will block insertion of *I* in plural contexts even if *I* is not specified as [SG]. The two spell-out rules would then look as follows:

(8) a. [φ: 1], [uFin] ↔ *I*
     b. [φ: 1, PL], [uFin] ↔ *we*

What these rules now capture is that 'singular' means the absence of a number feature. In other words, 'singular' is in a way unmarked. This makes sense if you think about it. Take a noun like *book*. You can make a plural of it by adding -s: *books*. The singular form, then, is quite literally unmarked. You mark a plural by adding something, but before you add something there is nothing, just the absence of plurality. In addition, we established that *it* can act as a dummy subject. The fact that it does not necessarily refer to a singular entity squares nicely with the statement that it is unmarked for number. The same reasoning pertains to tense. Note that the form -s in (4) is associated with [Fin: Pres]. However, English lacks an overt affix that expresses present tense, just as it lacks an affix expressing 'singular' on a noun. The notion 'present', then, is best captured as the absence of [Fin: Past]. This means that, just as there is no subfeature [SG] present on pronouns, there is no feature [Fin: Pres]. The term used for these oppositions is **markedness**. 'Singular' is unmarked with respect to 'plural', and 'present' is unmarked with respect to 'past'. As a consequence, the morpho-phonological rule for -s can be simplified, as in (9), where [Fin] no longer has a subfeature [Pres] (but still contains the subfeature [SG] on its φ-feature):

(9) [Fin], [uφ: 3, SG] ↔ -s

Note that, although we have erased the feature [SG] from the spell-out rule for *I* in (8), we cannot do so yet in (9) for -s. The reason is that, if we did this in (9), we would also expect the -s form to appear in 3rd-person plural contexts, as insertion of -s would no longer be restricted to singular contexts. This is obviously not the case: *They treasures their health* is ungrammatical. Although markedness allows us to leave out [SG] from some spell-out rules for pronouns, it does not allow us to leave it out from *all* spell-out rules. And yes, that is annoying. We will therefore note that our desire is to get rid of the subfeature [SG] altogether but that before our wish can be granted we have to solve the problem raised by *-s*. In other words, we will come back to this (and succeed, no worries).

Singular and present are unmarked not just morphologically but also conceptually. We conceptualise the here and now as the basic, unmarked situation, and the past, as well as the future, as deviations from that. Likewise, when you are asked to visualise the concept of 'dog', you presumably conceptualise this as a single creature, not as a whole pack. Singular is therefore conceptually unmarked. It is probably not a coincidence that in language (and the concrete case we are looking at is English) conceptual (un)markedness often correlates with morphological (un)markedness. The notion of markedness will become important later on.

Let us now go over the insertion of forms for the rest of the tree in (1) for *He treasure-s his health*. We have covered *he* and *-s*, so this leaves *treasure, his* and *health*. Of these three, the possessive pronoun *his* is the easiest because it is again a pronoun, a form that only spells out φ- and case features. Insertion of *his* is ensured once it wins out in the competition with other possessive forms, such as *her*, *'s* and *its*. This competition proceeds along the same lines as we have seen above. Insertion of *treasure* and *health*, however, requires a bit more discussion because these are not functional but lexical items, which generally have more semantic content than functional items. Now, if syntax is not interested in how things are expressed, then the question arises how we should represent the syntactic elements that underlie *treasure* and *health*.

One approach would be to use features. We should then create bundles of semantic features that together express the concepts of *treasuring* or *health*. It is not, however, easy to do this. It is much easier to establish the featural make-up of *he* and *his* than it is to semantically decompose concepts like *treasure* and *health*. It is actually debated by scholars if it even makes sense to undertake such decomposition for lexical items. From the perspective of the grammatical model we are building, it is very unlikely that such detailed decomposition is necessary. After all, would it be feasible to say that when morphology is confronted with the feature [Meowing] in a syntactic tree, it will spell out the feature bundle as *cat*? Most likely not. Moreover, we have seen that functional features, such as case and agreement, have an impact on the syntax: they are involved in syntactic dependencies. There is nothing that enforces the syntactic visibility of the feature [Meowing], however. Therefore, we had better give up this approach.

Luckily, there is an alternative option, one that makes more sense. We can take the word *cat* as representing the concept of a cat, and we will show this with SMALL CAPITALS, as CAT. The concept of a cat is the idea of a cat that we have in our heads when we talk about one (recall that when we think about a cat, we don't think about a group of cats). The morpho-phonological forms *treasure* and *health* (written in *italics*) are the realisations of the concepts of TREASURE and HEALTH. This is all we need for the grammatical model we are building. Of course, everybody will have more fine-grained ideas about what these particular concepts entail, and everybody knows that cats meow. This is just part of our encyclo-paedic knowledge (our knowledge about the world we live in). It is not necessary, however, to put this in the syntax, or in the spell-out rules that morphology consults. Since we have reason to believe that there is a distinction between what the syntax combines and what morphology expresses, the only thing that we need is a way to represent the concepts of TREASURE and HEALTH, so as to distinguish them from the actual, audible forms. The relevant spell-out rules then look as follows.

(10) a. TREASURE   ↔   *treasure*
     b. HEALTH   ↔   *health*
     c. CAT   ↔   *cat*
     d. DOG   ↔   *dog*

Once we have inserted all the morpho-phonological forms and utter the result, (1) comes out as follows.

(11) He -*s* treasure his health.

But this is not quite where we need to be yet, is it? The problem with (11) is that -*s* still does not appear on the verbal stem *treasure*. As it stands, these two forms are inserted into different syntactic heads and this is obviously the wrong result. The question, then, is how -*s* ends up on the verbal stem.

Before we continue with this problem, let's introduce a second prob-lem here too. Suppose we have a past-tense context, such as the struc-ture in (12):

(12)

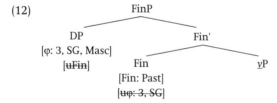

The problem here is that there are two forms that we could insert in Fin. We could insert the agreement form -*s* to spell out the feature [uφ: 3, SG]. Alternatively, we could insert the tense form -*ed* to spell out the fea-ture [Fin: Past]. Neither form is optimal in the sense that it does not spell out all the features of Fin. Each form spells out two syntactic features in total. Nevertheless, it is clear that -*ed* wins: (13a) is grammatical in a past-tense context, whereas (13b) is not. Also observe that generating both forms is not an option, since (13c) is ungrammatical as well.

(13) a. Yesterday, he still treasured his health.
     b. *Yesterday, he still treasures his health.
     c. *Yesterday he still treasureds his health.

Nothing we have said so far captures the facts in (13). Although -*ed* is specified differently from -*s*, it is not more specified. Therefore, the 'Elsewhere' principle has nothing to say here.

We will address these two problems in the next section, where we will endow the morphological component of the grammar with a bit more technical content.

Exercises

A3 a. Provide the tree structure for *She loves him* and indicate how *she* and *him* can be correctly inserted, given the pronominal paradigm for English in the main text (4).

b. Draw the tree structure of the sentence *We love them* and show what the relevant realisation rules are for the pronouns.

B4 Take the morpho-phonological forms that make up the present tense paradigm of *to be* and try to formulate the realisation rules for the three forms *am, are* and *is* with the use of the (sub-)features [1], [2], [3], [SG] and [PL]. You will run into a problem with *are*. What is that problem?

B5 Returning to the problem with *are*, you could assume that English has two *are* forms, each with its own specification. This means that we need four realisation rules for this paradigm (*am, is, are*1 and *are*2), not three. Alternatively, you could assume that *are* in English functions as an 'elsewhere' form. The advantage would be that you can go back to only having three realisation rules. Provide the realisation rules for both these analyses.

B6 The English present-tense agreement paradigm is very defective and only has one overt form, the famous 3rd person *-s*. This form occurs in the singular. You could say this is unexpected, given the notion of markedness introduced in this section. Explain why.

C7 In the realisation rules you provided in B5, did you need to specify any forms as [SG], or could you simply assume that singular was the absence of plural?

8.3 Consequences

So far, we have looked at morphology as merely an interpretive part of grammar. Morphology looks at the feature bundles that define the syntactic terminals (i.e. the lowest nodes in the tree) and inserts the most appropriate morpho-phonological forms. Now, if morphology is a separate module of the grammar, then in principle nothing forbids this module to do a bit more. Compare this to syntax. We have seen that this module can remerge constituents into the structures that it creates. Once a particular uninterpretable feature cannot be checked off, for instance because the matching interpretable feature does not c-command it, syntax can decide to remerge the constituent carrying the interpretable feature higher into the structure, so that the interpretable feature can c-command the uninterpretable one and feature checking can proceed. This was for instance the trigger for movement of the subject from spec-*v*P to spec-FinP. This remerger higher in the structure allows the [uφ] feature on Fin to be checked off. You could say, therefore, that Remerge is syntax's way to solve a problem.

Now, if we endow syntax with the ability to solve problems, we might want to endow morphology with similar powers. In fact, it would be weird if one grammatical module were able to further manipulate its building blocks, but another module weren't. So let us see what morphological operations we can propose to solve our problems, and how we can independently argue in favour of these operations.

8.3.1 Morphological Merger

As the analysis stands, morpho-phonological forms can realise [uφ] features in the Fin position, away from the verbal stem that it needs to be a part of. This cannot be the correct result, though. Whereas *treasure* is an unbound morpheme (a full word that you can, for instance, look up in the dictionary), the *-s* is a **bound morpheme**. It cannot appear on its own but needs to be combined with another morpheme. In addition, *-s* cannot be part of just any unbound morpheme, it needs to be part of a lexical verb. This is a property of the morpho-phonological form *-s* itself, and not of the morpheme that it spells out. After all, if Fin is spelled out by an unbound morpheme instead, such as an auxiliary, no host has to be found to which the auxiliary must attach. We therefore add this specific information about *-s* to the relevant spell-out rule on the right side of the arrow, as in (14), where '__' indicates the location in which *-s* must occur, on the right side of the verbal stem.

(14)   [Fin], [uφ: 3, SG]   ↔   *-s*/[V-__]

We established earlier that syntax does not care about how feature bundles are expressed. It certainly does not care, therefore, that some morpho-phonological forms need to be hosted by unbound morphemes. Syntax cannot know when Fin will be spelled out by a bound or unbound morpheme because it only has access to the features in Fin, not to the forms expressing those features. The problem created by the bound morpheme *-s* (namely, how does it end up on a host?) is therefore not something that syntax can solve, and so it must be morphology that solves it. How does morphology do this?

Take a look at the following structure:

(15)

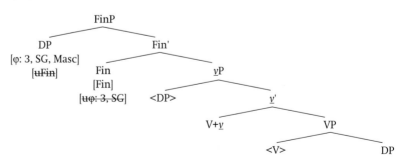

For morphology to be happy, Fin and V (sitting in *v*) need to come together. Let us propose, therefore, that this is exactly what morphology can do: bring these two heads together. When you have two syntactic projections, with one projection immediately dominating the other one, then the heads of these two projections can be merged by the morphology. This process is known as **morphological merger**, or M-merger. What happens is that Fin, with all its features, descends (or, as syntacticians say, 'lowers') onto the head of its sister. The sister is *v*P, so Fin can lower onto V+*v*. This gives us the representation in (16):

(16)

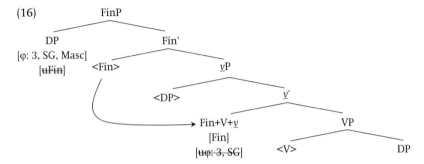

How do we know that Fin lowers onto V+*v*, and that it is not V+*v* rising to Fin? Because of facts like the following:

(17) a. John can really treasure his health.
　　　b. John really treasures his health.

In (17a), we see the adverb *really* sitting between *can* and *treasure*. If *can* sits in Fin and *treasure* in *v*, then *really* must sit somewhere at the left edge of the *v*P. In (17b), we see *-s* occur on *treasure* and *treasure* is on the right side of the adverb. In order to account for (17a) and (17b) at the same time, we must assume that *-s* is lower than expected, namely in *v*P rather than in Fin, and not that *treasure* is higher than expected.

Note that lowering Fin onto V+*v* looks very much like a syntactic movement, but it is not; it is a morphological movement. First of all, when we take into consideration the various syntactic movements that we have seen in previous chapters (verb movement, subject movement, *Wh*-movement), then there is one clear generalisation: syntactic movement is always upwards. Here, we have a case of lowering. The exceptionality of the direction of movement is directly captured if we maintain that syntactic movement is always up, but that morphological movement is always down. This way, we can even take it as a way of distinguishing syntactic movement from morphological movement.

Once morphology has lowered Fin onto V+*v*, it can spell out *-s* as part of the verb, as desired. Note that in (14) '__' occurs on the right side of V, not on the left side. *-s* is a **suffix**, and not a **prefix**. Therefore, it ends up being pronounced at the end of the word rather than at the beginning. It is important to note that under this analysis it is not the -*s* that has low-ered: -*s* is the morpho-phonological form that spells out features and it is these features that have undergone lowering by a morphological opera-tion. It is only after morphology has done the lowering that -*s* is inserted into the structure. In this particular example, then, -*s* has never been in the *v*P-external Fin position.

Okay, it is time to take stock. We had a problem and now we have a solution. The problem was that -*s* got inserted too high into the struc-ture, and the solution is to let morphology lower features from Fin to V+*v* and only then to insert the relevant morpho-phonological form. This is a solution, of course, that has all the appearance of brute force. Do we need the features to lower down? Well, morphology, go ahead and lower them down. The question, therefore, is the usual one. Is there any sup-port for this analysis? Actually, there are two facts about English that this analysis accounts for in a straightforward manner: (i) the fact that English has *do* support and (ii) the fact that it also accounts naturally for irregular verbs. Let us go over these in turn.

First of all, M-merger, which involves lowering, is a very specific and localised operation. Morphology can move features from a head to the head of its sister, and that is it. This means that M-merger of Fin and V-*v* is blocked as soon as a syntactic projection intervenes between FinP and *v*P. This is exactly what happens in a negative clause, in which FinP and *v*P get interrupted by NegP. The consequence of the presence of nega-tion is that the features in Fin cannot lower onto V+*v*, as indicated in (18). This, then, is responsible for the ungrammaticality of (19).

(18)

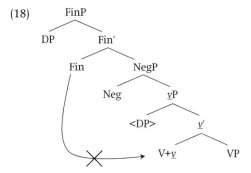

(19)   *He not treasures his health.

The sister of Fin is NegP, so the only head that can undergo M-merger with Fin is Neg, and not V+*v*. Even if this happened, -*s* could not be inserted, given (14): -*s* needs a verb. This means that in a clause with negation, insertion of -*s* is effectively blocked. Morphology, however, still wants to spell out the features in Fin. The solution that English has found for this predicament is a 'dummy verb'. It uses a meaningless form of *do* that is inserted just to spell out the features of the Fin head. The spell-out rules, then, also contain the following entry for 3SG contexts:

(20)   [Fin], [uφ: 3, SG] $\leftrightarrow$ *does*

Note that (20) is less specific than (14): *does* is not a morphological form that has to be attached to the left side of a lexical verb, like *-s*. Therefore, *does* can be considered an 'elsewhere' form: it is inserted whenever *-s* cannot be inserted. But whenever *-s* can be inserted, namely after M-merger has applied successfully, insertion of *does* is blocked. A natural consequence of this analysis is that in *Wh*-questions *does*, not *-s*, is inserted. If Fin moves to C syntactically, Fin moves away from, rather than to, the lexical verb. Sitting in the C position, Fin cannot undergo M-merger with V+*v* any more. After all, in the C position it can only undergo M-merger with the head of the sister of C, but that would be the base position of Fin, and not V+*v*. This is the reason why (21a) is bad as a regular yes/no question. This sentence simply cannot be derived by M-merger. What needs to happen instead is insertion of *does* as the realisation of Fin sitting in the C position. This gives us (21b), which we recognise as a regular yes/no question.

(21)   a.   *[$_{CP}$ [$_{FinP}$ He [$_{vP}$ treasures his health?]]]
       b.   [$_{CP}$ Does [$_{FinP}$ he [$_{vP}$ treasure his health?]]]

The *do* support facts, then, follow naturally from a restriction on M-merger. Note, by the way, that adverbs do not trigger *do* support. It seems that the features of Fin can undergo lowering despite the fact that these constituents intervene.

(22)   He really treasures his health.

This actually gives weight to the proposed analysis. Although in one sense *really* intervenes between Fin and V+*v*, it does not intervene in the relevant sense. *Really* sits in the *v*P, not in a projection in between *v*P and FinP. FinP thus immediately dominates *v*P. But this predicts that the head of FinP may undergo morphological merger with the head of *v*P. Therefore, Fin can lower onto V+*v* without any problems:

(23)

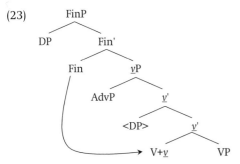

In addition to the facts involving *do* support, a second piece of support in favour of the proposed analysis particularly addresses the claim that what lowers onto V+*v* is Fin and its abstract features, and not the actual morpho-phonological forms. To see this, assume the opposite (namely that the actual morpho-phonological forms lower down) for a moment. This would mean that in a past-tense environment the morpho-phonological form, the suffix *-ed* lowers down to the verbal stem:

(24)

a. [FinP he -ed [vP ~~he~~ treasure+*v* [VP ~~treasure~~ his health]]] SYNTACTIC STRUCTURE
b. [FinP he -ed [vP ~~he~~ treasure+*v*+-ed [VP ~~treasure~~ his health]]] LOWERING

This would work well, as the expected outcome is the one we actually have, namely *He treasured his health*. The point is that this only works for regular verbs. Suppose we have a sentence that contains an irregular verb, such as *run*. There is no way we could analyse this if the past tense form *-ed* lowered onto the verbal stem. In fact, we would predict the outcome in (25a), not the one in (25b).

(25)   a.   *He runned a health check.
       b.   He ran a health check.

In order to account for (25b), we would have to assume that, during its descent towards V+*v*, *-ed* undergoes some serious metamorphosis and has the power to change the /u/ of the verbal stem into an /a/. Not only would our theory start to resemble science fiction, but just imagine how many storylines we would need to account for the existence of *thought* (rather than *thinked*), *slept* (rather than *sleeped*), *spoke* (rather than *speaked*), etc. If, alternatively, we assume that it is Fin and its abstract features that lower to V+*v*, and that morpho-phonological forms are inserted after this, then we can simply say that morphology inserts whatever it can find in the spell-out rules. These will contain dedicated forms to spell out certain past-tense forms. The relevant list for our toy example in (25) looks like that in (26):

(26)   TREASURE   ↔   *treasure*
       RUN   ↔   *run*
       [Fin: Past]   ↔   *-ed*
       RUN + [Fin: Past]   ↔   *ran*

To spell out the past form of *treasure* (*treasured*), morphology needs to insert two morpho-phonological forms, the stem *treasure*, and the past tense suffix *-ed*. To spell out the past form of *run*, however, morphology can take a shortcut, since the spell-out rules mention one morpho-phonological form to do just that, *ran*. Therefore, morphology will insert this form and be done with it. It takes the same shortcut with the past tenses of *think*, *sleep*, etc. Note that even though the elements on the left side of the arrow are different types of elements, CONCEPTS and [features], neither of them is a *morpho-phonological form*. These are represented on the right side of the arrow.

Now, it also follows that the regular past tense of *run, runned*, is ungrammatical. Or, put differently, we can now also understand why RUN + [Fin: Past] could not be realised as *runned*. When a morphological shortcut is available, it must be taken. This is really nothing but the application of the 'Elsewhere' principle: only use a general form if a more specific form is not available. Obviously, if you want to spell out RUN + [Fin: Past], then the most specified form you can have is the one form that spells out the concept of RUN in the past tense, and *ran* will win out over insertion of the general, regular form for the past tense, -ed. The availability of the specific form *ran* will therefore block the regularly formed past tense form *runned*.

To sum up this section: we had the unresolved problem that our theory expected agreement and tense morphemes, such as -s and -ed, to appear in a higher position than the verbal stem. We solved this problem by proposing M-merger, a morphological lowering operation that allows a syntactic head to become part of the head of its sister. We showed how *do* support and the behaviour of irregular past tense forms both provide evidence for M-merger as an operation that applies to features that are only subsequently realised by particular morpho-phonological forms. In this way, M-merger not only solves our initial problem but also offers a handle on some additional facts about English. What we have not properly analysed yet, though, is the fact that in English agreement morphology disappears in the past tense: you cannot say **He walkeds*. Why not? Let us turn to this next.

8.3.2 Impoverishment

In the previous subsection, we argued that it makes sense to think of morphology as a grammatical component in its own right with its own set of rules and operations. One such operation is the insertion of morpho-phonological forms; another, as we have just seen, is M-merger. We have shown how the introduction of this operation leads to an increased understanding of the syntax of English verbs, in the sense that more facts fall into place. The recognition that morphology is able to manipulate syntactic representation before it inserts morpho-phonological forms has led to the exploration of other operations that may be useful for understanding patterns of English. In this subsection, we will explore the usefulness of yet another morphological operation, known as **impoverishment**. It is this operation, we will argue, that underlies the disappearance of agreement morphology in the past tense.

To see how one would get the idea for this second operation, let us look at the relevant syntactic structure for a 3rd person singular in a past-tense context, namely (12), repeated here as (27a). Recall that we analysed present tense as the unmarked form, just as we did for singular number: 'present' entails the absence of a [Past] subfeature. This means that there is no feature [Fin: Present] but just [Fin], and that -s is simply not associated with a tense feature.

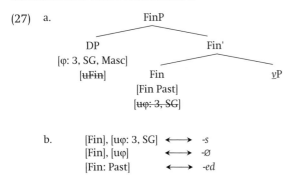

(27) a.

b.   [Fin], [uφ: 3, SG] ⟷ -s
        [Fin], [uφ]   ⟷ -ø
        [Fin: Past]   ⟷ -ed

The three forms in (27b) are in complementary distribution with one another, so one cannot occur in the presence of another. Structurally, this makes a lot of sense. After all, there is one syntactic head position, Fin, so intuitively you would say that only one morpho-phonological form fits there, just as there can only be one verbal stem in the V position. Put differently, the three morpho-phonological forms represent different morphemes, each with their own specifications. It is these morphemes that carry the feature [Fin] heading FinP in the syntax. Now, if there can be only one morpheme doing that in a particular clause, there can only be one morpho-phonological form realising that morpheme.

Although we have good reason for restricting insertion to one form only, the question is which one. Given the realisation rules in (27b), we could either insert *-s* or *-ed*; *-s* because of [uφ: 3, SG] and *-ed* because of [Fin: Past] on Fin. The 'Elsewhere' principle is of no help here, because these two forms spell out a different subset of the features present in Fin. The *-s* form spells out agreement features and the *-ed* form spells out a Fin feature. Therefore, we cannot say that one is more specific than the other, or that one is an 'elsewhere' form with respect to the other. The question is how we can ensure that we get the right outcome for (27), namely *treasured* and not *treasures*.

As a way towards understanding this, we will take the same route as before with M-merger (section 8.3.1). First, we will introduce the operation that gives the right outcome. After that, we will see what else this operation gets us, and to what extent we can understand it. In other words, first we are going to describe the facts, and then we will try to explain them.

When two forms are in competition and the usual diagnostics of specificity do not help us pick one, we should do something that blocks insertion of the wrong one. Now, what would block the insertion of *-s* in past-tense contexts? The absence of the [uφ: 3, SG] feature on Fin. If this feature is absent, then insertion of *-s* is no longer triggered by the syntactic context and only insertion of *-ed* becomes possible. What morphology needs to do, then, is simply delete the [uφ: 3, SG] feature from the syntactic representation. Let us therefore assume that it can, by using a so-called **impoverishment rule**, a rule that deletes a specific syntactic feature from the tree. The one that we need is given in (28):

(28) [uφ]   →   ∅ / [Fin: Past]__

How should we read this? This rule gives the relevant, targeted feature before the arrow ([uφ] in this case), it states what happens to it after the arrow (namely deletion, indicated by the symbol ∅), and it specifies after the oblique ('/') in which context this happens, namely when [uφ] sits in the __-spot, next to the feature [Fin: Past]. So (28) reads as 'Turn the feature [uφ] to zero (that is "delete it") when it occurs next to a [Fin: Past] feature.' Like M-merger, impoverishment is an operation on the syntactic representation that takes place before insertion of morpho-phonological forms.

After (28) has been applied, the original structure in (29a) looks like that in (29b), and the regular spell-out rules in (30) apply to this representation:

(29) a.

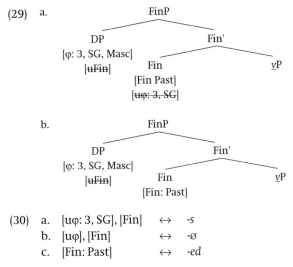

b.

(30) a. [uφ: 3, SG], [Fin]   ↔   -s
      b. [uφ], [Fin]   ↔   -ø
      c. [Fin: Past]   ↔   -ed

Now the choice is easy. Insertion of -s is blocked and therefore insertion of -ed can take place without competition. Note, by the way, that (28) blocks insertion not only of -s but also of -ø. This is without empirical consequences: since -ø is a non-overt form, there is no way of telling whether insertion of -ø is indeed blocked in [Fin: Past] contexts. The reason for adopting an impoverishment rule that deletes [uφ], and not a rule that only deletes this feature when it has the values [3, SG], is that (28) is simpler. And since the simpler rule is not contradicted by empirical facts, we will adopt it.

The next question is why morphology impoverishes tense rather than agreement features to solve the impasse: why does it delete [uφ] in the context of [Fin: Past], and not [Fin: Past] in the context of [uφ]? A first guess is that tense features on a verbal head are simply more important than [φ] features. After all, the [Fin: Past] feature is interpretable, whereas [uφ] is not. However, this would mean that morphology makes a choice that is semantic in nature, thereby caring about something that it is not supposed to care about. Morphology has to insert appropriate morpho-phonological forms, given the features that the syntax provides, independent of meaning, just as syntax merges and remerges feature bundles irrespective of what they end up sounding like. It is completely counterintuitive, therefore, to let morphology make a choice based on a *semantic* criterion; it needs to make a choice based on some *morphological* criterion.

It is hard to say what criterion this would be with only one case of impoverishment to go by. It would help us, therefore, to consider a second case of impoverishment. The resemblances between these two cases can then guide us towards the morphological factor that is at play here. To put it differently, instead of making some statement about the impoverishment of [uφ] over [Fin: Past], we would be standing on more solid ground if we made a generalisation first.

Let us therefore turn to pronouns. We can observe that these elements express three features in English; person, number and gender. Take a look at the paradigm for nominative personal pronouns in (31). The three features needed to describe the morpho-phonological contrasts have the potential for creating at least eighteen different pronouns: person (1st, 2nd, and 3rd) times number (singular and plural) times gender (masculine, feminine and absence of gender). English, however, only uses seven.

(31)   Paradigm of English nominative pronouns

	SINGULAR			PLURAL		
	MASCULINE	FEMININE	NEUTER	MASCULINE	FEMININE	NEUTER
1ST PERSON	*I*			*we*		
2ND PERSON	*you*					
3RD PERSON	*he*	*she*	*it*	*they*		

What we can observe is that not every person has a number contrast: 2nd person does not express the difference between singular and plural. And of the pronouns that do express a number distinction, only 3rd-person pronouns express a gender distinction – however, only in the singular.

Generalising, whether you express number depends on person, and whether you express gender depends on number and person. These dependencies suggest a hierarchy: person > number > gender. You could say that person is robustly expressed in English, in the sense that every person has at least one unique form. Apparently, it is more special (or more marked) to express number, because only 1st and 3rd persons make that distinction. Gender is the most special property for English pronouns to express, since only 3rd-person singular pronouns make gender distinctions. Now, the interesting fact is that these observations do not only pertain to nominative personal pronouns. When we look at accusative personal pronouns, the same regularities reappear. The 2nd person still does not express number (there is only *you*). As for the gender property, *him* and *her* express gender, but the 3rd person plural only has *them*. When we turn to reflexive pronouns, number reappears in the 2nd person: *yourself* vs. *yourselves*. Gender, however, remains absent in the 3rd person plural: *himself* and *herself* vs. *themselves*. And finally, the pattern extends to possessive pronouns: *his* and *her* express gender whereas 3rd person plural only has *their*.

It seems, then, that, in English pronouns, gender is generally absent in the plural. Now, we could express this absence in the spell-out rules by simply not adding a gender feature for those pronouns that do not express it, namely the plural ones. The differences between nominative 3rd-person pronouns would then look as follows:

(32)   [φ: 3, Masc], [uFin]   ↔   *he*
       [φ: 3, Fem], [uFin]   ↔   *she*
       [φ: 3, PL], [uFin]   ↔   *they*

We could then do the same in the paradigms for accusative personal pronouns, reflexive pronouns and possessive pronouns. However, the fact that gender does not play a role in the plural of any of these paradigms would then be rather coincidental. We could just as well have lived in a world in which English sometimes expresses gender in the plural and sometimes not, depending on the paradigm. After all, these are distinct paradigms, and what happens in one paradigm should not have any effect on other paradigms. What we see, however, is that gender is *systematically* absent in the plural dimension of any English paradigm. This strongly suggests that this is not a coincidence but simply a rule in English. How would we formulate this rule? You can probably guess: as an impoverishment rule. Suppose that the following rule is part of English grammar:

(33) [Masc]/[Fem] $\rightarrow$ $\varnothing\,/\,[\varphi\text{: PL, \_\_}]$

This one rule, which basically says that the subfeature [gender] disappears when there is a subfeature [PL] present, is able to capture an exceptionless pattern in English, so that the absence of gender across plural paradigms is no longer coincidental. If (33) exists, we could not live in a world in which English sometimes but not always expresses gender, depending on the paradigm. In short, the impoverishment rule captures a generalisation about English that is not captured by encoding in the spell-out rules along the lines of (32).

With this second case of impoverishment under our belt, let us now return to the tense vs. agreement debate that we put to one side. Why is it that in past-tense contexts English prefers insertion of *-ed* over insertion of *-s*? And what could be the *morphological* motivation for this? The discussion about pronominal paradigms now gives us an idea. Apparently, it is the case that gender systematically disappears in 3rd-person plural, but not in 3rd-person singular, contexts. Now, recall that 'singular' is unmarked and entails the absence of number. Using the hierarchy that we established earlier (person > number > gender), we could then schematically represent this contrast as follows:

(34) a. *he/she*:   [3rd person] > [Masc/Fem] $\rightarrow$ no impoverishment of gender

    b. *they*:   [3rd person] > [Plural] > [Masc/Fem] $\rightarrow$ impoverishment of gender

You could say that the lowest φ-subfeature on the hierarchy (namely [Masc] or [Fem]) disappears in the presence of the marked φ-subfeature [Plural]. Once [Plural] is present, [Masc] or [Fem] goes. Now note that this way of looking at impoverishment allows us a trigger for impoverishment that is purely morphological. What morphology does is keep a lid on the overall complexity of syntactic nodes: one subfeature in, one subfeature out. It does not look at what these features actually express semantically: it does not act on semantic properties. It only looks at the morphological hierarchy and decides to restrict the overall complexity by impoverishing the lowest φ-subfeature on it: gender ([Masc]/[Fem]), not number ([Plural]).

We have now manoeuvred ourselves into a position in which we can analyse the tense/agreement issue along the exact same lines. The difference between present-and past-tense contexts is that the present tense is morphologically simpler. After all, 'present' is unmarked and entails the absence of a past-tense marker. The contrast between *treasures* and *treasured* can therefore be represented as follows. The first, *treasures*, is a morpho-phonological form that spells out a feature bundle that has not been impoverished, whereas *treasured* is the spell-out of a feature bundle that has been impoverished.

(35)   a.   *treasures*:   [V+*v*] > [Fin] >   →   no impoverishment of
                          [uφ: 3, SG]   agreement

       b.   *treasured*:   [V+*v*] > [Fin: Past] >   →   impoverishment of
                          [uφ: 3, SG]   agreement

As before, morphology can impoverish a feature when another feature is added to the structure, so as to keep the overall complexity stable. In this case, the impoverished feature is [uφ: 3, SG] and the feature whose presence triggers this impoverishment is a subfeature, namely [Past] on [Fin]. It is only when this subfeature is present that [uφ: 3, SG] becomes impoverished. This captures the fact that agreement only disappears in the past tense; it is always visible in the present tense.

But is it really the case that agreement only disappears in the past tense? Remember that in section 8.2.1 we had a discussion about markedness. The idea was that in spell-out rules we could get rid of features like [SG] and [Pres] because they represent unmarked values: 'singular' is the absence of number, and 'present' is the absence of tense. This led to the simplification of these spell-out rules. But there was one annoying problem. We still had to include [SG] in the spell-out rule for the agreement form *-s*, repeated here:

(36)   [Fin], [uφ: 3, SG]   ↔   *-s*

If we delete [SG] in this rule, we immediately predict *-s* to show up in 3rd-person plural context, contrary to fact. For this reason, we could not conclude what we were so eager to conclude, namely that [SG] simply does not exist. But now we have a solution, and the solution is called impoverishment. Here's how it goes. Let us assume that [SG] indeed does not exist. In this case, the spell-out rule for *-s* looks as in (37):

(37)   [Fin], [uφ: 3]   ↔   *-s*

How do we ensure that *-s* does not show up in the plural? Well, earlier we had a rule that impoverished agreement in past-tense contexts. We can now add a specific rule for English agreement that states that person agreement is impoverished in plural contexts:

(38) [3] → ∅ / [uφ: PL, __]

After (38) has impoverished the relevant feature from the syntactic node, (37) can no longer apply, with the result that *-s* cannot be inserted in the plural. And this is the right result. As before, impoverishment works to keep the overall complexity stable. It is only in the presence of an additional feature (in this case [PL]) that impoverishment is triggered.

To sum up, this section has exploited the hypothesis that morphological operations exist that apply before the insertion of morpho-phonological forms. We have argued that morphology has the power to apply M-merger and impoverishment rules. The former ensures that affixes can be spelled out on the relevant host. Impoverishment rules target features that sit low on the morphological hierarchy and serve to reduce overall morphological complexity. We have seen two examples of the latter: impoverishment of gender features in the plural parts of nominal paradigms, and impoverishment of agreement and agreement features in the past-tense paradigm. Both M-merger and impoverishment rules are a useful tool for making sense of particular morphological regularities, as they capture these regularities in a very straightforward manner.

Exercises

A8   Draw the tree structures of the following two sentences and state which operations take place in morphology.
  a.   He does not know it.
  b.   He knows it.

B9   We could hypothesise that the absence of an overt person marker in the plural is not a coincidence. In this section, we have seen for the pronominal domain that featural distinctions have a tendency to disappear in the plural. It could be that something similar happens in the verbal domain. How can we use irregular verbs to provide more evidence for the idea that the absence of person marking in the plural is perhaps not coincidental?

C10   Formulate the realisation rules for the regular present-tense paradigm, as well as for the present tense of the verb *to be*, and use impoverishment to capture generalisations about the plural in the verbal domain.

C11   Answer question C7 from section 8.2 again, but now taking into consideration the spell-out rules you provided in question C10.

Summary

In this chapter, we have shown how syntax and morphology are related to one another. We have focused on one phenomenon that constitutes a real syntax–morphology mismatch, namely tense and agreement. On the one hand, we have syntactic evidence to think that the tense and agreement features reside outside of vP, in a position we know as Fin. On the other hand, the morphological evidence suggests that tense and agreement can be spelled out inside vP, namely on the lexical verb sitting there. We have taken our time to analyse this discrepancy and solve it. In this attempt, we have come to learn a lot about what syntax and morphology are and what they are not. In essence, we conclude that syntax is the machine that merges and remerges abstract feature bundles, and that morphology is the grammatical component that steps in after this is done to provide concrete forms, thereby consulting the spell-out rules of the English language. This means that in our inverted Y-model we have to locate morphology after syntax, on the 'sound' side of our model, and replace 'words' with 'features and concepts', as indicated in (39):

(39)   FEATURES AND CONCEPTS

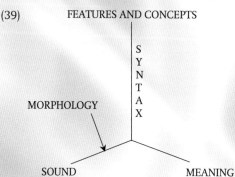

We have also argued that morphology can do a bit more than just insert morpho-phonological forms that featurally match the terminal nodes of the syntactic representation. It can also manipulate the feature bundles that it receives from the syntax. We have discussed two operations in some detail, namely morphological merger and impoverishment, and these take place before morphology inserts morpho-phonological forms. Zooming in a bit, then, the picture is as follows:

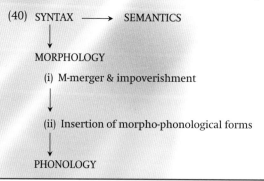

The independently supported operations listed in (40(i)) are both involved in the realisation of English verbal morphology. M-merger allows Fin and V+$\underline{v}$ to merge, so that tense and agreement features can be spelled out on a host verb. Impoverishment is the operation that accounts for the fact that English shows no agreement distinctions in the past tense and no gender distinctions in plural pronouns.

In the final two chapters, we are going to look in more detail at how syntax is relevant to grammar's sound and meaning components, also known as phonology and semantics.

Further Reading

The idea that parts of words can originate in different syntactic positions (so that there is not a neat one-to-one correspondence between syntax and morphology) was already part of Chomsky's 1957 analysis of the verbal syntax of English.

The more advanced idea that syntax operates with feature bundles, and that morphology inserts concrete forms later, is the cornerstone of Distributed Morphology (Halle & Marantz 1993; Noyer 1997; Marantz 1997, among many others). It is within this framework that morphological merger was formulated (see Embick & Noyer 2001 for the explicit analysis adopted in this chapter). Although distributed morphology is a prominent and influential approach to morphology, it is not without its critics, and some scholars feel that it is not sufficiently constrained.

Bonet (1991) is responsible for the hypothesis that morphology impoverishes syntactic structures before insertion of morpho-phonological forms. For more discussion on person–number–gender hierarchies, see Baker (2008).

9 Syntax and Phonology

CHAPTER OUTLINE

KEY TERMS

linear order
linearisation
head-initial
head-final
parameter
selection
adjunct
filler-gap pattern

In the previous chapter, we showed how morphology provides concrete, pronounceable forms for the abstract feature bundles that syntax merges. Once the grammar knows which morpho-phonological forms to use, it starts to care about how exactly to pronounce them. In this chapter, we will not concern ourselves with the actual way these morpho-phonological words are realised acoustically. The reason is that there is simply no connection with syntax here. The concept CAT in English is pronounced as K-A-T (or in the International Phonetic Alphabet as /kʰæt/), the pronoun *he* is pronounced as H-E or /hi:/. This is in no way related to the syntactic structure, and therefore of no interest to a syntactician. There is one aspect of sound, however, that a syntactician should care about, and which therefore deserves a closer look. It concerns the fact that the morpho-phonological forms that morphology has provided (i.e. the words of the sentence) have to be pronounced in a particular order (call it the word order). This order is not random but obeys certain rules. This raises the question of how to formulate those rules. It turns out that we run into a bit of a paradox here. On the one hand, it seems clear that the word orders we end up with are not entirely independent of the structures created by syntax. On the other hand, these word orders are not fully determined by the syntactic hierarchy either. After all, a hierarchy is not a linear order. This means that, in order to understand how linearisation works, we have to study the relation between syntax and phonology carefully. Which part of word order is due to syntax, and which is due to phonology? This is the topic of this chapter.

9.1 Insight: Syntax is not about Word Order

Syntax is not about word order? Yes, this is what we mean. This statement may come as a bit of a surprise because many dictionaries will define syntax in exactly that way: syntax is the study of word order. Are these dictionaries all wrong, then? Well, yes and no. It is certainly the case that what happens in syntax has effects on word order, but it is not the case that syntax itself cares about word order. To see why this is so, consider the 'inverted Y-model' (1) once more. Syntax builds structures that are then expressed (which is what morphology and phonology take care of) and semantically interpreted (which is what semantics does).

(1)

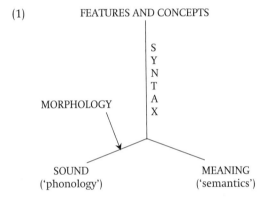

Grammar, then, consists of several subcomponents, each with their own requirements, and each with their own operations. In chapter 2, we looked in detail at the core operation of syntax. What did it need to look like if we wanted to account for the facts? We argued that Merge makes better predictions than other theories, and concluded from this that the essential syntactic operation is therefore Merge. What Merge gives you is hierarchical structures. That is, application of Merge only determines what belongs together, not what is uttered first. For instance, we have shown that the constituent *expensive delicious sausages* has an internal structure, [expensive [delicious sausages]], due to its creation by means of the Merge operation. This tells us that *delicious sausages* is one constituent and that *expensive delicious sausages* is another, but that *expensive delicious* is not. Merge creates internal structure. That is quite a lot, but limited at the same time.

What Merge does not produce is a **linear order**, an array of words. If it did, we would have a much easier time figuring out how to pronounce the products of syntax: just say the words in the order in which they appear in the string. This, however, is not what syntax does. It creates structural hierarchies. So the question becomes how we utter a hierarchy. Well, obviously, we can't. We can only utter a linear string of words that is derived from the hierarchy. This means that before we can utter the output of syntax, we have to linearise it. **Linearisation** is, among other things, what phonology takes care of.

Now, let us be very clear what we mean by 'syntax does not care about word order'. Take a look at another syntactic structure, this time one that results from merging a verb with an object:

(2)

Consider again what Merge does. It takes two constituents, puts them together, and then the categorial properties of one of these constituents determines the categorial properties of the newly created constituent. Full stop. Merge does not say 'Oh, and put the object to the right of the verb.' This means that we could equally well represent the merger of a verb and object as in (3):

(3)

Syntactically speaking, (3) expresses exactly the same as (2): they both involve a merger of a verb and a DP, with the verb being the head. The representations in (2) and (3) are different drawings of the same object, much as you do a drawing of the front and the back of the same tree. A better comparison may even be paper mobiles, where elements hanging on the same hanger can turn around. We could have used structures like (3) throughout the entire book when drawing a VP. Syntactically (2) and (3) are simply identical. There is really nothing in the syntactic structure that tells you that *fire* should be uttered to the left of *Ethan*. Syntax only tells us that *fire* and *Ethan* belong together, but there is nothing in the structural representation that tells us in which order they have to be pronounced. Now, take a slightly more complicated structure.

(4)

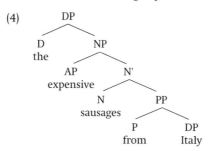

In this structure, *the* sits in a hierarchically higher position than *Italy*. After all, *the* c-commands *Italy* but *Italy* does not c-command *eat*. In the structure in (4), we have put *the* on the left side of the direct object, as in (2). But syntactically speaking, that does not mean anything. We might as well represent the tree as in (5), and it would not make the slightest difference, because in (4) the same syntactic relations are expressed as in (5).

(5)

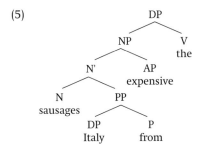

Again, (4) and (5) tell us that *from* and *Italy* belong together, just as *sausages* and *from Italy* belong together. And we can establish that *the* c-commands *Italy* but not vice versa, just as in (4). But the representation does not tell us which word is uttered to the left or the right of the other. Of course, we have used structures like (2) and (4) throughout, and not structures like (3) and (5), because the former two seem to more transparently reflect the linear order. In (2), the verb *fire* is placed to the left of the object *Ethan* because in English you say *fire* before *Ethan*, and in English you read from left to right. But what we are then in effect doing is linearising the tree; we are not expressing a hierarchy, a syntactic object. We are making decisions that are not made by syntax (and its main operation, Merge). It is these decisions that we will make explicit in this chapter.

In short, human grammars have a technical problem to solve. The problem is that we speak. A consequence of this is that our syntactic representations must be linearised. After all, we can only utter words in order, one after the other. What we need, therefore, is an algorithm, a technical procedure that allows us to linearise our syntactic structures. In section 9.2, we will look at what that algorithm must be able to do. We will also see how this affects differences between languages. After we have put such an algorithm in place, we can in 9.3 turn to a related issue, namely how to linearise remerged constituents.

Exercises

A1 The syntactic structure below tells us nothing about how to linearise it. This gives four possibilities, provided that elements that belong to the same constituent are uttered together. What are these four ways?

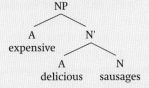

B2 Draw the tree structure of the VP *like the red car* and indicate how many linearisations are possible.

9.2 Implementation: A Linearisation Algorithm

We are at the point when the grammar has built a syntactic representation and morphology has done its job. It has inserted morpho-phonological forms into the syntactic terminal nodes, after the application of operations like M-merger and impoverishment. These forms now have to be put into a linear string, and this is when phonology becomes active. What does it look at? In section 9.2.1, we will discover that the notion of sisterhood is central to the linearisation procedure. The algorithm looks at sister nodes and determines an ordering for them. In section 9.2.2, we will discover that the linearisation algorithm also needs to have access to the featural content of the sister nodes to be put in order. This, among other things, will enable it to correctly linearise constituents whose presence is required by a particular syntactic head (so-called selected constituents) and constituents that are optionally present (non-selected constituents). As we will see, non-selected constituents have more freedom than selected constituents with respect to the head of the phrase they are in.

As a result, we will have an algorithm that is able to correctly derive the basic word-order facts not only of English, but also of other languages. There will be word-order patterns, however, that the algorithm can derive but for which there is no evidence. This is where other considerations, ones that go beyond what the grammar can do, play a role. Section 9.3, which focuses on the linearisation of moved constituents, discusses one such case in some detail.

9.2.1 The Relevance of Sisterhood

What information does phonology use when it creates a linear order? There are two options. Phonology could look at specific morpho-phonological forms themselves, or it could look at the syntactic positions in which they have been inserted. It takes little to see that linearisation must operate on the latter, for two reasons.

First of all, suppose that it only looks at morpho-phonological forms, and suppose for the sake of the argument that there are two forms on which phonology has to impose a linear order, namely *Ethan* and *fired*. If phonology were to impose an order based on just the morpho-phonological forms, this would essentially mean that every time *Ethan* and *fired* are in the same sentence *Ethan* must be ordered before or after *fired*. Phonology must make a similar decision for *Cindy* and *fired*, and for *Masha* and *fired*, etc. This would entail a massive number of ordering rules, one for every combination of two morpho-phonological forms. And that would be ridiculous. For the same reason, we argued in chapter 1 that syntax looks at features and not at individual words so that the number of necessary grammatical rules can be hugely reduced. What is true for syntax must also be true for phonology.

Second, we do not want fixed orderings for any two forms anyway. After all, *Ethan* can be the person firing somebody, or the person getting fired (*I fired Ethan* vs. *Ethan fired me*). This shows that the syntactic position of *Ethan* (whether it is in FinP or in VP) determines whether it is going to precede or follow *fired* in the linear string, and not the fact that it is *Ethan*.

We conclude, therefore, that the linearisation algorithm must be able to see the syntactic representation. Let us get a bit more precise now. What properties of the syntactic representation does phonology base its decisions on? A first guess would be hierarchy: the higher you sit in the tree, the more you will precede other constituents in the linear order. The relevant notion, then, would be c-command. We have this structural relation anyway, so we might as well exploit it. Could it be, then, that some constituent X is going to be linearised before constituent Y if X c-commands Y? This is not so obvious.

First of all, note that in the representations (2) and (3) V c-commands the DP but the DP also c-commands V. If the linearisation algorithm worked on c-command, it would simply get stuck here: it would not know which one to linearise first. Second, it is quite easy to construct example pairs showing that c-command relations do not determine word order. Have a look at the following VP structures.

(6) a.

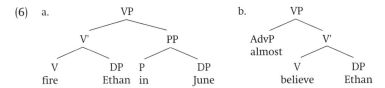

In (6a), we can observe that the PP *in June* asymmetrically c-commands the verb *fire*, as well as the DP *Ethan* (where 'asymmetrically' means that neither V nor the DP c-command the PP back). After linearisation, *in June* follows both *fire* and *Ethan*: *fire Ethan in June*. In (6b), on the other hand, the AdvP *almost* asymmetrically c-commands both V and NP. Nevertheless, *almost* precedes both *believe* and *Ethan* in the linearised string.

If c-command determines linearisation, we run into immediate problems. First of all, it is not obvious how to linearise sisters that symmetrically c-command each other, as in (2) or (3). What determines that *fire Ethan* is correct and not *Ethan fire*? Second, whether a c-command relation is interpreted as 'precede in the linear order' or 'follow in the linear order', the trees in (6a) and (6b) constitute a paradox, as at least one of them would not be linearised as it should be. If we want to know how linearisation works, we should look elsewhere. C-command alone is not enough, although we will later see that c-command is not entirely without its uses either.

As a first step towards understanding how the linearisation algorithm works, we will start with a generalisation about linearisation in English. This generalisation will capture a significant part of the English word-order facts. After this, we will look at the word-order facts that are not captured by this generalisation in sections 9.2.2 and 9.3. The generalisation is as follows:

(7)   A head typically precedes its sister node.

As the most straightforward example of (7), consider the structures in (2) and (3) once more. We argued that these representations are syntactically equivalent in that syntax does not impose any word order. Apparently, a verb and its sister node are linearised by phonology with the head, namely the verb, preceding rather than following its sister. In English, we say *(Maud) fired Ethan*, and not *(Maud) Ethan fired*. This turns out not to be an isolated fact about verbal heads but a fact about heads in general. Prepositions also precede their sister nodes in the linearised string (8a), and so do nouns (8b), adjectives (8c), determiners (8d), complementisers (8e) and the heads projecting FinP (8f), as you can see in the examples below.

(8)		TYPE OF PHRASE	HEAD	SISTER
	a.	PP	in	the middle
	b.	NP	destruction	of Rome
	c.	AP	afraid	of the dark
	d.	DP	the	green shirt
	e.	CP	that/if	Paul McCartney has left The Beatles
	f.	FinP	may/to	leave the building

The choice that English phonology makes, therefore, is a categorical one: given the option of ordering the morpho-phonological form spelling out the syntactic head before or after the material that spells out whatever is in the sister of this head, English decides to order the form related to the head before the form(s) related to the sister of this head. In short, English can be characterised as a **head-initial** language: first pronounce the head, then its sister.

The consequence for the linearisation algorithm that we are trying to construct is straightforward. This algorithm looks at sister nodes and imposes an order on them. When an X is merged with a YP, phonology will spell out X before YP. It should be understood that the choice made by the grammar is language-specific. English has decided to be head-initial rather than **head-final**, but the logic that distinguishes hierarchies from linear orders predicts that different languages can make different choices here. This turns out to be correct. Japanese and Korean are languages that systematically make the opposite choice from English, and can be characterised as head-final languages. As you can observe in (9), Japanese linearises verbs to the right of the direct object, and (10) shows that a preposition follows its sister:

(9)   Japanese:
  a. sensei-wa   hon-o   yomimashita
    teacher-topic book-object read-past
    'The teacher read the book.'
  b. *sensei-wa   yomimashita hon-o
    teacher-topic read-past book-object

(10) Japanese:
    a. heya ni
       room in
       'in the room'
    b. *ni   heya
       in   room

You can say, then, that languages have a choice here between the two options, head-initial and head-final. We can capture this in the form of what we call a **parameter**, a rule with a choice between two options.

(11) THE HEAD PARAMETER
    A syntactic head must precede OR follow its sister.

English chooses the 'precede' option, whereas Japanese opts for 'follow'. The power of such word-order parameters is enormous. It enables us to capture fundamental word-order differences between two languages (which may look very different) just through one different setting of the head parameter. As of now, you know the major principle determining word order in Japanese without probably speaking a single word of the language.

9.2.2 The Relevance of Selection

The previous section (9.2.1) contains one serious oversimplification. It was stated that a head is always ordered before its sister node, but this statement needs to be reworked. The reason is that it is quite simple to think of a YP merged with an X that precedes X in the linear order. Two examples are provided below:

(12)   a. Tammy [$_{VP}$ [$_{AdvP}$ slowly][$_V$ walks away]]
      b. I ate [$_{DP∅}$ [$_{NP}$ [$_{AP}$ expensive]][$_N$ sausages]]

In (12a), the VP contains two constituents, with the AdvP *slowly* modifying the verb. In (12b), the NP also contains two constituents, with the AP *expensive* modifying the noun. Structurally, both the AdvP and the AP are sisters to the head that they are merged with: *slowly* and *walks away* symmetrically c-command each other, and the same is true for *expensive* and *sausages*:

(13)   a.   b.

Nevertheless, AdvP and AP precede the heads they are merged with, contrary to what we are led to expect by (7). The crucial difference between (8) and (12) that is not (yet) captured by (7) is that the XPs preceding the head in (12) are optional elements that express an additional quality about the constituents they are merged with. For this reason, *slowly* and *expensive* can easily be left out without causing these examples to become ungrammatical. Note that in this sense these constituents behave similarly to the adverbials we encountered and discussed in chapter 3. The cover term used for these optional adjectives and adverbials is **adjuncts**.

The sisters of the heads in (8), however, are significantly different in that they entertain a more fundamental relation to their heads. This is easy to see for the preposition in (8a). The preposition *in* cannot occur without for instance a DP like *the middle* following it: *John was standing in* is ungrammatical, whereas *John was standing in the middle* is fine. Likewise, a determiner, like *the*, cannot occur without an NP; a complementiser, like *that*, cannot occur without a FinP; and an auxiliary or *to* infinitive marker cannot occur without a VP. Sometimes, the distinction between adjuncts and these required elements may not be immediately clear. For instance, in what sense would a PP like *of the dark* be required by the adjective *afraid*? After all, you can leave out *of the dark* without causing ungrammaticality. The same is true for *of Rome* when it is preceded by a noun.

(14)   a.   Harry is very afraid (of the dark).
        b.   They caused the partial destruction (of Rome).

Nevertheless, if Harry is afraid, you immediately understand that he is afraid of something. And if they caused the destruction, we immediately understand that it involved the destruction of something. The adjectives *afraid* and *destruction* remind us of the verb *eat*, an optionally transitive verb that can quite easily leave out its THEME argument (as in *Mary is eating* and *Mary is eating a sandwich*). In a way, these sisters look more like the arguments from chapter 3.

The fact that the sisters of *afraid* and *destruction* have a closer tie to the head than the adjuncts in (12) can also be brought out by comparing these examples with their verbal paraphrases in (15):

(15)   a.   Harry very much fears *(the dark).
        b.   They partially destroyed *(Rome).

Here, *the dark* and *Rome* cannot be left out, clearly showing that they entertain a close relationship with the verb. Although it is not clearly understood why the sisters to nouns and adjectives are easier to leave out than those of verbs, it is very intuitive to say that the relation between *Rome* and *destroy* is similar to that between *of Rome* and *destruction*, and the same is true for (14a) and (15a).

Generalising, then, we can say that all the syntactic heads in (8) select their sisters, whereas *walks* and *sausages* in (12), by contrast, do not select *slowly* and *expensive*, respectively. Now, in chapter 4 we introduced a term that is quite handy to use here. We said there that the first XP that a functional head merges with is called a complement: VP is the complement to the head of FinP, and FinP is the complement to the head of CP. We can now extend this term and also use it for XPs selected by lexical rather than functional heads. *Ethan* is the complement of V in *Mary fired Ethan*, and *the middle* is the complement of *in* in *in the middle*. *Slowly* and *expensive*, then, are not complements of the heads they are merged with.

We now have a way of reformulating the generalisation in (7). As it turns out, the head-initialness of English only pertains to heads and sisters that are selected, i.e. complements, as now captured by the new generalisation:

(16)   A head typically precedes its complement.

The statement in (16) basically reflects the English choice for the head parameter, which we can now reformulate as in (17):

(17)   THE HEAD PARAMETER
       A syntactic head must precede OR follow its complement.

English sets this parameter to 'precede'; Japanese to 'follow'.

The head parameter, then, accounts for the bulk of the English word-order facts, namely the bulk that involves heads and complements. For other constituent types, the head parameter has nothing to say. So let us now turn to the ordering of non-complements and see what we need to say for these. There are two other types that can be distinguished, obligatory and optional non-complements. Let us now go over these in turn.

Some constituents are not heads, nor complements, but their presence within a particular phrase is nevertheless obligatory. Take for instance a subject in FinP. This constituent needs to be present in that position because it needs to check the [uɸ] features on the Fin head. In the same vein, a *Wh*-object needs to sit in CP because it must check the [uWh] feature on C. These constituents therefore entertain a special relation to a syntactic head, but they are not directly merged with this head, as are complements. Therefore, they are not complements, and structurally they are not sisters to a head. The cover term for these obligatory non-complements was already introduced in chapter 4: *specifier*. A *Wh*-object is the specifier of CP, and a subject is the specifier of FinP.

This leaves constituents that are not obligatorily present because the head neither directly (as with complements) nor indirectly (as with specifiers) requires their presence. We are talking about constituents that are not heads, nor complements nor specifiers. We already gave a name to these optional elements: *adjuncts*. The following table provides an overview:

(18)   Properties of complements, specifiers and adjuncts

	STRUCTURAL POSITION:	PRESENCE:	LINEARISED BY:
COMPLEMENT	Sister to an X	Obligatory with V and P, non-obligatory with N and A	Language-specific setting of the Head Parameter
SPECIFIER	Sister to an X'	Obligatory	?
ADJUNCT	Sister to an X or X'	Optional	?

Specifiers and adjuncts, then, have in common that their linearisation is not determined by the head parameter of English. In principle, they can either precede or follow their sisters. We therefore have to look in a bit more detail at the linearisation of specifiers and adjuncts. In the remainder of this section, we will determine what we have to say for the linearisation of adjuncts in English. We will show that they obey rules that are different from the rules set for complements but that these rules are still specific to English. In section 9.3, we will take a closer look at specifiers, and their linearisation will turn out to be determined by factors that are not specific to English.

The generalisation in (16) for English has the right consequences for adjuncts. First of all, since adjuncts are not affected by the head-initial nature of English, given (16), their ordering with respect to the head is not determined by anything we have said so far. This immediately explains why adverbs behave more freely than XPs with a complement status. We can, for instance, freely order *slowly* before or after the verb. There is nothing that would forbid it:

(19) a. Tammy slowly walks away.
     b. Tammy walks slowly away.

Second, the effect can be repeated with more than one adverb in the same sentence. Take a look at the sentences in (20), in which two VP adjuncts, *occasionally* and *completely*, can either precede or follow the verb and the object (with the appropriate intonation patterns). In (21), you can observe that it is also possible to put one adverb in front of the verb and the object and the other after them:

(20) a. Adrian occasionally completely lost his mind.
     b. Adrian lost his mind completely occasionally.

(21) a. Adrian occasionally lost his mind completely.
     b. Adrian completely lost his mind occasionally.

This may give the impression that anything goes, but this is not really the case. It is for instance impossible to invert the order of adverbs in (20a):

(22) *Adrian completely occasionally lost his mind.

This suggests that *occasionally* must occupy a hierarchically higher position than *completely*: *occasionally* must c-command *completely*, not the other way round. For this reason, *occasionally* appears to the left of *completely*. It seems, therefore, that c-command is useful for understanding the differences in grammaticality between (20)/(21) and (22). In addition, we can now make a prediction. If *occasionally* sits higher in the tree than *completely*, and is for that reason spelled out to the left of *completely* in (20a), and if *occasionally* and *completely* can both either precede or follow the verb and its object, then only one order should be possible if both *occasionally* and *completely* follow the verb and its object. It should be the one in which *occasionally* follows *completely*. And this is exactly what we find. Whereas (20b) is grammatical, (23) is not:

(23) *Adrian lost his mind occasionally completely.

What we see here is a so-called mirror-image effect. When both adverbs precede the verb and its object, *completely* must follow *occasionally*.

However, when they both follow the verb and its object, *completely* must precede *occasionally*. This mirror-image effect is caused by syntax. The hierarchical relation between the two adverbs is fixed, with *occasionally* appearing structurally higher than *completely*. The ordering between them depends on their ordering with respect to the verb and its object. This is shown in the tree in (24):

(24)

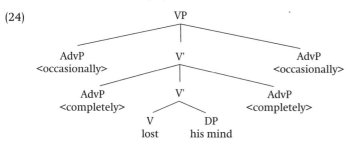

The ordering of the two AdvPs is freer than the ordering of direct objects, because they are not complements. At the same time, however, their ordering is constrained by syntax, so that orderings in which *occasionally* appears between *completely* and the verb plus object are ruled out. *Lost his mind* is first merged with *completely* and then the result of this merger (*lost his mind completely*) undergoes merger with *occasionally*. So although syntax is not the part of the grammar that cares about word order, it does restrict word-order possibilities to a significant extent. Syntax cares about constituents and, all things being equal (that is, if we forget about movement for the time being), all elements belonging to a constituent must be uttered next to each other. These mirror-image examples illustrate this point very nicely. A constituent that is hierarchically higher than two other constituents cannot end up between those two other constituents in the linear order.

These mirror-image effects make a more general point. Although we established that c-command cannot form the sole basis on which the algorithm linearises syntactic constituents, it is of course not the case that effects of c-command are absent altogether. On the contrary, they are very visible. The fact that a subject is hierarchically higher than a verb and an object for instance excludes the possibility of linearising the subject between the verb and the object, for the same reason that you cannot linearise *occasionally* between *completely* and the verb plus object. A PP adjunct (like *right* in *right in the middle*) can never be linearised between P and its complement, etc. Hierarchies, then, exclude a lot of possible word orders (or linearisations). Since the linearisation algorithm operates on sisters, it must determine how to linearise these sisters. If the input consists of A and B, A and B both being constituents, then there are simply two options: A precedes B or B precedes A. What is excluded is ordering A somewhere in the middle of constituent B, as this would ignore the hierarchical relations (*in right the middle* is bad). Hierarchies, therefore, severely restrict the options from amongst which the algorithm can choose. But there is an important difference between, on the one hand, restricting the options and, on the other, determining linearisation from A to Z. C-command (and therefore hierarchy) does the former, not the latter.

So far, we have seen that adjuncts show more freedom in their ordering with respect to other constituents in the same phrase than heads and complements, and that this freedom is caused by the fact that these adjuncts are insensitive to the ordering rules pertaining to syntactic heads. This does not mean that there are no rules regulating the positioning of these adjuncts in English. There certainly are. The crucial point about non-complement constituents is that in principle their ordering is free. Two scenarios are then possible. Either a particular language exploits this freedom, or it restricts this freedom by means of additional, language-specific linearisation rules. English does both. We have just seen the exploitation of freedom, illustrated by the ordering possibilities for adverbs. Let us now look at two relevant cases in which additional ordering rules are at play. The first case concerns adjuncts that are ordered with respect to their sister based on their categorial status. Then there are cases in which the semantic content of the adjuncts matters. We will look at these two cases in turn and conclude that the first case can be handled by the linearisation algorithm, but not the second.

To see that the categorial status of adjuncts matters for their linearisation, consider the case of a modified noun. A noun can be modified by an AP, and it can be modified by a PP. APs generally precede the noun, whereas PPs follow the noun:

(25)   a.   expensive sausages
       b.   *sausages expensive

(26)   a.   sausages from Italy
       b.   *from Italy sausages

It is very unlikely that the semantics of these adjuncts matters. Consider, for instance, the following examples. Here we see that the ordering of the AP and PP is the same as in (25) and (26), although they express similar content semantically.

(27)   a.   doubtful men/*men doubtful
       b.   men in doubt/*in doubt men

It appears, then, that the linearisation algorithm must make its choice based on the categorial features of the sister nodes that it has to linearise: PP adjuncts, carrying [P], follow the noun that they are merged with, whereas AP adjuncts, carrying [A], precede the noun that they are merged with. Looking at other languages, we can again establish that the choices made by English phonology are language-specific. French, for instance, allows (certain) APs to precede and follow the noun:

(28) a. la   jeune   fille
         the   young   girl
         'the young girl'
     b. la   fille   jeune
         the   girl   young
         'the young girl'

There are, however, complex restrictions in French with respect to which adjectives can and which cannot follow the noun, and which adjectives can appear on either side, with subtle variations in meaning, showing that these language-specific rules can become quite complex. This is the point where we are in luck to be writing a book about English, because English is simpler: N precedes a modifying PP and a modifying AP precedes the nominal constituent that it merges with, full stop.

That the algorithm inspects the featural status of the sister nodes and makes its decisions on the basis of the information encoded in these nodes is also clear from the fact that what is true for the nominal domain is not necessarily true for the verbal domain. PP adjuncts can just as well precede and follow the verb, even though they obligatorily follow the noun they modify, as we just saw:

(29)   a.   John [$_{PP}$ in all likelihood] never snores.
      b.   John never snores [$_{PP}$ in all likelihood].

(30)   a.   I will not [$_{PP}$ under any circumstances] resign.
      b.   I will not resign [$_{PP}$ under any circumstances].

Adjuncts in the verbal domain are thus more flexible than adjuncts in the nominal domain, showing that the linearisation algorithm must indeed have access to the categorial features [N] and [V].

It is not the case, however, that every PP in the verbal domain behaves in this way. Place and time adverbials, for instance, do not sit very comfortably in front of a verb (although it may be too strong to call these orders ungrammatical, hence the two question marks), as the following two contrasting pairs of examples demonstrate:

(31)   a.   Eventually, the Duke died in the summer.
      a′. ??Eventually, the Duke in the summer died.
      b.   Eventually, the Duke died in Hungary.
      b′. ??Eventually, the Duke in Hungary died.

These examples show that the semantic content of PPs sometimes matters. But is this also something that our linearisation algorithm predicts or makes possible? Actually, no, it doesn't. Just realise again what our algorithm tries to do. It tries to order constituents into a linear string based on the syntactic representations. The syntactic features in the tree do not reflect the meaning of the elements that carry them; they are independent of that. Just as syntactic and morphological rules only look at the syntactic features and not at the semantic features, phonology does not care about the meaning of the elements that it linearises. *In Hungary* and *in the summer* are just PP adjuncts for syntax or phonology. Nothing more, nothing less. Even if phonology wanted to look at the semantics, it couldn't. That information is simply not present in syntactic features.

Consequently, as far as our linearisation algorithm is concerned, there is nothing wrong with the examples in (31). The fact that they do not sound good must mean that there are other factors at play, having to do with language use, i.e. the properties of language outside of grammar. When we speak, we simply prefer not to use some of the word orders that the grammar can in principle allow, and we settle for particular ways in which we present the information we want to get across. The job for the linguist, then, is to figure out if we can make a meaningful difference between word orders that are ruled out because the grammar of English (and more specifically the linearisation algorithm) does not generate them, and word orders that are ruled out because they deviate from the ways in which speakers like to package their information when they speak. The fact that the word orders in (31) are certainly better than those in (25b) and (26b), especially with heavy emphasis on the preverbal PPs, may already be a first hint in that direction. A second hint might be that in certain languages close to English, such as our beloved native tongue Dutch, examples like (31) are fine, but (25b) and (26b) are still horrible.

9.2.3 Interim Summary

In section 9.2 we have laid down the essentials for the algorithm that derives the basic word-order facts of English. We have seen that there is a strict rule for the linearisation of complements (or selected constituents), determined by the head-initial parameter setting of English. Since the linearisation of adjuncts is not regulated by the head parameter, their ordering is freer, although English has some additional rules restricting this freedom. For instance, English nouns rigidly precede PPs that modify them, but follow modifying APs, even though English verbs in principle allow both modifying PPs and AdvPs to their left and right. Both the rule affecting the ordering of complements and the rules affecting the ordering of non-complements are language-specific. English makes certain choices that are distinct from the choices made by other languages. Japanese has complements precede their heads. And French has no problem with AP adjuncts following nouns.

In addition, we have established that there are limits to what a phonological algorithm can linearise. Although it has access to syntactic features, and can therefore distinguish selected from non-selected constituents, and APs from PPs, it cannot order constituents on the basis of their meanings. This means that whenever we see ordering effects that are semantic, these are arguably the result of grammar-external factors. In the next section (9.3), we will argue that such additional factors are also needed to account for an interesting restriction on the linearisation of remerged constituents. And this will be an area in which, interestingly, languages as distinct as English and Japanese no longer differ.

Exercises

A3 Draw the trees for the following examples and indicate for each pair of sisters what property of the English linearisation algorithm determines their ordering.
   a. almost in danger
   b. the completely unexpected liberation of Holland
   c. beautiful plastic flowers
   d. (Beatrice) will quit her job eventually

A4 State which constituents in the sentences in A3 are complements, specifiers or adjuncts.

B5 Did you have to add ordering rules for English in your answer to A3 that were not mentioned in the main text?

B6 It was stated that modified nouns are linearised by a rule that is specific to English: AP > N. Alternatively, we could argue that an adjective is a head selecting a noun phrase as its complement. In this case, the AP > N ordering can be seen as a consequence of the head parameter. Can you see problems with this analysis?

B7 Draw the tree structures for the following Japanese sentences. Remember that this language is head-final. List all sister nodes that are linearised according to the Japanese head parameter.
   a. John-wa   Mary-ga   sono hon-o   nakushita-to   omotteiru.
      John-topic Mary-nom   that book-acc   lost-that   thinks
      'John thinks that Mary lost that book.'
   b. sensei-ga   kuruma-o   kai-mashita   ka.
      teacher-nom   car-acc   buy-past   Q
      'Did the teacher buy a/the car?'

C8 Did you stumble upon any difficulties when drawing these Japanese trees, or can you blindly switch the head parameter to get the right results? Do any issues arise that are purely syntactic, that is issues that do not pertain to linearisation as such?

C9 Consider the data from Old English below and find as much evidence as you can for the head-parameter choice of this language. What is the problem you run into? And what is the theoretical consequence of this?
   a. astrece ðine hand ofer ða sæ
      stretch your-acc/sg/fem hand over the sea
      'Stretch your hand over the sea.'
   b. … þæt Darius hie mid gefeohte secan wolde
      … that Darius them for battle visit wanted
      '… that Darius wanted to seek them out for a battle.'
   c. [hwi] sceole we oþres mannes niman
      why should we another man's take
      'Why should we take those of another man?'

9.3 Consequences: The Linearisation of Remerged Constituents

In section 9.2, we saw that syntactic heads play a crucial role in the linearisation procedure, in that they directly determine the ordering of their complements. The head parameter predicts for constituents that are not directly selected by a head that their ordering is either free or that it is regulated by additional ordering rules. These additional rules are then predicted to be language-specific, just like the choice between head-initial and head-final. This turned out to be correct.

In this section, we will look at specifiers, constituents that are not directly selected by a head but are nevertheless obligatorily present in a particular phrase. We will determine what the consequences of our line-arisation algorithm are for the linearisation of specifiers. It will turn out that none of these consequences gives us a handle on specifiers. So the consequence is basically that we have to start work again, to figure out what is going on.

Let us characterise the problem. The thing that XPs sitting in the speci-fier of CP or FinP have in common is that they have been remerged in that position: they involve moved constituents. If you move some phrasal element (like a *Wh*-constituent), will it end up to the left or to the right of its sister? In other words, will movement be to the left, or to the right, or are both options possible? To study this, let us abstract away from concrete examples (like moving *Wh*-constituents) and focus on the underlying trees. In an abstract way, movement creates structures as in (32), in which the (a) and (b) examples are again syntactically identical.

(32)   a.   b.

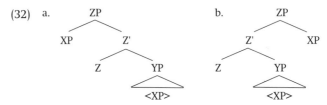

Now, is XP uttered to the left or to the right of Z'? Since XP is remerged with Z', and not with Z, it cannot be linearised with the head-parameter. The higher remerged XP can never be a complement. Therefore, the lin-earisation between XP and Z' is not determined by this part of the lineari-sation algorithm. We expect, therefore, either of two scenarios: (i) the linearisation of remerged XPs is unconstrained (as with certain English adverbs) or (ii) the linearisation of remerged XPs is determined by lan-guage-specific rules that take into consideration the category of the remerged XP (as English does with APs and PPs). The interesting fact is that neither scenario applies. Let us see why.

First of all, the ordering of remerged XPs is of course not free. In fact, all the examples of movement we have seen are examples in which, as a consequence of Remerge, the constituent ends up more to the left, not more to the right. Movement appears to be leftward. We can therefore make the following generalisation about remerged constituents:

(33)   A remerged constituent precedes its sister.

What this generalisation says is that an XP that has been remerged into an YP always precedes its sister, or: movement is always to the left. We have seen two concrete cases of this. One is movement of the subject from spec-*v*P to spec-FinP. The same can be said for a *Wh*-constituent that has been moved out of the VP into the CP. This *Wh*-constituent appears in clause-initial position, preceding all other constituents dominated by CP (34b).

(34)	TYPE OF XP	YP	X'
a.	FinP	Paul McCartney	has <Paul McCartney> left The Beatles.
b.	CP	Which band	did Paul McCartney leave <which band>?

The generalisation extends to cases in which we move a constituent for special emphasis (the ones we used in chapter 2 to test for constituency). Take a look at the following examples, in which movement to the left is completely natural but movement to the right horrible:

(35) I would not hesitate to give Harold flowers on his birthday but …
     a. … MARY I would never give flowers to on her birthday.
     b. *… I would never give flowers to on her birthday MARY.

(36) I would have no problem having to rely on my family but …
     a. … THE GOVERNMENT I would not rely on right now.
     b. *… I would not rely on right now THE GOVERNMENT.

Again, it seems that the linearisation of remerged constituents is not unconstrained.

The second scenario is one in which English grammar would have linearisation rules for remerged constituents that look at the category or the semantics of the remerged XP. We have seen that English has such rules for nominal adjuncts. This scenario is also very implausible for specifiers. A subject in FinP has moved to this position from one within $\underline{v}$P/VP, following the VP-Internal Subject Hypothesis (see section 6.3). This subject can be a DP, a FinP or a CP (as shown in (37)), and a *Wh*-constituent in CP can be a DP, PP or AdvP (as shown in (38)):

(37) a. [$_{DP}$ The neighbours] regularly <DP> show their shortcomings.
     b. [$_{CP}$ That the neighbours don't like my trumpet] <CP> shows their shortcomings.
     c. [$_{FinP}$ To play the trumpet] is <FinP> to overcome one's shortcomings.

(38) a. [$_{DP}$ Which instrument] do my neighbours hate <DP> most?
     b. [$_{PP}$ For which instrument] do my neighbours care <PP> the least?
     c. [$_{AdvP}$ Why] do my neighbours hate my trumpet <AdvP> so much?

In all these cases, as illustrated above, the remerged constituent ends up in the same position, to the left of its sister. It is clear, then, that the category-sensitive ordering rules we saw earlier (cf. discussion of (25) and (26)) are of little help in explaining (33).

There is a further difference between the ordering rules that must pertain to non-remerged constituents and those that pertain to remerged constituents. We have seen that with respect to non-moved constituents the ordering rules can be quite language-specific. Languages are either head-initial or head-final, and they can make their own choices for the ordering of adjuncts. When we look at the linearisation of remerged constituents, however, we see that languages behave in a surprisingly similar manner. Syntactically triggered movement is robustly to the left, and not to the right. We can schematise this as follows:

(39) a.   XP   ...   <XP>

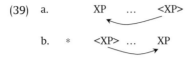

      b.   *   <XP> ...   XP

And this is just as true for other languages as it is for English. In every language that has *Wh*-movement, for instance, this movement is to the left. Examples are given below for French and for Greek (the example in Greek is only grammatical when it is not a real question but utters surprise, as in English sentences in which the *Wh*-constituent does not move):

(40) French:
      a. Qui as-tu vu?
          whom have you seen
          'Whom have you seen?'
      b. *As-tu vu qui?
          have you seen whom

(41) Greek:
      a. Pjos   nomizis oti agorase   kenurjo kanape?
          who.nom think.2sg that bought.3sg new   couch
          'Who do you think bought a new couch?'
      b. *Nomizis oti agorase   kenurjo kanape pjos?
          think.2sg that bought.3sg new   couch   who

This means that what explains (33) must be much more fundamental than an arbitrary choice between two options. We need to explain why all languages make the same choice here. Why is syntactically triggered movement always to the left?

This significant preference for leftward over rightward movement may be strange from the perspective of our linearisation algorithm, which otherwise allows quite a bit of language-specific freedom. Now, if linearisation rules are language-specific but there is no language-specific choice for remerged constituents (because they must precede their sisters), maybe that is a good reason to assume that the rules behind the linearisation of remerged constituents are not rules of grammar, but something else. We saw this before, when we said that certain word orders were acceptable to the linearisation mechanism, but independently blocked because they do not comply with the way speakers like to package their information (whatever the rules of language use are here). If we adopt the hypothesis that robust movement to the left has some grammar-external explanation, i.e. it has nothing to do with the grammar itself, it may actually not be so hard to understand why remerged constituents always precede their sisters. Here is why.

If, owing to syntactic requirements, constituents have to move, then we constantly talk to each other using sentences with displaced elements. In order to properly understand such sentences, we must relate the moved constituents to the positions that they have moved from. A *Wh*-object, for instance, is selected by a verb as a direct object, and it receives its θ-role from this verb. A proper interpretation of a moved *Wh*-object therefore involves relating it to its thematic position inside the VP.

Now, putting a moved constituent back into its base position is a relatively easy task if you first hear the moved element and then have to find the place from which this element has moved in the sentence you are currently listening to. If, on the other hand, the moved element appears towards the end of the sentence, then you have to put it back into a position somewhere in the sentence that you have just listened to and has now finished. Basically, you would then have to go back in the sentence, link the moved element to its original position and start over again. This requires a lot of short-term memory: it is generally less effort to keep in your memory a constituent that you have to find a place for than to keep in your memory an entire sentence that the moved element is a part of. In psychology they call this a **filler-gap pattern**: a filler (a moved element) should in principle precede its gap (its previous position).

Now we can go back to the generalisation in (33) and see if we understand it. The question that it poses for linearisation is the following: why are remerged constituents linearised to the left of their sister? Well, a remerged constituent has been moved from a position lower down in the structure into a position that c-commands the original position. Consequently, this base position is always contained in the sister of the remerged constituent. Just take a look at (32a) and (32b) again. In both representations, XP occurs twice, once as spec-ZP and once in a position dominated by Z'. Because every remerged constituent is by definition the sister of a constituent that contains the base position of that remerged constituent, the choice between (32a) and (32b) becomes an easy one. The desire to create a linearisation in which the filler linearly precedes the gap means that a remerged constituent is favourably linearised to the left of its sister, because the sister always contains the gap.

It is unfortunately not the case that the desire to create filler-gap patterns explains the linearisation of all specifiers. We have seen a few specifiers that have not remerged. Remember that it is usually the case that subjects move out of the *v*P/VP to spec-FinP. However, we have also seen that subjects sometimes appear lower down in the structure, for instance when spec-FinP is filled by an expletive subject, as in (42a). In addition, we have seen that subjects sometimes only partly move to spec-FinP, and that they can strand a quantifier in a lower position, as in (42b):

(42) a. [$_{FinP}$ There were [$_{vP}$ *two men* swimming in our pool]]
      b. [$_{FinP}$ The men were [$_{vP}$ *both* swimming in our pool]]

Now, *two men* is an argument of the verb *swimming*, and *both* is part of an argument. Therefore, they count as specifiers, here occupying spec-*v*P. Both specifiers are linearised to the left of their sister, *swimming in our pool*. Since they have not moved, the desire to create a filler-gap pattern cannot be what determines their linearisation. This means that there must be a second factor involved in the linearisation of specifiers. One hypothesis we could pursue is to say the following. A prototypical definition of a sentence is that of a linguistic unit consisting of a subject and a **predicate**. The subject is what the sentence is about and the predicate (basically the rest of the sentence) is the statement about this subject. Now, if you define a sentence in these 'aboutness' terms, it makes a lot of sense to first introduce the entity and then the statement about this entity rather than the other way around. If so, the linearisation of these non-moved specifiers has little to do with their syntax but is again determined by grammar-external factors, in this case having to do with a fundamental information-packaging strategy that first introduces an entity and then the statement about this entity. This hypothesis makes a prediction and raises a question. Let us look at these in turn.

If English speakers find it so much more logical to first introduce an entity and then the statement about this entity rather than the other way around, then so should a Japanese speaker, or a speaker of Swahili. To put it differently, if this way of packaging the information of a sentence is so fundamental, we expect that non-moved subjects are universally linearised to the left of their sister. In order to test his hypothesis, we should therefore look at the rest of the world's languages. It is interesting to note that the position of the subject is significantly more fixed than the position of the object. Whereas there is ample evidence for both V–O and O–V orders, Subject–Verb–Object (S–V–O) and Subject–Object–Verb (S–O–V) orders are each much more common than all other word orders (V–S–O, V–O–S, O–V–S, O–S–V) combined. We can conclude, therefore, that word orders in which the subject precedes the verb and object are by far the most common pattern. This certainly goes in the direction of our hypothesis. Note, however, that a superficial glance will not suffice. What we should investigate is to what extent this generalisation is a consequence of subjects that have moved. What happens if we look at non-moved subjects? In other words, is the dominance of S-V-O and S-O-V orders a consequence of filler-gap patterns, fundamental information-packaging, or both? Further research is required, and this is actually something that syntacticians are currently working on.

Exercises

A10   Show that the constituents in italics are specifiers. Also say whether they precede their sister because of the filler-gap mechanism or something else.
   a.   *That John left her* upset Denise deeply.
   b.   *Ahmed* seems to have the highest grade.
   c.   *What* did you tell him?
   d.   *There* is somebody waiting for you.

C11   This section has readdressed the notions 'complement' and 'specifier', and introduced the notion 'adjunct'. These notions turned out to be useful for the formulation of generalisations about linearisation and the rules that the linearisation algorithm uses. Discuss to what extent the following contrasts can be used to independently justify the three-way distinction between complements, specifiers and adjuncts.

- a. (i) What do you think Colin wrote a book about?
  - (ii) *What do you think that a book about caused an uproar?
- b. (i) Colin looked for a good reason. A good reason was looked for.
  - (ii) Colin snored for a good reason. *A good reason was snored for.

C12 We argued in this section that specifiers come in two flavours: remerged ones and non-remerged ones. For the first type, we argued that their linearisation is determined by the desire to create filler-gap patterns. For the second type, we needed a different story because non-remerged specifiers do not leave gaps. Discuss the relevance of indirect objects in double object constructions (e.g. *Mary gave John a book*) in this discussion and try to determine how they may have an effect on our analysis.

Summary

In the previous chapter, we determined how morphology inserts morpho-phonological forms into the syntactic tree structure. In this chapter, we have determined how phonology orders these morpho-phonological forms into a linear structure.

We have shown that syntax restricts linearisation options but does not determine them. What does this mean again? It means that the component responsible for linearisation, namely phonology, cannot linearise morpho-phonological forms in a way that ignores syntax. Phonology has to determine for each pair of sister nodes how they are ordered, but it cannot distort the existing sisterhood relations. Given the tree in (43a), there are four possible orderings, not six, as indicated in (43b).

(43) a.   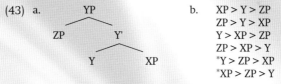   b.   XP > Y > ZP
                                              ZP > Y > XP
                                              Y > XP > ZP
                                              ZP > XP > Y
                                              *Y > ZP > XP
                                              *XP > ZP > Y

The possibilities arise out of making different choices for the ordering of the two pairs of sister nodes: ZP and Y', and Y and XP. The impossible orders are those in which the existing sisterhood relations are distorted. We cannot squeeze ZP in between Y and XP because ZP is the sister of Y', the node that dominates both Y and XP. It is in this sense, then, that syntax puts a restriction on the possible word orders.

However, syntax has nothing to say about the orderings of the sister nodes themselves. Which of these four orders is the one actually seen is up to phonology, not syntax. For this reason, we looked at the properties of the linearisation algorithm that phonology employs. This algorithm, we established, has access to selectional information of syntactic heads. It can see, for instance, that the verb *love* selects a DP, that C selects a FinP, and that the adjective *afraid* can select a PP. In this way, the algorithm can treat complements differently from adjuncts. In addition, we have seen that the algorithm looks at categorial features, so that it can order PPs to the right of N, and APs to the left, and so that it can order (some) PPs on both sides of the verb, but not on both sides of a noun.

We have also seen that the relative freedom that the algorithm allows for the positioning of non-complement constituents must sometimes be restricted by factors outside grammar, such as memory restrictions or information-packaging preferences. We have looked in some detail at specifiers and noted that the factors responsible for the linearisation of these may be less language-specific than what determines the linearisation of complements and adjuncts. If the reason for linearising remerged constituents to the left of their sister is psychological, this would explain why all languages prefer movement to the left: in all relevant respects, a Japanese speaker has the same kind of brain, and the same short-term memory, as an English speaker.

We can summarise linearisation as in (44):

(44) Properties of complements, specifiers and adjuncts

	STRUCTURAL POSITION:	PRESENCE:	LINEARISED BY:
COMPLEMENT	Sister to an X	Obligatory with V and P, non-obligatory with N and A	Language-specific setting of the Head Parameter
SPECIFIER	Sister to an X'	Obligatory	Non-language-specific preferences for filler-gap and subject–predicate patterns
ADJUNCT	Sister to an X or X'	Optional	Language-specific rules (may be grammar-external)

Linearisation is sensitive to the complement–specifier–adjunct distinction and makes its choices on the basis of a mixture of language-specific and language-universal factors. As soon as we start using words like 'universal', however, we must ensure that our claims live up to the facts. What (44) minimally does is provide a testable theory with which we can approach the rest of the world's languages.

Further Reading

The linearisation algorithm presented in the text is loosely based on Bobaljik (2002). See Richards (2004) for a detailed exploration of the hypothesis that ordering choices are made in the phonological component and not in the syntax. See Koster (1974) for an early exploration of mirror-image effects.

The claim that syntactic structure determines word order, contrary to the view adopted in this book, has been extensively explored by Richard Kayne (1994 and following work). He proposes that a syntactic phrase consisting of a specifier, head and complement universally leads to the linear order specifier > head > complement. A consequence of this is that all languages are predicted to have a basic SVO word order. His work has been very influential, but it is not generally embraced. The claim that languages universally have a specifier > head > complement order can only be upheld if we assume additional syntactic movements, and larger tree structures, for those languages that deviate from this base pattern, so that the elegance achieved by having a universal base order does not always lead to the most elegant analysis of a single language.

For the claim that *Wh*-movement in spoken language is universally to the left, see Cecchetto, Geraci & Zucchi (2009) for references. Petronio & Lillo-Martin (1997) claim that the same fact holds for American Sign Language, despite first impressions.

For the claim that the preference of syntactic movement to the left is related to parsing considerations, see for instance Ackema & Neeleman (2002).

The Japanese examples in (9) and (10) are from Helen Gilhooly (personal communication). The Greek example in (41) is from Marika Lekakou (personal communication). The Japanese example (a) in exercise B7 is from Aoshima, Phillips & Weinberg (2004), example (b) from Shirahata (2003). Example (a) in exercise C9 is from Denison (2006), examples (b) and (c) from Haeberli (2002).

For the world-wide distribution of word orders involving a subject, verb and object, refer to Dryer (2011): http://wals.info/chapter/81.

CHAPTER OUTLINE

KEY TERMS

Principle of Compositionality

scope

reconstruction

Quantifier Raising

covert movement

locality

syntactic domain

phase

phase edge

In the previous chapters, we focused on the relation between syntax and the way syntactic structures are expressed: how do concrete morpho-phonological forms get inserted into the syntactic representation, and how do these forms get linearised in the order we hear them in? But sentences are not only expressed; they also have a meaning. Semantics is the grammatical component that assigns an interpretation (i.e. a meaning) to a sentence. How does it do that? Crucially, like morphology and phonology, semantics is also based on the output of the syntax: the way words and morphemes with their interpretable features are merged determines the meaning of a sentence. This sounds like a pretty straightforward procedure, but we will see that the relation between syntax and semantics is not always transparent, as was also the case for syntax and morphology. In order to get to the right interpretations of sentences we sometimes need more syntax than syntax seems to give us.

10.1 Insight: Compositionality

How does a sentence get the meaning it has? This is a question that has interested philosophers and linguists for centuries. And even though there are many complex issues at stake, at least on two points consensus has arisen. These two points may sound obvious at first sight, but appear to be very powerful in explaining all kinds of semantic effects.

The first point is that the meaning of a sentence is determined by the meaning of the words or morphemes it consists of. If you have the sentence *John love-d Mary*, the meaning of the entire sentence follows from the meaning of components like *John, love, -d* and *Mary*. This sentence cannot all of a sudden mean that some guy hated Bill. No meaningful elements are removed or added when we interpret this sentence. In that sense, sentence meaning is like a linguistic fruit salad. If you mix bananas, strawberries and apples, the salad is not going to taste like oranges. Now, you may wonder, though, what exactly we mean when we say that semantics is interested in the meaning of words and morphemes. Wasn't it the case that words are sometimes formed after the syntax, for instance by morphologically merging the features in Fin with V+*v*? And surely, by morphemes we cannot mean the concrete forms that morphology inserts (which we referred to as morpho-phonological forms), because that happens after the syntax too. All processes that happen after the syntax on the sound side of the model are invisible to the meaning side of the model. Now, take a look at (1), which provides the underlying structure for the sentence *John loved Mary*.

(1)

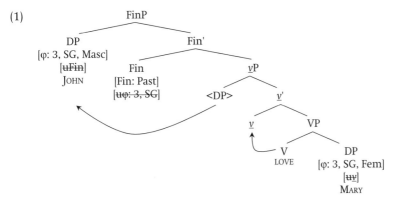

This tree will be interpreted by morphology, which inserts morpho-phonological forms with the use of the following realisation rules:

(2) a. JOHN   →   *John*
  b. [Fin: Past]   →   *-ed*
  c. LOVE   →   *love*
  d. MARY   →   *Mary*

On the right side of the arrow we find the morpho-phonological forms that morphology inserts. On the left side we find the concepts and feature bundles that together we can refer to as morphemes. What semantics is interested in, though, is not the stuff on the right side but the stuff on the left side of the arrow, the (abstract) morphemes. Since all these features and concepts are expressed by words, we may sometimes simply write down the words in the tree, but that's just shorthand for a tree that contains abstract morphemes only.

The choice of morpheme (or semantic properties underlying them) is not the only thing that determines the meaning of the sentence, however. To see this, take the following two sentences:

(3)   a.   John loved Mary.
       b.   Mary loved John.

These two sentences consist of the same words, but clearly have a different meaning. Now, this might be due to the fact that, as we know by now, *John* in (3a) is a nominative constituent, whereas it is an accusative in (3b); and the reverse holds for *Mary*. But that is not the issue here. Case features are uninterpretable features and therefore lack any semantic content. The only reason for the meaning difference is their structural difference. In (3a), *John* is in a higher position than *Mary*, and in (3b) it is the other way round. That brings us to the second point on which scholars generally agree: the meaning of a sentence not only depends on the meaning of its parts, but also on the way these parts are *syntactically structured*. The combination of these two factors is known as the **Principle of Compositionality**, attributed to the German philosopher Gottlob Frege (1848–1925).

(4)   PRINCIPLE OF COMPOSITIONALITY:
      The meaning of a sentence follows from the meaning of its parts and the way they are structured.

This Principle of Compositionality tells us that the meaning of the sentence is fully compositional. You only have to look at the syntactic structure and the semantic elements in there to figure out what the meaning of the sentence is. As said, this may look obvious, but its consequences are enormous.

One effect we have already seen is behind the examples in (3). That is the θ-hierarchy. As established earlier, the order in which the arguments are merged within the verbal projections ($\underline{v}$P, VP), before merger with the Fin head, determines what θ-role they receive. In a sentence like (5), the verb first merges with *a lecture*, then [$_{V'}$ *give a lecture*] merges with *John*, yielding [$_{VP}$ *John* [*give a lecture*]]; after that, $\underline{v}$ is merged with VP, to which the verb moves, giving [$_{v'}$ *give* [$_{VP}$ *John* [*<give> a lecture*]]]; finally, the subject merges and creates [$_{\underline{v}P}$ *Mary* [$_{v'}$ *give* [$_{VP}$ *John* [$_{V'}$ *<give> a lecture*]]]].

(5)   Mary gave John a lecture.

Recall from chapter 3 that we established a θ-hierarchy that looked like (6):

(6)   AGENT > RECIPIENT > PATIENT/THEME > GOAL

Since GOALs require phrases that generally start with *to* ('to John'), the lowest θ-role available here is the PATIENT/THEME and that is the role that is first assigned, to *the lecture*. Then follows *John*, which will receive the next θ-role in line, the RECIPIENT. Finally, we have *Mary*, present in *v*P, who will receive the AGENT role. The same applies to the examples in (3): the argument that is merged with the verb first becomes the PATIENT (*Mary* in (3a), *John* in (3b)), the next one the AGENT. The θ-roles of the arguments, then, are fully determined by the meaning of the verb (which determines which θ-roles it can assign) and the syntactic structure, which tells us which argument receives which θ-role. θ-role assignment, then, is a good example of the two components that according to the Principle of Compositionality determine the meaning of a sentence: word or morpheme meaning and syntactic structure.

Exercises

A1 What are the meaningful features and (abstract) morphemes in the following three sentences?
 a. Mary left Peter.
 b. She finally arrived.
 c. Whom did you see?

B2 The following sentence has two meanings:
   Bill hit the dog with a stick.
 a. What meanings does it have?
 Given the Principle of Compositionality these different meanings must be the result of two different underlying structures.
 b. What are these structures and how do they give rise to the two readings?

C3. One might argue that idioms, such as the examples below, violate the Principle of Compositionality.
   (i)   The shit hit the fan.
   (ii) All hell broke loose.
   (iii) Elvis has left the building.
 a. Why might these idioms violate the Principle of Compositionality?
 b. Are there ways to reconcile the existence of idioms with the Principle of Compositionality?

10.2 Implementation: The Scope–C-Command Principle

The θ-hierarchy forms a nice illustration of how the syntactic structure determines the meaning of the sentence. But there are many more cases to be found in which differences in syntactic structure trigger differences in meaning. Let us give a few more examples:

(7) a. Edith often doesn't eat breakfast.
    b. Edith doesn't often eat breakfast.

(8) a. Bill never deliberately teased Mary.
     b. Bill deliberately never teased Mary.

(9) a. It may be the case that Anna must leave.
     b. It must be the case that Anna may leave.

In all these sentences the (a) and (b) readings are different. In (7a), it is often the case that Edith doesn't eat breakfast, in (7b) it is not the case that Edith often eats breakfast. Even though the sentences look similar in meaning, they are not. Suppose that Edith only eats breakfast every second day. And suppose that we define 'often' as 'more than 50%'. In that case (7b) is true: it is not often the case that she eats breakfast. But (7a) is not true. It would be way too strong to say that it is often the case that she doesn't eat breakfast, because she has breakfast on 50% of the days. Similar effects arise in (8) and (9). In (8a) Bill may have teased Mary, but not deliberately; in (8b) Bill never teased her, and that was his choice. And in (9a) there is a good chance that Anna has to leave, whereas in (9b), it is certain that Anna is allowed to leave. Now why is it that the (a) and (b) readings of these sentences are so different? Again, given the Principle of Compositionality, this must be the result of differences in the syntactic structure only, since in (7)–(9) the (a) and (b) sentences contain the same words. In section 10.2.1, we will introduce the ingredients that are necessary for understanding these meaning differences. In sections 10.2.2 and 10.2.3, we will introduce some problems and subsequently solve them.

10.2.1 Semantic Scope

Let us first determine the precise semantic differences between the (a) and (b) sentences. In order to express these differences, we need to introduce the notion of semantic scope. Scope refers to the domain to which some semantic element applies. For instance, the scope of *often* concerns everything that happens often, and the scope of negation concerns everything that is negated. Now, in (7a), what is often the case is that Edith does not eat breakfast, so the part of the sentence *doesn't eat breakfast* is in the scope of *often*. In (7b), by contrast, it is negated that it is often the case that Edith eats breakfast, so here *often* is in the scope of the negation. Formally we may express the meaning differences as in (10), where '>' means 'has scope over'.

(10) a. often > not   ((7)a)
      b. not > often   ((7)b)

Similarly, in (8a) *never* takes scope over *deliberately*, whereas in (8b) *deliberately* takes scope over *never*:

(11) a. never > deliberately   ((8)a)
      b. deliberately > never   ((8)b)

(11a) gives us the meaning that it is never the case that something deliberately happens, whereas (11b) gives us the meaning that it is deliberately the case that something never happens. Finally, in (9a), *may* scopes over *must*, whereas in (9b), *must* takes scope over *may*. Note that in (9) we also see something else: the left modal (*may* in (9a), *must* in (9b)) has a different kind of meaning from the right modal. The right modal expresses an obligation or permission, whereas the left modal says whether something is possible or necessary given what we know about the world. (9a) says that, given what we know, it is possible that Anna has an obligation to leave; by contrast, (9b) says that, given what we know, it is inevitable that Anna has permission to leave. When a verb expresses our knowledge of the world it is called an **epistemic modal**; a modal verb that tells us something about somebody's permissions and obligations is called a **deontic modal**.

Most modal auxiliaries can have both an epistemic and a deontic reading. For instance, (12) can be uttered by a teacher who tells a pupil in a language class that s/he is required to speak Spanish (the deontic reading), or by somebody commenting on the ability of someone who grew up in a Spanish-speaking environment (the epistemic reading).

(12)   You must speak Spanish.

Now, when two modal verbs appear in one sentence, as is the case in (9), the higher (left) modal must receive an epistemic interpretation and the lower (right) modal a deontic interpretation. (9a) cannot mean that there is some permission that, given our knowledge of the world, it is possible that Anna leave. The fact that the previous sentence is kind of impossible to understand illustrates just that.

So, it is not only the meaning of the words that determines the meaning of a sentence, but also the way in which they are put together, the order in which they were merged into the structure. Different word orders, as we have seen above, may give rise to different scope relations. But what exactly determines how different elements take scope? For that, let's look at the structure of (7):

(13)   a.

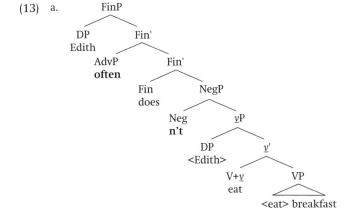

b.

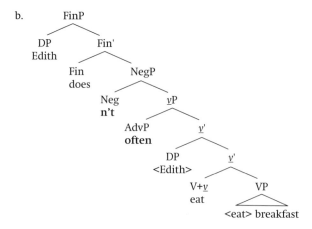

What we can observe is that in (13a) *often* c-commands *n't*; in (13b) *n't* c-commands *often*. In fact, c-command seems to be the only structural relation that there is between *often* and *n't*. Therefore, on the basis of the trees in (13), we may already hypothesise that scope relations are the result of c-command relations. If some element X c-commands another element Y, X also seems to take scope over Y. This hypothesis is actually quite interesting. So far, we have seen that every syntactic dependency involves c-command. And now that we have established that syntactic relations underlie semantic relations, it turns out that again the relevant syntactic relation is c-command. C-command helps us to get the different interpretations for (7a) and (7b). But does this also work for (8) and (9)? We will not give the trees here, but invite you to draw the relevant parts of the trees yourself and convince yourself that in (8a) *never* c-commands *deliberately* and that in (8b) *deliberately* c-commands *never*. And, as a follow-up exercise, you can figure out what the c-command relations are between *may* and *must* in (9a)–(9b).

We can now summarise our conclusion in terms of the following principle:

(14)   THE SCOPE–C-COMMAND PRINCIPLE:
       If some element X has scope over some other element Y, X must c-command Y.

Now we have seen a second case, besides the θ-hierarchy, in which the syntax clearly determines semantic interpretation.

10.2.2 Reconstruction Effects

However, there are some examples that seem to run against the Scope–C-Command Principle, which did such good work for us in the previous section. Take for instance the following examples:

(15)   a.   Somebody may leave.
       b.   Everybody didn't go.
       c.   Nobody must stay.

The examples in (15) are all **ambiguous**. An ambiguous sentence is a sentence that has two different meanings. For instance, (15a) can mean that there is some person, say Fred, who has permission to leave. But (15a) can also be uttered in a situation in which you need to collect a group of people to do some work and at some point you need one person fewer. Then some person is allowed to leave. In the first interpretation, you have a specific person in mind, like Fred, but in the second interpretation it does not matter who the person is that may leave. This ambiguity is the result of two different scope relations. In one scope relation, *somebody* > *may*, the first reading emerges: there is somebody who has permission to leave (namely Fred). The second reading results from the reverse scope relation: *may* > *somebody*. Under that reading, it is allowed that somebody leaves (but it doesn't matter who). We conclude that, even though *somebody* precedes *may* and therefore c-commands *may*, at the same time *may* can also have scope over *somebody*.

The same is true for the second example in (15). This sentence also has two readings: one reading in which nobody went, and one reading where not everybody went. Again, the two readings follow from different scope relations:

(16) a. everybody > not
      b. not > everybody

(16a) says that for *everybody* it is the case that s/he/they did not go. And if for every person it holds that they didn't go, nobody went. (16b), on the other hand, says that it is not the case that everybody went. Reading (16a) reflects the c-command relations that we see in (15b), because if you draw the structure for it *everybody* in FinP c-commands *not*, the head of NegP. But the reading in which not everybody went requires the inverse scope relation in (16b), with *not* c-commanding *everybody*. In fact, this is the most salient reading, the one that most speakers prefer, and this reading does not seem to adhere to our scope principle based on c-command.

And finally, for many speakers of English (15c) is ambiguous too. Under one reading, *nobody* > *must*; it is for nobody the case that they must stay. That means that everybody can leave if they want. But the other reading, *must* > *nobody*, paints a less pleasant picture, because it must be the case that nobody stays. In other words, everybody has to leave. This second reading, again the one that does not seem to adhere to our Scope–C-Command Principle, is the strongest. For some speakers of English it is in fact the only possible reading.

So the question arises why the sentences in (15) can have more than one reading, one of them requiring a c-command relation that is not reflected by the syntactic structure. Actually, this question suggests a problem that does not really exist. The ambiguity of the sentences in (15) should not be that surprising and has in fact been expected since chapter 6. Why? Well, in the syntactic representations for all three examples in (15) there is a subject that c-commands either a modal verb or a negation.

We know from chapter 4 already that a modal auxiliary (or to be more precise: the modal feature that will be realised as a modal auxiliary) resides in the head of FinP. And we know from chapter 8 that the negative marker (or to be more precise: the negative feature that will be realised as the negative marker) is hosted in NegP, a projection between FinP and *v*P. Therefore, the subject in spec-FinP c-commands both the head of the phrase that it sits in, Fin, and the head of NegP. We therefore expect the readings in which the subject takes scope over the modal and/or negation. But we have also known since chapter 6 that subjects move from a position inside *v*P to spec-FinP. In (17), the relevant structures are provided:

(17)   a.

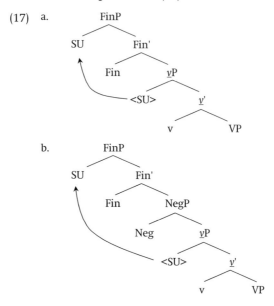

The presence of a lower subject position entails that both the modals and the negation in (15) are c-commanded by the subject in its overt position, but at the same time they c-command the original subject position in spec-*v*P. Now, just as the morphological and phonological components interpret the outputs of the syntactic component, so does the semantic component: it sees the entire structure, including all positions of remerged constituents. But then the Scope–C-Command Principle can apply in two ways here. The subject in the highest position c-commands the modal and/or negation and should thus take scope over them, but the subject in the lowest position is c-commanded by the modal and/or negation and should thus take scope under them. The fact that both scope relations can be arrived at with c-command is what underlies the ambiguity of the sentences in (15); the two readings reflect the two underlying scope relations. The reading in which the subject takes high scope is called the **surface scope reading** (since it reflects the readings of the elements as we see them on the surface); the other reading is called the **inverse scope reading**. The phenomenon where an element is interpreted in its lower position is called (scope) **reconstruction**, since the movement of the subject is in a way undone: the subject is semantically reconstructed into its lower position, so that it scopes under the modal and/or negation.

Semantic reconstruction happens often and is an insightful way to understand ambiguities in sentences with two scopal elements. It follows directly from the Principle of Compositionality (through the Scope–C-Command Principle) and from the fact that Merge may apply internally as well, i.e. the fact that the same element may be merged more than once into the structure. It would therefore be tempting to hypothesise that, in general, ambiguity is the result of reconstruction. However, this is not the case. There are instances of scopal ambiguity that do not follow from reconstruction, as we will now see. At the same time, it will turn out that those cases can also be handled by our theory. The next sections will show that.

10.2.3 Quantifier Raising

Take a look at the following sentence:

(18)   Every woman loves some man.

The sentence in (18) is also ambiguous. It has one reading in which for every woman it is the case that she loves some man, for instance Mary loves Bill, Sue loves Peter and Edith loves Rob. But it has another reading too, namely one in which there is some man, say Peter, who is loved by every woman. The first reading reflects the surface scope: if for every woman it is the case that there is some man such that she loves him, then *every woman* takes scope over *some man*. This reading follows straightforwardly from the syntactic representation, since *every woman* c-commands *some man*. Now, the second reading is a bit of a surprise. In that interpretation, some man is such that every woman loves him: the object *some man* takes scope over the subject *every woman*. But given our Scope–C-Command Principle, that should mean that the object c-commands the subject, and that is clearly not the case. At the same time, there is no position lower than the object that the subject started out in: the base position of the subject is still higher than the object position, so the trick we used in the section 10.2.2 (to look at the base position of the subject) is useless here.

Now, there might be one way out of this problem. It could be the case that the second reading, which looks like an inverse scope reading, is actually a special case of the surface scope reading. Suppose that it is true that for every woman there is some man such that she loves him. Then nothing excludes that Mary loves Peter, that Sue loves Peter, and that Edith loves Peter. Nothing requires that the men being loved by these women must be different men. When every woman happens to love the same man, this is just a special situation in which for every woman there is a man that she loves. If so, there is no reason to assume that the inverse scope reading exists in its own right. This would be good news because we then don't need a syntactic representation in which the object c-commands the subject, and we can be relieved to conclude that our Scope–C-Command Principle has not been violated.

But unfortunately, this relief is only short-lived. The following exam-ple is just as ambiguous as example (18):

(19)   Some woman loves every man.

This sentence also has two readings: a surface scope reading in which there is some woman who loves all the men, and an inverse scope read-ing in which for every man there is some woman that loves him. There are then two ways to continue this sentence, as (20) illustrates:

(20)   a.   Some woman loves every man, and her name is Edith.
       b.   Some woman loves every man, because Edith loves Harold, Deirdre loves Tom and Anne loves Andy.

But unlike in (18), the inverse scope reading of (19), namely (20b), can never be a special case of the surface scope reading ((20a)). The reason is that the surface scope reading requires the presence of one woman, and this one woman loves all the men. The inverse scope reading, however, requires the presence of several women. Now, if we want the inverse scope reading to be a special case of the surface scope reading, we end up saying that in some special situation one woman turns out to be several women. And that is simply impossible. Nevertheless, we can utter (19) truthfully in a situation in which there are several women loving several men. This shows that the inverse scope reading exists in its own right, not as a special case of the surface scope reading. But given our Scope–C-Command Principle, this should mean that the object must take scope over the subject, in contradiction to the c-command relation of the sub-ject and object provided by the syntactic structure.

So where do we stand? It turns out that sentences containing quanti-fiers such as *some* and *every* can give rise to scopal ambiguity even if one quantifier clearly does not c-command the other. So what to do? We could throw away our Scope–C-Command Principle, but that would be rather drastic. Not only did it make rather precise and correct predic-tions for the cases of reconstruction, it also followed from the Principle of Compositionality, and we certainly don't want to get rid of that.

So we seem to be stuck. But there is a solution. Take again the so-called inverted Y-model with which we ended chapter 8:

(21)   FEATURES AND CONCEPTS

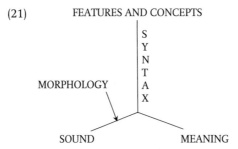

What we saw in chapter 8 was that the ability to apply Merge does not stop after syntax has done its work. Remember M-merger, the operation that applied in the morphology, after syntax? But if Merge can apply on the morphology/phonology branch after syntax, we may also find applications of Merge on the meaning branch. In fact, it would actually require some extra explanation if we didn't find any cases of Merge there. Why would the relation between syntax and semantics (or morphology) have special status when it came to Merge?

Just as the grammar can first manipulate the syntactic structure before it inserts morpho-phonological forms, so it can apply additional Merge operations before it interprets the structure. Now, what semantics cannot do is merge new elements into the structure. Note that this additional Merge operation takes place on the meaning side of the model. This means that whatever we merge into the structure after syntax has done its work will not be expressed by any morpho-phonological forms. But then it is hard to see how these new and invisible constituents can be recognised. If merger of non-expressed elements is generally possible, *John will leave* could actually mean *John will not leave*, with the negation merged into the structure after syntax is done. Clearly, we do not want this. But this does not immediately exclude remerger of constituents that are already part of the syntactic structure. It is this operation, we propose, that grammar allows.

So here we go. The structure of the sentence in (19) is as in (22).

(22)

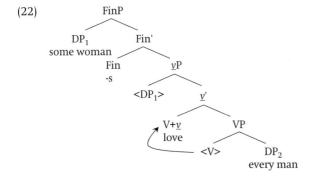

This structure only gives rise to the reading in which some woman is such that she loves every man (e.g. Edith loves all the men in the world). But now, let's apply Remerge and merge the object [$_{DP}$ every man] to the entire FinP [$_{FinP}$ some woman loves every man]:

(23)

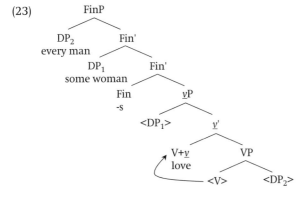

The consequence of this remerger is that the object now also c-commands the subject. And if that is the case, the object is also expected to have scope over the subject. Note that this is not an instance of movement that you see or hear: it takes place after the moment when the syntactic tree is going to be expressed (i.e. after the moment when the syntactic structure is interpreted by the morphological and phonological components). The object will still be expressed in its base position but in the trajectory from syntax to semantics the object is remerged in clause-initial position, bypassing the sound components of the grammar. In essence, then, *every man* moves invisibly (or: covertly).

The same operation can now be applied to derive the inverse scope reading of (18). After all, even though this inverse scope reading may still be seen as a special case of the surface scope reading, nothing now excludes that it exists in its own right:

(24)

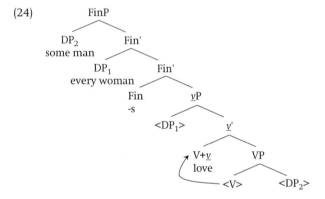

In this structure, the object [$_{DP}$ some man] is both in its base position c-commanded by the subject and in a position in which it c-commands the subject. Therefore, the sentence is again predicted to be ambiguous, a prediction that we have seen is indeed borne out.

You only apply this kind of semantic movement (also known as **covert movement**, since you do not see or hear it) to elements if covert movement gives rise to a proper semantic effect. In effect, this can only happen if you want to change the scopal relations between scope-taking elements. Now, the most likely cases in which scope relations are inverted are cases in which we have quantificational subjects and objects (as all the previous examples with inverse scope readings have shown). After all, there is no reason to covertly move *Mary* in *John loves Mary*. It would not lead to a different interpretation. Covert movement is therefore mostly restricted to quantifiers and is therefore often referred to as **quantifier raising**.

Let us have another look at the inverted Y-model in (21). You may now have an improved understanding of why it looks the way it does. To see its virtue, let us compare it with some alternatives. We could have a model that looks like in (25a), with the meaning component following the sound component, or perhaps the one in (25b), with the meaning and sound components reversed.

(25) a.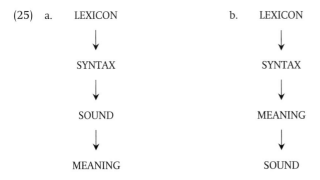

One of the motivations for separate, instead of sequentially ordered, sound and meaning components is that phonology is not interested in the meaning of syntactic structures (in fact, phonology must destroy syntactic hierarchies, because you cannot utter a hierarchy, only a linear string) and that semantics is not interested in how syntactic structures are expressed (in fact, semantics blatantly ignores many features that are expressed, such as agreement (5.2.1) and case (5.2.3)). We now have an additional argument in favour of the inverted Y-model. We have analysed quantifier raising as a covert movement, a movement you cannot see or hear. It is therefore a straightforward sound–meaning mismatch. The inverted Y-model provides a natural place for quantifier raising, whereas the alternative models presented in (25) are unable to account for it. Let us spell out why.

If our grammatical model looked like the one in (25a), we would always interpret what we hear. Why would that be? Well, remember what the sound component does: it 'flattens' the syntactic tree: it interprets the hierarchical representation that syntax provides and linearises its constituents. After this is done, there is no longer any syntactic tree, and therefore it is impossible to have the additional Merge operations necessary to create the inverse scope relations. In essence, then, quantifier raising could not exist.

If, on the other hand, the model looked like the one in (25b), we would always utter what we mean, and every constituent would be expected to be in the position in which we interpret it. If we interpret *Some woman loves every man* with inverse scope ('For every man there is some woman that this man loves'), we would expect it to come out as *Every man some woman loves*. In essence, then, quantifier raising should always be visible, and this is clearly not the case.

Quantifier raising, then, shows that we need a grammatical model in which the sound and meaning parts are independent, so that mismatches can exist. The inverted Y-model offers just that.

We can now conclude that the Scope–C-Command Principle holds without exception. Every scopal relation in the meaning of a sentence corresponds with a syntactic c-command relation, and every scopal relation in the semantics corresponds to a similar c-command configuration in the syntax. This achievement, however, comes at a cost. We have to assume the existence of covert, invisible movement. Whenever you make a special assumption – and let's face it, covert movement is a big one – you must make sure that you do not just assume it to keep your theory working. In other words, we should ask if we have evidence for the claim that certain elements, like quantifiers, may move covertly. The following section will look into this and give an affirmative answer.

Exercises

A4 Give the scope relations between the underlined elements in the following sentences using proper paraphrases ('it is … the case that … '):
a. Bobby did<u>n't</u> <u>always</u> drink.
b. <u>Perhaps</u> you <u>want</u> to drive <u>more safely.</u>
c. <u>Unfortunately</u> I <u>have</u> to leave.

A5 Do the scope relations in the sentences in A4 reflect c-command relations?

B6 What are the different readings of the following sentences? Try to sketch contexts where one reading is true and the other is false, or vice versa.
    (i)   A teacher might be around.
    (ii) Every girl did her homework.
    (iii) Few students did all the homework assignments.
    (iv) I took pictures of the man with a digital camera.
a. What are the different readings?
b. Do the ambiguities arise because of semantic reconstruction, quantifier raising or something else (and if so, what)?

B7 The following sentence is ambiguous as well:
    Some students must leave.
What is the surface scope reading and what is the inverse scope reading? Illustrate each reading with a possible scenario where that reading is true.

C8 The following sentence is ambiguous for many speakers of English:
    Three boys lifted four tables.
a. What would be the two scope readings that this sentence has?
b. How can these readings be explained, given the Scope–C-Command Principle?
c. Draw the tree for the inverse scope reading.

10.3 Consequences: Overt Movement and Syntactic Locality Conditions

The question we should ask ourselves is how we know that inverse scope readings that cannot be explained by reconstruction follow from invisible Merge operations. Can we provide additional evidence for this in some way? And how do we know that the existence of inverse scope readings in sentences like (18) and (19) does not follow from some fancy, alternative, semantic mechanism? What we need is a testing ground, so to speak, to independently confirm the claim that covert movement exists. In this section, we will develop such a test, and it turns out that covert movement passes the test with excellent grades.

10.3.1 Finite Clauses as a Syntactic Domain

Movement is a syntactic phenomenon. To be more precise, movement is a syntactic dependency, just like agreement and binding. Syntactic dependencies are relations between two elements that are based in different positions, with some distance in between them. A good example is binding: the relation between an antecedent and a reflexive can take place over some distance, but this distance, at the same time, may not be that great:

(26) a. Mary likes herself.
      b. Mary seems to like herself.
      c. *Mary thinks that he likes herself.

On the basis of the examples in (26) and similar examples in chapter 5, we reached the conclusion that binding relations are restricted to finite clauses: i.e. the antecedent and reflexive must sit in the same FinP with the feature [Finite] in its head position. In (26b), *herself* can be bound by *Mary* because the FinP that *herself* sits in is not finite and therefore binding (or binding agreement) by an antecedent in the main clause is not blocked. In (26c), on the other hand, *herself* sits in an embedded clause that is finite, and must therefore find an antecedent within that finite clause, which it fails to do.

The restriction to finite clauses is not something that is specific to the binding of reflexives. Binding, as we have seen, is an instance of agreement, and agreement is restricted to finite clauses as well. Take the sentences in (27), involving case agreement:

(27) a. I heard him.
      b. I heard him cry.
      c. *I heard that him cried.

Him carries the accusative feature [u$\underline{v}$], and this feature can be checked by $\underline{v}$ either in the same (finite) clause (27a), or in a higher clause. The latter option is only available, however, if *him* sits in the non-finite clause itself. If *him* sits in an embedded finite clause, a syntactic dependency with $\underline{v}$ in a higher clause is blocked. Hence the contrast between (27b) and (27c).

And to really drive home the message that we are dealing with a generalisation here: movement follows the same pattern. Take, for instance, argument movement. An object can move within a finite clause by becoming the subject of a passive sentence, as in (28a). We can also move an argument from an embedded clause into a main clause, an operation we have seen in so-called raising constructions, even when the embedded clause is a passive as in (28b). But, if we try to make the subject undergo a similar movement but now from an embedded finite clause, the result is hopeless, as you can see in (28c).

(28) a. Mary was killed <Mary>.
      b. Mary seems <Mary> to have been killed <Mary>.
      c. *Mary seems that <Mary> has been killed <Mary>.

On the basis of all these examples we can conclude that a finite clause constitutes a **syntactic domain**, i.e. a part of the syntactic structure in which a syntactic dependency must be realised. Binding, agreement and movement are all syntactic dependencies between two elements within the same domain.

Now let's look at quantifier raising. If quantifier raising is indeed an instance of covert movement, it should be subject to the same kinds of restrictions that hold for overt (i.e. visible or audible) movement. If quantifier raising violated all these so-called syntactic **locality conditions**, it would probably not be a movement phenomenon. So, let us see what happens. Consider the following sentences:

(29) a. Someone loves every student.
　　　 b. Someone seems to love every student.
　　　 c. Someone believes that Mary loves every student.

We already know that (29a) can have a reading in which every student is loved by somebody else. This shows that the inverse scope reading is available. The same holds for (29b). This sentence can have a reading in which every student is such that some student seems to love him/her. So this sentence would be true in a situation in which Peter seems to be loved by Mary, Bill seems to be loved by Charles and Edith seems to be loved by Henry. We again conclude that the inverse scope reading is available too (with, for the technicians, both *someone* and *every student* taking scope above *seems*). But now let us look at (29c). The reading that this sentence clearly has is one in which some person, say Olga, believes that Mary loves all students. This is the surface scope reading: *someone > believes > every student*. What it lacks, however, is a reading in which for every student it is the case that someone believes that Mary loves this student. Say that again? Well, that would be a reading in which, say, for Peter, Olga believes that Mary loves him, and for Charlotte, Bill believes that Mary loves her, etc. This reading, which requires the scopal order *every student > someone > believe*, is completely absent.

What does this tell us? It tells us that the following instances of covert movement are allowed:

(30) a. [Every student [someone loves <every student>]]
　　　 b. [Every student [someone seems to love <every student>]]

But it also tells us that the following instance of covert movement is forbidden:

(31) *[Every student [someone believes that Mary loves <every student>]]

This is exactly what we expect if inverse scope readings are the result of covert syntactic movement. If quantifier raising did not involve covert syntactic movement, why would the availability of an inverse scope reading be dependent on the same constraints that hold for overt movement, and syntactic dependencies in general? Syntactic constraints on quantifier raising, then, provide independent evidence for the idea that movement can take place in that part of the grammar where spell-out and linearisation play no role, namely where syntax meets semantics.

10.3.2 *Wh*-**Movement and Locality**

So far, we have seen that covert movement is just as sensitive to syntactic domains as any other syntactic operation. The main piece of evidence for this concerns the fact that it is clause-bound, i.e. restricted to finite clauses. But there is one case in which quantifier raising does not seem to be clause-bound. And that concerns cases with *Wh*-constituents. It may not be completely obvious, but *Wh*-constituents are also quantifiers. To see this, compare the following three sentences:

(32) a. Mary saw Bill.
      b. Mary saw every student.
      c. Which student did Mary see?

(32a) can readily be rephrased by 'the person Mary saw was Bill'. But (32b) cannot be rephrased by 'the person Mary saw was every student'. That shows that *every student* is not a regular object. The fact that you cannot rephrase it in this way, but that you must rather rephrase it in the way of (33), is a classical test for quantifierhood. It shows that *every student* is a quantifier.

(33) Every student is such that Mary saw him/her.

Now, let's look at (32c). This sentence cannot be rephrased as 'the person Mary saw was which student'. Again, you have to use a paraphrase that is very similar to the one in (33):

(34) Which student is such that Mary saw him/her?

This shows that *Wh*-constituents are also quantifiers. Now, this may not tell us all that much about *Wh*-constituents and quantifier raising, because *Wh*-constituents already overtly move up to the highest position in the sentence. However, in sentences with more than one *Wh*-constituent this is not the case. And here the facts get exciting.

Take, for instance, the sentences in (35):

(35) a. Who loves whom?
      b. Where did she kiss whom?
      c. Where did you see what?

A natural answer to (35a) would be that Aubrey loves John, Charles loves Bill, and Peter loves Susanne, etc. The corresponding question has a meaning like: 'for which person x and for which person y is it the case that x loves y?' The same applies to (35b)–(35c). The answer to (35b) would be, for instance, that she kissed Bill in the garden and Edith in the kitchen. The question in (35b) can be logically characterised as 'for which place x and for which person y is it the case that she kissed y at x?' Asking (35c) would amount to asking 'for which place x and for what thing y is it the case that you saw y at x?'

Semantically speaking, as you can tell from the logical descriptions, both *Wh*-constituents in each of the questions in (35) take scope over the rest of the clause. Now, in English only one *Wh*-constituent can syntactically move to the clause-initial position, and the other *Wh*-constituent remains in its base position. To ensure that the last *Wh*-constituent also ends up taking scope over the rest of the clause, we must use covert movement. This is indicated in the following examples:

(36) a. Whom who loves <whom>?
      b. Where whom did she kiss <whom>?
      c. Where what did you see <what>?

So far, so good. Nothing speaks against the instances of covert movement in (36). They are just regular cases of the phenomenon, so are predicted to be possible. But now take a look at the following examples:

(37) a. Who do you think loves whom?
      b. Whom did you say that she kissed where?
      c. What did you believe you saw where?

Again, the same kinds of answers are available. 'Mary loves John, Charles loves Bill, and Peter loves Susanne' is just as good an answer to (37a) as it is to (35a). And the same holds for the answers to (37b)–(37c). They could just as easily have served as answers to the questions in (35b)–(35c), respectively.

Now, if that is the case, we should conclude that the questions in (37) also involve covert movement of the second *Wh*-constituents into the main clause. But if this is what is happening, we seem to have an instance of quantifier raising that violates the restriction on syntactic dependencies. It involves movement from an embedded finite clause into the main clause. Wouldn't this be forbidden and therefore a problem for what we have said so far?

Well, yes and no. We predict that the same locality conditions hold for overt and covert movement. So, this is only a problem if overt *Wh*-movement were indeed restricted to finite clauses. But it isn't. Already in chapter 6 we saw examples in which *Wh*-constituents moved out of an embedded finite clause into the main clause. They are repeated below:

(38) a. Which yellow chair did you say that Adrian has always liked?
      b. Which yellow chair do you think that I said that Adrian has
          always liked?

Which yellow chair in both examples starts out as the object of *like*, and subsequently moves out of the finite embedded clause into the highest one.

(39) a. Which yellow chair did you say
              that Adrian has always liked <which yellow chair>?
      b. Which yellow chair do you think
              that I said that Adrian has always liked <which yellow
              chair>?

So, the fact that quantifier raising of *Wh*-constituents is not sensitive to syntactic locality conditions can't be that much of a surprise. It is actually expected, since we predict that overt and covert movement are subject to the same kinds of restrictions. If overt *Wh*-movement across the finite clause boundary is acceptable, so should covert *Wh*-movement. And this is what we observe.

The fact that we can establish this parallel between overt and covert *Wh*-movement does not mean, however, that nothing more needs to be said. What we have just observed is that one particular class of elements, *Wh*-constituents, can for some reason escape from finite clauses, whereas other, non-*Wh*-constituents, cannot. This raises an obvious question: why?

In order to answer this question, we have to see in which way *Wh*-movement is different from other types of movement. This is not an easy task. It cannot have anything to do with the kind of feature that triggers *Wh*-movement, for instance. Overt *Wh*-movement is just as much triggered by uninterpretable features as are other instances of movement. Moreover, *Wh*-constituents start out in positions from which other elements can also undergo movement, for instance from an object position as in (39). But whereas a *Wh*-constituent can move from an object position out of the finite clause into a higher clause, non-*Wh*-objects never undergo raising out of their finite clause, as was for instance shown in (28c). The only difference between *Wh*-movement and non-*Wh*-movement seems to be their landing site: CP for *Wh*-constituents; FinP, for instance, for other constituents.

Both in main clauses and in embedded clauses, *Wh*-constituents move into the specifier of CP:

(40)   a.   [$_{CP}$ Whom did [$_{FinP}$ you see <whom>]
       b.   [I wonder [$_{CP}$ why [$_{FinP}$ he will leave you <why>]]]

Now, could there be anything special about CP such that it can explain why elements moving there can undergo raising across the finite clause border, whereas other elements cannot? Actually, yes. We have said that all syntactic dependencies (except for *Wh*-movement) are restricted to finite clauses. But what is a finite clause? Obviously, it is a clause that contains a marker for finiteness. But which projection in the syntactic tree corresponds to the finite domain relevant for the locality constraint that we observed? One answer would be to say that this domain must be FinP. After all, the head of this projection contains the agreement and tense features that define finiteness. The presence of the feature [Finite] projecting FinP is what makes a finite clause finite. At the same time, we would not want to say for an embedded clause that CP is not part of a finite clause. Even stronger, the C head is spelled out by elements, like *that* and *if*, that can only appear in finite clauses, suggesting that they are finite elements themselves, belonging to this finite clause. We conclude, therefore, that it is not so easy to pin down the relevant notion of 'finite clause' to a specific projection in the syntax, as both FinP and CP are relevant. This is exactly what is going to help us explain why *Wh*-constituents can move from an embedded clause into a main clause.

Let us now look at the embedded clause of (40b) in detail. The structure of the clause before movement of *why* is as in (41a) (as can be evidenced by the answer *he left me for no good reason*). Subsequently, *why* moves into spec-CP and outside FinP in (41b).

(41)   a.   [$_{FinP}$ he left you <why>]
       b.   [$_{CP}$ Why [$_{FinP}$ he left you <why>]]

Now, here is a question: has *why* left the finite clause? On the one hand, no, since *why* is still part of the embedded CP; but on the other hand, yes, as *why* has left FinP, the locus of finiteness. In other words, the hard constraint that an element cannot leave a finite clause has been obeyed. But at the same time, if *why* moved further, it would not move out of a finite clause again, since it is already outside FinP. And therefore, nothing forbids further movement of *why*, as is the case in (42).

(42)   [$_{CP}$ Why do you think [$_{CP}$ <why> [$_{FinP}$ he left you <why>]]]

What does this all mean? It means the CP is some kind of an escape hatch for finite clauses; FinP is a syntactic domain and the CP that immediately dominates FinP is some kind of a domain edge. Once you land in this domain edge, you can move further into the main clause. The result is known as **successive-cyclic movement**. The *Wh*-constituent moves from the embedded clause into the main clause but makes an intermediate landing at the edge of each 'cycle'. And one cycle can be equated with CP here. *Wh*-constituents, then, can travel over long distances, as long as they use all the escape hatches (spec-CPs) on the way to their final destination. Theoretically, there is nothing wrong with this. We can simply propose it. But this brings us to an important rule of the syntactic (or any other scientific) game: whenever you hypothesise something, you should look for independent evidence. Is there anything showing us that in the sentence *Why do you think he left you?* the *Wh*-constituent *why* makes an intermediate landing at the edge of the embedded clause, as indicated in (42)?

What our theory predicts is that *Wh*-constituents can move from an embedded finite clause into a main clause, but only if they land in every intermediate spec-CP position that they meet on their way. It is not possible to directly move from the embedded clause into the main clause, because that would qualify as a syntactic dependency across a finite clause boundary. How can we test this prediction? Here is an idea. We are going to make sure that the *Wh*-constituent on the move cannot make the required intermediate landing. How do we do this? By putting some other *Wh*-constituent in that position. Remember that in English only one *Wh*-constituent can syntactically move to clause-initial position. Now, if we move one to the beginning of the embedded clause, the landing site is blocked for any other *Wh*-constituent that wants to escape the embedded finite clause. This other *Wh*-constituent is then forced to move into the main clause without making this intermediate landing. Since this is what our hypothesis forbids, the resulting sentence is predicted to be ungrammatical.

Let us set up the experiment. We start by taking a clause with two *Wh*-constituents, *what* and *who(m)*:

(43)   [_{FinP} She gave whom what]

Then we make it an embedded clause by adding CP and we move *who(m)* into the CP:

(44)   [_{CP} whom [_{FinP} she gave <whom> what]]

Next, let us embed the clause into a main clause and ensure that the lexical verb we add is one that can select a *Wh*-clause object, such as *wonder*:

(45)   Do you wonder [_{CP} whom she gave <whom> what]

Now comes the decisive step: if *Wh*-movement into the main clause can take place directly, *what* should be able to undergo raising into the main clause CP. If, however, *what* needs to make an intermediate landing in the embedded CP first, then movement of *who(m)* into the main clause is effectively blocked. The only way *what* could move into the main clause is by moving there directly, but that would mean movement out of a finite clause, which is forbidden in general. Let us see what the outcome is:

(46)   *[_{CP} What do you wonder [_{CP} whom she gave <whom> <what>]

The ungrammaticality of this sentence is indeed as predicted. The result therefore serves as independent confirmation of our theory. We can now maintain our generalisation that movement out of a finite clause is strictly forbidden, unless movement can use the CP as an escape hatch. *Wh*-movement takes place cyclically. First embedded clauses are built, the *Wh*-constituent then moves to the edge of this clause, after which it moves into another clause. This process can take place multiple times, as long as the *Wh*-constituent makes an intermediate stop at the edge of every finite clause. The proper representations for the sentences in (38) are therefore as in (47).

(47)   a.   Which yellow chair did you say
             <which yellow chair> that Adrian has always liked <which
             yellow chair>?
       b.   Which yellow chair do you think
             <which yellow chair> that I said
               <which yellow chair> that Adrian has always liked <which
               yellow chair>?

Let us sum up. What we have seen is that all syntactic dependencies are constrained and subjected to the requirement that a syntactic dependency between two elements is realised within the finite clause that contains them. In this respect, overt and covert dependencies act alike. Finite clauses offer an escape hatch for movement of constituents that end up in spec-CP. As a consequence, *Wh*-constituents can move from lower to higher clauses in a cyclic fashion: the construction of one CP must be completely finished before the next clause can embed it. For this reason, a clause is sometimes called a phase, and the specifier of the CP of that clause a **phase edge**, which forms the escape hatch. We have now studied one syntactic domain in some detail. The study of domains in which syntactic operations must apply is called the study of **locality**. Part of the work of contemporary syntax is to identify which local domains play a role in locality, and it looks as if there is more to this than just finite clauses, something we will come back to in our afterword. Crucial for now is the observation that all locality conditions work the same for all syntactic dependencies, from binding and agreement to overt and covert movement.

Exercises

A9   In this chapter, we established that a finite FinP is a syntactic domain. Give three more sentences that show this, one involving binding, one involving overt movement, and one involving covert movement.

A10   Explain the ungrammaticality of the following sentence:
*John says that left Mary.

A11   The sentence below is ambiguous:
How did you figure out that Mary stole the wallet?
a.   What are the two readings?
b.   What is the cause of this ambiguity?

B12   Draw the tree for the following sentence. Tip: look for instances of covert movement.
Where did you do what?

Summary

In this chapter, we saw that the output of the syntactic component forms the input to the semantic component. Semantics assigns a meaning to a sentence by looking at the meaning of the words or morphemes and the way these words and morphemes are syntactically combined. One important notion in semantics is scope. Scope determines the domain to which some semantic element applies. In the sentence *Mary didn't see everything, everything* is in the scope of negation (hence the paraphrase: it is not everything that Mary saw). Strikingly, semantic scope reflects c-command relations in the syntax.

However, sometimes the overt syntax does not reflect the scopal orders. We have found evidence that such scope mismatches can result from (scope) reconstruction, where a scope-taking element is interpreted in a position from which it has moved in the syntax (for instance, inside *v*P, in the case of a scope-taking subject).

Alternatively, a mismatch can be the result of a so-called covert movement operation, a form of movement that is not visible on the surface. Focusing on these rather mysterious instances of invisible movement, it turns out that they are subject to exactly the same locality conditions as overt movement, or any other syntactic dependency, which provides evidence that such covert operations exist. One of the conclusions of this chapter, then, is that there is syntax that we do not see, a possibility that is actually predicted by the inverted Y-model of the grammar.

Further Reading

The Principle of Compositionality has been attributed to Gottlob Frege, even though he never explicitly stated it (see Frege 1879, see also Janssen 1997). The connection between c-command and scope was introduced by Reinhart (1976) and has been further explored by May (1977, 1985), who posited the idea that there is a level in the syntax where scope relations are determined, after instances of covert movement have taken place. See also Fox (1999) for a discussion and overview of the literature on quantifier raising. For a discussion on scope reconstruction, we refer the reader to Dominique Sportiche's seminal overview paper (Sportiche 2006) and references therein.

Most of the work on syntactic locality started out with the PhD dissertation by Haj Ross (1967). The idea that *Wh*-movement is cyclic or phasal, i.e. you can only move from an embedded clause into a main clause through an intermediate landing site in the embedded CP, comes from Chomsky (1977, 2000, 2001). For arguments that *Wh*-constituents undergo covert movement, see Huang (1982).

Afterword

In this book, we have moved from looking at the grammar of English as a set of basically arbitrary rules toward looking at the grammar of English as a set of rules that are the result of a restricted set of principles underlying them. To put it differently, we have uncovered several fundamental patterns *underneath* the surface rules.

Here is an example. The fact that in English a *Wh*-constituent must be in clause-initial position is a surface rule that is caused by the underlying fundamental principle for interpretable features to c-command their uninterpretable counterparts. The former (surface) rule is not fundamental for English, the latter is: the former is a consequence of the latter and not the other way around. And the latter principle captures not just the surface rule that *Wh*-constituents appear in clause-initial position, but it captures all syntactic dependencies.

Another one. The rule that in English you must say *eat a sausage* and not *a sausage eat* is not an arbitrary fact about verbs and objects in English but follows from the more fundamental choice in English to linearise complements after their heads. This is not just true for verbs and objects but also for determiners and nominal phrases, and for complementisers and clauses. It is, in fact, the rule within English phrases in general.

Many more examples can be given. Syntacticians try to capture general, underlying patterns on the basis of the surface patterns we observe, and formalise these into a theory. The theory we developed in this way for English meets a couple of requirements we can set for any scientific theory:

(i) The theory is uniform in a lot of ways because it is based on generalisations that go beyond the surface data, as just explained. Syntax, we conclude, is not a machine with 200 distinct operations but offers a highly constrained way of building phrases and sentences: it is basically Merge plus a constraint on feature checking (every uninterpretable feature needs to be checked by a matching local c-commanding interpretable feature).

(ii) The theory is highly explicit. It does not say 'Well, we have certain constituents in some kind of structure that have to be able to see each other in some way or other.' No, we say that an interpretable feature must c-command its uninterpretable counterpart. We explain what an interpretable feature is, what an uninterpretable feature is, and we define c-command in a highly specific way. This explicitness allows us to arrive at a third property of the theory, namely …

(iii) The theory makes testable claims. It is precise enough to formulate meaningful predictions. These predictions we can subsequently test, and this is what we have done throughout the book.

After this ten-chapter 'good news' show, we would like to leave you with the message that the work is not finished. In fact, it has only just started. This is another way of saying: oh yes, there are problems. Now, these are problems that we have caused ourselves. After all, it is only in the presence of our concrete, explicit theory that we stumble upon them. Without such a theory, every new fact about English is just that: a new fact. A new fact is neither dull nor surprising, because without a theory we don't know what to expect. Now that we have a theory, however, every new fact can and must be evaluated. It can be something that fits in nicely with the theory as we have it, or it can be problematic for this theory.

It is important to realise that the situation in which we have a theory – and therefore also problems – the one that we deliberately put ourselves into, is very advantageous. Without a theory, problematic facts do not exist, and new facts will therefore never provide an impetus to change our minds about things. As a consequence, our understanding of English will not deepen (and in fact, without a theory, you may wonder how much understanding there could have been to begin with). If, however, we want to deepen our understanding, problematic facts are the trigger for re-evaluating what we thought we understood. Problems are therefore exactly what science needs, and whenever science solves such problems, it generally leads to a better understanding.

Now, in this book, we have obviously focused more on achievements than on problems, and when we introduced problems we set out to solve them. An introduction to syntax that mentioned more problems than solutions would easily give the newcomer the impression that (s)he was diving into a highly problematic scientific area. As a consequence, the problems would obscure the achievements. However, now that you have ten chapters of mainly insights and solutions to problems under your belt, we feel sure that this will not happen. So let us look at four real, concrete problems that we, as syntacticians, will have to face and deal with, so that we can develop an even better theory than the one you have worked your way through.

Hybrid Verbs

We have argued that verbal heads in English come in two kinds. Some of them, namely lexical verbs, belong to category V and project a VP. Other verbal heads, such as modals, belong to category Fin and project a FinP. This distinction was justified by evidence showing that these heads appear in different positions in the clause. Most notably, Fin heads precede negation, whereas V heads always follow negation:

(1) a. Hans will not eat eggs.
     b. *Hans not will eat eggs.
     c. *Hans eats not eggs.

On the basis of this test, we concluded that finite forms of the auxiliaries *have* and *be* belong to the category Fin, as these forms must precede negation:

(2) a. Hans is not eating eggs.
     b. *Hans not is eating eggs.

(3) a. Hans has not eaten eggs.
     b. *Hans not has eaten eggs.

So far, so good. The problem is that the auxiliaries *have* and *be* occur not only as finite forms; they can also occur in non-finite forms, namely as infinitives, past participles or progressive participles. Whenever they occur in a non-finite form, they must follow negation. Some relevant examples are given below (note that the (b) examples are ungrammatical as paraphrases of the (a) examples; they are grammatical in an irrelevant interpretation in which just the lexical verb is negated):

(4) a. Hans has not been eating eggs.
     b. *Hans has been not eating eggs.

(5) a. Not having eaten eggs, Hans collapsed.
     b. *Having not eaten eggs, Hans collapsed.

(6) a. Hans may not be eating eggs.
     b. *Hans may be not eating eggs.

We are therefore forced to conclude that finite forms of *to be* and *to have* (e.g. *am*, *has*) are Fin heads but the non-finite forms (namely *be* and *have*) are V heads. This means that we allow for tree structures in which a V head is able to select a VP or *v*P as its complement. An example is given in (7):

(7)

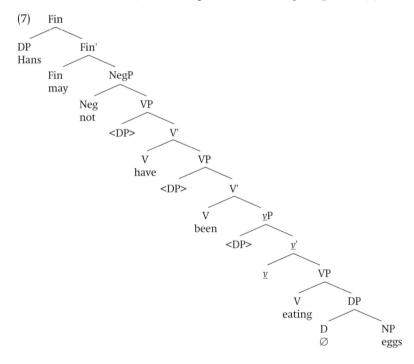

The problem is that we now have two verbs, the auxiliaries *have* and *be*, that are hybrids, behaving like Fin heads when they are finite and behaving like V heads when they are not. In other words, we are forced to conclude that *am* is a Fin head but *be* a V head. We need a three-way distinction to correctly describe the facts: (i) lexical verbs project VPs, (ii) modal auxiliaries project FinPs and (iii) auxiliaries *have*

and *be* project either a FinP or a VP, depending on their finiteness. We can be happy with this description. However, we should acknowledge that describing the facts is not the same as understanding them. The real work begins after your description is done. That's when the questions arise.

It cannot be a coincidence, for instance, that two verbs belonging to the same class of verbs (non-lexical, non-modals) show this hybrid behaviour. It is *have* and *be* that do this, not *have, be* and *sing*. This raises the question as to which property of these verbs is the cause of this hybrid behaviour. We could try to get rid of these 'hybrid' verbs and restrict the number of verb classes to two, Fin heads and V heads. We could then hypothesise that auxiliaries *have* and *be* are basically V heads but move to an abstract Fin head to pick up their finiteness features. Intuitively, making use of V movement is not unappealing. A question we would then have to answer is what makes these verbs distinct: why is it that only these two can move to Fin? Some property of a lexical verb like *sing* blocks a similar movement to Fin, and we should be on the look-out for this property.

In short, we conclude that our theory ideally has to explain why *have* and *be*, and only *have* and *be*, are special. Although we can describe the facts in different ways, as we just did, it is not so clear at the moment what explains these facts. Work in progress, therefore.

Wh-Subjects

In chapter 6, we looked in detail at *Wh*-movement. We analysed these constructions as a ballet of two movements. The *Wh*-constituent moves to the specifier of CP, and the head of FinP moves to the head of CP. If there is no modal or finite form of *have* or *be* in Fin, a form of the auxiliary *do* is inserted instead, and moved to C:

(8)   [CP Which yellow chair did [FinP Adrian <did> [vP like <which yellow chair>]]]

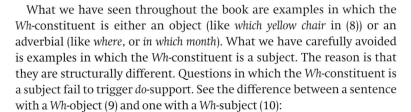

What we have seen throughout the book are examples in which the *Wh*-constituent is either an object (like *which yellow chair* in (8)) or an adverbial (like *where*, or *in which month*). What we have carefully avoided is examples in which the *Wh*-constituent is a subject. The reason is that they are structurally different. Questions in which the *Wh*-constituent is a subject fail to trigger *do*-support. See the difference between a sentence with a *Wh*-object (9) and one with a *Wh*-subject (10):

(9)   a.   Which actress did the jury like?
       b.   *Which actress the jury liked?

(10)   a.   Which actress won a prize in Cannes?
       b.   *Which actress did win a prize in Cannes?

As you can see, *Wh*-objects trigger *do*-support, whereas *Wh*-subjects block it. Under the assumption that all *Wh*-questions contain the same C head, which carries the feature [uFin], the head in Fin is triggered to move to C and enter into a position from which it can c-command the [uFin] feature on C. Therefore, the absence of Fin-to-C movement in (10) should come as a surprise. Obviously, something has to give. The current debate among syntacticians is about where exactly in the grammar the difference between (9) and (10) arises. Let us discuss two approaches, an older one, and a newer one.

The older approach starts off with the observation that in a sentence with a *Wh*-constituent, this *Wh*-constituent must occupy the highest specifier position of the clausal structure. If the *Wh*-constituent is an object or adverbial, the subject in FinP will be the highest specifier. What needs to happen, therefore, is that *Wh*-objects or *Wh*-adverbials move to a projection that dominates FinP, namely CP, so that they become the highest specifier. However, if the *Wh*-constituent is a subject, it already is the highest specifier when it sits in the structural subject position, the specifier of FinP. Therefore, there is no reason to move it. The features in Fin can undergo morphological merger with $\underline{v}$+V and no *do* support is triggered.

In essence, this is not a bad story at all, as it allows us to make the following elegant generalisation: in all sentences that contain a *Wh*-constituent, it is a *Wh*-constituent that occupies the highest specifier position of the clausal structure. The problem, of course, is that it states that *Wh*-movement is a different kind of movement from all the other cases of movement discussed in the book. What we then lose is a uniform way of characterising syntactic dependencies in terms of feature checking, including movement phenomena. Next to Remerge triggered by the necessity to bring the interpretable feature to a position from which it can c-command its uninterpretable counterpart, we now have an additional, rather vague, potential trigger for movement: the necessity to become the highest specifier. In other words, our theory becomes less elegant. And this is not a trivial consequence. If for every problem we can in principle come up with a new story, then our theory easily becomes a collection of short stories rather than, well, a theory. The question for this approach, then, is whether we can formulate this particular story in such a way that it fits in with the general pattern again. Not a trivial task.

The second, more recent approach is fully in line with the idea that movement is the result of Remerge triggered by the need to check uninterpretable features. Under this approach the distinction between *Wh*-subjects and other *Wh*-constituents follows as a result of *do* support being a last-resort rescue operation. Take (9) and (10) again. The only difference between sentences with a *Wh*-subject and sentences with other *Wh*-constituents is that the latter display *do* support. Now, the idea is as follows. If you have a FinP and linearise its components, then the features in Fin will be **adjacent** (i.e. next) to $\underline{v}$+V unless a negation head intervenes. In the latter case, negation blocks the morpho-phonological form -*s* from being spelled out on the verb.

(11) a. [$_{FinP}$ Adrian -s [$_{vP}$ like these yellow chairs]]

ADJACENT

b. [$_{FinP}$ Adrian -s [$_{NegP}$ not [$_{vP}$ like these yellow chairs]]]

NON-ADJACENT

The consequence is that *do* support is triggered to ensure that *-s* has a host. If *-s* cannot undergo M-merger to *v*+V, a dummy *do* is realised in the Fin head. Let us suppose, as we did in chapter 7, that all *Wh*-constituents move to the specifier of CP and that the features in Fin are triggered to move to C to check some uninterpretable [uWh] and [uFin] features, respectively. Then we maintain the uniformity of syntactic dependencies that we have used throughout, in contrast to the previous approach. The distinction between adjacency and non-adjacency in the linear string we used in (11) can be used to make the distinction between *Wh*-subjects and other *Wh*-constituents as well. If a *Wh*-subject moves to CP, then the features in C will be spelled out by *-s*, and this morpho-phonological form is string-adjacent to *v*+V, as there is no other element intervening. If on the other hand a *Wh*-object or *Wh*-adverbial moves to CP, then the morpho-phonological form in C will not be string-adjacent to *v*+V for the simple reason that the subject in the specifier of FinP intervenes:

(12) a. [$_{CP}$ who -s [$_{FinP}$ [$_{vP}$ like these yellow chairs]]]

ADJACENT

b. [$_{CP}$ which chairs -s [$_{FinP}$ Adrian [$_{vP}$ like]]]

NON-ADJACENT

This means that only in the latter case will *do* support be triggered, which is the right result.

Great story, right? So where is the problem? Well, it is about the interveners for M-merger. Note that negation is a syntactic head but the subject is a specifier. In this analysis, this difference does not matter, as the spell-outs of both constituents can count as interveners and trigger *do* support. But this predicts that *any* morpho-phonological form between *-s* and *like* will act as intervener and trigger *do* support. And this is not the case. Adverbials can easily appear between *-s* in Fin and the verb in *v*. Otherwise, a simple sentence like *John often eats delicious sausages* would be ungrammatical. We must conclude, then, that both negation and subjects count as interveners for M-merger (and yield *do* support) but that adverbials are exempt for some reason. It is, however, unclear what this reason would be. What is needed, then, is a theory that sets adverbials apart from subjects and negation. And it is not so clear what assumption or theory could do this in a natural way.

The Uniformity of Syntactic Dependencies: What about Selection?

In this book, we have argued for a uniform treatment of syntactic dependencies. They all involve an interpretable feature that c-commands its uninterpretable counterpart. Subject–verb agreement can be stated in these terms, and so can case relations and binding. The hypothesis to pursue, therefore, is that this uniformity holds for all syntactic relations in which some syntactic constituent is dependent on another. We have come a long way, but we are not quite there yet. Take the relation of selection, introduced in chapter 9, which holds between a syntactic head and its complement. Transitive verbs need to be combined with a complement, be it a DP, CP, FinP or PP. A preposition needs to be combined with a DP, a complementiser needs a FinP complement, and Fin needs a *v*P or VP complement, etc. These are all clearly syntactic dependencies in the sense that the head cannot survive without the complement being there. The question is whether these dependencies can be characterised in the same terms as the other dependencies.

Given the way we have defined a syntactic dependency, a head that needs a complement should carry an uninterpretable feature that is checked against the interpretable counterpart present on its complement. After all, uninterpretable features encode the presence of elements that carry a matching interpretable feature. We could, for instance, say that a preposition or transitive verb has a [uD] feature, and that Fin has a [u*v*] feature, and so forth. This way, it is ensured that prepositions or transitive verbs need the presence of a DP, and that Fin needs a *v*P. Under this analysis, the feature on the complement must c-command the feature on the syntactic head that it is selected by. Since a complement to a particular syntactic head does not obligatorily move, it must be the case that feature checking can proceed successfully without movement. Put differently, the interpretable feature must be able to c-command the uninterpretable feature from its complement position. Now, take a look at the structures in (13):

(13) a.

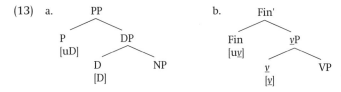

The head carrying the interpretable feature does not c-command the head carrying the uninterpretable feature. Rather, it is the other way around; the head with the uninterpretable feature c-commands the element that carries the interpretable feature. The only way we can account for the fact that feature checking proceeds successfully in these structures is by assuming that the interpretable features are also visible on the phrasal nodes, DP and vP respectively, as indicated in (14).

(14)   a.   PP   b.   Fin'

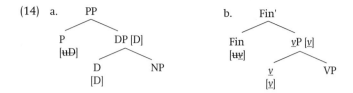

Now, the DP node c-commands P straightforwardly, and the $\underline{v}$P node c-commands Fin. Note that this idea is much in line with what we assumed about features in the first place: the features of an entire constituent are the same features as the ones of its head.

If this is correct, selection is also a syntactic dependency that fits the general pattern, a nice result in itself, but only under the assumption that the top nodes of complements enter into a checking relation with the heads that they are selected by. Although this does not sound at all unreasonable, the necessary assumption that we have now made explicit gives rise to a paradox.

As we argued in chapter 7, a Fin head moves to C in a question because the [uFin] feature on C must be checked by the interpretable [Fin] feature on the Fin head. But if this interpretable feature is also visible on the top node, namely FinP, then this node should be able to check the uninterpretable feature on the C head without anything moving:

(15)   C'

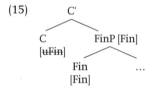

In other words, we then lose the trigger for Fin-to-C movement, the fact that in all *Wh*-sentences (except for the ones with a *Wh*-subject) the auxiliary ends up in the head of the CP. This gives us the paradox: in order to unify selection with other syntactic dependencies, we seem to lose the unification of head movement with other syntactic dependencies. So, we can make selection fit in with the general pattern of syntactic dependencies, but we then have to rethink our analysis of Fin-to-C movement.

Syntactic Islands

In chapter 10, we concluded that syntactic dependencies need to be established within a finite clause. In other words, a finite FinP seems to act as a syntactic domain within which feature checking must proceed. It is impossible to establish an agreement or binding relation across a finite clause boundary. Likewise, it is impossible to raise a quantifier like *every man* out of a finite clause.

For some reason, only *Wh*-constituents can move to spec-CP. This position functions as an escape hatch for movement out of a finite clause, accounting for the fact that only *Wh*-constituents can move long distances. This singling out of *Wh*-constituents predicts that movement of a *Wh*-constituent from an embedded clause into the main clause becomes impossible if another *Wh*-constituent already occupies the escape hatch, thereby creating an island from which another *Wh*-constituent cannot escape. This prediction was confirmed by examples like (16):

(16)   a.   *[$_{CP}$ Whom do you know [$_{CP}$ when she killed <whom> <when>]]?
       b.   *[$_{CP}$ When do you know [$_{CP}$ whom she killed <whom> <when>]]?

On the basis of these observations, we concluded that a finite FinP is a syntactic domain and that only *Wh*-constituents are in principle able to escape it. This account makes two predictions. First of all, *Wh*-movement out of a constituent that is smaller than a finite FinP should *always* be possible. Second, *Wh*-movement out of a finite CP with an empty escape hatch should *always* be possible. Unfortunately, these predictions turn out to be too strong.

Let us start by looking at the examples in (17):

(17)   a.   *Whom was [$_{DP}$ the story about <whom>] funny?
       b.   *Whom was [$_{CP}$ <whom> that John saw <whom>] a surprise?

In (17a), a *Wh*-constituent has moved out of a subject DP into spec-CP, and in (17b) it has moved out of a subject CP. Both lead to an ungrammatical sentence. We cannot simply say that DP and CP, like FinP, are syntactic domains that function as islands for movement. After all, movement out of the same DP or CP is unproblematic if these function as objects:

(18)   a.   Whom did you read a story about?
       b.   Whom do you think that John saw <whom>?

What seems to matter is that the movements in (17) are out of subjects. In other words, subjects seem to behave like islands for movement, just like the embedded *Wh*-clauses in (16).

Something similar can be said for adjuncts. These seem to behave like so-called islands too. Consider the following two examples:

(19)   a.   *Which film did you have dinner [$_{PP}$ during <which film>]?
       b.   *Which film did you meet Natasha [$_{CP}$ after you saw <which film>]?

In (19a), we have moved a *Wh*-constituent out of an adjunct PP. In (19b), we have moved a *Wh*-constituent out of an adjunct clause. The results of both are ungrammatical. Although as far as we can tell the spec-CP of the adjunct clause (19b) is not occupied (complementiser *after* functions as the head of the CP), *Wh*-movement out of it still gives a bad result. The generalisation, therefore, seems to be that adjuncts also function as islands.

To conclude, we have three different island types: *Wh*-islands, subject islands and adjunct islands. We cannot account for these island effects by simply referring to finite FinP being a syntactic domain out of which movement is impossible, because this statement would only account for

Wh-islands. In essence, then, we do not have a good syntactic generalisation over these different island types on which we can base an explanation for them.

Some scholars, though, do not take islands to be very revealing about the grammar itself. It could be that the examples above are judged to be ungrammatical by speakers not because their grammar forbids these movements but because it is very hard to parse these sentences. In other words, these sentences are all grammatical as far as the grammar is concerned but are taxing for our short-term memory (an explanation that is quite similar to the one we provided for the ban on rightward movement in section 9.3). Take the *Wh*-islands in (16). What a speaker hearing such a sentence has to do is put not one but two *Wh*-constituents back into their base positions, so as to interpret the sentence correctly. This could lead to a working memory overload, with the result that you don't like that sentence.

The current debate is about finding out how many of the island effects must be ascribed to the grammar, and how many are due to short-term memory limitations. The more of these effects are accounted for by grammar-external factors, the more we can hope for a relatively simple grammar. And isn't that what we all want? At the moment, it is not obvious how far we will succeed with this. Note for instance that it is not so clear why moving out of a subject island would be taxing for your short-term memory. After all, there is no second *Wh*-constituent that you also have to keep active, as was the case in a *Wh*-island, and the distance between the moved constituent and its base position is quite small. On the other hand, it could be that subjects are islands because you move something out of a constituent which itself has moved, from spec-*v*P to spec-FinP.

To make the issue even more hairy, it is also not always so clear what the right generalisations are. The example in (19a) involves movement out of an adjunct and is therefore expected to be bad if adjuncts function as syntactic islands. The example in (20), however, sounds much better to quite a few native speakers, probably because the role of the film in the event is more prominent: it is the film that put us to sleep.

(20)   ?This is the film we fell asleep during.

It is subtleties of this type that may turn out to be very relevant for the debate, because you do not really know what to explain if you don't know what the facts are first.

Final Remarks

We have shown you four problems that arise out of the theory we have developed. And we could have presented many more. What they show us is that the theory as it stands cannot be entirely correct. There is more work to do. That is nothing weird; it is the usual situation in science.

Every scientific theory that we know of has problems that need to be solved.

The consequences of the existence of these syntactic problems are not very clear at the moment. We may need a few small ingenious tweakings of the theory so that we can accommodate these recalcitrant facts. It is also possible that the problems are more fundamental, and that we have to make some core changes to the theory. And it is also possible that the changes we make to solve these problems cause facts that we now think we understand to suddenly become problematic. We simply don't know. But what we do know is that we always need some person who suddenly sees the solution to particular problems, or who sees problems that others haven't seen. And that person could be you.

Further Reading

For a discussion about the hybrid nature of the English auxiliaries *have* and *be*, see Pollock (1989). Grimshaw (1997) proposes that *Wh*-subjects do not have to move to CP because they already satisfy the relevant syntactic constraints in a lower position. See Bobaljik (1995, 2002) for the analysis that relates the absence of *do* support in *Wh*-subject questions to adjacency of inflectional material and the verb. In his (2002) paper, he argues that adjuncts do not count as interveners for the relation between inflection and the verb (in contrast to subjects and heads) because they can be more freely linearised. His solution hinges on a structural assumption (namely, that adjuncts are sisters to VP nodes) that is not generally accepted.

Island effects were first studied in depth by Ross (1967) and have since led to a fully-fledged exploration of restrictions on syntactic movement (see Chomsky 1986a and Rizzi 1990 for significant proposals). Hofmeister & Sag (2010) defend the idea that at least some island effects are due to memory overload. See Phillips (2013) for an excellent overview of the issues in this debate. See Truswell (2007) for an analysis of legitimate extractions from adjunct islands.

Glossary

abstract nouns: nouns that lack a concrete (say, pointable) reference. *Peace* and *democracy* are abstract nouns; *house* and *dog* are not.

accusative: the form in which a nominal constituent appears when it occurs in an object position, within a prepositional phrase, or when it is the overt subject of a non-finite clause. Accusative forms contrast with **nominative** forms.

active sentences: sentences in which all the obligatory arguments of the verb are realised. The lexical verb appears in the active, not passive voice: it does not show up as a passive participle.

adjective: grammatical category that consists of elements that can modify a noun, such as *beautiful* or *black* (*a beautiful song, the car is black*).

adjuncts: constituents that are neither directly nor indirectly selected by a syntactic head and therefore have an optional status in the structure: you can easily leave them out. Adjectives modifying a noun and adverbs modifying a verb are examples of adjuncts.

adverb: grammatical category that consists of elements that can modify non-nominal categories, such as a verbal constituent (as in *speak softly*), an adjectival constituent (as in *quite ill*), a prepositional constituent (as in *right in the middle*) or an adverbial constituent (as in *rather unexpectedly*). In English, many (but not all) adverbs end in *-ly*.

adverbial: a constituent whose presence in a clause is not required by the syntactic head of the phrase it is in, usually a verb. This constituent can therefore easily be left out without causing ungrammaticality. Adverbials are not always adverbs (*in the car* isn't), but can always be replaced by adverbs.

AGENT: the θ-**role** assigned to the **argument** that undertakes the action. A helpful test to distinguish AGENTs from non-AGENTs is the *-er* test. The suffix *-er* can be attached to a verb creating a noun that refers to an AGENT only.

agreement: a term that plays a dual role in this book: (i) it refers to the phenomenon of subject–verb agreement, the fact that the finite verb in English agrees with the subject of the clause, and (ii) it refers more abstractly to the relation between two constituents in a syntactic dependency involving feature-checking. In the latter sense, case and binding relations are also considered agreement relations.

ambiguous: the property of a syntactic structure of having more than one meaning. The sentence *I hit the dog with a stick* is an ambiguous sentence, because it has two readings (one where the hitting took place with a stick, and one where the dog has a stick).

antecedent: a constituent (grammatically or contextually present) to which a reflexive or a non-reflexive pronoun refers back. *Suzanne* is the antecedent of *herself* in *Suzanne likes herself*; and *Harry* can be the antecedent in *Harry said that he would come over*.

argument:	a constituent whose presence is required by the semantics of the verb. It is hard (but not always impossible) to leave out this constituent without causing ungrammaticality.
article:	grammatical category that consists of elements, such as *the* and *a(n)*, that indicate whether a noun refers to a unique or a non-unique element. *The* is a definite article and refers to unique elements (*the car* refers to a unique car); *a(n)* is an indefinite article that states that the noun is not unique: *there is a red car in the street* does not mean that there is only one red car.
associated subject:	the semantically contentful subject in a *there* construction (like *a man* in *There is a man walking down the street*).
base-generated position:	the position in which a constituent is merged before undergoing remerger. A constituent is base-generated in its base position.
binding:	the phenomenon in which a pronoun is in a relationship of syntactic dependency with another constituent and in which the interpretation of the pronoun is determined by the interpretation of the constituent the pronoun depends on. *John* binds *himself* in *John dislikes himself*.
bound morpheme:	a morpheme, like the agreement marker *-s*, that cannot appear on its own; it always needs to be attached to another **morpheme**.
branch(ing):	a **node** in a **tree** has never just one daughter; it has either zero daughters (because it is the terminal, lowest node in the tree) or it has two. If it has two, we say that the node branches, and it branches into two daughters.
Burzio's Generalisation:	a generalisation, first noted by the Italian linguist Luigi Burzio, that links the presence of an AGENT argument to the availability of accusative case. A transitive verb like *investigate* appears in a sentence with an AGENT subject and an object appearing in the accusative case. In the passive counterpart, the AGENT disappears and the object appears no longer in the accusative case but in the nominative case by becoming the subject. A similar pattern can be observed with **ergative verbs**.
by phrase:	a prepositional phrase starting with *by* that occurs in a passive sentence (as in *Mary was kissed by Bill*). The *by* phrase contains the constituent carrying the θ-role that is assigned to the subject in the corresponding active sentence.
case:	the form in which a nominal constituent appears. English provides evidence for two cases, **nominative** (like *she, he* and *they*) and **accusative** (like *her, him* and *them*).
Case Filter:	the filter that states that every nominal argument must be assigned either nominative or accusative case.
categorial:	having the property of belonging to a particular word category such as nouns, verbs, adjectives, etc. For this reason, [N] is referred to as a categorial feature.
category:	the property of a word, e.g. verb, noun or preposition, that determines its syntactic behaviour. All prepositions behave syntactically in the same way, because they all belong to the same category, P.

c-command:	a structural relation between two constituents in a syntactic structure which holds if the node immediately dominating constituent A also dominates constituent B, and A does not dominate B.
circular reasoning:	a form of invalid reasoning where the assumption is based on the conclusion. For instance: 'Nobody gives me a C, because I am an A person. – But why are you an A person? – Because nobody gives me a C.'
clause:	a constituent that contains at least a lexical verb and a subject. A clause corresponds to a **FinP** (in non-interrogative main clauses) or a **CP** (in embedded clauses or interrogative main clauses). Clauses can be finite or non-finite.
clause-bound:	the property of occurring in the same clause. A syntactic dependency is clause-bound if all participants in the dependency must appear in the same clause.
clause type:	the type of a clause (embedded vs. non-embedded; interrogative vs. declarative).
closed class:	a categorial class with a small number of elements and to which no new elements can easily be added. The class of determiners (*the, an, this, that,* …) is an example of a closed class. Closed classes contrast with **open classes**.
co-index:	a subscript added to a nominal expression to indicate that it refers to the same entity as another nominal expression, for example the use of $_i$ in *Kyle$_i$ thinks that he$_i$ has the best theory.*
complement:	the constituent that must merge with a syntactic head and which appears on the right side of the head in English (because it is a **head-initial** language). The verb *kill*, for instance, requires an object referring to the person being killed, and the preposition *under* requires a constituent that can refer to a location. Complements contrast with **specifiers** in that the latter are usually not merged directly with a head, but with a projection of that head.
complementary distribution:	two elements are in complementary distribution if the presence of one element in a particular position excludes the presence of the other.
complementiser:	a grammatical category that consists of elements like *that* or *whether* which make a clause become an embedded clause.
concept:	the meaning of a particular content word, written in SMALL CAPS. For instance, CAT is the concept that is spelled out as the word *cat*.
constituent:	one or more words that behave syntactically as a unit. A constituent coincides with a node in the tree structure. Constituents can sometimes (but not always) be moved or replaced by a pronominal form.
control construction:	a construction in which a lexical main verb has as its object argument an infinitival clause with an empty **PRO** subject. This construction requires a lexical main verb that assigns a θ-role to its subject (like *hope* or *expect*), thereby contrasting with a **subject-raising construction**. The interpretation of PRO is

determined ('controlled') by one of the arguments of the verb in the main clause.

coreference:
a semantic relation that holds between two nominal expressions because they refer to the same person or thing in the real world. In the sentence *Johnny said he was ill*, *Johnny* and *he* can corefer, i.e. point to the same individual. In a sentence like *Johnny hates himself*, coreference between *Johnny* and *himself* is obligatory, owing to the reflexive nature of *himself*.

count(able) noun:
a noun that can be both singular and plural, such as *cat: one cat, two cats*.

covert movement:
movement that you do not hear or see because the constituent that has undergone covert movement is not expressed in the highest position where it occurs. Covert movement contrasts with overt movement in that the latter involves a constituent that is pronounced in the highest position where it occurs. An example of overt movement is a *Wh*-object, which appears at the beginning of the clause and not in the object position where we interpret it. An example of covert movement is **quantifier raising**.

CP (Complementiser Phrase):
This is a syntactic projection that is headed by a complementiser. Since in actual analysis CP can also be the structure for a main clause, in which case the C head is filled by an auxiliary, 'clause-type phrase' may be a more appropriate term.

cross-categorial:
a property that holds across different categories.

declarative clause:
a clause that declares or asserts something. A declarative clause contrasts with an **interrogative clause**.

definite determiner:
an article or other determiner that refers to contextually unique elements (e.g. *the* or *those*).

degraded:
the property of a phrase or sentence that is not fully grammatical but not fully ungrammatical either. This status is usually indicated by one or two question marks (rather than an asterisk).

deontic modals:
modals that express somebody's obligation or permission (like *may* in *You may leave now*).

determiner:
an element (like *the, an, this, that*) that maps a particular noun to a particular referent. *The car* refers to a unique car, *this car* to a unique nearby car, etc.

direct object:
the grammatical function taken on by the selected **sister** of a lexical verb, which generally receives a PATIENT or THEME role, for instance, *a book* in *She gave him a book* or *She read a book*.

distribution:
all syntactic positions in which an element can occur.

ditransitive verb:
a verb (such as *assign* or *give*) whose semantics requires the presence of three arguments, one realised as the subject and two as objects (one direct object and one indirect object).

domain:
a piece of structure that is important for the establishment of **syntactic dependencies**. The idea is that constituents that stand in a dependency (such as an agreement marker and a subject, or a reflexive like *herself* and the nominal expression that *herself* refers to) must be in the same domain. In this book, **FinP** is identified as an important domain for syntactic dependencies.

dominate:	a structural relation between two nodes of a syntactic representation. Node A dominates node B if you can reach B from A by only going down in the tree.
double object constructions:	constructions that involve both a direct and an indirect object.
DP:	Determiner Phrase. This is a functional projection, a piece of syntactic structure, that sits on top of an NP. The head of this DP can be expressed by elements such as *the, a, this* and possessive *'s*.
embedded clause:	a clause that needs to be part of another clause, e.g. a clause headed by a complementiser such as *that* or *if*.
empty:	the property of being syntactically present but not having a phonological realisation. An element like **PRO**, to give one example, syntactically fills a position but you cannot hear it.
epistemic modals:	modals that express our knowledge of the world (like *might* in *It might be raining tomorrow*).
ergative verbs:	verbs that show an active–passive alternation without appearing in a passive form (i.e. with the lexical verb showing up as a passive participle). An example is *break: John broke the glass* vs. *The glass broke*.
exceptional case marking:	accusative assignment to a **DP** in a non-finite clause by a verb in a higher clause (e.g. *I heard her sing a song*, in which *heard* assigns accusative case to *her*).
expletive subject:	a subject that does not receive a θ-role and whose presence is merely due to the desire to have a subject, also known as 'dummy subject'. For instance, *it* in *it is raining*.
feature:	a property of a word (part) that has consequences for its syntactic behaviour, the way it is uttered and/or the way it is interpreted. Every word (part) therefore consists of syntactic, phonological and semantic features.
feature checking:	a process that takes place when an uninterpretable feature is c-commanded by a matching interpretable one (in the same syntactic domain). We then say that this uninterpretable feature is checked. Feature checking is what takes place in the second definition of **agreement**.
filler-gap pattern:	the pattern in which a moved element (the filler) appears before the base position it has vacated (the gap) in the linear string of words.
filter:	a rule ensuring that a structure we can in principle build is correctly characterised as ungrammatical. Using Merge, we can for instance create the sentence *Me like this* but it is ungrammatical. We therefore assume the existence of a filter (in this example Case theory) that makes sure that in a main clause an accusative subject leads to ungrammaticality.
finite:	being marked for either tense or agreement. Forms like *was, wishes* and *had* are finite, whereas their infinitival counterparts (*(to) be, (to) wish* and *(to) have*) are not.
finite verbs:	verbs that are marked for tense, agreement or both.
FinP:	Finiteness Phrase (also abbreviated to FiniteP). This is a functional projection, a piece of syntactic structure, that sits on top of a **VP**.

	It is the location for features that are involved in the expression of finiteness, namely tense and agreement. The head of FinP can be expressed by finite forms of *have* and *be*, modal auxiliaries and the *to* infinitive marker.
floating quantifier:	a quantifier (e.g. *all*) that is left behind when the subject moves, as in *the teachers are all dancing*.
functional categories:	closed-class categories, whose members form a finite list. Their meaning is not always easy to construct because these words have a grammatical function. Complementisers and determiners are functional categories. They stand in contrast to **lexical categories**.
functional projection:	a constituent whose head is an XP headed by a functional element (e.g. **FinP, DP** or **CP**).
GOAL:	the θ-role assigned to the argument that forms the natural endpoint of an action: *to Mary* is the goal in *I gave the book to Mary*. A GOAL can be distinguished from a RECIPIENT by appearing lower in the syntactic tree structure than a THEME or PATIENT. A RECIPIENT appears higher than a PATIENT or THEME.
grammatical:	every sentence that can be created by following the rules of grammar is grammatical; all other sentences are ungrammatical.
grammatical module:	a separate component of the grammar with its own rules. Syntax, morphology, phonology and semantics are different grammatical modules.
grammaticality:	the grammatical status of a constituent. A sentence, for instance, is either grammatical or ungrammatical.
head:	the word (or morpheme) within a constituent that is responsible for the syntactic behaviour of that constituent.
head-final:	the property of ordering the head after its complement in a linear string. Japanese and Korean are languages with this ordering strategy.
head-initial:	the property of ordering the head before its complement in a linear string. English is head-initial, in that verbs and prepositions, for instance, precede their complements.
hierarchy:	a structure in which certain elements may appear in a higher position than others. A hierarchy contrasts with **linear order**. If you put all the constituents of a sentence in a linear string, there is no internal order (and therefore no constituents).
hypothesis:	a scientifically based guess/assumption that you can test by evaluating its predictions.
imperative clause:	a clause that generally lacks a subject and conveys an order (e.g. *Give me the keys!*).
impoverishment:	an operation by which the grammar takes the syntactic tree and deletes one or more syntactic features from it. This operation takes place after the syntactic tree has been built and before **morpho-phonological forms** are inserted that make the syntactic features audible. Impoverishment therefore has the effect that certain forms that you may expect on the basis of the syntactic representation do

	not appear. For example, if the syntax contains the feature bundle [3SG, Past], and 3SG is impoverished, the verb on which these features are spelled out comes out as *walked*, and not as *walkeds*.
impoverishment rule:	a morphological rule that expresses which syntactic feature is deleted, and in which context.
indefinite determiner:	an article or other determiner that refers to contextually unspecified elements (e.g. *a(n)* or *some*).
indirect object:	the grammatical function taken on by the second highest **DP** argument within a **VP**, which generally receives a RECIPIENT role, for instance, *him* in *She gave him a book* or the grammatical function taken on by a GOAL argument, for instance *to Mary* in an example like *She gave a book to Mary*.
infinitive:	a verb that expresses non-finiteness, such as *to swim, to kill* and *to be*. In English infinitives are often but not always preceded by the infinitival complementiser *to*.
interpretable feature:	a feature that contributes to the meaning of a constituent. An interpretable feature contrasts with an **uninterpretable feature**.
interrogative clause:	a clause that poses a question, and starts with a complementiser (like *if* or *whether*), a *Wh*-constituent, or a finite verb form (as in *Will Harold leave?*).
intransitive verb:	a verb (such as *snore*) whose semantics requires the presence of one argument, realised as a subject. Intransitive verbs contrast with **transitive** and **ditransitive verbs**.
inverse scope reading:	a scope reading that is the inverse of a **surface scope reading**: for instance, *Every boy didn't sing* can mean 'Not every boy sang'. This meaning requires a scope relation, namely *n't* > *every*, that is the inverse of the scope relation given by the tree structure of the surface order (namely *every* > *n't*, which would yield the meaning 'No boy sang').
island:	a syntactic constituent from which you cannot move a subconstituent. It is for instance very hard to move a constituent that is part of a subject or part of an adverbial.
lexical:	lexical elements are words that reflect concepts and not features. Nouns, like *cat*, and verbs, like *kiss*, reflect the concepts CAT and KISS respectively. Lexical elements contrast with functional elements (such as determiners like *the* and complementisers like *that*) in that the latter reflect grammatical features.
lexical categories:	open-class categories in the sense that the list of words belonging to them is basically endless. Lexical categories have a clear meaning and relate to something in the real world, no matter how abstract. Verbs and nouns are examples of lexical categories.
lexical semantics:	the meaning of a content word (e.g. that a cat is an animal, meows, is aloof, etc.).
linear order:	the order in which elements (such as words) appear one before the other.
linearisation:	the process by which **morpho-phonological forms** that morphology inserts into the tree structure are ordered before and after each other. In this process, the hierarchical relations between

syntactic constituents get lost. This process takes place in the phonological component of the grammar.

locality:
: domain restrictions on **syntactic dependencies**. If syntactic dependencies can only take place in a particular syntactic domain, they are subject to a locality constraint.

locality conditions:
: the exact conditions, referring to a specific syntactic domain, under which a **syntactic dependency** can be established. A reflexive, for instance, has to be bound by an antecedent in the same finite **FinP**.

logical object:
: a constituent functioning as a subject of a clause that we interpret as the object of the lexical verb in that clause. In a passive construction, for instance, the subject carries the θ-role that we associate with the object position in the active counterpart of this construction. *Hella* in *Hella was fired* corresponds with the object (carrying the **THEME** role) in the active sentence *The company fired Hella*.

logical subject:
: see **associated subject**.

main clause:
: a clause that can stand on its own (and that is not dependent on another clause). A main clause contrasts with an **embedded clause**.

marked(ness):
: the property of requiring an extra feature. For instance, 'plural' is marked, because a plural noun carries a feature [Plural], whereas a singular noun does not carry a feature [Singular].

mass noun:
: a noun that is not countable, such as *milk*. One cannot say *two milks*.

match(ing):
: having similar features or feature values. *Cecilia* and *she*, for instance, match in person, number and gender features, whereas *Cecilia* and *he* do not have a matching gender feature. And Cecilia matches with the presence of a [3SG] *-s* affix on the verb, whereas *two girls* does not.

Merge:
: a syntactic operation that creates a new constituent by combining two subconstituents and ensures that the feature(s) of one of the subconstituents become(s) the feature(s) of the new constituent.

minimal pair:
: a pair of words/sentences that differ in only one respect. If one of two sentences that form a minimal pair is grammatical and the other is not, you know what the culprit is.

Minimal Search:
: the condition that states that when you need to remerge a constituent with some interpretable feature [F] to check off some uninterpretable feature [uF] on some other constituent, you have to take the closest constituent with [F] that is c-commanded by the element with [uF].

mirror-image effect:
: constituents that appear in an inverse order. For instance, when two adverbs occur in a particular order with respect to one another in one situation but appear in the opposite order in another, they are displaying a mirror-image effect.

modal auxiliaries:
: non-lexical verbs that convey information about the likelihood, possibility or necessity of the event described by the sentence. Examples are *can, may, will* and *must*.

morpheme:
: the smallest unit of meaning, as the standard definition will tell you. The word *uninteresting* for instance consists of three morphemes, *un-, interest* and *-ing*, and each of these adds meaning: the noun *interest* is the core, *-ing* makes out of it an adjective expressing a quality, and *un-* negates this quality. Despite this standard definition,

there are morphemes in respect of which it is very hard to express what meaning they contribute, if any. Morphemes that belong to functional categories are clear examples, such as *to* (in *I want to live*), or *for* (as in *For Andrew to leave would be surprising*). In chapter 8, the notion of a morpheme becomes more abstract and coincides with the feature bundles of syntactic terminals. [1, PL], [uFin] for instance, would be a morpheme and *we* the **morpho-phonological form** realisation of this morpheme.

morphological component:
that part, or module, of the grammar where concrete **morpho-phonological forms** are inserted into the abstract syntactic representation. The syntactic tree can for instance contain the feature [Past]. The morphological component then has to ensure that this feature becomes audible, for instance by inserting the form *-ed*.

morphological merger (M-merger):
a morphological operation by which one syntactic head is merged with a lower syntactic head. Fin for instance can be M-merged with V and the consequence is that features of Fin (like 3SG or Past) can be expressed on the verb (*walks* or *walked*). M-merger is only possible if the lower syntactic head is the head of a projection that functions as the **complement** of the higher head.

morphology:
the set of grammatical rules that pertain to the building of words.

morpho-phonological form:
the form that indicates the way in which particular features are realised (e.g. *-s* is the morpho-phonological form corresponding to [uφ: 3, SG] for the verb *love: he love-s*).

movement:
a syntactic operation that places, or **remerges**, a constituent in a position different from its original, **base-generated position**.

negation:
using words such as *not* that may change true sentences in false sentences and vice versa.

node:
a node in the tree that represents a constituent. We can distinguish top nodes (which are not dominated by other nodes and are referred to as '_P'), terminal nodes (which do not dominate other nodes and are referred to as **heads**) and intermediate nodes (which at the same time dominate and are dominated by other nodes and are referred to as '_').

nominal expressions:
constituents like **NP** or **DP**, where the noun has a central function.

nominative:
the form that a nominal constituent appears in when it is the subject of a finite clause. Nominative forms contrast with **accusative** forms.

non-reflexive pronouns:
pronouns that do not need to be bound within the same finite **FinP**, such as *him* or *us*.

nouns:
one of the two major categories in (English) syntax. Nouns are elements that can be preceded by the article *the* and often, but not always, refer to some particular individual or entity.

NP:
Noun Phrase.

number:
the category that determines whether some constituent is singular or plural.

object:
the **argument** of the verb that appears as the **sister** of the verb in a transitive construction (e.g. *the kitchen* in *Deirdre rebuilt the kitchen*). Such direct objects carry the thematic role of PATIENT or THEME. Ditransitive verbs, like *give* or *send*, require the presence of a second

object, the indirect object, which takes on the RECIPIENT or GOAL role (as in *David gave Estella a present* and *David sent the present to Estella*, respectively).

open class: a categorial class with a large number of elements and to which new elements can easily be added. Verbs (*to google, to skype, to syntactify, …*) provide an example of an open class. Open classes contrast with **closed classes**.

overgeneration: a syntactic theory, rule or mechanism can be said to overgenerate if it produces phrases and sentences that are ungrammatical and should therefore be ruled out. The opposite is also possible: if there are grammatical examples that are not predicted to be grammatical, the theory suffers from undergeneration and is too restrictive.

paradigm: a collection of morphological forms that express the same lexical or grammatical notion in different contexts. *Am, are* and *is*, for instance, form the present-tense paradigm of the verb *to be*. The morphemes *-ø* and *-s* are the two variants that together form the regular present-tense paradigm for verbal agreement.

parameter: a choice between two options that a language can choose from (e.g. the Head Parameter gives languages the choice between head-initial and head-final linearisations).

participle: a non-finite form of a verb that is not the infinitive. There are two kinds: perfect participles (regular form ending in *-ed*) that have to be combined with a form of *have* (as in *I have given this up*) or *be* (as in *He was given some credit*); and progressive participles (ending in *-ing*) that have to be combined with a form of *be*, as in *John was fishing in the wrong pond*.

passive sentences: sentences in which the argument associated with the hierarchically highest θ-role of the lexical verb either goes missing or shows up in a *by* phrase. The lexical verb appears as a passive participle. *Horrible things were said (by Deirdre)* is the passive counterpart of the **active sentence** *Deirdre said horrible things*.

PATIENT: the θ-role assigned to an animate argument that undergoes the action (the word therefore does not have the connotations of sickness in linguistics that it has in everyday life). A helpful test to distinguish PATIENTs from non-PATIENTs is to use the paraphrase 'what happens/happened to X is/was that …'. *Her daughter* is a PATIENT in the sentence *Mary kissed her daughter*, as it can be rephrased as *What happened to her daughter was that Mary kissed her*. THEMES are similar to PATIENTS, except that they are inanimate.

perfect participle: a verbal participle like *killed* or *fought* that requires a form of the auxiliary *have*: *(to) have killed, He has fought*, etc.

phase: a syntactic domain with an escape hatch. A **CP** is a phase, because elements that are at the edge of the CP can still establish syntactic dependencies with elements outside the phase.

phase edge: the highest head or specifier position of a phase, from where elements can still establish syntactic dependencies with elements outside the phase.

φ-features: the cover term for person, number and gender features.

phonological feature: the property that pertains to how something is uttered (the fact that *cat* has a t-sound in it, for instance).

phrase: a constituent that is complex, and generally consists of more than one word. Since all constituents have at least a head, it goes without saying that every phrase has a head. The difference between 'phrase' and 'constituent' is that the syntactic head of a phrase is also a constituent (a unit in the tree structure) but not a phrase. Strictly speaking, not every phrase is an **XP**, because the _P notation is reserved for a constituent that is not part of a bigger constituent with the same head. In the sentence *I like delicious expensive sausages, delicious expensive sausages* and *expensive sausages* are both constituents with the same head. They are both phrases but only the first is an **NP**. Although a phrase, *expensive sausages* is not the highest [N] category and is therefore referred to as N' rather than NP in the tree structure.

plural: having the property 'more than one'. A plural noun is a noun that refers to more than one element, e.g. *cats* refers to more than one cat. Other categories than nouns can also have plural forms, such as *are* in *we are*.

predicate: the part of the clause or sentence that says something about a subject argument. In the sentences *Adrian probably likes yellow chairs* and *Adrian is a fool, Adrian* functions as the subject in both, and *probably likes yellow chairs* and *is a fool* function as predicates.

prefix: a **bound morpheme** that sits on the left side of the stem that it attaches to. *de-* is a prefix to *hydrate* in the word *dehydrate*, and *pre-* is a prefix to *prefix*. Prefix stands in opposition to **suffix**.

preposition: a grammatical category that consists of elements that precede nominal expressions and often indicate a spatial or temporal property of that nominal expression: *in the closet, before midnight.*

Principle A: the principle that states that a reflexive must be bound by a c-commanding antecedent that is dominated by the closest finite **FinP** that also dominates this reflexive.

Principle B: the principle that states that a non-reflexive pronoun may not be bound by a c-commanding antecedent that is dominated by the closest finite **FinP** that also dominates this non-reflexive pronoun.

Principle of Compositionality: the principle stating that the meaning of a sentence follows from the meaning of its parts and the way they are structured.

PRO: the unpronounced pronominal subject of the non-finite clause in **control constructions**.

progressive participle: a verbal participle like *walking* or *singing* that requires an auxiliary *to be* (*to be walking, is singing*). Progressive participles refer to ongoing actions.

pronominal subject: a subject that expresses person, number and sometimes gender features but has no descriptive, or lexical, content beyond that. *He* is an example of a pronominal subject, whereas *The caretaker* is a nominal subject.

pronoun:	words that can replace nouns and refer to some previously mentioned or contextually understood noun. *I, you, us* and *his* are well-known pronouns. For instance, *I* refers to the speaker or writer; *his* to some previously introduced male.
proper name:	names of people, places, etc., such as *John, Barack Obama* or *Amsterdam*. A proper name is special kind of noun.
quantifier:	expressions like *some ...* or *every ...* .
quantifier raising:	covert movement of a quantifier that takes place when a quantifier takes **scope** from a higher position than where it is pronounced in the sentence.
raising construction:	a construction in which the embedded infinitival clause contains a subject that has moved into the main clause. This is possible because the main clause verb does not assign θ-roles to the subject in the main clause. In an example like *Janice seems/appears/is likely to leave, Janice* is the subject of *leave* but has moved into the main clause.
RECIPIENT:	the θ-role assigned to the argument that benefits from the action. Often, indirect objects are RECIPIENTs. An example is *Estella* in *David gave Estella a present*. The benefit is not always positive, by the way. *Estella* is also the RECIPIENT in *David gave Estella the creeps*.
reconstruction:	the process by which a remerged element is interpreted in its lower (base) position.
reflexive:	a pronoun such as *herself* or *ourselves* that refers back to a **DP** in the same finite clause. We say that reflexives have to be bound within their finite clause.
Remerge:	a syntactic operation that creates a new constituent by combining two subconstituents, both of which are already part of the syntactic structure. The consequence of Remerge is that it creates a **movement** effect.
salient:	the most natural. Salient usually refers to readings. The most salient reading is the most natural one.
scope:	the domain to which some semantic element applies. For instance, the scope of negation concerns everything that is negated.
select:	to require as a **sister**. A verb like *love* for instance selects a constituent expressing the person or thing that is loved. This makes the THEME/PATIENT constituent a selected sister. Another term for these constituents is **complement**.
selection:	the process that makes a syntactic head merge with another constituent because it has to. **Arguments** of the verb are selected because their presence is necessary, given θ-theory. **Adverbials**, on the other hand, are not selected and appear only optionally in a sentence.
semantics:	the set of grammatical rules that pertain to determining the meaning of a sentence.
sentence:	a clause that can stand on its own and is not embedded in another clause.
singular:	having the property of referring to one element, e.g. *one car*. Other categories than nouns can also have singular forms, such as *am* in *I am*.

sisters:	two nodes in a tree structure that are immediately **dominated** by the same node.
specifier:	a constituent that can be indirectly selected by a head. It is therefore not (always) a sister to the head (so not a complement), but like complements their presence is obligatory. Subjects, as well as *Wh-*constituents in **CPs**, are examples of specifiers.
spell-out rules:	rules that determine which morpho-phonological forms must be used to spell out, or realise, a syntactic **terminal node**. Sometimes also called 'realisation rules'.
subject:	the constituent that controls agreement in finite clauses. It appears in the specifier of *v*P and/or **FinP** and in principle has the highest available θ-role.
subject drop:	the phenomenon where you don't utter the subject.
subject-raising construction:	see **raising construction**.
substitution test:	a test to see whether elements belong to the same category (i.e. share the same feature(s). If two elements can always be substituted for each other (while retaining grammaticality), they belong to the same category.
suffix:	a bound morpheme that sits on the right side of the stem that it attaches to. *-er* is a suffix to *kill* in the word *killer*, and *-s* is a suffix to *eat* in the word *eats*. Suffix stands in opposition to **prefix**.
surface order:	the order in which we hear words being uttered.
surface scope reading:	a scope reading which reflects the surface ordering of the scope-taking elements. An example is *must > not* in *You must not leave* (meaning: *you must stay*). Surface scope reading stands in opposition to **inverse scope reading**.
syntactic dependency:	a relation between two constituents, one of which requires the presence of the other. Most syntactic dependencies are the result of the fact that certain elements carry uninterpretable features that need to be checked. An agreement feature like [3SG] needs a 3rd-person subject in the same clause, for instance, and *herself* requires the presence of a nominal constituent referring to a feminine being.
syntactic domain:	the domain in which a syntactic dependency can be established (e.g. a finite **FinP**).
syntactic feature:	the property of a constituent that is relevant for how this constituent is merged with other constituents. The presence of the feature [3SG], for instance, requires that the constituent carrying [3SG] is merged with a constituent carrying a matching feature.
tense:	the feature of verbs that indicates time reference.
terminal nodes:	the nodes in a tree where branching stops. These nodes correspond with the bound or unbound morphemes that will determine which morpho-phonological forms will be inserted.
thematic role (θ-role):	the semantic function of an argument (e.g. AGENT, THEME, etc.). Every argument must receive a unique θ-role.
Theta Criterion (θ-criterion):	the principle stating that every θ-role must be assigned to a unique argument and every argument must receive a θ-role.

theta hierarchy (θ-hierarchy):	the hierarchical order of θ-roles. In the book we established the following θ-hierarchy: AGENT > RECIPIENT > PATIENT/THEME > GOAL. When more than one θ-role is assigned within a clause, the θ-hierarchy is mapped onto the syntactic structure, so that the highest θ-role is assigned to the argument that is syntactically highest in the tree structure, etc.
THEME:	the same θ-role as a PATIENT, with the difference that PATIENTs are animate, and THEMES are not.
transitive verb:	a verb (like *love* or *kill*) whose semantics requires the presence of two arguments, realised as subject and object. Transitive verbs contrast with **intransitive** and **ditransitive verbs**.
tree:	an alternative name for a syntactic representation that is hierarchically organised.
trigger:	the reason why a particular syntactic operation takes place. In this book, the notion comes up primarily in the context of Remerge or movement. A constituent is moved because otherwise some uninterpretable feature remains unchecked. We can then identify the uninterpretable feature as the trigger for Remerge.
unbound morpheme:	an unbound morpheme is a morpheme, like *cat*, that can be a word on its own. An unbound morpheme contrasts with a **bound morpheme**.
undergeneration:	see **overgeneration**.
underspecification:	the property of not being specified for a particular feature, in contrast to other forms that are part of the same **paradigm**. *You*, for instance, belongs to the same set of forms as *he* and *they* (the paradigm of nominative pronouns) but is not associated with number. Therefore we say that it is underspecified for number.
uninterpretable feature:	a feature that does not contribute to the meaning of the phrase or sentence and that requires the presence of a matching c-commanding **interpretable feature** in the same **syntactic domain**.
verbs:	one of the two major categories in (English) syntax. Verbs are elements that can appear in finite and non-finite forms and often, but not always, refer to some particular event or action.
VP:	verb phrase.
*v*P:	verb phrase in which the verb has undergone merging.
VP-Internal Subject Hypothesis (VISH):	the hypothesis to the effect that nominative subjects start out in VP/*v*P and are subsequently remerged in a functional projection dominating VP/*v*P (namely, **FinP**).
Wh-clause:	a clause that contains a *Wh*-element, such as *who* in <u>*Who*</u> *kissed Mary?*
Wh-constituent:	a constituent that contains a *Wh*-element, such as *which yellow chairs*.
Wh-questions:	questions including the interrogative words *what, when, where, who, whom, which, whose, why* and *how*.
XP:	X Phrase, where 'X' stands for an arbitrary **categorial** label. Whenever we want to make a generalisation about NP, VP, PP, FinP, etc., we can use XP as the term referring to any of these phrases. It has the same function as _P.

References

Abney, S. P. 1987. *The English Noun Phrase in its Sentential Aspect*. Doctoral dissertation, MIT.

Ackema, P. & A. Neeleman. 2002. Effects of Short-term Storage in Processing Rightward Movement. In S. Nooteboom, F. Weerman & F. Wijnen (eds.), *Storage and Computation in the Language Faculty*. Dordrecht: Kluwer.

Ackema, P., A. Neeleman & F. Weerman. 1993. Deriving Functional Projections. In A. Schafer (ed.), *Proceedings of NELS 23*. Amherst: GSLA. 17–31.

Adger, D. 2003. *Core Syntax. A Minimalist Approach*. Oxford: Oxford University Press.

Alexiadou, A. & T. Kiss (eds.). 2015. *The International Syntax Handbook*. Berlin: Mouton de Gruyter.

Aoshima, S., C. Phillips & A. Weinberg. 2004. Processing Filler-Gap Dependencies in a Head-Final Language. *Journal of Memory and Language* 51: 23–54.

Baker, M. 1989. Object Sharing and Projection in Serial Verb Constructions. *Linguistic Inquiry* 20: 513–53.

Baker, M. 2008. *The Syntax of Agreement and Concord*. Cambridge: Cambridge University Press.

Baker, M., K. Johnson & I. Roberts. 1989. Passive Arguments Raised. *Linguistic Inquiry* 20: 219–51.

Bjorkman, B. 2011. *BE-ing Default: The Morphosyntax of Auxiliaries*. Doctoral dissertation, MIT.

Bobaljik, J. 1995. *Morphosyntax: The Syntax of Verbal Inflection*. Doctoral dissertation, MIT.

Bobaljik, J. 2002. A-Chains at the PF-Interface: Copies and 'Covert' Movement. *Natural Language and Linguistic Theory* 20: 197–267.

Bobaljik, J. & I. Landau. 2009. Icelandic Control is not A-movement: The Case from Case. *Linguistic Inquiry* 40: 13–132.

Boeckx, C. & N. Hornstein. 2004. Movement under Control. *Linguistic Inquiry* 35: 431–52.

Bonet, E. 1991. *Morphology after Syntax: Pronominal Clitics in Romance*. Doctoral dissertation, MIT.

Bošković, Ž. 2007. On the Locality and Motivation of Move and Agree: An Even More Minimal Theory. *Linguistic Inquiry* 38: 589–644.

Büring, D. 2005. *Binding Theory*. Cambridge: Cambridge University Press.

Burzio, Luigi. 1986. *Italian Syntax*. Dordrecht: Reidel.

Carnie, A. 2013. *Syntax. A Generative Introduction*. Malden, MA: Blackwell.

Cecchetto, C., C. Geraci & S. Zucchi. 2009. Another Way to Mark Syntactic Dependencies: The Case for Right Peripheral Specifiers in Sign Languages. *Language* 85: 1–43.

Cheng, L. 1991. *On the Typology of Wh-questions*. Doctoral dissertation, MIT.

Chomsky, N. 1957. *Syntactic Structures*. The Hague: Mouton.

Chomsky, N. 1970. Remarks on Nominalizations. In R. Jacobs & P. Rosenbaum (eds.), *Readings in English Transformational Grammar*. Waltham, MA: Ginn & Co. 184–221.

Chomsky, N. 1973. Conditions on Transformations. In S. Anderson & P. Kiparsky (eds.), *Festschrift for Morris Halle*. New York: Holt, Rinehart & Winston. 232–86.

Chomsky, N. 1977. On Wh-Movement. In P. Culicover, T. Wasow & A. Akmajian (eds.), *Formal Syntax*. New York: Academic Press. 71–132.

Chomsky, N. 1980. On Binding. *Linguistic Inquiry* 11: 1–46.

Chomsky, N. 1981. *Lectures on Government and Binding*. Dordrecht: Foris.

Chomsky, N. 1986a. *Barriers*. Cambridge, MA: MIT Press.

Chomsky, N. 1986b. *Knowledge of Language*. New York: Praeger.

Chomsky, N. 1995. *The Minimalist Program.* Cambridge, MA: MIT Press.

Chomsky, N. 2000. Minimalist Inquiries. In R. Martin, D. Michaels & J. Uriagereka (eds.), *Step by Step.* Cambridge, MA: MIT Press. 89–155.

Chomsky, N. 2001. Derivation by Phase. In M. Kenstowicz (ed.), *Ken Hale: A Life in Language.* Cambridge, MA: MIT Press. 1–52.

Chomsky, N. & M. Halle 1968. *The Sound Pattern of English.* New York: Harper & Row.

Cinque, G. 1999. *Adverbs and Functional Heads: A Cross-Linguistic Perspective.* New York: Oxford University Press.

Contreras, H. 1987. Small Clauses in Spanish and English. *Natural Language and Linguistic Theory* 5: 225–44.

Corbett, G. 1981. Syntactic Features. *Journal of Linguistics* 17: 55–76.

Corbett, G. 2006. *Agreement.* Cambridge: Cambridge University Press.

Corbett, G. 2012. *Features.* Cambridge: Cambridge University Press.

D'Alessandro, R., I. Franco & Á. Gallego (eds.). Forthcoming. *The Verbal Domain.* Oxford: Oxford University Press.

Den Dikken, M. (ed.). 2013. *The Cambridge Handbook of Generative Syntax.* Cambridge: Cambridge University Press.

Denison, D. 2006. Category Change and Gradience in the Determiner System. In A. van Kemenade and B. Los (eds.), *The Handbook of the History of English.* Oxford: Blackwell. 279–304.

Ding, N., L. Melloni, H. Zhang, X. Tian & D. Poeppel. 2015. Cortical Tracking of Hierarchical Linguistic Structures in Connected Speech. *Nature Neuroscience* 19: 158–64.

Dryer, M. 2011. Order of Subject, Object and Verb. In M. Dryer & M. Haspelmath (eds.), *The World Atlas of Language Structures Online.* Munich: Max Planck Digital Library, chapter 81. Available at http://wals .info/chapter/81

Edmonds, J. 1976. *A Transformational Approach to English Syntax.* New York: Academic Press.

Embick, D. & R. Noyer. 2001. Movement Operations after Syntax. *Linguistic Inquiry* 32: 555–95.

Everaert, M., H. van Riemsdijk, R. Goedemans & B. Hollenbrandse (eds.). 2013. *The Blackwell Companion to Syntax, Volumes 1–5.* Oxford: Wiley-Blackwell.

Fillmore, C. 1968. The Case for Case. In E. Bach & R. Harms (eds.), *Universals in Linguistic Theory.* New York: Holt, Rinehart & Winston. 1–88.

Fox, D. 1999. *Economy and Semantic Interpretation.* Cambridge, MA: MIT Press.

Frege, G. 1879. *Begriffsschrift, eine der arithmetischen nachgebildeten Formelsprache des reinen Denkens.* Halle: Nebert.

Gelderen, E. van. 1993. *The Rise of Functional Categories.* Amsterdam: Benjamins.

Gelderen, E. van. 2009. Renewal in the Left Periphery: Economy and the Complementiser Layer. *Transactions of the Philological Society* 107: 131–95.

Goldberg, Adele. 1995. *Constructions: A Construction Grammar Approach to Argument Structure.* Chicago: University of Chicago Press.

Grimshaw, J. 1990. *Argument Structure.* Cambridge, MA: MIT Press.

Grimshaw, J. 1997. Heads, Projection and Optimality. *Linguistic Inquiry* 28: 373–422.

Gruber, J. 1965. *Studies in Lexical Relations.* Doctoral dissertation, MIT.

Gruber, J. 1967. *Functions of the Lexicon in Formal Descriptive Grammars.* Santa Monica: Systems Development Corporation.

Haeberli, E. 2005. Clause Type Asymmetries in Old English and the Syntax of Verb Movement. In M. Batllori and F. Roca (eds.), *Grammaticalization and Parametric Change.* Oxford: Oxford University Press. 267–83.

Haegeman, L. 2006. *Thinking Syntactically. A Guide to Argumentation and Analysis.* Malden, MA: Blackwell.

Halle, M. & A. Marantz. 1993. Distributed Morphology and the Pieces of Inflection. In K. Hale & S. J. Keyser (eds.), *The View from Building 20.* Cambridge, MA: MIT Press. 111–76.

Harley, H. & E. Ritter. 2002. Meaning in Morphology: Motivating a Feature-Geometry Analysis for Person and Number. *Language* 78: 482–526.

Harris, Z. 1951. *Methods in Structural Linguistics.* Chicago: University of Chicago Press.

Hofmeister, P. & I. A. Sag. 2010. Cognitive Constraints on Syntactic Islands. *Language* 86: 366–415.

Hornstein, N. 1999. Movement and Control. *Linguistic Inquiry* 30: 69–96.

Huang, C.-T. J. 1982. *Logical Relations in Chinese and the Theory of Grammar.* Doctoral dissertation, MIT.

Iatridou, S. 1990. About Agr(P). *Linguistic Inquiry* 21: 551–77.

Jackendoff, R. 1972. *Semantic Interpretation in Generative Grammar.* Cambridge, MA: MIT Press.

Jaeggli, O. 1986. Passive. *Linguistic Inquiry* 17: 587–622.

Janssen, T. M. V. 1997. Compositionality. In J. van Benthem & A. Ter Meulen (eds.), *Handbook of Logic and Language.* Amsterdam, Cambridge, MA: Elsevier, MIT Press. 417–73.

Katz, J. & J. Fodor. 1963. The Structure of Semantic Theory. *Language* 39: 170–210.

Kayne, R. 1994. *The Antisymmetry of Syntax.* Cambridge, MA: MIT Press.

Kitagawa, Y. 1986. *Subjects in Japanese and English.* Doctoral dissertation, University of Massachusetts, Amherst.

Koeneman, O. 2000. *The Flexible Nature of Verb Movement.* Doctoral dissertation, Utrecht University.

Koopman, H. 1984. *The Syntax of Verbs.* Dordrecht: Foris.

Koopman, H. & D. Sportiche. 1991. The Position of Subjects. *Lingua* 85: 211–58.

Koster, J. 1974. Het werkwoord als spiegelcentrum. *Spektator* 3: 601–18.

Kratzer, A. 1996. Severing the External Argument from its Verb. In J. Rooryck & L. Zaring (eds.), *Phrase Structure and the Lexicon.* Dordrecht: Kluwer. 109–37.

Kratzer, A. 2009. Making a Pronoun: Fake Indexicals as Windows into the Properties of Pronouns. *Linguistic Inquiry* 40: 187–237.

Langacker, R. 1987. *Foundations of Cognitive Grammar, Volume 1, Theoretical Prerequisites.* Stanford: Stanford University Press.

Langacker, R. 1991. *Foundations of Cognitive Grammar, Volume 2, Descriptive Application.* Stanford: Stanford University Press.

Landau, I. 2003. Movement out of Control. *Linguistic Inquiry* 34: 471–98.

Larson, R. 1988. On the Double Object Construction. *Linguistic Inquiry* 19: 335–91.

Lasnik, H. 1992. Case and Expletives: Notes toward a Parametric Account. *Linguistic Inquiry* 23: 381–405.

Marantz, A. 1997. No Escape from Syntax: Don't Try Morphological Analysis in the Privacy of your own Lexicon. In A. Dimitriadis, L. Siegel, C. Surek-Clark & A. Williams (eds.), *Proceedings of the 21st Annual Penn Linguistics Colloquium: Penn Working Papers in Linguistics* 4:2. 201–25.

May, R. 1977. *The Grammar of Quantification.* Doctoral dissertation, MIT.

May, R. 1985. *Logical Form: Its Structure and Derivation.* Cambridge, MA: MIT Press.

Milsark, G. 1974. *Existential Sentences in English.* Doctoral dissertation, MIT.

Mitchell, B. & F. C. Robinson. 2011. *A Guide to Old English.* Oxford: Wiley-Blackwell.

Moro, A. 1997. *The Raising of Predicates.* Cambridge: Cambridge University Press.

Noyer, R. 1997. *Features, Positions and Affixes in Autonomous Morphological Structure.* New York: Garland Publishing.

Pesetsky, D. & E. Torrego. 2004. Tense, Case, and the Nature of Syntactic Categories. In J. Guéron & J. Lecarme (eds.), *The Syntax of Time.* Cambridge, MA: MIT Press. 495–537.

Pesetsky, D. & E. Torrego. 2007. The Syntax of Valuation and the Interpretability of Features. In S. Karimi, V. Samiian & W. Wilkins (eds.), *Phrasal and Clausal Architecture.* Amsterdam: Benjamins. 262–94.

Petronio, K. & D. Lillo-Martin. 1997. Wh-Movement and the Position of Spec-CP: Evidence from American Sign Language. *Language* 73: 18–57.

Phillips, C. 2013. Some Arguments and Non-arguments for Reductionist Accounts of Syntactic Phenomena. *Language and Cognitive Processes* 28: 156–87.

Pollard, C. & I. Sag. 1994. *Head-driven Phrase Structure Grammar*. Chicago: University of Chicago Press.

Pollock, J.-Y. 1989. Verb Movement, Universal Grammar and the Structure of IP. *Linguistic Inquiry* 20: 365–424.

Postal, P. 1970. On Coreferential Complement Subject Deletion. *Linguistic Inquiry* 1: 439–500.

Postal, P. 1974. *On Raising*. Cambridge, MA: MIT Press.

Postal, P. 1986. *Studies of Passive Clauses*. Albany: State University of New York Press.

Preminger, O. 2013. That's Not How You Agree: A Reply to Zeijlstra. *The Linguistic Review* 30: 491–500.

Radford, A. 2009. *Analysing English Sentences. A Minimalist Approach*. Cambridge: Cambridge University Press.

Reinhart, T. 1976. *The Syntactic Domain of Anaphora*. Doctoral dissertation, MIT.

Reinhart, T. & E. Reuland. 1993. Reflexivity. *Linguistic Inquiry* 24: 657–720.

Reuland, E. 2001. Primitives of Binding. *Linguistic Inquiry* 32: 439–92.

Reuland, E. 2011. *Anaphora and Language Design*. Cambridge, MA: MIT Press.

Richards, M. 2004. *Object Shift and Scrambling in North and West Germanic: A Case Study in Symmetrical Syntax*. Doctoral dissertation, University of Cambridge.

Richards, N. 1997. *What Moves Where When in Which Language?* Doctoral dissertation, MIT.

Rizzi, L. 1990. *Relativized Minimality*. Cambridge, MA: MIT Press.

Rizzi, L. 1997. The Fine Structure of the Left Periphery. In L. Haegeman (ed.), *Elements of Grammar: A Handbook of Generative Syntax*. Dordrecht: Kluwer. 281–337.

Roberts, I. 2010. *Agreement and Head Movement: Clitics, Incorporation, and Defective Goals*. Cambridge, MA: MIT Press.

Rooryck, J. & G. vanden Wyngaerd. 2011. *Dissolving Binding Theory*. Oxford: Oxford University Press.

Rosenbaum, P. 1967. *The Grammar of English Predicated Complement Constructions*. Cambridge, MA: MIT Press.

Ross, J. R. 1967. *Constraints on Variables in Syntax*. Doctoral dissertation, MIT.

Shirahata, T. 2003. The Acquisition of a Second Language C-system by Japanese Learners of English. In S. Wakabayashi (ed.), *Generative Approaches to the Acquisition of English by Native Speakers of Japanese*. Dordrecht: Mouton de Gruyter. 109–42.

Sportiche, D. 1988. A Theory of Floating Quantifiers and its Corollaries for Constituent Structure. *Linguistic Inquiry* 19: 425–49.

Sportiche, D. 2006. Reconstruction, Binding and Scope. In M. Everaert et al. (eds.), *The Blackwell Companion to Syntax, Volume 4*. Oxford: Blackwell. 35–93.

Steele, S. 1978. Word Order Variation: A Typological Study. In J. Greenberg, C. Ferguson & E. Moravcsik (eds.), *Universals of Human Language, Volume 4: Syntax*. Stanford: Stanford University Press. 585–623.

Tallerman, M. 2011. *Understanding Syntax*. Abingdon: Routledge/Taylor & Francis.

Travis, L. 1984. *Parameters and Effects of Word Order Variation*. Doctoral dissertation, MIT.

Truswell, R. 2007. Extraction from Adjuncts and the Structure of Events. *Lingua* 117: 1355–77.

Vergnaud, J.-R. 2008. Letter to Noam Chomsky and Howard Lasnik on 'Filters and Control', April 17 1977. In R. Freidin, C. Otero & M.-L. Zubizarreta (eds.), *Foundational Issues in Linguistic Theory: Essays in Honor of Jean-Roger Vergnaud*. Cambridge, MA: MIT Press. 3–15.

Williams, E. 1983. Semantic vs. Syntactic Categories. *Linguistics & Philosophy* 6: 423–46.

Wells, R. 1947. Immediate Constituents. *Language* 23: 81–117.

Wurmbrand, S. 2012. Parasitic Participles in Germanic: Evidence for the Theory of Verb Clusters. *Taal en Tongval* 64: 129–56.

Zeijlstra, H. 2008. On the Syntactic Flexibility of Formal Features. In Th. Biberauer (ed.), *The Limits of Syntactic Variation*. Amsterdam: Benjamins. 143–73.

Zeijlstra, H. 2012. There is Only One Way to Agree. *The Linguistic Review* 29: 491–53.

Index

Page numbers in **bold** refer to Glossary entries.